Ototoxic Drugs Exposed

The Shocking Truth About Prescription Drugs, Medications, Chemicals and Herbals That Can (and Do) Damage Our Ears

Fourth Edition

Volume 1 of 3

Neil G. Bauman, Ph.D.

Integrity First Publications

Lynden, WA

https://IntegrityFirstPublications.com

Ototoxic Drugs Exposed

The Shocking Truth About Prescription Drugs, Medications, Chemicals and Herbals That Can (and Do) Damage Our Ears

Fourth Edition

Volume 1 of 3

Another **Integrity First** book in the series:

Everything You Wanted to Know About Your Hearing Loss But Were Afraid to Ask
(Because You Knew You Wouldn't Hear the Answers Anyway!)

ISBN 978-1-935939-30-6 (Volume 1)
ISBN 978-1-935939-33-7 (3 Volume Set)

Integrity First Publications
1013 Ridgeway Drive,
Lynden, WA 98264-1057
Phone: (360) 778-1266
FAX: (360) 389-5226
Email: info@IntegrityFirstPublications.com
Website: https://IntegrityFirstPublications.com

Printed in the United States of America

Warning—Disclaimer

This book is for your education and reference. It is neither a medical manual nor a guide to self-treatment for medical problems. Do not construe this book as giving personal medical advice or instruction. The author is not a medical doctor and neither prescribes treatment nor treats medical problems and does not intend that you attempt to do so either. If you suspect that you have a medical problem related to your ears, seek competent professional medical help. Use the information in this book to help you make informed decisions, not as a substitute for any treatment that your doctor may have prescribed for you.

The information and opinions expressed in this book are the result of careful research. They are believed to be accurate and sound, based on the best judgment available to the author. If you fail to consult appropriate health professionals, you assume the risk of any injuries. Neither Integrity First Publications, the Center for Hearing Loss Help nor the author assumes any responsibility for damages or losses incurred as a result of using the information in this book, nor for any errors or omissions. It is the responsibility of each reader to exercise good judgment in using any information contained in this book.

Trademarks

Trademarked names appear throughout this book. Rather than list all the names and entities that own the trademarks, or insert a trademark symbol with each mention of the trademarked name, the publisher states that it is using the names with no intention of infringing upon that trademark. To this end, all the brand names of drugs and chemicals are printed in italics with the initial letter capitalized. These brand names are the registered trademarks of their respective pharmaceutical and chemical companies.

About the Author

Neil G. Bauman, Ph.D., (Dr. Neil as he is often called), is the Founder and CEO of The Center for Hearing Loss Help. He is a hearing loss coping skills specialist, researcher, author and speaker on issues pertaining to ears and hearing loss. No stranger to hearing loss himself, he has lived with a life-long, severe, hereditary hearing loss, not to mention life-long tinnitus.

Dr. Neil did not let his hearing loss stop him from achieving what he wanted to do. He earned several degrees in fields ranging from forestry to ancient astronomy (Ph.D.) and theology (Th.D.).

For the past 30 years he has extensively researched and studied the side effects of ear-damaging (ototoxic) drugs in addition to subjects related to hearing loss, tinnitus, hyperacusis, Meniere's disease, Musical Ear Syndrome and various other ear conditions.

He has dedicated himself to helping hard of hearing people understand and successfully deal with these and related ear conditions. To this end, he provides education, support and counsel to hard of hearing people through his books, articles and presentations. He annually answers thousands of queries and questions via personal contact, phone, email and through his website.

A prolific writer, Dr. Neil is the author of eleven books (in multiple editions) and more than 1,000 articles on hearing-loss-related topics (https://hearinglosshelp.com/blog/). (See the back of this book for a list of his books or go to https://hearinglosshelp.com/shop/category/books/.)

You can reach him at:

Neil Bauman, Ph.D.
The Center for Hearing Loss Help
1013 Ridgeway Drive
Lynden, WA 98264-1057
Phone: (360) 778-1266 FAX: (360) 389-5226
Email: neil@hearinglosshelp.com
Web site: https://hearinglosshelp.com

Contents

VOLUME 1

Preface

Each year an estimated 1,500,000 people in the United States end up in the hospital as a result of the adverse side effects from taking drugs? Another 100,000 people die each year from these adverse side effects![1] According to another source, these figures are too conservative. They estimate that in 1999, 2,000,000 people were hospitalized and 140,000 died from the side effects of, or reactions to, prescription drugs!

The 140,000 figure was the total for all drug deaths, which included wrongly prescribed drugs, wrongly administered drugs, drug overdoses, people not taking the drugs according to their doctor's orders, etc. However, a more-detailed study revealed that this figure is still much too low.

In fact, the number of deaths resulting just from taking properly-prescribed, properly-taken drugs is roughly this much. For example:

> In 1998, researchers at the University of Toronto, led by professor Bruce Pomeranz, concluded that properly prescribed and correctly taken pharmaceutical drugs were the **fourth** leading cause of death in the U.S.... In all, they calculated that somewhere between 76,000 and 137,000 American patients died each year from **correctly administered drugs**.[2]

This is further confirmed by Donald Light, a medical sociologist and author, who reported:

> About 2,460 people die each week as a result of taking prescription medications.[3]

Multiply this figure by 52 weeks and you get 127,920 people dying per year—right in the middle of the above estimate. Note, this figure does not include the multitudes that died from errors in drug prescriptions, from self-medication, or from drug overdoses.[4]

Yet another source says that at least a million people in the USA are severely injured each year by the medications they take and an additional million people are harmed by drugs given to them during their hospital stays.[5]

Put another way, doctors estimate that between 3 and 7% of adverse drug reactions require hospitalization. What's even more outrageous is that while in hospitals, about 20% of these patients experience additional adverse drug reactions. About 1% of these patients die from these drug reactions.[6]

These are shocking statistics. The cost of this drug-induced carnage is more shocking still. Current estimates tell us that adverse drug events and medical errors cost more than 100 billion dollars a year![7] Not only is this totally ridiculous, it is also totally unnecessary.

Of the people who survive this drug assault on their bodies, some soon discover to their shock and dismay that prescription drugs have also insidiously attacked their ears leaving them condemned to the eerie world of semi-silence filled with incessant, nerve-wracking tinnitus, not to mention plagued with all sorts of balance problems.

In the course of talking with, and helping, thousands of people with hearing losses, I am appalled at the enormous number of people who have lost some (or all) of their hearing or balance from taking drugs prescribed by their doctors. Most of these unfortunate people were never told that taking such drugs could (and often would) damage their ears. In fact, many doctors don't even know that many of the drugs they prescribe can, and do, damage ears.

The technical name for drugs that have side effects that can damage your ears is ototoxic drugs. (The correct pronunciation is OH-toe-TOKS-ik, although, depending on where you live, people may pronounce it as AWE-toe-TOKS-ik).

One lady told me that when challenged, her doctor couldn't name even one ototoxic drug! Yet ototoxic drugs are not unknown. In 1999, audiologist Richard Carmen wrote that there were at least 130 drugs and chemicals already identified as ototoxic.[8] (This book you are now reading lists a whopping 1,812 ototoxic substances.)

Ototoxic?

Doctors don't know anywhere near as much as they should about drugs that can damage our ears. Shari once asked her doctor if a drug he was prescribing for her was ototoxic. He replied, "Oto *what*?"

How come so few people seem to know about these ototoxic drugs? There is abysmal ignorance concerning ototoxic drugs by both health care professionals and the public in general. Doctors need to realize that the indiscriminate use of numerous prescription and over-the-counter drugs has been responsible for many people suffering from unnecessary hearing losses, tinnitus, balance problems and kindred conditions.

In order to fill this gap, I have attempted to make this book as comprehensive as possible. To this end, I have included all the known (to me) ototoxic drugs used in Canada, the United States, Great Britain and indeed, from any country in the world where I could find reasonably-reliable information in English.

If you live or travel elsewhere in the world, you should know that there are more than 10,000 prescription drugs that are not available in the USA.[9] No doubt, many of these drugs are also ototoxic. Unfortunately, I haven't been able to find much ototoxic information about them, so the information on foreign drugs contained in this book is generally rather sparse and thus, is often grossly underreported. In any case, I have included all the ototoxic information I have come across.

Although drugs can be useful in the treatment of various disorders, at the same time you need to have a realistic understanding of what drugs can and cannot do. Very seldom do drugs miraculously reverse a fatal illness. "Aside from antibiotics for a few infections, drugs that make a disease totally and permanently disappear are almost unknown."[10]

Furthermore, drugs usually only relieve the **symptoms** of an illness such as pain, anxiety, angina, etc.,[11] but they do **not** remove or fix the underlying **cause**. At the same time, they cause adverse side effects. This is the reality of drug treatment. You need to decide if you want to risk your precious ears in order to treat a symptom rather than do something to root out the cause and thus fix your disorder.

The rule in buying goods and services is *caveat emptor*—let the buyer beware. This is the same warning I leave with you concerning any drugs you may consider taking.

The purpose of this book is not to scare you, or make you afraid to take any drugs since almost all drugs can have ototoxic side effects. Rather, I want to give you a realistic understanding of the risks of the many drugs out there. Then, instead of blindly taking all the drugs your doctor offers you, you can do your own due diligence and wisely choose the amount of risk you are willing to take in any given situation.

Sometimes taking drugs may be the wise choice. However, many times lifestyle changes, dietary changes or herbals and other supplements may be the wiser course of action. In order to reduce the risks of drug side effects, I normally opt for the latter, but the ultimate choice is up to you. Choose wisely.

For the record, I am not a medical doctor, audiologist, pharmacist or biochemist, nor do I pretend to be any of these. However, I have spent the past 30+ years ferreting out and reporting on the ototoxic side effects of drugs. My expertise lies in educating people and helping them understand and successfully live with their hearing losses, tinnitus, hyperacusis, etc. If this book helps you save even some of your precious hearing or balance, or prevents you from getting tinnitus, hyperacusis or other ear conditions, I will have achieved my goal.

Neil Bauman, Ph.D.
Lynden, WA

Preface Endnotes

1 Waltermire, 1998. p. 1.
2 Mercola, 2022b. p. 6.
3 Mercola, 2019b. p. 1.
4 Mercola, 2019b. p. 1.
5 Freundlich, 1998. p. 1.
6 DiSogra, 2001. p. 5.
7 Rybacki, 2001. pp. xvii, xxiii.
8 Carmen, 1999. p. 37.
9 International Retail Prices for Prescription Drugs, 2001. p. 1.
10 Flieger, 1995. p. 5.
11 Flieger, 1995. p. 2.

Section I

Getting Started—Read This Section Before You Do Anything Else

Chapter 1

How to Effectively Use This Book

This book is actually a 3-volume book-set. Volume 1 consists of everything before Chapter 19. Volume 2 contains the detailed drug listings (Chapter 19), while Volume 3 consists of everything from Chapter 20 to the end of the book.

This book is divided into four sections. The first section—this chapter—teaches you how to effectively use this book. The second section explains what ototoxic drugs are, what you need to know about them, and what you can do to help yourself lessen their effects on your ears. The third (and major) section (Chapters 19 through 21) lists specific information of which I'm aware on the ototoxic side effects of each drug, herbal and chemical in this book. The fourth section contains two appendices. Appendix 1 consists of 21 tables of the relative ototoxic drug risk of the drugs in some of the more-commonly-prescribed classes of drugs, while Appendix 2 contains a glossary of terms used in this book.

Quick Start

If you want to dive right in and look up a specific drug or chemical and find out what its ototoxic properties are, here's how to do it fast. (However, I strongly urge you to read this entire chapter first or read along as you are looking up a drug, since this chapter explains what the various headings, authorities and risk assessment classes mean.)

In order to quickly find any drug, herbal or chemical in this book, go to the Index (first set of black tabs in Vol. 1, beginning on page 277) and look up the substance (whether drug, herbal or chemical) you are interested in. All the drug, herbal and chemical names are combined in this one alphabetical "Index" listing. It includes generic names, brand names, common names, scientific names, chemical names and trade names so you can quickly and easily find the substance you are interested in no matter what name you know it by.

Note that after each name there is either a C, D or H in parentheses. This indicates whether the substance you are looking for is listed as a drug (D) (Chapter 19), herbal (H) (Chapter 20) or chemical (C) (Chapter 21).

Legend

Throughout this book, I use certain conventions. Drug classes are in SMALL CAPITAL LETTERS. The first letter of each generic drug name (apart from the Index) is capitalized. If the drug is also ototoxic, it is shown as both capitalized and in **bold**. The few generic drug names mentioned in this book that are not known to be ototoxic are not bolded so it is easy to tell them apart. Brand (trademarked) names of drugs are in *italics* to show that they are registered trade names.

For example, the AMINOGLYCOSIDE ANTIBIOTIC **Tobramycin** is sold under such trade names as *Nebcin, TOBI, Tobradex* and *Tobrex* while the LOOP DIURETIC **Furosemide** is sold under such brand names as *Diuremida, Furix, Impugan* and *Lasix* (among others).

Drugs

Specific information on each ototoxic drug is found in Chapter 19, the main drug section (Vol. 2, pages 435–1444). Drugs are listed in alphabetical order by their **generic** names. You will find the details of each drug under the drug's generic name. If you don't know the generic name, look up the brand name in the Index and it will "point" you to the correct generic drug where you will find the details about this drug's known ototoxic properties and other information. Note that since some drugs have many brand names, not all brand names are listed in this book, but hopefully, the most common ones are.

Herbals

Chapter 20 contains information on ototoxic herbals (Vol. 3, pages 1495–1522). Follow the same procedures explained above for looking up drugs. The detailed herbal listings are in alphabetical order by their genus and species (**bold**), while common herbal names are in regular type.

Chemicals

Chapter 21 contains information on ototoxic chemicals (Vol. 3, pages 1523–1579). The detailed chemical listings are in alphabetical order by the most common generic chemical name (in **bold**). Alternate chemical names are in regular type, while any trademarked names are in *italics*.

If you don't know the generic chemical name, look for a known brand name or other alternate chemical name in the Index and it will "point" you to the generic chemical name used in this book where you will find the details about this chemical's known ototoxic properties and other information.

Now the Details for the Drugs

Each drug listing follows the same standard format to make it easy for you to find the information you want. This also makes it easy to compare between drugs.

This standard format has the following headings in this order: "Generic drug name," "Pronunciation guide," "Drug classification," "Brand name(s)," "Ototoxic effects," "Risk assessment", "Notes" (if there are any) and "Anecdotal Reports" (if any). The following sections explain the contents under each of these headings.

Generic Drug Name

Drugs generally have two kinds of names. First, they have an "official" generic name. Second, each drug generally has a brand or trademarked name. For example, **Azithromycin** is the "official" generic drug name of a particular antibiotic. It is sold under the brand name of *Zithromax*. These two names refer to exactly the same drug.

A few drugs have more than one generic name. When this happens, I have chosen the more commonly-used name in North America and put it as the preferred generic name. Any alternate generic names are in parentheses beside it, e.g., **Paromomycin (Aminosidine)**. In this case, **Paromomycin** is the more commonly-used generic name, and it is under this name that you will find the ototoxic details of this drug. If all you know is the lesser-used name, look up this name in the Index (e.g., **Aminosidine**), and it will refer you to **Paromomycin**.

Most drugs have two-part generic names. For example, **Acebutolol** is really **Acebutolol hydrochloride**. **Morphine** is really **Morphine sulfate**. The first part of the name is the important part. Therefore, in order to keep things simple, and thus easier to understand, I typically only use the first part of the name as the generic drug name.

However, to further complicate matters, some drugs have more than one chemical formulation—

Generic Name vs. Generic Drug

Don't confuse the term "generic name" with the terms "generic drug" and "generic product". The generic **name** of a drug is the "official" chemical name for the active ingredient of a given drug. A generic **drug** or generic **product** is a drug that is not sold under a specific brand or trade name. (They are often called "no name" brands). A few drugs don't have any trade names and are just sold under their generic names. This is commonly done when a drug's patent expires and other companies begin to manufacture it but cannot use the trademarked name under which it was originally sold.

In any case, whether a drug is sold by its generic name, a specific brand name or as a generic drug, the active ingredient is identical.

e.g., **Metoprolol tartrate** and **Metoprolol succinate**. Although these different forms basically have the same active ototoxic ingredient, they may have slightly different degrees of ototoxicity, but their basic ototoxic properties are there in any case. Likewise, **Erythromycin estolate**, **Erythromycin ethylsuccinate**, **Erythromycin gluceptate** and **Erythromycin stearate** are just slightly different forms of the active ingredient, **Erythromycin**. In such cases, I combine them all under one generic name, in this case, **Erythromycin**.

In a few cases, I include a generic drug with very minor ototoxic properties under the listing of another generic drug rather than giving it a separate listing of its own. For example, suppose you want to find the ototoxic properties of the generic drug **Antipyrine**. When you look for it, you will see it listed as "**Antipyrine** (see **Benzocaine**)". This means you will find the details of this drug in the "Notes" section of the drug **Benzocaine**. Note that typically, such drugs are taken together, often combined in one pill.

Combination Drugs

Combination drugs complicate things. There are many brands of medications that now contain two or more drugs combined into one "pill". One or more of these drugs may be ototoxic.

As far as I have been able to determine, just because two or more drugs are combined into one medication does not change the fundamental ototoxic properties of each separate drug. However, depending on the exact combination, the ototoxic properties of one (or more) of these drugs may make the ototoxic side effects of another drug in the combination more severe (the synergistic effect).

If your doctor prescribes a medication that contains more than one drug, in order to be safe, look up each of the drugs that are included in the combination and see if any of them are ototoxic. If you don't know what drugs a given medication contains, ask your doctor or pharmacist to give you a list of the generic names of the drugs in the medication, or you can often look it up on the Internet.

I list the brand name for a combination drug under the listing for the **main** ototoxic ingredient in that drug (in my opinion). In the notes section of that drug, I then list the other drugs in that combination. If any of these drugs are ototoxic, I refer you to the appropriate drug listing for the ototoxic details of those drugs.

If an ototoxic side effect is only listed for a combination drug and not separately for each drug in the combination, it is difficult to know to which drug to assign the ototoxic property. I typically assign it to what I feel is the most-likely drug in the combination. This is my opinion only.

Pronunciation Guide

Hard of hearing people have a tough time understanding unusual words so they never quite hear how to pronounce all the "fancy" drug names. Many of these drug names are real tongue twisters if you are not already familiar with them.

To make it easier for you, I have included a pronunciation guide for each drug. Just be aware that in some cases there is more than one "official" way to pronounce a given drug's name. Thus, the American, Canadian and British ways of pronouncing the same drug name can be quite different, depending on which syllable the accent is placed. Furthermore, different people pronounce these names differently anyway. Sometimes they use short vowels and other times long vowels or break the syllables in different places. Therefore, use this as a guide only.

Pronounce the name just like it appears. For example, pronounce **Fenofibrate** as "fen-oh-FYE-brate". Put the stress on the syllable(s) in CAPITAL letters.

Drug Classification

I have attempted, whenever possible, to classify drugs by their chemical similarities, since drugs with similar chemical properties typically have similar ototoxic side effects. Often, by convention, these chemically-similar drugs all end with the same letters—thus all beta-blocker drugs end in the letters "lol", and most end with "olol" e.g. Atenolol, Nadolol, Sotalol, Timolol, etc. This makes it easy to see they all belong to the same class of drugs.

If I can't find a chemical class for a drug, I classify it by its main use classification (since numbers of drugs are used for various conditions so it is hard to know where they fit).

The drug classification helps you find other drugs that are in the same class of drugs. Thus, if your doctor prescribes a certain drug, you can see whether there is another drug with similar medicinal properties that may be less ototoxic, and thus might be better for your ears, yet still do the intended job.

Furthermore, since drugs in the same class tend to have similar ototoxic risks, you can see at a glance which drug classes you might want to avoid (if possible) in order to protect your ears.

The information under the "Drug classification" heading refers you to the appropriate section in Table 19.1 (the second set of "tabbed" pages—Vol. 2, pages 1445–1493). This table shows all the drugs grouped by their chemical (or use) classification. Within each group, the drugs are in alphabetical order by their generic names.

Brand Names

Brand names are the registered trade names of specific drug formulations manufactured by specific pharmaceutical companies. In this book I primarily list the more common brand names in use at this time in the USA and Canada, but these are by no means all, or even most, of the brands that may be used for that drug.

Note that some drugs only have one brand name. Other drugs can have more than 100 brand names that are used in various countries around the world. However, when a given ototoxic drug has multiple brand names, in order to save space, and not to bore you unduly, under the drug listings I typically list the more commonly-used name(s) in the USA. However, I also may list some brand names that are used in other parts of the world—typically the ones listed in any of the ototoxic side-effect sources I consulted.

Some Drugs Have Many Brands

Just to show you that some drugs can have enormous numbers of brand names, here is a listing of all the brand names I found for the drug **Furosemide**. There is quite a pile of them—102 to be exact.

Aldic, Aluzine, Anfuramaide, Apo-Frusemide, Apo-Furosemide, Aquarid, Aquamide, Aquasin, Arasemide, Bioretic, Cetasix, Dirine, Discoid, Disemide, Diural, Diuresal, Diurema, Diurin, Diurolasa, Diusil, Dranex, Dryptal, Durafurid, Edenol, Errolon, Eutensin, Fluidrol, Franyl, Frumex, Furmid, Frusedan, Frusema, Frusemid, Frusemide, Frusetic, Frusid, Frusix, Furantril, Furanturil, Furetic, Furex, Furix, Frumide, Furo-Basan, Furocot, Furodiurol, Furomen, Furomex, Furomide M.D., Furo-Puren, Furorese, Furosan, Furoside, Furosix, Furoter, Furovite, Fusid, Golan, Hissuflux, Hydrex, Hydro, Impugan, Kofuzon, Kutrix, Lasemid, Lasiletten, Lasilix, Lasix, Lasix Retard, Laxur, Liside, Marsemide, Naclex, Nadis, Nelsix, Nephron, Nildema, Novosemide, Odemase, Odemex, Oedemex, Promedes, Promide, Radisemide, Radonna, Rasitol, Retep, Rosis, Salinex, Salurid, Seguril, Sigasalur, Trofurit, Uremide, Urenil, Uresix, Urex, Urex-M, Urian, Uridon, Uritol, Yidoli.

Note also that when I list a particular brand name, it does not indicate in any way that the brands I list are superior or more highly recommended or less ototoxic than any brand names I may have omitted.

Therefore, if you are taking a certain brand of a drug and it is not listed in this book, don't assume that it is not ototoxic until you check the listing under that drug's generic name.

If you only know the brand name and cannot find it listed in the Index, either look it up on the Internet or ask your pharmacist for that brand's generic drug name. Then look under the generic drug name (if it is listed) for its ototoxic properties.

Be aware that the **same brand name** of a combination drug can have different formulations in different countries. When this occurs, a formulation using a given brand name may be slightly ototoxic, whereas the same brand name used in another country may be quite ototoxic depending on its formulation.

For example, in the USA, *Chlor-Tripolon Decongestant* is a combination of **Chlorpheniramine** and **Phenylpropanolamine**. However, in Canada, *Chlor-Tripolon Decongestant* is a combination of **Chlorpheniramine** and **Pseudoephedrine**.

This is why you shouldn't take a brand name combination medication at face value. You need to specifically check the ingredient list on the bottle and then look up each generic drug to see whether any of them are ototoxic.

Things get even worse when a brand name in one country refers to totally different drugs, not just a slightly different formulation in another country. Thus, never assume that all drugs with the same brand names always have the same formulations or generic drugs.

For example, consider the combination drug *Gaviscon*, an antacid. In the USA, *Gaviscon* has two active ingredients—**Aluminum hydroxide** and magnesium trisilicate, while in the UK, *Gaviscon* contains three active ingredients—sodium alginate, **Sodium bicarbonate** and **Calcium carbonate**. In this case, note that none of the drugs are the same or even similar.

You have to be careful even with single-ingredient drugs. Depending on where you are, medications with the same brand name can have totally different generic drugs. Here's an example. The brand name drug *Tavor* is used for four totally different drugs, depending on which country you are in. In Chile, Colombia and Ecuador the brand name drug *Tavor* is the generic drug **Fluconazole** (an ANTIBIOTIC) whereas in Cyprus, Greece and Italy it is **Lorazepam** (a BENZODIAZEPINE). In Mexico it is **Oxybutynin** (a MUSCARINIC RECEPTOR ANTAGONIST), and in Venezuela it is **Simvastatin** (an HMG-CoA REDUCTASE INHIBITOR).[1] You sure wouldn't want to get these drugs mixed up because although they all have the same brand name, they have totally different uses and ototoxic properties!

The use of the same brand name for various drugs around the world is not all that uncommon. Here's a couple of more examples. The brand name drug *Depas* is used for **Diclofenac** (an ACETIC ACID) in India, while in Italy, Japan and South Korea it is used for the generic drug **Etizolam** (a THIENODIAZEPINE). Furthermore, the brand name drug *Mioflex* is used for **Methocarbamol** in Colombia, while in Spain it refers to the generic drug Suxamethonium.

Thus, in order to avoid confusion, I generally don't list drug brand names when I know they contain different drugs or have different drug formulations than are used in the USA.

However, it is your responsibility to always check that the brand name of a drug you are taking correlates with the generic drug name used in this book so you don't mistakenly assume the wrong ototoxic side effects for that drug.

Furthermore, note that sometimes there are minor spelling differences between brand names in different countries. For example, *Lopresor* is the Canadian version of **Metoprolol** while *Lopressor* is the United States counterpart.

If a drug only goes by its generic name and has no brand name, or I can't find a brand name, I show this simply as "—".

Here's something else of which you need to be aware. Some people have noticed a difference in the ototoxic side effects they experience between using a brand name drug and the equivalent generic drug. Theoretically, they have exactly the same active ingredient, so the side effects should be the same when taken in the same dose.

However, you have to watch out. These different side effects can be the result of other "filler" ingredients added to the "pill". These are typically called "inactive" ingredients. Note—and this is very important—that the inactive ingredients are not necessarily inert (i.e., have no effect on your body) like you might think. Rather, "inactive" in this case just means that ingredient is not listed as being used to actively treat the condition for which the drug you are taking is approved.

These other ("inactive") ingredients may be very active on your body and cause ototoxic side effects. For example, sometimes an "inactive" ingredient in one pill may be **the** "active" ingredient in another pill approved for use for another condition.

One example would be a typical cough medicine such as *Robitussin* that contains two drugs that are listed as active ingredients, namely **Dextromethorphan** and **Guaifenesin**. So far so good. But when you look in the list of inactive ingredients you find **Propylene glycol** and **Polyethylene glycol**, both of which are ototoxic drugs in their own right. You'll see this when you look them up under their appropriate generic names in this book.

Thus, although some of these ingredients may be listed as "inactive", they certainly are not inert! That is why a brand name drug can give you different (or additional) ototoxic (and other) side effects than what you get from taking the equivalent generic drug which has different "inactive" ingredients.

Therefore, to be safe, you should check all the "inactive" ingredients against the drugs and chemicals listed in this book to see if they have any known ototoxic side effects.

Ototoxic Side Effects

This is the real "meat" of each listing. This is where you find out how this drug can affect your ears. For example, the side effects of some ototoxic drugs can kill or damage the sensitive hair cells and/or underlying support cells in your cochlea and/or in your vestibular (balance) system. Thus, they are actually toxic to the ear and can cause permanent harm to your ears. This can result in a number of ototoxic side effects appearing including tinnitus, hyperacusis, hearing loss and balance problems. Other drugs produce tinnitus as a side effect, supposedly without damaging your inner ears,[2] but upset the normal balance in the auditory processing parts of your brain that results in tinnitus.

In this book I have collected the numerous terms researchers have used describing ototoxic side effects under four basic headings in each of the drug listings, namely "Cochlear", "Vestibular", "Outer/Middle Ear" and "Unspecified/ General Ear Conditions".

Cochlear side effects include side effects that have to do with hearing while vestibular side effects encompass those side effects that affect your balance. The other two headings are self-explanatory. If I have no information available for a specific heading, I do not use that heading.

Under these four headings I have collected the various terms used to describe ototoxic side effects. This was necessary because researchers often use a variety of vague terms. Since there are so many such vague terms, and numbers of them are apparently synonyms, in order to simplify things and remove some confusion as to what is meant by these various terms, I have narrowed these down to 30 "standardized" ototoxic terms that I use in the drug listings in this book.

Here are these 30 simplified terms collected in alphabetical order under each of the above four main headings. I describe and explain these 30 standardized terms in Chapter 4.

Note: If you want to do your own research, there are around 120 different terms used to describe ototoxic side effects, so looking all of them up for each drug is a real chore.

Cochlear Ototoxic Side Effects

Auditory hallucinations: includes Musical Ear Syndrome (MES) sounds and so-called "musical tinnitus" which is really MES.

Hearing disorder: includes nebulous terms such as auditory damage, auditory defects, auditory disorders, auditory disturbances, auditory ototoxicity, hearing disorder, hearing abnormality, hearing alterations, hearing disturbance, hearing dysfunction, hearing problems and inner ear disorder—whatever they mean by these terms.

Hearing loss: includes hearing loss, decreased hearing, diminished hearing, hearing disability, hearing impaired, hypoacusis, sensorineural or neurosensory hearing loss, deafness, transitory deafness, and similar terms.

Hyperacusis: includes both (loudness) hyperacusis and loudness recruitment.

Phonophobia: otherwise known as fear hyperacusis.

Tinnitus: includes neurophysiologic tinnitus, somatosensory tinnitus and somatosounds such as "pounding in ears" and "pulsatile tinnitus".

Vestibular Ototoxic Side Effects

Ataxia/Gait disturbance.

Balance disorder: also includes the terms equilibrium disorder, equilibrium dysfunction and loss of balance.

Dizziness.

Labyrinthitis: including labyrinthine disorders.

Nystagmus: (eyes jerking sideways).

Oscillopsia: including "bouncing vision".

Vertigo: (spinning or rocking sensation when no movement present).

Vestibular disorder: includes vague terms such as vestibular disorder, vestibular dysfunction, vestibular disturbance, acoustic neuritis and vestibular neuronitis.

Outer/Middle Ear Ototoxic Side Effects

Burning/Stinging: in ear canal.

Ceruminosis: (ear wax) includes ceruminosis, cerumen impaction and excessive ear wax.

Cholesteatoma.

Ear blocked: includes the terms ear blocked, ear congestion, ears feel plugged, feeling of fullness in ears and middle ear pressure.

Ear discomfort/Ear pain: includes ear pain, earache and ear discomfort.

Ear infection: includes ear infections whether bacterial, fungal or viral and otitis.

Eustachian tube dysfunction.

Otitis externa: (outer ear infection) includes both otitis externa and itching ears.

Otitis media: includes otitis media (middle ear infection), fluid in ears, middle ear disorder.

Otorrhagia: (bleeding from the ear canal) includes both otorrhagia and ear hemorrhage.

Otorrhea: (purulent discharge [puss] from the ear canal) includes both otorrhea and ear puritus.

Otosclerosis.

Perforated eardrum: includes the terms perforated eardrum and tympanic membrane perforation.

Unspecified/General Ototoxic Side Effects

Ear disorder: includes such nebulous terms as ear disorder, ear disease–unspecified, cochlear lesion and cochlear damage.

Meniere's disease.

Ototoxicity: ototoxicity not otherwise specified.

Ototoxic Side Effect Details

For each drug, I list the ototoxic side effects I have found. I compiled these from numerous sources. Even when using these 30 standardized terms, often the results are still somewhat vague. For example, under the heading "hearing loss" you don't know whether it refers to permanent or temporary hearing loss; whether it is mild or severe hearing loss or total deafness; or, whether it is a sensorineural or conductive hearing loss. This is because I have no way of knowing since it is typically not stated by the researchers.

In addition, if a percentage was given for frequency of occurrence, I state it. If no statistics were given, I am unable to determine whether the side effect is relatively common or extremely rare so only note how often people report that side effect.

Keep in mind that drug books such as the CPS and PDR typically do not list all the ototoxic side effects for a given generic drug, nor do they necessarily list them all in any one place. For example, both the CPS and PDR list drugs by brand name rather than by generic name. Thus, ototoxic side effects can be scattered throughout the various brand names for the same generic drug.

To make things simpler to understand, I have gathered all the ototoxic side effects from the various brand-name listings of each generic drug and compiled them under the generic drug. Note that information on a given drug can vary all over the place. For example, one brand may list several ototoxic side effects while another brand of the identical generic drug may list one (or none).

Therefore, if you or your doctor look up the ototoxic side effects of a drug under a particular brand name, you may not find all those side effects there. Consequently, you may think I have padded the results. Rest assured that all the side effects I list have indeed been reported by the authorities cited, sometimes even just from a different listing in the same book edition.

Also, be aware that the same side effects are not always reported consistently from year to year. Therefore, if my listing shows "Tinnitus: (PDR)," for example, and you look in the current PDR and do not find it listed—this is **not** a mistake. It just means that this side effect was listed in a previous edition (or perhaps for a different brand) but is not listed in the current edition for whatever reason.

The ototoxic effects of a given drug can vary greatly depending on how it is taken. For example, ototoxic effects may not be apparent if you take a certain drug as a tablet, but if you take the same drug as an intravenous injection, it could be quite ototoxic. Many ototoxic effects also depend on the dose—both how much you take at a time, and for how long you take the drug. For example, the greater the dose and/or the longer the time you take a drug, generally the greater the risk of ototoxic effects showing up.

It is important you realize that the ototoxic side effects picked up during the drug trials are generally in people taking the drug at the **recommended** frequency, duration and dosage. A drug may be ototoxic at higher than recommended dosages, but this information may not be known or readily available since the drug trials are conducted at the recommended dose. As a result, if your doctor prescribes a drug at a higher dose, or for longer than the recommended time, you may experience ototoxic side effects that are not listed in books like the PDR!

After each ototoxic side effect, I give one to three pieces of information about that side effect. First, if known, I provide an estimate of frequency of ototoxic occurrence. Second, I show a comparison to placebo results. Third, I provide the source where I got this information.

Here is how to interpret this information.

Symbols Used

The symbol “<” before a number means “less than”. Likewise, the symbol “>” means “greater than”. Therefore, you would read “<4%” as “less than 4%” and “>0.1%” as “greater than 0.1%”.

Frequency of Occurrence

Some drug studies report how many people have experienced a given ototoxic side effect. If I can find the results of such studies, I include the results and convert them to percentages. If there are two or more studies, I combine the results and show the range. This makes things easier to understand. Therefore, if one study reports that hearing loss is 1% and another reports it is less than 3%, I combine these results and show the range as between 1% and 3%. If the reported frequency is from a data base I simply list the number of people reporting this side effect (and an 3 letter abbreviation indicating where I got this information). If I do not have any information on of frequency of occurrence, I leave this blank.

Comparison to Placebo Results

In order to know whether a given ototoxic side effect is really a result of taking a certain drug or not, researchers often conduct special double-blind studies. In double-blind studies, a group of patients or study volunteers are divided into two sub-groups. One group gets the drug under study. The other group gets a “dummy” pill or “placebo” (commonly called a “sugar pill”). Neither the people taking the drugs/placebo nor the researchers examining the people and reporting the side effects know which group a person was in until after the study is completed. This eliminates obvious bias on the part of researchers and “wishful thinking” on the part of the study volunteers.

When reporting on such studies, I show the drug results as compared to the placebo results in square brackets. It might look like this: "Dizziness: 6.8% [1% above placebo results]". This means that in the drug study 6.8% of all the people who received the drug had resulting dizziness whereas only 5.8% of the test (placebo) group had dizziness. Thus, the drug under consideration is responsible for 1% of all the cases of dizziness observed.

I want to emphasize that these results only apply to the studies reported. They are not necessarily indicative of how another group of people might respond, or how the population in general would respond, but this is the best information we have at the moment.

Authorities Cited

The third piece of information beside any ototoxic side effect is the source from which I got that information. It is usually in the form of two three-character abbreviations in parentheses like this: "(CPS, PDR)".

I use these same abbreviations throughout this book. Table 1-1 lists all the abbreviations and acronyms used.

In order to keep this list of abbreviations manageable, I use footnote references instead of abbreviations if a source is only quoted a couple of times.

The six main references I quote are the CPS and PDR plus four on-line lists, the DCC, DIO, EHM and FMR. In addition, I have compiled information from a number of other drug books, and from various other sources (see Table 1-1).

I cite a maximum of two sources if they are available (in addition to the DCC, EHM or FMR) and place them in alphabetical order. This keeps things from getting too cumbersome. My first choices are typically the PDR and the CPS. If one or both of these two sources do not list that ototoxic side effect, I cite any other sources I have. If I only cite one source, that is the only source I have for that side effect.

Note that the figures listed for DCC, EHM and FMR are the number of incidents reported to the Food and Drug Administration (FDA) in the USA. Since, according to one FDA commissioner, the side effects reported to the FDA are less than 1% for major side effects, you can expect that it is far less than 1% for the "minor" ototoxic side effects. Thus, the figures shown are the absolute minimum results, not the real incidence of such side effects which will be much higher. Furthermore, the figures in the FMR are compiled from data between January 2004 and October 2012 so they represent just the reports sent to the FDA and FactMed in that 9-year period. (See Chapter 6 for much more detail about the grossly under-reported incidence of ototoxic side effects.)

Table 1-1. Authorities Cited (Abbreviations & Acronyms)

AHF	AHFS Drug Information. 2002, 2009.
ATS	Agency for Toxic Substances and Disease Registry. 2001.
BNF	British National Formulary. 2002, 2009.
CP2	Clinical Pharmacology 2000. 2001.
CPS	Compendium of Pharmaceuticals and Specialties. 1998, 2000, 2003, 2010.
DCC	DrugCite.Com 2012.
DFC	Drug Facts and Comparisons. 2009.
DIN	Drug Informer. www.druginformer.com. 2014
DIO	Drug Information Online. www.drugs.com. 2010-2022.
DMED	Daily Med. 2013.
EHM	eHealthMe. Real World Drug Outcomes. www.ehealthme.com. 2010, 2022, 2023.
Eps	Epstein. 2002. Drugs That Can Cause Hearing Loss/Drugs That Can Cause Tinnitus.
FMR	FactMed Reports. FactMed.com (data from between January, 2004 and October, 2012) (Information no longer on-line.)
GIP	Cianfrone. 2011. Guide for Italian Physicians. Pharmacological drugs inducing ototoxicity, vestibular symptoms and tinnitus: a reasoned and updated guide.
Ka7	Kaufman. 1997. Ototoxic Medications: Drugs That Can Cause Hearing Loss and Tinnitus.
Ka8	Kaufman. 1998. Ototoxic Drugs.
Med	Medscape DrugInfo. 1998-2013.
Med+	Medline Plus. 2001.
NDH	Nursing 2010 Drug Handbook. 2010, 2012.
Nia	Niall, Paul. 1998. The Effects of Industrial Ototoxic Agents and Noise on Hearing.
NTP	National Toxicology Program. 2001.
NVC	National Vaccine Information Center. 2023. https://www.medalerts.org/vaers-db/findfield.php; https://www.medalerts.org/index.php
PDR	Physicians' Desk Reference (PDR). 1997, 2000, 2002, 2003, 2007, 2008, 2009, 2010, 2012 (and PDR.COM on-line 2001).
PDR-H	Physicians' Desk Reference for Herbal Medicines. 2000, 2007.
PDR-N	Physicians' Desk Reference for Nonprescription Drugs and Dietary Supplements and PDR for Nonprescription Drugs, Dietary Supplements, and Herbs. 2002, 2008, 2009.
RXK	RxISK. http://wp.rxisk.org/category/stories. 2014.

Table 1-1. Authorities Cited (Abbreviations & Acronyms) (Cont'd.)

RXL	RxList Monographs. 1997-2023 RxList.com.
Ryb	Rybak, Leonard. 1992. Hearing: The Effects of Chemicals.
San	Sanders, Melodie. 1997. Drugs Which Can Cause Ototoxicity and/or Tinnitus.
She	Shemesh, Zecharya. 2001. List of Drugs Which May Cause Tinnitus.
Str	Strain, George. 1996. Aetiologies of Deafness.
USP	United States Pharmacopeia. 1997, 2001. Complete Drug Reference.
WIK	Wikipedia. 2024.
	Note: See the "Literature Cited" section at the back of this book for complete citations for these authorities.

Risk Assessment

Before you take a drug that might be ototoxic, you probably want to know two things. First, you want to know what your chances are of experiencing one or more of its ototoxic side effects. Second, you want to know how bad those side effects could be if you do experience any. You want to know, for example, if you will just experience a bit of temporary dizziness, or if your world will be flipped upside down as a result of permanently losing all your hearing or balance.

Unfortunately for us, not much is known about the risks of many ototoxic drugs. Therefore, I have come up with a **very rough** guide to assessing that risk. Note that this is my own personal subjective assessment of a drug's risk based on my knowledge and experience. Feel free to disagree with my risk assessment if you so choose. You and/or your doctor may come to an entirely different conclusion. That is quite all right. However, if you don't have a clue as to a drug's risk of ototoxicity you can use this one as a rough guideline.

I assign each drug a risk assessment class ranging from Class 0.5 (very low risk) to Class 5 (very high risk) in half-step increments based on the probability of a person experiencing an ototoxic side effect from taking that drug. Note: If a drug does not have any reported ototoxic side effects, I have not included it in this book.

I base the largest share of this risk assessment on how frequently people report these side effects—specifically biasing the rating in favor of two particular side effects, namely "hearing loss" and "tinnitus", and giving lesser emphasis to vestibular (balance) and other ototoxic side effects since most people want to know whether a given drug will cause them (further) hearing loss or give them tinnitus or cause their existing tinnitus to become much worse.

Fortunately for our ears, most drugs are in the lower risk classes but so much depends on the dose. As the dose increases, so does the risk of experiencing more/worse ototoxic side effects. Fortunately for us, as you can see, roughly half of all ototoxic drugs have a very low risk of producing ototoxic side effects. Also, again fortunately for our ears, relatively few drugs are in the high risk classes—Classes 4, 4.5 and 5. Table 1-2 shows the risk classes, together with the number of drugs in this book in each risk class and the percentage of drugs in each class.

Table 1-2: Number of Drugs by Risk Class

Risk Class	Number	Percent
0.5 (very low)	793	49.4%
1	259	16.1%
1.5 (low)	176	11.0%
2	104	6.4%
2.5 (moderate)	82	5.1%
3	80	5.0%
3.5	54	3.3%
4 (high)	42	2.8%
4.5	5	0.3%
5 (very high)	9	0.5%

Note: Sometimes I don't feel I have enough reliable information to make a reasonable assessment for a given drug. In such cases I take an educated guess as to what class it likely is and to show my significant degree of uncertainty I put a question mark ahead of the risk rating—thus ?2. This question mark indicates a considerable degree of uncertainty as to the completeness (or accuracy) of the specific ototoxic properties of this drug, but I think it would probably be in this risk class if I had more information available.

Some of these drugs may be new, foreign, experimental, restricted or withdrawn. As a result, there currently may be little information on their ototoxic side effects readily available. This is especially true if these drugs are foreign and there is not much information available on them in English. Thus, many of them are rated as 0.5 now, but as more information becomes available, they could rate higher in the future.

The higher the risk class, the more you need to be convinced that this drug is absolutely necessary. Never forget that even a Class 0.5 or Class 1 drug has a very real risk, and you may experience severe side effects from taking it as some people have found out to their sorrow. It's just that fewer people experience these side effects than do those taking higher-risk-class drugs.

Thus, don't assume that tinnitus (for example) resulting from a Class 0.5 drug will be mild and temporary and tinnitus from a Class 5 drug will be severe and permanent. That may or may not be true. This rating is not an estimate of severity—only frequency of occurrence no matter what the rating.

With Class 4 and 5 drugs, you have a much greater chance of getting one or more of the ototoxic side effects listed. Therefore, you need to carefully weigh the risk of developing adverse side effects from taking such drugs against the proposed benefits of taking them in order to satisfy yourself that the resulting trade-off will be worth it. Thus, it is a good idea to ask your doctor to prescribe the least ototoxic drugs that will do the job.

Furthermore, consider the various risk factors that may apply to you when making this decision. (See Chapter 5 for these risk factors and how you can help put the odds in your favor.)

Finally, you need to remember that this risk assessment only applies to **ototoxic** side effects—not to all the other adverse side effects these drugs may have. You may be shocked to learn that many drugs have 100 to 300 different side effects. Since **all** drugs can have adverse side effects, you want to weigh **all** adverse side effects when considering taking any medication, not just their ototoxic side effects I cover in this book.

Notes

The notes section gives additional information about a given drug. Many drugs do not have any notes.

There are three basic kinds of information I list here. First, for combination drugs, I list all the drugs contained in this compound. I indicate which of them are ototoxic and which listings to go to for further information on their ototoxic properties. Second, I give further information on this drug's ototoxicity and use if available. Third, I refer you to other chapters in this book for further information on this drug or things related to this drug.

Anecdotal Reports

Anecdotal reports are personal (anecdotal) stories of **real** people who have written to me about the side effects **they have experienced**—supposedly from taking a given drug. Take them at face value (or not) as you choose. The more anecdotal reports listed of a given drug, the more common those side effects likely are. Do not take the absence of anecdotal reports as indicating that the drug does not affect people—just that no one has told me of their experiences with that particular drug's side effect(s). If you search online, you may find many, many more such anecdotal reports than are listed here.

Ototoxic Drugs by Drug Class (Table 19-1 Explained)

Table 19-1 follows the drug listings. It is easy to find as it is the second set of "tabbed" pages (Vol. 2, pages 1445-1493). (The tabs are visible on the front edge of the pages in this table.)

Drugs in Table 19-1 are arranged in alphabetical order by drug class (except that the "Supplements" class is placed at the end) and by generic name within each drug class/subclass. Subclasses and sub-subclasses are grouped more by function than alphabetically.

As previously mentioned, many drugs fall into two or more use classes. However, I show each drug under only one class—it's main classification—so as not to make this table longer than it needs to be. Where possible, I've tried to arrange the classes so that they contain chemically similar drugs, since they will be more likely to have similar ototoxic properties. If their chemical classes are unknown, I've attempted to group them in classes by their most common use. In such cases, these drugs are not necessarily related chemically so can have widely varying ototoxic side effects.

You can use this table to quickly determine which drug(s) is likely to be the least ototoxic of the drugs listed in a given class as the column on the right lets you see the risk assessment class of each drug.

Here is an example of how you could benefit by using this table. Let's assume your doctor prescribed the ACE INHIBITOR **Ramipril** for your high blood pressure. You could turn to section 20.8.8 in Table 19-1 and see all the ACE INHIBITORS and their ototoxic risk classes at a glance. Upon inspection, you can see that **Enalapril** and **Ramipril** have the highest risk class (3.5) in this class of drugs. You can also see that **Cilazapril**, **Imidapril** and **Rescinnamine** have the lowest risk (0.5). Therefore, you might suggest to your doctor that all things being equal, and if one of these drugs would do the job, you would rather he prescribe one of them for you, as you want to save your ears from further damage as much as possible.

If those choices aren't acceptable for some reason, you could suggest drugs in risk class 1 or 1.5. However, before you decide on a specific drug, read the drug listings for the drugs you are thinking about taking to see their specific side effects and other pertinent information listed there.

What To Do If You Can't Find a Particular Drug/Chemical

There are five reasons why a drug or chemical for which you are looking might not be listed in this book.

1. The most obvious reason is that the drug or chemical is not known to be ototoxic. This book only contains drugs known to me to be ototoxic. However, don't assume that if a drug/chemical is not listed in this book, it is not ototoxic. It may be. Read on.

2. It is a new drug put on the market after I did the research for this book, or its ototoxic properties have been newly discovered/reported. Some existing drugs once thought to have no effect on our ears, later prove to be ototoxic months, years or even decades after they are released. A good recent example is the drug **Acetaminophen**. It wasn't listed at all in the second edition of this book (2003) as it wasn't then known to be ototoxic, but it has now been found to be quite ototoxic. **Amoxicillin** is another such drug.

3. It is a foreign drug. There are a number of ototoxic drugs used in foreign countries that are not listed in this book. This is because I have a difficult time getting reliable information on many foreign drugs. However, I have listed all the foreign ototoxic drugs I have come across.

4. It is an "old" drug or chemical that is no longer used. There are a number of drugs that have been used in the past and are not used any more or are no longer used in Canada and the USA. When this happens, current drug publications such as the CPS, PDR or on-line databases cease listing these drugs. However, just because they are no longer being used does not mean that they were not ototoxic. In fact, some of these were highly ototoxic. The problem is that since they are no longer listed, it is hard to dig up the specific ototoxic properties of these drugs. Therefore, reliable information on some of these discontinued drugs may be meager or non-existent.

5. I missed it somehow. I'm certainly not infallible. Furthermore, I don't have access to all the ototoxic drug information that is squirreled away in various places all over the planet. Thus, I have no idea how many ototoxic drugs I may have missed while compiling this book.

If you are suspicious that a drug may be ototoxic yet it is not listed in this book, there are a couple of things you can do. First, realize that this book will be obsolete before it is even published since there are new ototoxic drugs coming on the market all the time.

Therefore, look up any drug not listed here in the latest version of the PDR if you are in the USA or the CPS if you are in Canada, or better yet, look it up on the Internet as information on new drugs appears on the Internet quite fast. You may find that Drugs.com is a good place to start.

Second, you can often make an educated guess as to a drug's ototoxic properties since drugs that are chemically similar in a given class of drugs likely have similar ototoxic side effects to some degree or other.

Begin by determining what class of drug you have or ask your pharmacist. Then turn to Table 19-1 and find that class of drugs and see what the ototoxic properties of the various drugs in that class are. You could make a reasonable assumption that any new drugs in that class (especially if they are chemically similar) will likely have similar ototoxic properties—although this is not always true. Some of the newer drugs are more ototoxic and some of them are less ototoxic.

Let's say you are wondering about the drug *Terramycin*. You don't find it listed in the drug listings. You know that *Terramycin* is the brand name of the generic drug Oxytetracycline. You have discovered that it is a member of the **Tetracycline** class of drugs. You turn to the TETRACYCLINES (section 7.4.60) in Table 19-1. There you see seven drugs listed. You could assume that *Terramycin* has much the same chance of causing ototoxicity. as the drugs listed in this class, although that has not yet been reported.

Next, look up the various drugs in this class and see what the individual drug listings say about the ototoxic side effects of each of these drugs. At this point, decide if you want to risk taking that drug. What you are really doing is making an educated guess, but by doing so, you are helping to put the odds in your favor.

Herbals

The herbal section (Chapter 20) follows the same general format as do the drugs. They are in alphabetical order by their scientific names. Herbs do not have headings for "Drug classification," "Pronunciation guide," "Brand names" and "Risk assessment".

Two new headings they do have are: "Common name" and "Main active ingredient".

Common Name

This is the common English name(s) by which most people know this herb.

Main Active Ingredients

These are the active chemical constituents that can cause ototoxic side effects.

Chemicals

The chemical section (Chapter 21) also follows the same general format as does the drug section, but with a few differences. There are no headings for "Drug classification" and "Risk assessment," but I have added two other headings, namely "Other Names" and "Uses".

Other Names

The "Brand names" heading used for ototoxic drugs is now the more general heading, "Other names". This is because it includes not only trade names, but alternate chemical names for this substance. Trade (brand) names (at least what I think are trade names) are in *italics*. Other chemical names are in normal type.

Sometimes it is hard to tell which is the most commonly-used name for a chemical. In these cases, I have chosen one and placed the synonyms listed under "Other names".

Uses

Unlike drugs, which you basically take when you are sick, chemicals are used all the time and can be found everywhere. As a result, knowing where a given chemical is used gives you a clue as to whether you may have been exposed to it or not.

Drug Comparison Tables

Appendix 1 contains tables of 21 selected common classes of drugs so at a glance you can see the relative ototoxic risk of the various drugs in that class. For example, there are tables covering anti-hypertensive (blood pressure) drugs; cholesterol-lowering drugs; nonsteroidal anti-inflammatory (NSAID) drugs; selective serotonin reuptake inhibitor (SSRI & SSNRI) drugs; some of the common antibiotic drugs; and benzodiazepine drugs.

Glossary

If you come across unfamiliar words, see Appendix 2 for a brief definition.

Chapter 1 Endnotes

1 Tavor, 2022. p. 1.
2 American Tinnitus Association, 2002. p. 2.

Section II

What You Need to Know About Ototoxic Drugs

Chapter 2

Ototoxic Drugs—What Are They?

Ototoxic Drugs Defined

Drugs whose side effects can damage your ears, particularly your inner ears, go by the name of ototoxic drugs. "Oto" refers to ears, and "toxic" means something that is poisonous. Therefore, technically, ototoxic really means "ear poisoning". However, it is not necessarily used in quite that literal a sense.

The *American Heritage Dictionary* currently defines "ototoxic" as "having a toxic effect on the structures of the ear, especially on its nerve supply".[1] Consequently, in a restricted sense, ototoxicity refers to drugs and chemicals that damage the inner ear and/or the hearing and balance nerves (vestibulo-cochlear nerve) going from your inner ears to your brain.

However, the authoritative source, *Stedman's Medical Dictionary*, simply defines ototoxicity as "the property of being injurious to the ear".[2]

As a result, your view of ototoxicity depends on which dictionary definition you use.

The Two Opposing Schools of Thought Regarding Ototoxicity

If you use the *American Heritage Dictionary* definition, then you believe there are few ototoxic drugs. This is the view of many doctors. However, if you use *Stedman's Medical Dictionary*, then you will tend to believe there are many drugs that are ototoxic.

The same holds true for the number of ototoxic side effects a drug may have. If you hold the former view, you may narrowly define ototoxicity as causing hearing loss and vertigo, and maybe tinnitus. In contrast, if you hold the latter view, you identify at least 30 different ototoxic side effects.

These two opposing views of ototoxicity gives rise to some confusion as to exactly what constitutes an ototoxic drug and an ototoxic side effect.

For example, in an online chat room for hard of hearing people, one lady asked me if a certain drug was ototoxic. I replied, "It can cause hyperacusis, tinnitus, ataxia, dizziness, vertigo and ear pain". She typed back, "But is it ototoxic?" You see, to her, ototoxicity was hearing loss and nothing else. Other people consider tinnitus also to be an ototoxic side effect. To me, all of the above are symptoms of ototoxicity.

Ototoxic Drugs Aren't New

Ototoxic medications have been around for a long time. In fact, ototoxic substances have been recognized for more than 3,500 years—since the 15th or 16th century B.C.![1] However, it was only in the past 130 years that have doctors recognized the ototoxic potential of certain drugs.

For example, for centuries the natives in South America have used **Quinine**, found in the bark of the cinchona tree, to treat malaria. About 1630, Europeans also began using this drug for treating malaria. Even so, it wasn't until the late 1800s that doctors began to realize the ototoxic effects of **Quinine**.

Here is another example. In 1829, researchers discovered salicin, the active ingredient of SALICYLATES (of which **Aspirin** is one), but it took another 48 years (until 1877) before they first noticed its ototoxic properties.[2]

References

1 Haybach, 1998. p. 6.
2 Haybach, 1999. pp. 16-17.

Another lady remarked:

> I'm confused because I've read some other opinions (from MDs) that for example **Trazodone** or BENZODIAZEPINES are not ototoxic in the sense that they do not cause physical damage of ear structures. They explained that these medications just change some brain chemicals and thus can cause tinnitus. Or it can be because they cause excess release of some chemicals in the brain that are ototoxic.

I explained that many doctors consider ototoxicity to be only those conditions that affect the inner ear and associated nerves (auditory nerve and vestibular nerve). To them, the structures of your ears subject to ototoxicity include your cochlea, vestibule, semicircular canals and related structures.[3]

So whether you or your doctor consider a given side effect ototoxic or not basically boils down to whether you limit your definition of ototoxicity to drugs that physically damage the auditory or vestibular systems in your inner ears, or whether you use Stedman's broad definition and include in your definition of ototoxicity, drugs that disrupt the normal functioning of any part of the auditory and vestibular systems in any way whether there is physical damage or not.

View 1: Few Drugs Are Ototoxic

It appears that most medical doctors hold the view that few drugs are ototoxic; that there are few ototoxic side effects; and even if ototoxic side effects appear, they are almost always temporary—with a few exceptions.

As a result, when you are proactive and ask your doctor whether a drug he is prescribing for you is ototoxic, he may assure you that the drug is not ototoxic, then, when you take this drug you are blindsided by the appearance of a severe ototoxic side effect. This is exactly what happened to one man. He reported:

> Three years ago, after taking **Bupropion** for six months, I woke up with tinnitus and a few days later with vertigo. I was told by my doctors that there was **no connection** to my tinnitus, but stopped anyway because I broke out in a rash. I have had tinnitus ever since. A few weeks ago I started taking **Bupropion** again, believing it wasn't related, and now my tinnitus is a louder shrieking sound. I will never take this drug again because now I have to listen to this terrible sound for the rest of my life—it is so loud and unpleasant. I would never have chosen this over depression if I had even the slightest idea this could be a side effect. That I took this drug for depression is so ironic. I should have been warned!

This leaves the patient confused and ultimately not trusting his doctor.

Here's another example. A man read my article, *The Ototoxicity of Drugs Ending in -mycin.*[4] In it, I mentioned that all of the drugs listed there (which included **Clindamycin**) are ototoxic to some extent or other.

He then referred me to Dr. Tim Hain's article *Ototoxic Medications*[5] where Dr. Hain had written, "**Clindamycin** has not been reported to cause ototoxicity, by itself, and is probably safe."

Confused, this man then lamented,

> This article says that there is no reported hearing loss from **Clindamycin**, and you say differently. I don't know what to believe anymore.

I explained to this man that even on the good sites like Dr. Hain's, there are differences of opinion, and that Dr. Hain is ultra-conservative and defines ototoxicity very narrowly.

I further explained that ultra-conservative doctors, don't believe a drug is ototoxic unless it has been written up by another doctor as being ototoxic, and/or there are formal studies to prove it. Thus, they discount anecdotal reports of ototoxicity by members of the public that have actually experienced ototoxic side effects from a given drug. They typically put such side effects down to "coincidence". Thus, you need to exercise a measure of wisdom to discern the truth.

Dr. Stephen Nagler is another ultra-conservative doctor on the topic of ototoxicity. When asked:

> Do you know if there is a website that contains information about the ototoxicity of common prescription and OTC drugs? If so, I'd love to be able to share that with my doctors and also with friends.

He answered:

> This is a very important issue that comes up time and time again because tinnitus sufferers typically feel that they "just don't want to take any chances". And who can blame them?
>
> The problem, as I see it, is that lists like you describe tend to promote the avoidance of any risk whatsoever, which in my opinion is not a good idea ... because **every medication we take has some risk**.... So in terms of medications and tinnitus, the real question comes down not to how to avoid all risk but rather to what are and are not acceptable risks in any given situation. And none of the ototoxic lists available in print or on-line makes that distinction. So while websites like you seek do exist, I never refer to them.

I agree with Dr. Nagler that just having a list of ototoxic drugs or having a list of drugs as having a given side effect—for example, tinnitus (such as my on-line tinnitus list[6] are not very useful without qualifying information on the resulting ototoxicity of each drug. This is because 100% of the top 200 prescription drugs can be ototoxic. Thus, in order to avoid all ototoxic drugs, you'd have to avoid taking any drugs in the first place!

What you really need is an annotated list detailing the kinds of ototoxic side effects a given drug can cause. For example, is the drug known to cause tinnitus or hearing loss or hyperacusis or vertigo or ear pain, or all of them. You want to know how likely any given side effect will occur—is the risk of occurrence 15% or just 1 in 10,000? You also want to know how severe a side effect is likely to be if it does occur—will it just be mild dizziness or severe intractable vertigo. In addition, you want to know whether the resulting side effects are likely to be temporary or permanent.

As far as I know, the only reasonably complete source of such information that is readily available in one place and is in an easy-to-read format is contained in this book you are now reading. However, such lists do serve to raise awareness of the vast number of drugs that can cause tinnitus—whether permanently or temporarily.

Dr. Nagler continues:

> Instead, I recommend that tinnitus sufferers do exactly what I myself do when it comes to medications, which is to avoid if possible those medications known to potentially cause irreversible auditory damage. As far as those medications not known to potentially cause irreversible auditory damage but that might nonetheless still aggravate tinnitus, my thinking is that since it would be extremely rare that the increased tinnitus would not return to baseline upon cessation of the drug, I just don't worry about it.
>
> With the above paragraph in mind, then, here are the drugs that I would absolutely avoid unless the situation were life-threatening and no acceptable alternative could be found that would effectively address that life-threatening condition.[7]

He then lists a handful of drugs he considers to be ototoxic—a mere 10 drugs. These include Aminoglycosides such as **Gentamycin**, **Streptomycin**, **Amikacin** and **Tobramycin**; quinine-based drugs such as **Chloroquine** and **Quinidine**; platinum-based Anti-neoplastic drugs such as **Cisplatin** and **Carboplatin**; and **Azithromycin**; and **Nabumetone**.

View 2: Most Drugs Are Ototoxic

In contrast to the narrow view of what comprises ototoxicity, this book follows Stedman's definition when considering whether a drug side effect is ototoxic or not. I think this reflects the desire of the average person to know all the side effects a given drug can cause to their ears.

When doctors take the narrow view of the definition of ototoxicity, they do not consider ear pain to be an ototoxic side effect even though 772 drugs are reported to cause it. I think most readers would want to know this fact before they take one of these drugs.

Furthermore, doctors taking the narrow view of ototoxicity would not consider a drug to be ototoxic if it blocked the ion-gates that prevent sound signals from being passed to your brain (but which do not cause physical damage to your ear structures—yet you'd be just as deaf as if the drug had caused the death of the hair cells in your inner ears. You'd want to know that fact too, wouldn't you?

Thus, for the purposes of this book, I use the term "ototoxicity" in its broadest sense (as per Stedman). Simply put, I take a pragmatic view of ototoxicity. If a drug causes your ears (both hearing and balance systems) to function abnormally in **any** way, it is ototoxic whether it physically damages your ear structures or not.

Therefore, using Stedman's definition of ototoxicity, a drug that causes hearing loss by producing excessive ear wax (ceruminosis) so it blocks your ear canal is ototoxic (but very mildly so) as are drugs that cause middle ear congestion.

In addition, drugs that damage the auditory or balance circuits in the base of your brain are also ototoxic since they result in your inability to maintain your balance or to understand what you hear.

When you take this view of ototoxicity, you will find that most drugs can have ototoxic side effects whether there have been formal studies done on them or not.

The truth is that up to now many drugs have not been screened for ototoxicity. According to neuroscientist Allison Coffin:

> There are a number of different drugs that cause hearing loss, but we only know that because patients receive these drugs and start reporting hearing loss.

She further explained:

> Hearing loss is not tested for as a possible side effect during drug development or clinical trials.[8]

In other words, there are few (or no) clinical studies to show whether a drug causes hearing loss or not, so doctors assume they don't.

To add insult to injury, few doctors accept anecdotal reports. Thus, they discount anecdotal reports of hearing loss and other ototoxic side effects (such as are reported in this book).

The result is that untold millions of people suffer drug side effects, report them to their doctors, and instead of taking their complaints seriously, their doctors often ignore them and write their observations off as a "coincidence", another condition or categorically declare "that drug doesn't/can't cause that side effect" and send the patients on their (not so) merry way.

Fortunately, some medical professionals take a much more all-encompassing view and accept anecdotal reports as having validity even if no formal studies have been done. After all, a drug that is ototoxic is still ototoxic whether a study has been done to prove it or not. As you can tell, this is my philosophy also.

Therefore, I typically accept a person's report of experiencing drug side effects at face value. If only one person ever reports a certain side effect for a given drug, I tend to write it off as a coincidence or an anomaly. However, when several, or many, people all tell me essentially the same thing, I take this as strong circumstantial evidence that this is indeed a valid ototoxic side effect and needs to be taken seriously. Note that circumstantial evidence is accepted in a court of law, so why can't medical doctors accept circumstantial evidence in relation to ototoxicity? There is no valid reason for not doing so.

How Common Are Ototoxic Drugs?

As it stands today, ototoxic drugs have been largely ignored. Few doctors can name more than a handful of ototoxic drugs if even that many.

However, ototoxic substances are much more common than people realize. For example, researchers estimate that between 1.5% and 16% of the more than 1,000,000 different chemical compounds (which includes drugs, industrial chemicals and metals) may be sensory toxicants. This means that between 15,000 and 160,000 chemical compounds likely affect our senses.[9]

Those chemical compounds that specifically damage our ears are a subset of this number. We have five senses, with our eyes and ears being the major ones. I am going to take a guess (this is just my own personal unsupported opinion here, and it may be totally wrong) and say that our eyes and ears respectively each account for 35% of this total and that our other three senses (taste, touch and smell) account for approximately 10% each.

If my 35% figure is in the ballpark, there may be between 5,200 and 56,000 ototoxic chemical agents out there. (Even if we assume that each of the 5 senses has an equal share at 20%, these figures would still range between 3,000 and 32,000 ototoxic agents.)

This book contains information on the 1,812 ototoxic agents known to me at the time of writing, but obviously this is a small fraction of the ototoxic agents that exist—just 3% to 35% (or 6% to 60% if you take the 20% figure) of the ototoxic substances thought to be out there. No matter which way you figure it, there are still an lot of ototoxic agents of which we know nothing at this time!

The 1,812 ototoxic substances in this book break down into three categories: 1,604 drugs, 64 herbals and 144 chemicals.

As I mentioned previously, some drugs have only one brand name; others have more than 100! (I've included the more common brands—a total of about 3,959 brand names.) In the "Ototoxic Chemicals" section I list a total of about 676 brand names and alternate chemical names and 99 alternate names of herbals.

As you might expect, drug manufacturers release a number of new drugs each year. Unfortunately, many of these new drugs are ototoxic. A number of years ago I was looking at the 1998 edition of the *Complete Drug Reference*. They included a number of "Introductory Version Patient Education Leaflets" in their Appendix I. These are leaflets for the new drugs that have not yet gone through the formal review process yet. This is a great idea since it provides consumers with relevant information on medications as soon as possible after these new drugs hit the market.

In their Appendix I, they listed 53 new drugs. I was shocked to see that fully 28% already had known ototoxic side effects.[10] Remember, these are all new drugs. Field testing of new drugs (meaning we are the guinea pigs) often reveals a host of further ototoxic side effects.

In fact, we knew by 2001 that a whopping 62% of these drugs had ototoxic side effects. This means almost two-thirds of the new drugs that come on the market each year are found to be ototoxic within 3 years of their release! (Note that these figures are very conservative. The true figure is close to 100%—see page 395.) This is scary and something we all need to know. I would have hoped that new drugs would be safer for our ears, not the other way around. However, this does not seem to be the case.

As further corroboration, *Supplement A*, the semi-annual supplement to the *Physicians' Desk Reference*, listed 15 new ototoxic drugs in the 2000 edition.[11] Therefore, it is likely that at a very minimum, 30 new drugs with ototoxic properties are coming on the market each and every year in America alone!

Warning Ototoxic Side Effects

Ototoxic drugs often damage the sensitive hair cells in your cochlea and/or in your vestibular (balance) system. This can result in a number of side effects, depending on the exact site of the damage. Some ototoxic drugs cause permanent damage while others only have a temporary effect on your ears. A few of the ototoxic side effects you may experience include temporary or permanent hearing loss in both ears, generally, but not always, in the higher frequencies; ringing or other noises in your ears; dizziness or vertigo; eye problems; and balance problems. (Chapter 4 gives a comprehensive list and explanation of the many ototoxic side effects.)

Often the first warning you get of impending damage to your ears is when your ears begin to ring (tinnitus) or, if you already have tinnitus, your tinnitus gets worse.[12] Tinnitus usually appears first as a continuous high-pitched sound. The reason for this is that ototoxic drugs generally damage the hair cells at the base of the cochlea which is where the high-frequency sounds are detected and passed on to your brain. If your ears begin to ring, you should immediately report this to your doctor, then together you and your doctor should decide what to do—

whether to reduce the dose, change the medication or stop taking that medication altogether in order to prevent ear "damage" from getting worse.

If your tinnitus is not very loud to begin with, or if you are quite sick, you may not even be aware of this warning signal until after it is too late.

The same holds true for some of the warning symptoms of vestibular damage. If you are bedridden, or in the hospital, you may not notice that your balance is affected until later when you are feeling better and try to get up. By then, it may be too late to do much to mitigate the damage.

Unfortunately, doctors often attribute this unsteadiness to the results of your sickness, or to your being bedridden, not to drug-induced damage to your vestibular system. As a result, doctors may overlook such ototoxic damage, or fail to diagnose it right away.[13]

Therefore, if you find that you have balance problems after you get out of the hospital, both you and your doctor need to carefully review your hospital records for any ototoxic drugs you may have taken. Be aware that symptoms may not appear until several days after you get home.[14]

Another warning you may have is a feeling of fullness or pressure in your ears. Your ears may feel "blocked" or "full". In contrast, your first warning typically will not be a noticeable hearing loss.

If you complete a course of drug therapy with apparently no ill side effects to your ears, don't assume that the drug did not harm your ears in any way. The time for ototoxic damage to show up varies tremendously. For example, intravenous Loop diuretics or high-dose Salicylate therapy can bring on hearing loss in a matter of minutes. The shortest time I've come across is just 7 minutes later. The ototoxic effects of other drugs such as **Erythromycin** and **Cisplatin** normally show up in the first 4 days of therapy.

Unfortunately, the ototoxic side effects of some drugs don't show up for several days, weeks or months after you **stop** taking them. By then, it is typically much too late for your doctor to do anything about it. The ototoxic effects of Aminoglycoside antibiotics can take from a few days to 6 months[15] or more to reveal themselves.[16] Also, be aware that when you take various drugs from time to time over many years, each different drug may have a minor effect on your ears, but taken together, they may result in noticeable hearing loss or other ear damage as the years roll by.

However, don't blame drugs for all of your ear problems. You do not want to automatically assume that there must be a cause-and-effect relationship between any drug you are taking and any symptoms of ear damage you are experiencing.

For example, just because tinnitus develops while you are taking a certain drug does not necessarily mean that the drug caused the tinnitus. It might have. Then again, your tinnitus might have come from an entirely different source—for example, being overtired, or stressed out, or from exposing your ears to loud sounds.

If you are in doubt as to whether a drug is causing ototoxic damage to your ears or not, stop taking the medication (with your doctor's permission of course) and see if the symptoms go away. You need to allow your body time to get rid of the drug so give it at least two weeks or so. If the symptoms become less pronounced or go away, begin taking the drug again and watch if the symptoms come back. If they return, that is a strong indication that this drug is indeed ototoxic to your ears.

Just be aware that for certain drugs, and based on your body chemistry and other factors, some ototoxic side effects can prove to be permanent and thus do not go away when you stop taking those drugs, so the above experiment won't work in such cases.

Some Common Ototoxic Drug Classes

There are a few classes of ototoxic drugs that doctors commonly recognize today (although there are many more drugs in other classes that they should recognize). These classes include the Aminoglycoside antibiotics (**Amikacin**, **Gentamicin**, **Neomycin**, **Tobramycin**, etc.), Salicylates (**Aspirin**, etc.), Quinines (**Chloroquine**, **Quinine**, etc.), Loop Diuretics (**Ethacrynic acid**, **Furosemide**, etc.), and some Anti-neoplastics (anti-cancer drugs such as **Buserelin**, **Cisplatin**, **Vinblastine**, **Vincristine**, etc.).

In addition, NSAIDs (Non-steroidal anti-inflammatory drugs), Antibiotics, Antihistamines, Cardiovascular drugs, Anti-convulsant drugs, Anti-depressant drugs and Anti-psychotic drugs (tranquilizers) are also ototoxic.

Furthermore, there are many drugs in other classes that are ototoxic to some degree or other. To see the risk assessment of the ototoxic drugs in this book by their classes, see Table 19-1 (page 1445—second set of tabbed pages).

Ototoxicity Often Minimized

Most people, many doctors included, do not think about ototoxic drugs. In fact, ototoxic drugs are so far removed from the stream of human consciousness that until very recently the word "ototoxic" was not even listed in regular dictionaries!

This begs the question, "How is the average person supposed to find out about ototoxic drugs when the word isn't even mentioned?" Thus, it should be no surprise that drug books downplay the seriousness of ototoxic side effects. For example, in the 2006 edition of *The Essential Guide to Prescription Drugs* the author compiled 12 tables of drugs that cause "important" side effects for various conditions.

Does this book have a special table for ototoxicity? Definitely not! There are tables for such important things as drugs that may cause damage to your blood, nerves, heart, lungs, liver and kidneys. There are tables for drugs that might increase your sensitivity to sunlight; drugs that can adversely affect your sexuality; and drugs that may interact with alcohol. There is even a table for drugs that may adversely affect your vision. To be sure, good vision is vital to people with poor hearing. Hard of hearing people use their eyes as their ears. However, there is no table specifically for drugs that adversely affect ears. This needs to change!

Because the incidence of ototoxicity is minimized, it is easy to fall into the trap of believing that because ototoxic side effects have not been reported for a given drug, it must be safe for your ears. A good quote to remember is, "absence of evidence does not equal evidence of absence". In other words, just because an ototoxic side effect has not been reported for a specific drug does not mean that that drug never causes ototoxic damage. In fact, as you will see in Chapter 6, the **vast majority** of occurrences of ototoxic side effects are **never** reported.

Deaf People and Ototoxicity

I've been asked by deaf people if they have to worry about taking ototoxic drugs. Their thinking is that they are already deaf so what further damage can drugs cause. The truth is that just because you may be deaf already doesn't mean that you are immune to the side effects of ototoxic drugs. True, you may not experience any further hearing loss if your hearing is already totally gone. However, ototoxic drugs can still cause ear pain and middle ear congestion, not to mention cause damage to your vestibular (balance) system. Most of the drugs in this book are known to affect the vestibular system in some way. Therefore, whether you are deaf or not, you still want to be very careful when taking any ototoxic drugs if you value your balance.

If you are almost deaf (severe or profound hearing loss), you certainly don't want to lose your remaining precious bit of hearing or cause it to become even more distorted than it already is. Some health care professionals might wonder what difference a little hearing makes. To them it may be insignificant. To us, it is extremely important.

How Ototoxic Drugs Damage Your Ears

Ototoxic drugs can damage your ears in a variety of ways. Not all of these are known, but here are three known ways drugs can damage your ears.

1. Free Radicals

Free radicals cause oxidative stress. Oxidative stress results when drugs, chemicals, loud sounds, etc. generate free radicals. Note: A free radical is an atom or molecule that has at least one unpaired electron in its outer orbit. This makes it highly unstable and reactive since it wants to become stable again. Thus, these unstable oxygen atoms/molecules steal electrons from nearby molecules in order to become stable.

Unfortunately, the hair cells in your inner ears are particularly susceptible to damage by free radicals. Think of these free radicals as tiny enemy bullets. If they "zap" (steal an electron) from a hair cell's fatty walls, this damages a cell. Enough of this thievery mortally wounds the hair cell. It then basically commits suicide through a process doctors call **apoptosis** in which it systematically shuts itself down and dies. With the death of each hair cell, a bit more of your hearing disappears too.

It is not necessarily that the drug itself is toxic to the hair cells, rather it can be the by-products of drugs (such as the AMINOGLYCOSIDES) that cause free radicals to form. In turn, it is these free radicals that cause the ototoxicity. This is why it is important to zap the free radicals before they do their dastardly deeds.

The good news is that taking antioxidants can largely prevent this damage. Antioxidants are the "good guys". They basically zap the free radicals by "shooting" an "electron bullet" at them, thus neutralizing them so they no longer try to steal an electron from the hair cells. As a result they cease causing damage to these inner ear structures.

One of your body's most powerful natural antioxidants is glutathione. Some drugs such as **Acetaminophen** deplete your body of glutathione., Thus, supplementing your diet with antioxidant building blocks such as N-acetyl-cysteine (NAC) can help protect your hair cells from free radical damage, and thus prevent hearing loss.

2. Ion Gates

Some drugs only temporarily cause your ears to malfunction. Thus, when you stop taking the drug in question, your hearing comes back. How can this happen? Note that this can only happen if the hair cells are "sick", not dead.

In some cases, an agent blocks the sound signals from getting through to your brain, thus you don't hear. When the blocking agent is removed, your hearing returns.

Here's how this can happen. In order for a sound signal to pass from your inner ears to your brain, it must first go through an ion gate (or ion channel) located at the entrance to each auditory nerve fiber. These ion gates are located at the bases of the tiny stereocilia on the hair cells. Tip links at the top of each cilia momentarily "yank" open these ion gates. When a ion gate opens, potassium ions rush in—causing a sound signal to be sent to your brain.

This is how it normally works. However, some drugs produce an excess of certain ions that love to "stand" in the ion gates and block the way so the potassium ions can't pass—think of a big goon standing in the gate and not letting the tiny potassium ions carry their message to your brain. (For example, heavy metals such as lead and mercury can do this.) The result is a temporary (or fluctuating) hearing loss.

However, if you carry out a detoxifying program and get rid of the heavy metals or the offending drugs, this effectively removes the "goons" blocking the ion gates and sound signals can once more pass to your brain. Thus, your hearing returns to normal. This scenario works because there is no physical damage to the inner ear structures—just the "goons" temporarily blocking the ion gates.

3. Decreased Blood Flow

Your hearing is dependent on an adequate supply of blood continually flowing to your inner ears. Some drugs decrease this blood flow. Since some of the smallest arteries in your body are in your inner ears, your ears are very sensitive to any reduced blood flow.

When not enough blood reaches your inner ears, they stop operating normally and one result is reduced hearing. By quitting the drug, and/or taking vasodilators, adequate blood flow is restored and hearing returns to normal.

Chapter 2 Endnotes

1 American Heritage Dictionary, 2000.
2 Stedman's Medical Dictionary, 2000. p. 1288.
3 Guidelines for the Audiologic Management of Individuals Receiving Cochleotoxic Drug Therapy, 1994. p. 1.
4 Bauman, 2015. p. 1.
5 Hain, 2001b. p. 1.
6 Bauman, 2021. p. 1.
7 Nagler, 2018a. pp. 1-2.

8 WSU Researchers to Build Ototoxic Drug Database, 2021. p. 1.
9 Environmental Impact on Hearing: Is Anyone Listening, 1994. p. 5.
10 United States Pharmacopeia, 1998. pp. 1672-1725.
11 Physicians' Desk Reference. 54th Edition. Supplement A, 2000.
12 Compendium of Pharmaceuticals and Specialties, 2000. pp. 1589, 1669.
13 Troost, 1998b. p. 1.
14 Troost, 1998b. p. 2.
15 Haybach, 1999. p. 62.
16 Haybach, 1998. p. 3.

Chapter 3

Factors Affecting Ototoxicity Vary from Person to Person

We are all different, so it should be no surprise that we all react differently to drugs. Therefore, just because a drug is listed in this book doesn't necessarily mean you will damage your ears if you take that drug. The truth is that ototoxic drugs do not always (or even mostly) cause ototoxic damage—but be warned, they can. Each person's body is slightly different and thus reacts somewhat differently.

For example, Marcia had been taking **Diclofenac** for **15 years** and did not have any noticeable ear damage, although the drug she had been taking could cause hearing loss, balance problems and tinnitus. She was one of the fortunate ones.

In contrast, "Sylvia" took **Diclofenac** for just **15 days** when she developed severe tinnitus, severe vertigo and severe hearing loss in her right ear. That's how different ototoxic reactions can be to the same drug.

This begs the question, "Why are drug reactions so varied and harmful?"

Why Can Drugs Be So Harmful?

There are a number of factors that affect why drugs can be so harmful to some people and not to others, and why the severity of any resulting side effects can vary so much between different people. A lot has to do with what doctors call pharmacodynamics, which is a fancy way of saying how drugs affect or act in your body.

According to one doctor, the reason why drug side effects are often so harmful typically boils down to four main reasons.

1. The drug in question should not be on the market in the first place as it causes significant risks with minimal benefits. (This typically occurs because it is very profitable to the drug company that makes this drug, not because it effectively helps you.)

2. The side effects of the drug are "conveniently" omitted from the literature doctors receive. As a result, when side effects occur (which suggest the person should stop taking the drug), doctors frequently don't believe the adverse side effects are linked to the drug. (This is especially true for the more subtle and chronic side effects drugs often create.[1] Thus, side effects are blamed on coincidence or other health conditions.)

3. Few drugs can be precisely targeted to the specific tissues your doctor is trying to treat. Instead, most medications are systemic, meaning they travel freely around your body. Thus, they can get into your ears and cause ototoxic side effects. For example, if you are treated with the antibiotic **Neomycin** for a cut on your leg, you can end up with hearing loss and tinnitus as the drug is absorbed into your bloodstream and travels to your ears. This happened to one young man in his twenties. He wrote:

   > I have experienced ototoxicity following a single application of **Neomycin** on a large, deep cut on my leg. I covered the cut completely with *Neosporin* and soon thereafter experienced tinnitus and dizziness. My hearing has worsened, and I have experienced a dramatic change in the way I perceive sounds.

4. The appropriate dose varies significantly from person to person and thus is often very different from the "standard" dose that doctors typically prescribe.[2]

This last point is very important. I have received numerous reports from people who found that their ototoxic side effects appeared when their drug dosage was increased, or conversely, went away when doctors reduced their drug dosage.

Getting the Dose Right Can Minimize Drug Side Effects

It is critical for you to receive the right drug dose tailored to your body in order to prevent side effects from occurring—not just the "standard" dose you likely received. Here's why.

Typically, in order for a drug to "work", enough of it has to be present in your body to trigger the desired (beneficial) effect of the drug. The question is, "Exactly how large/small does the dose have to be for that to occur?" The truth is, the proper dose for each person varies significantly because:

- Different people require different amounts of a drug in their systems to achieve the target concentration of a drug. (For example, this is why doctors often give higher doses to heavier people).

- The same drug concentrations affect people differently.

- The degree to which people absorb an oral drug varies significantly. (An example is how grapefruit juice affects certain drugs. See Chapter 16 for more on this.)

- The degree to which people eliminate a drug also varies significantly, especially as they age. Thus, in some people the drug may clear immediately, while in others (typically older people) it may persist for a long time and consequently build up to dangerous levels in their bodies.[3]

Not only does the drug dose vary widely in how well in works, but also the toxicity of a drug can widely vary from person to person for these same above reasons.[4]

Furthermore, it is often impossible to have an effective dose which is low enough so that it does not also create side effects in some people. That is why the drug companies do their best to downplay the toxicities that occur in their trials.

In order to do this, generally the drugs in clinical trials are often **only** tested on the healthiest members of the population (typically college age males). This is because college-age males are the least likely to experience adverse side effects to the trial medications. Drug trials would be more truthful if they tested the new drugs on the people most likely to be taking them (such as older people) and thus would be more likely be injured by them.[5] As one doctor explained:

> This is a longstanding issue in clinical trials (e.g., we rarely test drugs on the elderly—who are typically the most likely to suffer adverse reactions to them, but once the drugs go to the market, those are the groups they are most frequently pushed upon).[6]

Furthermore, doctors insist many side effects of drugs are not from the medications they prescribed, but from something else (e.g., pre-existing conditions or coincidence) because the dose they gave their patient was "appropriate."[7]

Most people don't realize that the drug dose they are given is a weighted average dose that does not take into account the needs of more sensitive people. As the above-mentioned doctor further explained:

> It would be very difficult to run a medical system which quickly sees a large volume of patients (e.g., it would take much more than 30 seconds to prescribe

the correct dose of a drug), but at the same time, it also makes a large demographic exist for which standard medicine care simply does not work.[8]

Why You Are More (or Less) Sensitive to Drug Side Effects

Some people are much more sensitive to the effects of drugs than others are. Here's why.

- **Age**—as you age, your body becomes less able to tolerate toxic drugs. For example, your kidneys and liver are responsible for clearing drugs from your body. Since their function declines with age, as you age you often cannot tolerate the same dose of a drug that you could when you were younger.

  Likewise, as you age, your arteries become less able to reflexively bring blood to your head when your blood pressure drops there. As a result, if your doctor medicates you down to a blood pressure level appropriate for younger adults, far too often you become lightheaded and pass out. This causes a huge problem because of the severe harm falls often cause to older people such as broken hips and head injuries.

  Conversely, premature infants are less able to tolerate vaccinations, for example, than can normal-weight infants. As a result, neurological disorders and sudden infant death syndrome following vaccination are much more common in those children. Nonetheless, because vaccines are assumed to be a 100% safe and effective, ways to prevent toxic doses (e.g., by vaccinating later in life or spacing out vaccinations) are never considered within the conventional medical system.

- **Gender and Race**—significant differences exist in how different genders and races respond to many medications. It is a rare drug trial that will note gender specific differences to a drug. It is rarer still that a drug trial will record and evaluate racial differences. Furthermore, in the name of diversity, equity and inclusion (DEI), there has recently been a push in the medical field to remove many of the metabolic differences that had been observed between different races (and affected their appropriate medical management).[9]

- **Genetic factors**—genetic variations can affect how you respond to a drug. For example, the P450 enzymes play a pivotal role in liver detoxification, and as a result, P450 function directly affects how long a drug will stay in your system and what your resulting appropriate dosage is for it. For example, certain drugs are known to increase or decrease P450 function.[10] (For more on this see Chapter 16 on grapefruit and such drugs.)

- **Constitutional Archetypes**—Throughout history, health practitioners of various persuasions have classified people under one of three constitutional archetypes based on their personalities and physiques. Each type requires a different treatment for their ailments than the other two types. It is not the "one size fits all" formula that is so typical of western medicine's use of drugs.

  These three constitutional types are Ectomorph, Mesomorph and Endomorph, also called Sattva, Rajas and Tamas in Hinduism and Vatta, Pitta and Kapha in Ayurvedaic medicine. These are not identical, but somewhat similar in their characteristics.

  Ectomorphs tend to be intelligent, gentle and calm, but self-conscious, introverted and anxious. Physically they tend to have a less solid or thin body type and personality and are much more sensitive to their environment and surroundings. They have the qualities of goodness, calmness and harmoniousness.

  Mesomorphs tend to be competitive, extroverted and tough. Physically, they tend to be muscular and lie somewhere between ectomorphs and endomorphs in their characteristics. They tend to be passionate, active and in motion.

  Endomorphs tend to be outgoing, friendly, happy and laid-back, but also lazy and selfish. Physically, they tend to be stocky/overweight and have a much denser and thick body type and are much less sensitive to the things around them. They tend to be ignorant, lazy and lacking in inertia.[11]

  Therefore, the way to care for each of these types is completely different from the other two types. For example, treating ectomorphs are basically opposite to treating endomorphs because ectomorphs tend to be sensitive to drugs and can easily develop side effects if given a "standard" dose, whereas endomorphs are more resistant to drugs and have few side effects when given the standard dose.

  This concept is generally misunderstood by those in the medical field, and as a result, ectomorph sensitivities are often interpreted as being psychiatric in nature. Further compounding this issue, since there are also many endomorphic patients (who respond quite well to conventional care), mainstream doctors tend to disproportionately remember those positive responses and assume they generalize to their entire patient population, and this is just not true.

  As a result, when the opposite of what the doctor intends ultimately happens due to their inappropriate treatment plan, these doctors tend to view it as being the fault of the patient rather than considering that they might be working with a different constitutional archetype which intrinsically requires a different treatment approach, or at the very least, a different dose.

This is why you and your doctor need to know your archetype and adjust your drug dose appropriately so you don't suffer from ototoxic (and other) side effects.[12]

Strategies for Selecting the Correct Dose

Due to the many factors influencing how your body utilizes drugs, how can your doctor determine what the correct dose is for you? Probably the single most important thing is simply to be aware that the dose they assume you should take probably is not correct and needs to be adjusted (typically downward) to fit the above-mentioned factors.[13]

Here are some strategies one doctor typically uses:

- Be aware of the size of the therapeutic window of the medication being used. Some medications are fairly safe and highly unlikely to cause side effects at normal doses in most people. However, others are much more likely to have side effects for some of the people that take them—especially ectomorphs. Note: Frequently doctors are able to spot if the drugs other doctors prescribe cause issues, but almost never are able to see when theirs do the same thing.[14]

- Be aware of what nutrients drugs commonly deplete in the body, and recognize if you have a pre-existing deficiency of that nutrient prior to when you start the drug.[15] Here's three examples. **Esomeprazole** depletes your body of magnesium while **Acetaminophen** depletes your body's stores of glutathione and **Atorvastatin** depletes your body of co-enzyme Q10.

- Furthermore, note that many of the side effects doctors attribute to medications are actually the result of drugs causing critical nutritional deficiencies.[16]

- Evaluate if you are dealing with a more sensitive person—typically an ectomorph. Often you can tell if this is the case as sensitive patients have a variety of unusual characteristics and a very distinctive presence. However, in many cases, you need to review their history and see if they've had any past experiences which suggest they are more susceptible than the average individual to a bad reaction from a drug.[17]

- Learn what side effects you can expect to occur when prescribing lower doses of drugs. [18]
- Start with a lower-than-normal drug dose, then evaluate what happens. If no side effects show up, there is no harm to the patient, and the benefits are not sufficient for the patient, gradually raise the dose.
- This approach is much less likely to create adverse side effects for a patient, but it is also much more time consuming to do, so doctors seldom do it. Numbers of doctors have had numerous cases where they escalated a dose for a desperate patient faster than they had originally planned to, and then regretted doing this when the patient had significant side effects to a still relatively-low drug dose.[19]
- Note: When slowly increasing the dose, your doctor frequently needs to carefully observe you for subtle signs of any changes. This is because subtle signs your body is not tolerating a medication typically emerge before more overt side effects appear.[20]

Figuring out how to balance all of these constraints is a bit of an art.[21]

If you are a patient, you should also consider the strategies laid out here. Then, if you experience an adverse side effect or something simply feels wrong to you, you should consider the possibility that it is due to the drug and not coincidence or something else and report it to your doctor. It's better to be safe than sorry! As one doctor explained:

> Many patients who developed chronic injuries from a toxic pharmaceutical have told me that one of their greatest regrets was listening to their doctor instead of their intuition or their body when they decided to go forward with taking the pharmaceutical that then ruined their lives.[22]

Ototoxic Drugs and You

Be careful about taking any drugs, especially ototoxic drugs, if you are hard of hearing. Be aware that most drugs coming on the market have not been thoroughly studied for potential ototoxic side effects. As a result, if you take them, you end up as the guinea pig. Is this what you want? Never forget that all drugs have side effects. Some of these side effects may be much worse for the rest of your body than are the effects of certain ototoxic ones on your ears.

Remember, at the beginning of the Preface I wrote:

> Each year an estimated 1,500,000 people in the United States end up in the hospital as a result of the adverse side effects from taking drugs. Another 100,000 people die each year from these adverse side effects![23]

You do not want to be a part of these statistics.

The reason for these gruesome statistics is because the prime motive of the pharmaceutical industry is **to make money, not to make you well**. According to Dr. John Abramson:

> In litigation involving Pfizer—although Pfizer is no different than other drug companies in this respect—internal Pfizer documents stated in stark language that "Pfizer-sponsored studies belong to Pfizer, not to any individual," and that the "Purpose of data [from those studies] is to support, directly or indirectly, marketing of our product." Not to ensure that the drugs will make people healthier or improve quality of life—or to ensure that they will do no harm—but to support the company's marketing.[24]

In other words, from the pharmaceutical industry's perspective, your taking drugs is not primarily for the purpose of making you better, but for making money for them—whether you get better or not! Thus, I emphasize again that you have to be very wary of "drug studies" that purport to show a drug's efficacy, knowing that the drug was **primarily** designed—not to make you better, but to make the maximum amount of money for the drug company.

There are many drugs that are ototoxic to some degree. For example, taking 6 to 8 **Aspirin** a day can cause ringing in your ears (tinnitus) and temporary hearing loss.[25] Other drugs will quickly and permanently damage your ears. You may be left with little or no hearing. This happened to Elizabeth after she took an AMINOGLYCOSIDE ANTIBIOTIC to fight a life-threatening infection. Now she cannot hear any high-frequency sounds whatsoever.

Other drugs can have both temporary and permanent effects. For example, while taking chemotherapy, Ruby temporarily lost most of her hearing. Fortunately, after her treatments were over, most of her hearing returned, but she was left with permanent and annoying tinnitus.

When looking at side effects, always look at **all** the side effects (ototoxic and otherwise) you may experience, then carefully weigh the good the drug is supposed to do you against its potential for causing permanent damage to your ears (and the rest of your body). Only then make your choice based upon how much risk you are willing to accept. Only you, yourself, know what you are willing to endure in order to avoid the risk of losing any more of your hearing or balance, or causing other ear damage from taking drugs.

Sometimes, the side effects of the drugs are much less severe than the result of not taking them, namely certain death. It's a no-brainer when the choice is either deaf or death. If it's not a matter of life and death, do your research, then make your informed decision.

Your informed decision needs to include researching whether the drug you are considering taking will even do a good job in helping you, or if it is basically just a ploy to make the drug manufacturers richer at your expense with minimal improvement in your condition. As Dr. Robet Steinbrook, MD warns:

> A study found that from 2015 to 2021, fewer than one-third of the most common drugs featured in direct-to-consumer television advertising were rated by independent health technology assessment agencies as "having high therapeutic value," which the researchers defined as "providing at least moderate improvement in clinical outcomes compared with existing therapies."[26]

In other words, at least 67% of the most popular drugs currently advertised on your television are basically almost worthless—they do not give you much relief/improvement and for this privilege, you pay the big bucks and often suffer from debilitating side effects. Thus, you will likely be better off making lifestyle and dietary changes, taking supplements and possibly using existing inexpensive (typically off-patent) drugs to achieve improvements in your conditions.

Furthermore, in order to make an informed decision, before beginning drug therapy, you need to know what drugs you are going to be taking. You need to know **all** the side effects of these drugs. You need to know the interactions that may occur between these drugs. Finally, and this is most important, you need to carefully consider the role that hearing and balance play in maintaining the quality of your life and how your quality of life could change when the drug treatment is over. Too often, people

Women and Drug Side Effects

It might not seem fair, but women have a 50% to 70% greater risk of developing adverse drug side effects than men do, and thus have a higher risk of developing ototoxic side effects. This is borne out by the fact that "of the 10 prescription drugs withdrawn from the US market between 1997 and 2000, eight caused statistically greater health risks for women than men."

The reason for this disparate reaction to drug use between women and men is due to differences in hormones, metabolism, biochemistry, anatomy, the use of oral contraceptives and where a woman is in her menstrual cycle. Besides, women typically consume more medications than men. Thus, the use of multiple medications is higher in women than in men.[1]

References

1 Secret 67 Special Reports, 2021. pp. 85-86.

neglect this important aspect until they lose their hearing or balance. At that point it is too late to say, "Oops, we should have thought of this before!"

It is not easy to determine what effects any ototoxic drug may have on your life. This is because there is enormous variation in how ototoxic side effects affect different people as we saw earlier in this chapter. The side effects you experience may be temporary or permanent; the symptoms may be mild or severe; and the ototoxic damage may affect both ears (bilateral) or just appear in one ear (or even be totally different in each ear).

After you have carefully considered all these factors, you need to sit down with your doctor and decide whether you are prepared to accept the risk of those side effects if you take the proposed drug(s).

Furthermore, be aware that damage to your ears can result in serious vocational, educational and social problems. You often can minimize or prevent these effects if you detect any ototoxic side effects early enough in the treatment process. Therefore, you and your doctor have to work together to closely monitor the effects of any drugs on your body. Unfortunately, monitoring for the effects of ototoxic drugs is not a common practice. This is something that needs to change!

Don't let your doctor railroad you into taking his recommended course of drugs without first doing your own research. Your body may react differently than he expects. For example, certain drugs may build up to toxic levels in your blood if your body does not metabolize them as expected. Each person's reaction to any given drug or medication is unique.[27] In fact, studies show that people vary widely in how much of a drug they need to take before it begins to adversely affect their ears.[28]

You may not have a single noticeable side effect from a given drug while the next person has several severe side effects. Betty found this out to her sorrow. Her doctor told her that a certain antibiotic he prescribed would only damage her hearing if taken in large doses for a prolonged time. What happened to her? The very first (relatively low) dose permanently damaged her hearing. For the past twenty-five years she has had to wear two hearing aids just to be able to catch most of what people say.

Always ask your doctor or pharmacist about the possible side effects of any medications (or combinations of medications) you are taking. Have them look it up in their "drug bibles" (the PDR in the USA, the CPS in Canada and the BNF in Great Britain) and show you. Remember, it's your hearing that is at risk. You are the one who will have to live with the results day after day, month after month, year after year, not your doctor or pharmacist. I know that I, for one, always want to err on the side of caution. I avoid all drugs (ototoxic and otherwise) if that is possible.

You also need to be aware that sometimes you do not find the ototoxic information where you would expect to find it. For example, I looked up the drugs *Ecotrin* (**Acetylsalicylic acid**) and *Demadex* (**Torsemide**) in the PDR. To my surprise, it did not list any ototoxic side effects for these drugs where you would normally look to find such information—under the section headed "Adverse Reactions". Yet these drugs are indeed ototoxic. I only found this out when I looked under "Warnings" on a different page. There I read "If ringing in the ears or a loss of hearing occurs..." and "Tinnitus and hearing loss...have been observed...". There was not even a "See WARNINGS" as is customary if side effects are listed elsewhere. If you want to be sure you have found all the ototoxic side effects, you need to read **all** the fine print on any drug, no matter what the heading says.[29]

Here is something else you should know. If you read the "Patient Product Information" sheets that come with your drugs, or if you read the "Patient Product Information" area on the manufacturer's web site, you likely are not getting much if any of the information you are wanting on ototoxic side effects. These information sheets are "dummied down" for the layperson, and also greatly shortened. Thus, a lot of information is left out. For example, one manufacturer's "Patient Product Information" sheet on their web site only listed one ototoxic side effect—dizziness—yet this drug has a number of other ototoxic side effects.

True, the manufacturer listed a bunch of "serious" side effects, but not the ototoxic ones about which you specifically want to know. Then, at the bottom of the page they gave this warning. **Be sure to heed it!** It said:

> The side effects described above **do not include all the side effects reported with this drug**. Consequently, do not rely on this leaflet alone for information about side effects. Your doctor or pharmacist can discuss with you a more complete list of side effects.

When you see something like this, you need to look elsewhere for a more complete list of the side effects. In this case, if you go to the "Physician Prescribing Information" page on this same web site, you will find the missing ototoxic side effects. These are the same side effects as those you find in the PDR. There you will discover that, in addition to dizziness, this drug could cause vertigo, tinnitus, otitis media and earache. Now you know you are getting nearer to the truth.

Since most drugs have upwards of 100 to 300 different side effects, if a source only lists 10 or 20, you know it is not a complete listing by any means!

Take Responsibility for Yourself

You, and you alone, are responsible for the body God gave you. Therefore, although you may go to doctors for help, the final decision on any treatment, including any drugs your doctor may want you to take, is up to you.

As a result, you need good information so you can make good decisions. Since doctors seldom are reliable sources of ototoxic drug information, you need to check things out for yourself. If you don't, it is your ears that will suffer—not the ears of your doctor, nor the ears of your pharmacist. You alone are ultimately responsible for everything that goes into your body.

Therefore, before you take a drug, check out the side effects listed on the box/bottle or the insert that comes with it. Do this with over-the-counter medications too. Better yet, check out the side effects in the CPS, PDR or Drugs.com (which basically gives the same information as the PDR gives. Even better, check out the drugs in this book as it is faster and more complete.

Some people take the time to check things out and thus save themselves a lot of grief later. One lady I know went to her local drug store to pick up some *Excedrin* (**Acetylsalicylic acid**) at her doctor's suggestion. Being diligent, she read the fine print on the box and was surprised to see that it could cause tinnitus and hearing loss. This is great—a bit of "ototoxic truth" on the boxes now! But you have to watch out. She told me that these side effects were listed on the larger box, but not on a smaller box of the same drug.

She was further surprised when she asked the pharmacist about these ototoxic side effects, and he immediately told her that *Extra Strength Tylenol* would be much less ototoxic for her.

This was so unusual (truth in labeling and a pharmacist that knew about ototoxicity) that she emailed me to see if both were telling the truth! (At the time this incident happened, both were telling the truth as far as anyone knew. However, since then researchers have discovered that *Tylenol* [**Acetaminophen**] is actually quite ototoxic—but they didn't know that back then.)

The unfortunate thing about this whole incident is that her doctor either didn't know or didn't care about the fact that he was recommending an ototoxic drug to a hard of hearing person, or perhaps he thought that the dose was low enough that no ototoxic side effects would surface. Therefore, I re-emphasize, check out every drug for yourself. Always ask yourself before choosing to take any medications or receiving any medical procedure, "Do the benefits outweigh the risks?" You may be extremely glad you did!

Chapter 3 Endnotes

1 A Midwestern Doctor, 2023d. p. 1.
2 A Midwestern Doctor, 2023d. p. 1.
3 A Midwestern Doctor, 2023d. p. 1.
4 A Midwestern Doctor, 2023d. p. 1.
5 A Midwestern Doctor, 2023d. p. 1.
6 A Midwestern Doctor, 2023g. p. 1.
7 A Midwestern Doctor, 2023d. p. 1.
8 A Midwestern Doctor, 2023d. p. 1.
9 A Midwestern Doctor, 2023d. p. 1.
10 A Midwestern Doctor, 2023d. p. 1.
11 A Midwestern Doctor, 2023f. p. 1.
12 A Midwestern Doctor, 2023f. p. 1.
13 A Midwestern Doctor, 2023d. p. 1.
14 A Midwestern Doctor, 2023d. p. 1.
15 A Midwestern Doctor, 2023d. p. 1.
16 A Midwestern Doctor, 2023d. p. 1.
17 A Midwestern Doctor, 2023d. p. 1.
18 A Midwestern Doctor, 2023d. p. 1.
19 A Midwestern Doctor, 2023d. p. 1.
20 A Midwestern Doctor, 2023d. p. 1.
21 A Midwestern Doctor, 2023d. p. 1.
22 A Midwestern Doctor, 2023d. p. 1.
23 Waltermire, 1998. p. 1.
24 Abramson, John. 2023. p 6.
25 Stanten, 1996. p. 16.
26 Steinbrook, 2023. p. 2.
27 Medroxyprogesterone acetate, 2001. p. 2.
28 Fausti, 1993a. p. 664.
29 Physicians' Desk Reference, 1997. pp. 2625-2626.; PDR, 2000. pp. 2629-2630.

Chapter 4

Ototoxic Side Effects and Your Ears

The Effects of Drugs

All drugs potentially have four kinds of effects on your body. First, there is the intended therapeutic effect. This is why you are taking this drug in the first place. Second, there are the side effects. These are relatively-mild reactions other than the intended effect. Third, there are the allergic effects. Fourth, there are the toxic effects. These are severe effects up to, and including, death.

According to Dr. Harold McPheeters,

> It has become fashionable in recent years to refer in drug advertisements and promotions to the latter three kinds of effects as "side effects". In reality, some of the toxic effects (such as damage to the liver, kidneys and nervous system) are becoming more dangerous as medications themselves become more powerful.[1]

The effects of drugs on our ears mostly fall in group 4, toxic effects rather than into group 2, side effects. However, in keeping with current usage, I'll refer to groups 2-4 simply as "ototoxic side effects," "adverse side effects" or just plain "side effects".

The Various Ototoxic Side Effects

When you think of ototoxic side effects, you likely think of things such as hearing loss and tinnitus, and you would be right. However, this is just barely scratching the surface. There are a whole host of other ototoxic side effects (see Table 4-1). Some of these give rise to problems that you might never suspect were related to your ears.

Drugs can damage or cause problems in various parts of your ears. I have broken these side effects down into four basic groups—cochlear, vestibular, central nervous system and outer/middle ears.

Table 4-1: The Ototoxic Side Effects Used in This Book by Their Frequency

Side Effect	No. of Drugs*	% of Ototoxic Drugs**
Dizziness	1,487	93
Ataxia/Gait disturbance	1,284	80
Vertigo	1,172	73
Tinnitus	1,126	70
Hearing loss	1,103	69
Balance disorder	950	59
Ear discomfort/Ear pain	772	48
Otitis media	611	38
Auditory hallucinations	602	37
Ear infection	569	35
Nystagmus	495	31
Otitis externa	415	26
Ear disorder	375	23
Ceruminosis	369	23
Labyrinthitis	324	20
Eustachian tube dysfunction	319	20
Vestibular disorder	299	19
Ear blocked	283	18
Meniere's disease	282	18
Hyperacusis	281	17
Otorrhea	277	17
Otorrhagia	256	16
Perforated eardrum	208	13
Hearing disorder	199	12
Ototoxicity	165	10
Phonophobia	112	7
Cholesteatoma	89	6
Oscillopsia	34	2
Otosclerosis	11	0.7
Burning/stinging	4	0.2

*The number of drugs in this book with this side effect.
**These percentages are based on the 1,604 ototoxic drugs mentioned in this book.

The ototoxic drugs in this book each have an average of 9.0 different ototoxic side effects.

Cochlear Side Effects

The cochlea is the part of your inner ear that converts mechanical sound vibrations into electrical signals. It contains thousands of tiny hair cells that relay hearing information to the auditory nerve and from there up to your brain.

Cochlear damage from ototoxic drugs can result in such side effects as tinnitus, hearing loss, distorted hearing, hyperacusis and auditory hallucinations.

Tinnitus

Tinnitus is a phantom sound. You "hear" it in your brain when there is no external sound present. Sometimes people refer to it as a ringing in their ears or ear noises.

Tinnitus can manifest itself as a wide variety of sounds. It may be a ringing, roaring, beating, clicking, banging, buzzing, hissing, humming, blowing, chirping, clanging, sizzling, whooshing, rumbling, whistling or dreadful shrieking noise in your head. It may also sound like rushing water, radio static, breaking glass, bells ringing, owls hooting or chainsaws running.[2] Some people hear several of these sounds at the same time.

Often tinnitus precedes or accompanies hearing loss from ototoxic drugs. In fact, tinnitus is the **number one** indicator that you may be doing further damage to your ears. It also may be the **only** warning you'll ever get. Pay attention to it!

Although tinnitus from ototoxic drugs is generally high-pitched, continuous and occurs in both ears, certain ototoxic drugs produce distinctive tinnitus sounds. For example, tinnitus caused by SALICYLATES is generally high-pitched and sounds like a continuous musical note. It usually stops when you stop taking the drug. Tinnitus from **Quinine** and related drugs produces similar sounds. In contrast, taking **Erythromycin** can produce a blowing-like sound while LOOP DIURETICS may produce a middle-frequency sound.[3]

Tinnitus arising from taking ototoxic drugs may or may not be permanent.[4] If you are taking an AMINOGLYCOSIDE ANTIBIOTIC, you are one of the lucky ones if it stops within a couple of weeks after you finish the drug therapy. For some people, it never goes away.

Tinnitus may show up very quickly after you begin taking an ototoxic medication or it may take several days to months to years to become apparent. For example, tinnitus from LOOP DIURETICS may start just seven minutes after you begin receiving it as an I.V. In contrast, tinnitus may not show up until 2 or 3 days after taking an AMINOGLYCOSIDE antibiotic. With the BENZODIAZEPINES, tinnitus may only show up **after** you stop taking the drug.

The third edition of *Ototoxic Drugs Exposed* listed 529 drugs that were reported to have triggered tinnitus in some people. If you think that is a lot of drugs that can cause tinnitus, hold onto your hat. This fourth edition lists 1,126 drugs that are reported as being associated with tinnitus. Even this is not all of the drugs that can cause tinnitus, just the ones that so far have been reported to have caused tinnitus.

For Further Information About Tinnitus

To learn more about tinnitus and how you can bring it under your control, get my comprehensive book on the subject: *Take Control of Your Tinnitus—Here's How*. (See the back of this book for ordering information.)

Hearing Loss

Hearing loss may be the first thing you associate with ototoxic drugs. Although it is not the most common ototoxic side effect, the results of hearing loss certainly can have an enormous effect on your life.

Hearing loss may occur as the only ototoxic side effect, but tinnitus almost always precedes or accompanies it. You should never ignore these side effects.

Typically, ototoxic drugs first damage the hair cells (cilia) at the base of the cochlea. The cilia at the base of the cochlea are sensitive to high-frequency sounds. The damage then progresses towards the tip where the cilia are sensitive to low-frequency sounds. This is why hearing loss typically begins in the very high frequencies and steadily moves down the frequency spectrum to the speech frequencies as the hearing loss progresses.

You may have a hearing loss from taking an ototoxic drug and never know it unless you have special high-frequency audiograms between 8,000 Hz and 20,000 Hz done. As your hearing loss progresses to the lower frequencies (below 8,000 Hz), a regular audiogram will begin to reveal your hearing loss. It is not unusual to be unaware of any hearing loss until it has reached mild to moderate status. By that time, your hearing loss will be more than 30 dB in the speech frequencies,[5] and it may be much too late to do anything to try to restore your hearing.

Ototoxic drugs almost always cause sensorineural hearing losses (SNHL) (the old term was nerve deafness). This is as opposed to conductive losses, which stem from damage to the middle ear. However, taking certain drugs may result in clogged middle ears with a resultant conductive hearing loss. Hearing loss can range from mild high-frequency loss to total deafness. Also, drug-induced hearing loss is generally the same in both ears (bilaterally symmetrical), although sometimes it can be different in each ear (asymmetrical),[6] or only affect one ear. Sensorineural hearing loss may be permanent or temporary depending on the drug and a number of other factors.

Hearing Disorder/Distorted Hearing

Even though an ototoxic drug may not cause a hearing loss, it can still damage your hearing. Sometimes it will cause you to experience distorted hearing—everything may sound "tinny" or "funny".

The typical "ski slope" hearing loss means you hear the lower frequency sounds close to normal, but you don't hear high frequency sounds much or at all. (Your audiogram looks like a ski slope that slopes down to the right.) This, by itself, will make speech sound distorted or different.

Furthermore, auditory system damage caused by ototoxicity may impair your ability to discriminate between spoken words. You may be able to hear speech, but don't understand some/most/all of the words you hear, even when they are loud enough for you to hear them.[7]

If you have a sensorineural hearing loss, generally the worse the loss, the worse your discrimination (word recognition) will be.

Hyperacusis

Although there are at least seven kinds of hyperacusis, since hyperacusis is neither well-known nor well-understood, most references to hyperacusis don't differentiate between them and instead just lump them all together as though there was only one kind of hyperacusis, namely loudness hyperacusis. Loudness hyperacusis is a condition where you perceive normal sounds as abnormally loud. In fact, many sounds may seem painfully loud. Yet these same sounds are at a comfortable level for those with normal hearing. It's as though your internal volume control is now stuck on high.

In this book there are at least 280 drugs that have been reported as causing hyperacusis—probably meaning loudness hyperacusis, but who knows what the researcher really had in mind in any given case.

Do not confuse loudness hyperacusis with recruitment.

For Further Information About Hyperacusis

To learn more about the various kinds of hyperacusis and how you can help bring them under control, read my book: *Hypersensitive to Sound?* (See the back of this book for ordering information.)

Recruitment is also clearly explained in this book.

Recruitment is an abnormal **rate of increase** in sound due to hearing loss. Sounds get too loud too fast. For example, when you double the volume of a sound a person with normal hearing perceives it as twice as loud. A person with recruitment may perceive it as four or seven or whatever times as loud. Generally, the worse your hearing, the worse your recruitment.

Hyperacusis of all kinds can occur whether you have normal or near normal hearing, or have a hearing loss. In contrast, recruitment is **always** a function of having a sensorineural hearing loss.

Auditory Hallucinations

A good number of drugs cause hallucinations—auditory or otherwise. There are two basic classes of auditory hallucinations. For lack of a better term, I'll call them "psychiatric" auditory hallucinations and "psychological" or "non-psychiatric" auditory hallucinations.

Psychiatric auditory hallucinations are where a person hears and understands voices speaking to or about him when no one is there. Often the person knows exactly who or what is talking to him—for example, a departed loved one, a chair or a tree, etc. Sometimes the person carries on a conversation or responds to these voices. These kinds of hallucinations are an indication of a mental illness such as schizophrenia. If you hear these kinds of voices, you should seek treatment by a competent psychiatrist.

Certain drugs can cause this effect. Therefore, if your medication is causing these voices, just stopping the drug (in consultation with your doctor) may be the best solution.

Much more common, in my opinion, but far less talked about for fear of being labeled mentally ill, are the non-psychiatric variety of auditory hallucinations, previously referred to as musical hallucinations or musical tinnitus, but now known as Musical Ear Syndrome (MES).

Musical Ear Syndrome is not a sign of mental illness, but rather is a by-product of something not working quite right in your auditory system. From time to time, numerous hard of hearing people hear such sounds. This is generally nothing to worry about. Many people hear tinnitus—one class of phantom sounds—but no one considers them to be "crazy". Unfortunately, the same is not true of MES. Musical Ear Syndrome is somewhat related to tinnitus but consists of complex (modulated) phantom sounds such as music and voices whereas tinnitus is comprised of simple (unmodulated) sounds. A person who hears these MES sounds is no more suffering from mental illness than a person who hears tinnitus.

If you have MES, you may hear what sounds vaguely like voices or singing or music. For example, you may hear what sounds like a radio program, but you cannot quite distinguish the words although it sounds like someone talking. Similarly, you might hear music. The tune is vaguely familiar, but you cannot quite place it.

At other times, you may clearly hear the phantom music. Generally, this music is pleasant to neutral. Two common tunes in America are "The Star-Spangled Banner" and "Amazing Grace". Sometimes you may hear classical music or songs you learned in your childhood. Older hard of hearing people seem especially prone to hearing these phantom sounds mainly due to advancing hearing loss as they age.

No doubt, some drugs cause psychiatric auditory hallucinations and others result in Musical Ear Syndrome. Since the drug reference books such as the PDR and CPS do not define what they mean by auditory hallucinations, they may be referring to either of the above classes. Furthermore, the professionals recording the side effects may not be aware of the difference between the two classes of hallucinations in the first place. As a result, they may just lump them together as "auditory hallucinations".

This book contains 602 drugs that are listed as causing hallucinations. Unfortunately, of this number, only a few specifically state that the resulting hallucinations are of the auditory variety. However, probably most of these 602 drugs do cause auditory hallucinations since auditory hallucinations are by far the most common kind of hallucinations.

For Further Information About Musical Ear Syndrome

If you hear phantom music, singing or voices that are not talking to or about you, you can learn more about your Musical Ear Syndrome and how you can help bring it under your control in my book: *Phantom Voices, Ethereal Music & Other Spooky Sounds*. (See the back of this book for ordering information.)

Vestibular Side Effects (Tabulated in the Drug Listings)

The vestibular (balance) system is that part of your inner ear that consists of the three semicircular canals (anterior, posterior and lateral), the saccule, the utricle and the vestibular nerve. Like the cochlea, these structures contain thousands of tiny hair cells that generate and relay balance signals to your brain.

As long as your vestibular system is working properly, you seldom give your ability to keep your balance a thought. However, if your vestibular system ever fails, it can impose enormous changes on your lifestyle.

Perhaps you weren't aware of this, but your vestibular system does not work alone to maintain your balance. Actually, you have three separate systems that help you maintain your balance. The other two systems are your ocular (visual) and your proprioceptive (proh-pree-oh-SEP-tiv) systems.

The vestibular portion of your inner ear continuously senses gravity and both straight and curved movement. Your eyes see both your position in space and movement. Your proprioceptive system uses special pressure sensors in the muscles, tendons and joints in your legs and feet to sense gravity and joint position.

Your vestibular system works together with your eyes in what doctors call the vestibulo-ocular reflex. This reflex instantly adjusts the position of your eyes to prevent blurred vision and to prevent your vision from bouncing (oscillopsia) when you move your head, walk or even breathe.

Your vestibular system also works together with the muscles of your body via your spinal cord in what doctors call the vestibulo-spinal reflex. This instantaneous reflex allows for continual, coordinated muscle adjustments so you can maintain your balance as you change position. It involves the vestibular system, vestibulocochlear nerve, brain, spinal cord and the muscles you use for standing and walking.[8]

In addition, your vestibular system works together with your vestibulo-sympathetic reflex to keep your blood pressure and respirations normal while you are moving.[9]

Your brain uses the separate signals from your vestibular, ocular and proprioceptive systems to instantly and subconsciously maintain clear vision and to make rapid muscle adjustments to prevent you from falling. You need at least two of these three systems working properly in order to effectively maintain your balance.[10]

When all three systems are working properly, you have no trouble keeping your balance. However, when you lose your vestibular system, your brain has to rely on the other two systems, but without the critical vestibular information, problems can arise.

One of the insidious things about taking ototoxic drugs is that vestibular damage may not show up right away. As a result, you may not stop taking an ototoxic drug soon enough to prevent severe vestibular damage. Vestibular ototoxicity may develop concurrently with cochlear ototoxicity or develop separately. Be aware that sometimes the onset of vestibular ototoxicity can be both sudden and severe.[11]

Ototoxic drugs can cause a number of vestibular side effects. Some of the more common ones include the inability to tolerate head movement, dizziness, lightheadedness, nausea, vomiting, vertigo, oscillopsia, visual problems, loss of balance, difficulty walking in the dark, nystagmus,[12] ataxia[13] and severe fatigue.[14] Note that many of these symptoms are not specific to ototoxic drug damage alone but can result from several other causes as well.

In general, vestibular side effects are worse in the first few weeks after vestibular damage occurs. As time goes by, your brain gets less confused by the loss of vestibular information because it learns to rely more on your visual and proprioceptive systems. Walking becomes easier. Your ataxia (staggering gait) will slowly resolve to some extent as your brain puts this alternative information to use. However, if you had severe vestibular damage, you will be left with permanent side effects that can alter your lifestyle dramatically.[15]

There are numerous ototoxic side effects that affect the balance system. The drug listings in this book only tabulate the effects of those ototoxic side effects more directly associated with the inner ear, namely: dizziness, vertigo, ataxia, nystagmus, labyrinthitis, balance disorders and oscillopsia.

Dizziness

Dizziness is a very common side effect of taking drugs. In fact, the vast majority of the drugs available today can cause dizziness.[16] Many of these drugs are ototoxic, so it should be no surprise that dizziness is also the most common ototoxic symptom. According to a pamphlet put out by Audiologic Consultants, fully 85% of dizziness symptoms can be attributed to inner ear disturbance (ototoxicity).[17] Of the 1,604 ototoxic drugs in this book, 1,487 (93%) are known to cause dizziness.

Because dizziness may or may not be an ototoxic side effect, and since I have no way of knowing for sure what the case is for any particular drug, I have not listed a drug in this book if its sole ototoxic side effect is dizziness. As a result, I will have left out a number of drugs that do indeed cause dizziness as an ototoxic side effect and thus should have been included.

Not only is dizziness a common ototoxic side effect, I also believe dizziness is one of the early symptoms of ear damage. Whether your dizziness is actually caused by ototoxic damage to your balance system or whether the vestibular damage results from the same cause as the dizziness you may be experiencing—namely a lack of oxygen getting to your inner ears—doesn't really matter. The end result is the same—very real damage to the delicate hair cells in the vestibular portion of your inner ears.

Dizziness comes in two basic types. With near-syncope dizziness, not enough blood gets to your brain. Symptoms usually appear over a few seconds. Typically, if you have this type of dizziness your vision dims, you are uncoordinated, confused, pale and perspiring. If these symptoms improve rapidly when you either sit down, squat down or lay down, you likely had this kind of dizziness.[18] You may describe it by such terms as feeling woozy, feeling you are going to faint, feeling light-headed, feeling that you are going to black out or feeling you have tunnel vision. For example, you could get this kind of dizziness from standing up too quickly (orthostatic dizziness). Also, some medications can lead to hypovolemia (which basically results in low blood pressure) or autonomic reflex loss with the resulting dizziness.[19]

The second type, non-syncope dizziness manifests itself as a feeling of vague disequilibrium. You can get this of dizziness from hyperventilating (breathing too fast or too deeply),[20] hypoglycemia, anxiety or migraine headaches, among other things.[21]

Unfortunately, sometimes people use the term "dizzy" when they really mean "vertigo" and vice versa. Unlike dizziness, if you have vertigo, you have a false sensation of moving or spinning.

Vertigo

Vertigo (VER-tih-goe) is a medical term reserved for the perception of movement when the body is really at rest. You most often experience vertigo as a spinning sensation much like what you experience after getting off of a merry-go-round. You have the sensation that your surroundings are continuing to spin even though they aren't.[22] If you have vertigo, you may feel that the room you are in is spinning around you, or that you are spinning around and the room is still. Sometimes, you may have the sensation that just the ceiling of the room is slowly spinning around. Vertigo can also appear as linear motion such as feeling that someone is pushing you, or it may even feel like a rocking motion.[23]

Benign Paroxysmal Positional Vertigo

If your vertigo is brought on by certain particular head positions, then you likely have benign paroxysmal positional vertigo.[1] This kind of vertigo occurs when the "rocks in your head" (the technical name is otoconia)—tiny crystals of calcium carbonate—get into the wrong places. They normally are in a tiny structure in your inner ear called the utricle. If they get jiggled out of the utricle and get into one of your semi-circular canals, you get benign paroxysmal positional vertigo. This kind of vertigo has nothing whatsoever to do with ototoxicity. It is typically treated with the Epley maneuver.

Reference

1 Bowen, 1998. p. 5.

Vertigo results from a mismatch of vestibular, ocular, and proprioceptive inputs. When all three are telling your brain the same thing, all is well. However, when your ears tell your brain one thing and your eyes and proprioceptive system tell it another thing, your brain doesn't know what to believe. In this case, your brain's confusion manifests itself as vertigo.

Symptoms of vertigo may start instantly, or they may develop over a few seconds. If you are experiencing vertigo, you typically become pale and may have some of the symptoms of motion sickness such as nausea, vomiting, headache and fatigue. The typical vertigo attack gradually goes away, often leaving you feeling queasy and tired for some time afterwards.[24]

Ataxia/Gait Disturbance

Ataxia (ah-TAKS-see-ah) is the loss of your ability to coordinate your muscles properly such that it affects your gait. As a result, when you walk you may stagger as if you were drunk.

Ataxia is one of the results of a damaged vestibular system. Normally, your vestibular system sends balance information to those areas of your brain and nervous system involved in the motor control of your muscles. This balance information allows your brain to continuously make little adjustments in muscle activity and body position to allow you to stand upright and maintain your balance.[25]

If your vestibular system doesn't pass this information to your brain or if it passes faulty information, your brain does not order these tiny adjustments. As a result, you will lurch and stagger (staggering gait) as the other two parts of your balance system try to compensate. You will likely have an unsteady gait and stumble a lot.

You may try to compensate by standing and walking with your legs farther apart than normal in order to give you better control of your balance (wide-based gait), and you may keep looking down while you are walking.[26] Even so, you may lose your balance or stagger when turning quickly (whole body or head only), and need to hold on to walls or furniture when you are walking.

In addition, you may have difficulty walking on slippery, soft or slanted surfaces or on uneven ground. You may have difficulty standing or walking in dim or dark places or when you have your eyes closed. Even under good lighting conditions, you will still tend to stagger. You may also feel unsteady, have problems standing with your feet together, be uncoordinated and clumsy and overreach when grabbing for objects.[27]

Nystagmus

Nystagmus (nye-STAG-muss) is another side effect that at first glance doesn't seem to have anything to do with your ears. Nystagmus is technically not a "ear" problem. However, it shows the powerful influence the vestibular (balance) system has on the motor neurons of the III (oculomotor), IV (trochlear) and VI (abducens) cranial nerves. These nerves control various eye movements.

Nystagmus refers to abnormal rapid rhythmic back-and-forth involuntary eye movements (eye jerking),[28] usually side to side, rarely in the vertical plane.[29] With nystagmus, both of your eyes drift slowly in one direction and then suddenly jerk in the opposite direction. When nystagmus is caused by vestibular problems, your eyes jerk horizontally (sideways).

You get nystagmus if only one side of your vestibular system is damaged, or if one side is damaged worse than the other side. Your eyes will jerk toward the undamaged (less damaged) side and will drift back towards the (more) damaged side. This abnormal eye movement can also result in vertigo, nausea, vomiting and a host of other visual complaints.[30]

Labyrinthitis

Labyrinthitis (lah-brin-THY-tis) is simply an inflammation of the labyrinth. The labyrinth includes all the structures in your inner ear (cochlear and vestibular systems).

Labyrinthitis may show up as many different symptoms some of which include vertigo, nystagmus, sensorineural hearing loss, nausea and vomiting.[31]

Balance Disorders

When you damage your vestibular system, one result is that you have difficulty keeping your balance. When your finely-tuned sense of equilibrium is damaged, you may suddenly lose your balance or stagger like you are drunk. You may feel unsteady. You may bump into things and have difficulty walking straight. In extreme cases you may not be able to stand erect without support.

Oscillopsia

You get oscillopsia (ah-sih-LOP-see-ah) when you are unable to sense minute head movements and thus make compensatory eye adjustments to keep the "picture" you are seeing stable. When your eyes can't maintain a stable horizon, you see a "jumbling of the panorama"[32] and have "bouncing vision".[33]

Oscillopsia is common if your vestibular system is severely damaged in both ears. Here is what happens. When you walk, your head moves up and down slightly with each step you make. Your vestibulo-ocular reflex (involving your vestibular system, vestibulocochlear nerve, brain and the muscles of your eyes) normally keeps your eyes clearly focused on your surroundings by instantly and continuously changing your eye position as you move.[34] You think nothing of this. It is totally subconscious and automatic. However, if your eyes and your ears lose this coordination due to vestibular damage,[35] your eye muscles do not receive the proper signals to automatically adjust to movement. As a result, your surroundings will appear to move, bounce, jiggle and jump about as you move, and your vision may be blurry.[36]

When your surroundings "bounce" it can make walking extremely difficult or even impossible. This is because under these conditions it is difficult to see and respond to obstacles in your path and to sense the exact location of the floor or ground.[37]

Vestibular Side Effects (Not Tabulated in the Drug Listings)

The following ototoxic side effects of vestibular damage are not tabulated in the drug listings, but they are just as much the product of ototoxic drug damage to the balance system as those mentioned previously. You may experience some, all or none of the following side effects when an ototoxic drug damages your vestibular system.

If you experience any of the following side effects after taking an ototoxic drug, very likely they were also caused by the same ototoxic drug that produced any of the above-listed side effects.

Emotional Problems

Damage to your vestibular system can result in emotional problems, especially if your lack of balance causes major changes in your life. For example, emotional problems may surface if you go from self-sufficiency to near total incapacitation. Your emotions can also take a beating if others don't understand your situation, or if your mental abilities change. You may experience anxiety, frustration, anger and depression.[38] You may mourn your loss of self-reliance. Your feelings of self-confidence and self-esteem may plummet.

You may also experience similar emotional problems as a result of hearing loss since hearing loss can cut you off socially from those around you.

Fatigue

A seemingly unlikely result of vestibular ototoxicity is fatigue. If your balance system is severely damaged, you may be exhausted all the time. This is because keeping your balance is now no longer a subconscious event, but something that you must consciously work hard to maintain. In addition, your ocular and proprioceptive systems must work overtime too. The result may be that everyday tasks are now exhausting.

Fatigue may also result from hearing loss. When you lose some hearing, you strain to hear and intently watch people's faces in order to speechread them. This, just by itself, is also exhausting.

Memory Problems

Strange as it may seem, vestibular ototoxicity can cause memory problems. Here is why. When you damage your vestibular system, keeping your balance is now largely a conscious effort, not the automatic effortless procedure it once was. Consequently, those areas of your brain that you once just used for thought and memory, now must constantly work on keeping you balanced. As a result, your memory may suffer. You may grope for words when talking. You may easily forget what is being spoken about during a conversation. You may be easily distracted. You may have difficulty comprehending directions or instructions. You may have trouble concentrating and may feel disoriented at times.

Older people may have similar problems as they age. However, you can't blame everything on aging if you are taking ototoxic drugs. Ototoxic side effects may be partly/largely responsible for these symptoms.

Muscular Aches and Pains

Another seemingly unlikely result of vestibular ototoxicity is muscular aches and pains and headaches. Your muscles may become sore and tense when your automatic vestibulo-spinal reflex (the reflex dictating automatic muscle changes in response to changing movement situations) no longer works automatically and you have to consciously control it. You may do this by making your muscles rigid and less relaxed as you strain to keep your balance. In addition, you may get headaches and a stiff/sore neck from trying to hold your head absolutely still so you won't feel dizzy or nauseous.

Nausea

You might not associate nausea with damage to your inner ears, but it is actually a relatively common side effect of vestibular damage.[39] When you damage your vestibular (balance) system, the confusion of sensory inputs your brain experiences can result in nausea. The nausea may be continual or intermittent. You may feel like you have a hangover all the time or you may feel "seasick".

Visual Problems

Whether you realize it or not, your eyes are inextricably tied to your ears. You need your eyes to help maintain your balance. At the same time, you need your ears (vestibular system) to maintain clear vision. Thus, when you damage your vestibular system, you will almost certainly have visual difficulties as well. In fact, visual complaints may be one of the first clues you have that you have damaged your vestibular system. These resulting visual problems may even cause you more trouble than the "normal" vestibular side effects.

Earlier in this chapter, you learned that one of the functions of the vestibular system is to send certain information to your brain and nervous system in order to control your eye movements (vestibulo-ocular reflex). This information helps stabilize your eyes in space when you move your head. It also reduces the movement of the image of a fixed object on your retinas thus giving you clear vision.[40]

You might not think just how important your balance system is to your eyes. Every time your heart beats or you breathe, your head moves a tiny bit. Your vestibular system senses these tiny changes in position and tiny movements (as well as all the major movements too) and your brain sends messages to your eye muscles to correct for it, all unknown to you.

Anything that disrupts your vestibulo-ocular reflex directly affects your vision.[41] Therefore, if your vestibular system is damaged, you will likely have fuzzy or blurred vision. Furthermore, you will likely have difficulty focusing on objects, or holding your eyes on a printed page since your hands can't hold a book completely steady.[42] This makes it very difficult to read, especially smaller print.[43] It can also make it difficult to write. Furthermore, you probably will have difficulty with depth perception, and focusing on, or watching, moving objects.

In addition, you may feel dizzy, experience nausea or have a sense of moving, particularly at the onset, especially if you move your eyes, move your head and eyes simultaneously, or watch moving objects. This can make being around traffic, riding in a vehicle, watching TV or watching a movie in a movie theater very unpleasant. You may find moving or flickering lights bother you.

You may find that you no longer can tolerate head movement, that you no longer can determine when movement has stopped, and that you no longer can determine your bodily position in space, especially with your eyes closed.[44]

Just the act of focusing your eyes may be difficult and can lead to dizziness and nausea. You may tend to look down because it is harder to focus on more distant objects. In addition, a visually "busy" scene may make you feel sick. Looking at the floor with its (generally) simple patterns makes it much easier to "take in". Your ability to accurately determine distances may also be disrupted. This can lead to even more difficulty when you are walking. Poor depth perception may result in your bumping into things. People may think you are clumsy.

Never underestimate how experiencing both eye and balance problems at the same time can have an enormous impact on your life and lifestyle.[45]

Vomiting

When you see a person vomiting, your first reaction is not, "Aha, that person has a damaged balance system!" You think stomach flu, food poisoning, sickness and anything else but ear damage, don't you? Yet vomiting may be the result of a damaged vestibular system—especially at the beginning.[46] As time goes by, your brain attempts to compensate for the vestibular damage and generally the vomiting ceases. Quite often vomiting and vertigo occur together. When the room is spinning around, you feel so sick you often "toss your cookies".

Vague Feelings of Unease

Sometimes you can't put your finger on exactly what is wrong. You may feel vaguely uneasy. You may feel that things seem wrong or unreal. You may feel tired and listless without knowing why. You may feel lightheaded or faint.[47] As unlikely as it may seem, all these symptoms may be the result of a damaged vestibular system.

By now you should have developed a sense of awe at the marvelous balance system God designed for you. At the same time, you now also realize the tremendous upsets that may come into your life and lifestyle if you allow ototoxic drugs to damage this wonderful system.

Central Nervous System (CNS) Side Effects

Ototoxic drugs can also mess up your brain and/or scramble the message as it passes along your auditory nerves. The PDR and CPS sometimes refer to this by the ambiguous term "CNS toxicity". Unfortunately, this may or may not have anything to do with your auditory system. Be aware that anything that affects your brain can just as easily affect your auditory network. However, since there is no way of telling whether "CNS toxicity" specifically includes ototoxic side effects, I have not included it as one of the ototoxic side effects for the purposes of this book.

Central Processing Disorder

Sounds may enter your ears and be processed correctly, but these sound signals may be delayed or scrambled after they leave your inner ears. This scrambling can occur as the sound signals are processed by the neuronal networks that make up your auditory nerves, or in the auditory parts of your brain. When this processed sound reaches the conscious level in your brain where you "hear", you may hear a bunch of gibberish. The proper name for this is a central processing disorder.

Several ototoxic chemicals have this effect. These chemicals do not necessarily cause a hearing loss as such, but they prevent your brain from processing sounds normally. As a result, you may not understand speech well (or at all).

Outer/Middle Ear Side Effects

Outer or middle ear side effects include such things as feelings of fullness in your ears, ceruminosis (excessive ear wax production), swelling or redness in your ear canals, middle ear infections and ear pain or earaches. Occasionally you will see terms such as otorrhagia (bleeding from the ear), otorrhea (purulent discharge or puss from the ear), ruptured or perforated tympanic membrane (hole in your eardrum) and cholesteatoma (tumor of the middle ear).

Ears Blocked/Feelings of Fullness in Your Ears

One ototoxic side effect of some drugs is a feeling of fullness in your ears or head. This may feel like pressure in your ears, your ears may feel "plugged up", stuffed up, clogged or blocked, or you may have a general feeling of pressure in your head.[48]

There are three reasons you can experience this side effect.

First, the drug may cause ear congestion, so you have a real feeling that your ears are blocked. This can occur if a drug causes middle ear infections that clog up your middle ears/Eustachian tubes.

Second, your ears feel "blocked" or "full". This is a psychological feeling as your ears are not really congested. This kind of feeling of fullness in your ears often precedes or appears at the same time you first notice a hearing loss.

The professional health care people seem baffled by this symptom. As one health care professional explained, "Not only is the reason for this sensation unknown, but no nerve able to sense a pressure change in the inner-ear areas has been identified".[49]

I think they are looking in the wrong place. They are expecting to find the Eustachian tube or the middle ear itself clogged due to an infection. This can certainly give a clogged-up feeling.

However, there is another reason of this feeling of fullness that few seem to understand, and that is a **psychological** feeling of pressure in response to hearing loss. When you suddenly lose some hearing, your brain tells you that your ears **must** be blocked (or else sounds would keep coming through, wouldn't they?). Hence, the stuffed-up feeling.

I get this same sensation when I take my hearing aids off—all of a sudden it is too quiet, and my ears may feel "blocked". This feeling soon goes away as my brain gets used to not hearing much of anything again.

Therefore, if your ears feel "blocked" after taking an ototoxic drug, you may be losing your hearing, and your ears are warning you in this manner. It's a good idea at this point to have your hearing checked by an audiologist.

A third reason comes under the general heading of Eustachian tube dysfunction. This is where an ototoxic drug causes the trigeminal nerve that innervates your Eustachian tubes to malfunction leaving the affected Eustachian tube either stuck open—patulous Eustachian tube, or failing to open, thus building up pressure in the Eustachian tube and middle ear making it feel "full" or a feeling of pressure.

Ceruminosis

This is the medical way of saying excessive ear wax production and build-up. A few drugs have this side effect. This can result in both temporary hearing loss and temporary tinnitus.

Ear Pain

The fancy word for ear pain is otalgia. Traditionally, ear pain can be a result of ear infections, particularly in your middle ears. Thus, ear pain and otitis (see below) often go together.

However, ear pain (and earache and ear discomfort) can be the result of taking an ototoxic drug that causes ear pain/discomfort apart from any ear infection. A lot of drugs (772) have ear pain associated with them.

Otitis

Otitis is an inflammation of the ear. Normally doctors define where this inflammation occurs by adding a modifier to the word "otitis". Thus, "**otitis**

externa" refers to conditions of the outer ear and ear canal. Typically, they include infections that have symptoms such as redness, swelling and itching.

"**Otitis media**" typically refers to infections of the middle ear. Terms used to describe this condition include fluid in ear, ear pressure, pressure/throbbing in ears and ear disorder.

Some of the drugs listed in this book as having otitis, otitis externa or otitis media as an ototoxic side effect do not directly cause these conditions. Rather, infectious agents come in and take over when an opportunity presents itself. Thus, these infections are sometimes called "opportunistic infections". For example, this could happen as the result of an ototoxic antibiotic killing off the "good bacteria" in the ear canal, leaving it wide open to an opportunistic invasion of "bad bacteria".

Another scenario is where an ototoxic drug suppresses the immune system to some degree, thus letting a "bad guy" get a foothold where it otherwise would not be able to do so. Sometimes these are classified under the heading of a "resistance mechanism".

Unspecified/General Ear Conditions

There are three nebulous conditions researchers have used to describe ear side effects. The first one is the undefined catch-all term called "Ear Disorder" whatever they mean by that. The second is the term "Ototoxicity" where the researchers also didn't specify the specific side effect other than to probably mean the drug caused an inner ear side effect. Neither of these terms is very helpful.

The third term they used inappropriately is the term "Meniere's Disease" (see below).

Meniere's Disease

Doctors typically don't clearly understand the underlying cause of Meniere's disease, and thus don't have any real insight into how they can effectively treat it.

The truth is that Meniere's disease isn't a disease at all. Rather, it is simply a collection of four symptoms—periodic bouts of vertigo, hearing loss, tinnitus and a feeling of the ear being blocked. If you exhibit these symptoms, when your doctor has exhausted all other known causes for such symptoms, he typically calls it Meniere's disease.

Since there are a number of drugs that can cause these same four side effects, if a person exhibits these side effects due to taking a given drug, the drug is often listed as causing Meniere's disease. This is why 282 drugs are listed in this book as causing Meniere's disease.

For Further Information About Meniere's Disease

You can learn more about the underlying cause of Meniere's Disease and the details of how to effectively treat it in my book *Say Good Bye to Meniere's Disease—Here's How to Make Your World Stop Spinning.* (See the back of this book for ordering information.)

However, don't be misled. These drugs do **not** cause Meniere's disease. Rather, Meniere's disease is caused by your top two cervical vertebrae (C_1 and C_2) being out of proper alignment (what chiropractors call a subluxation) and thus "pinch" some/many/all of the nerve fibers in the vestibulocochlear nerve. The result is that some or all of the above symptoms appear. Depending on which side effects appear, doctors call these conditions by various names including Meniere's disease, endolymphatic hydrops, cochlear hydrops or vestibular hydrops.

Therefore, in this book when you see Meniere's disease listed as a side effect of a given drug, just disregard it as not being true Meniere's disease. What is true is that these drugs produce some or all of the same side effects that are common to Meniere's disease. Consequently, these side effects should have been listed

---

Chapter 4 Endnotes

1 McPheeters, 2000-2001. p. 1.
2 Bauman, 2022. pp. 29-31.
3 Haybach, 1999. pp. 33-34
4 Haybach, 1998. p. 3.
5 Kalkanis, 2001. p. 2.
6 Kalkanis, 2001. p. 1.
7 Kalkanis, 2001. p. 8.
8 Haybach, 1998. p. 2.
9 Haybach, 1998. p. 2.
10 Haybach, 1999. pp. 6-7.
11 Troost, 1998b. p. 1.
12 Disorders of the Inner Ear, 2000. p. 8.
13 Compendium of Pharmaceuticals and Specialties, 2000. p. 1499; Physicians' Desk Reference, 2000. p. 2803.
14 Haybach, 1996. pp. 3-4.
15 Haybach, 1999. p. 36.
16 Haybach, 1999. p. 33.
17 Are You Dizzy, 2001. p. 1.
18 Bowen, 1998. pp. 2-3.
19 Bowen, 1998. p. 4.
20 Vestibular Frequently Asked Questions, 1995. p. 1.
21 Bowen, 1998. p. 9.
22 Haybach, 1998. p. 6.

23 Vestibular Frequently Asked Questions, 1995. p. 1.
24 Bowen, 1998. p. 3.
25 Vestibular Apparatus, 2000. p. 1.
26 Haybach, 1998. p. 6.
27 Haybach, 1998. p. 6.
28 Haybach, 1998. p. 6.
29 Hull, 2000. p. 1.
30 Haybach, 1999. pp. 7-8.
31 Disorders of the Inner Ear, 2000. p. 11.
32 Kalkanis, 2001. p. 2.
33 Haybach, 1998. p. 6.
34 Haybach, 1998. p. 2.
35 Troost, 1998b. p. 1.
36 Haybach, 1999. p. 7.
37 Haybach, 1999. pp. 36-37.
38 Haybach, 1999. p. 38.
39 Compendium of Pharmaceuticals & Specialties, 2003. p. 1612.
40 Vestibular Apparatus, 2000. p. 1.
41 Haybach, 1998. p. 4.
42 Haybach, 1998. p. 6.
43 Haybach, 1998. p. 6.
44 Haybach, 1998. p. 6.
45 Haybach, 1999. pp. 37-38.
46 Compendium of Pharmaceuticals & Specialties, 2003. p. 1612.
47 Haybach, 1999. p. 36.
48 Haybach, 1998. p. 3.
49 Haybach, 1999. p. 34.

Chapter 5

Are You at Risk?

Some people take ototoxic drugs with seeming impunity—with no obvious side effects. Others take one dose of an ototoxic drug and wham—there goes their hearing. Why? The short answer is, "We are all different". Therefore, it should be no surprise that we also vary in our sensitivity to ototoxic drugs.

As a result, you need to realize that there is an unavoidable degree of risk attached to all drug treatments.[1] This is why many people notice that their tinnitus or other ototoxic side effects begin while they are taking some form of medication.[2] For example, one person explained:

> I was recently prescribed **Atomoxetine** (*Strattera*). I asked my doctor if it could bother the tinnitus I got from taking **Bupropion** (*Wellbutrin*) because I don't want to take anything else that could make it worse.

He pointed out (truthfully, I might add):

> **All** medications have the potential to cause tinnitus. There isn't any medication that you can categorically say with 100% certainty that it won't cause tinnitus.

Therefore, the most you can say is that certain drugs are unlikely, or highly unlikely to cause tinnitus (or any other ototoxic side effects), but there is still a chance that any given drug may cause a side effect such as tinnitus if given the right conditions.

Unfortunately, many doctors have been brainwashed to believe that drugs have few ototoxic (and other) side effects. Furthermore, they are led to believe that even the side effects that do occur are typically relatively rare. Thus, they rationalize away most reports of ototoxic side effects.

One of their favorite ways of rationalizing away any ototoxic side effects of the drugs they prescribe for you is to tell you, "It was just a coincidence." Their thinking goes something like this:

> Having an ototoxic side effect such as tinnitus is fairly common and having to take a blood pressure medication (for example) is also common. It is, therefore, inevitable that some people's tinnitus should start while they are taking such drugs and thus they link the two together.[3]

Doctors that think this way blithely pass off any ototoxic side effects as a coincidence and do this in spite of the fact that hundreds or thousands of people have reported precisely this same side effect to the FDA's adverse drug reporting system (FAERS).

Two or three reports of a given drug causing a particular ototoxic side effect may indeed be coincidental or a case of mistaken causality, but when large numbers of people report the same side effect, it is time to realize that something is going on—it's not just a coincidence.

If all else fails, these doctors then may admit that "a tiny number of people do seem to have unusual reactions to the medication."[4] Tiny number? The FDA's data base is packed with thousands upon thousands of reports of people getting ototoxic side effects from taking various prescription drugs.

And to hide their ignorance, often your doctor will "reassure you that the drug is not the cause of your ototoxic side effect."[5] One patient of a doctor that took this deceitful approach lamented:

> I took **Bupropion** (*Wellbutrin*) for a very short time and now have tinnitus that seems to be irreversible. This is not fair as I made sure to ask my doctor about that side effect before going on it and he **assured** me it was not an issue.

With tactics such as these, no wonder many doctors are losing credibility with their patients! Thus, it is essential that healthcare providers understand that essentially all medications can have unwanted side effects. This is a universal truth of drug treatment.[6] They need to take their patients' reports seriously.

Risk Factors

Researchers have identified a number of factors that increase the risk of your having an ototoxic reaction when taking certain drugs.[7] These risk factors include medication dose, therapy duration, cumulative lifetime dose, impaired kidney function, infusion rate of certain medications (e.g., IV **Furosemide** and AMINOGLYCOSIDES), co-administration of multiple ototoxic medications, age, previous exposure to head and neck radiation (chemotherapeutic agents), genetic susceptibility, and family history of ototoxicity.[8] Thus, if any of these risk factors apply to you, you are more at risk of an ototoxic reaction to a given drug than the general population.

This chapter explains many of these risk factors (in no particular order of importance). The more that apply to you, the higher your potential risk.

1. Correct dose is critical. Did you know that the appropriate dose significantly varies from person to person and is often very different from the standard dose. This is because the degree to which people absorb an oral drug varies significantly. Furthermore, the degree to which people eliminate a drug varies significantly.[9] As a result, receiving the wrong dose (e.g. too high) can cause ototoxic side effects that otherwise would not appear.

2. The person is very young. This includes as yet unborn children. Thus, for example, if you are pregnant when you take an ototoxic drug, it can have devastating effects on your unborn child, including damaging both the auditory and vestibular systems resulting in permanent deafness and/or balance problems. Your unborn baby is particularly vulnerable during the first trimester, especially between weeks 6 and 8. **Quinine**, the SALICYLATE family, **Streptomycin** and **Dihydrostreptomycin** are among the drugs that do this.[10]

3. You are a senior (over age 60). Age makes a difference as the older you are, the slower your body typically metabolizes a given drug. Furthermore, as you age your liver and kidneys often don't function as well as they once did. Consequently, they don't eliminate drugs as fast as they used to. This causes drugs to stay in your body longer and thus causes drug concentrations to build up. Also, how much water and fat you have in your body changes as you age and this can put additional strain on your liver and kidneys.

   Furthermore, as you age, you tend to take more drugs and how these drugs interact with each other affects the frequency and severity of any resulting ototoxic side effects, especially when taken at higher doses. In addition, you very likely already have minor hearing problems. The effects of taking ototoxic drugs are additive and can compound your hearing loss.

4. You have certain hereditary (genetic) factors that make you more susceptible than the general population. This seems particularly true if you take AMINOGLYCOSIDE antibiotics. (For further information on this, see the section "Genetics and Aminoglycoside Ototoxicity" in Chapter 12.)

5. You already have a sensorineural hearing loss, balance problems or some other form of pre-existing ear damage.[11] People with a pre-existing

hearing loss may be at greater risk of incurring further hearing loss than people with normal hearing. This is the case with **Cisplatin** for example, and there is no reason to believe the situation is any different with other ototoxic drugs. One study found that people with pre-existing hearing loss on their baseline audiogram (taken before **Cisplatin** treatment) had greater subsequent hearing loss than those with normal hearing.[12]

Since ototoxic damage is often cumulative, pre-existing ear damage, whatever the cause, can result in measurable or observable damage more quickly. This could include ear problems such as Meniere's Disease (syndrome of fluctuating hearing loss, tinnitus and vertigo), endolymphatic hydrops (basically a subset of Meniere's Disease), Cogan's disease (a syndrome of visual, hearing and balance problems), Lermoyez syndrome (increasing deafness, interrupted by a sudden attack of dizziness, after which hearing improves), autoimmune inner-ear disease (AIED) and perilymphatic fistula (inner ear fluid leaking into your middle ear).[13]

6. You have had previous ear damage (hearing loss) from excessive noise.[14] The amount of noise predisposing you to more hearing loss from taking ototoxic drugs is not well defined. You could assume you are at greater risk if you have been around artillery fire, jet aircraft, rock concerts (as either a performer or a fan), or use jackhammers, fire guns, work at construction sites, or work or play in noisy environments.

7. You have problems with either your liver or kidneys (whether pre-existing or developing during drug treatment). If your liver or kidney function is reduced, the drug may not be broken down or eliminated from your body as quickly as it otherwise would. Thus, the drug can build up to toxic/ototoxic levels in your blood.

   You increase your risk if you take drugs that cause nephrotoxicity (kidney toxicity) because this, in turn, increases the likelihood of ototoxicity. For example, people with kidney problems have an unusually high incidence of hearing loss, even without drug use.[15] Chinese herbalists have known this for hundreds of years. They still teach that your ears and your kidneys are "connected".

   This is corroborated by modern research. As Dr. Ghent explains, "It is important to remember that any chemical that is ototoxic is also likely to be poisonous to your kidneys, because your inner ears and kidneys arise from the same germ layer during embryonic development. While kidney damage is rare, it can result from a serious complication of chemical [drug] exposures and is often presaged by hearing difficulties resulting from the same causes."[16]

Another way your ears and kidneys are "connected" is that both your inner ears and your kidneys use the same ion transporters. The stria vascularis in your inner ears is responsible for generating and maintaining your "cochlear battery's" charge. To do this, it uses ion transporters. Since many of the ion transporters in the stria vascularis are the same as those in your kidneys, drugs that affect your kidneys often damage your inner ears as well.[17]

Therefore, if you are taking any medications that affect your kidneys, or if your kidneys are not working properly (possibly from taking nephrotoxic [kidney-damaging] drugs such as the Aminoglycoside antibiotics), watch out for any ototoxic changes to your ears.

Furthermore, your body eliminates many drugs through your kidneys. If your kidneys aren't working properly, ototoxic drugs can spend more time in your body, thereby increasing your chances of ototoxic side effects.[18]

8. You are extremely sensitive to drugs or have a low tolerance for drugs in general.

9. You have previously used ototoxic drugs, or you have taken repeated courses of the same ototoxic drug. This is especially true if you have previously used Aminoglycoside antibiotics.

10. You have previously had ototoxic reactions to drugs. This proves your ears are particularly sensitive to ototoxic drugs. Your risk of ototoxic reactions to current or future drug therapy is much higher. Not only does the risk increase, but the resulting ototoxic damage has a tendency to be more severe and is more likely to be permanent.[19]

11. You have taken certain drugs for a long time, especially if you have taken a drug for longer than the manufacturer recommended. You have to watch this as doctors often prescribe drugs for longer periods than the manufacturer recommends.

    For example, Benzodiazepines are only recommended to be taken for up to two weeks, yet many people have been on them for months or years and are thus prone to ototoxic side effects, especially when they try to get off these drugs.

12. You can be at higher risk if an ototoxic drug isn't administered properly. Proper administration is critically important if you want to avoid permanent, severe ototoxic damage.[20] For example, you increase your risk if you have taken ototoxic drugs in larger doses than recommended; if you have been given a larger single dose of an ototoxic drug than recommended; if you

have been given a higher than recommended cumulative (total) dose; or you have been given a rapid or faster than recommended dose (injection or intravenous). This could show up as higher than recommended peak serum levels and/or higher than recommended trough serum levels.[21]

13. You have been given an inappropriate dose (children, elderly people, obese people)—e.g., a child given an adult's dose.

14. You are overweight. Your weight can make a difference as some drug doses are determined by your lean body weight. Thus, if you are overweight and if the drug is fat-soluble, how much fat you have in your body can make a big difference. For example, if you have extra fat, and if your doctor/nurse forgets and calculates your dose by your total weight, you'll get an overdose which can show up as ototoxic side effects.

Medication Error

"Medication error is **not** just giving the wrong pill or the wrong dosage—it is also giving the **wrong medication** to a person who cannot tolerate ototoxic drugs"—Malisa Janes, Rh.D.

That is why it is important that your doctor calculates the drug dose based on your lean muscle mass, not on your total body weight including fat.[22]

Furthermore, if you have a lot of fat, the drug can be stored in your fat. Consequently, you get a higher concentration of the drug. Also, the drug can stay in your body fat longer and thus have a continuing effect after you stop taking the drug.

15. You are at a higher risk if the drug you are taking has a small therapeutic index or window. Let me explain. When a drug company designs a new drug, it has to decide what constitutes an appropriate dose for this new drug. Ideally the company wants this new drug to have minimal side effects, and at the same time, it wants the majority of people taking it to experience the intended benefits of this drug.

Sometimes, this is fairly easy to accomplish. This occurs when the toxic dose (where side effects begin to show up) is much higher than the effective dose (where the drug's benefits show up). In other cases, it's virtually impossible to accomplish, such as when the effective dose and the toxic dose are very close to each other.[23]

This gap between the effective dose and the toxic dose is called the therapeutic index or therapeutic window. With a drug that has a wide therapeutic index, it is relatively unlikely that if you take this drug at the prescribed dose will experience any negative side effects. In contrast, if you take a drug that has a narrow therapeutic window, you will have a relatively high risk of experiencing negative side effects.[24] In such cases, even a slight drug "overdose" just due to changes in the water (you are dehydrated) or fat content of your body can cause ototoxic side effects to appear.

Since drugs vary in their effective doses, you should know the therapeutic index of the drugs you take. A high therapeutic index lets you know that the effective dose is well below the toxic dose so you have a lot of "wiggle room" to adjust the dose before side effects appear. On the other hand, a low therapeutic index tells you that the therapeutic dose is close to the toxic dose so there isn't much "wiggle room" to adjust the dose. Thus, unless your doctor carefully tailors your dose to your body's characteristics, you could inadvertently be prescribed a toxic dose and thus experience serious ototoxic (and other) side effects. Examples of drugs with low therapeutic indices are **Lithium** and various cancer drugs.

16. You are dehydrated. If the drug you are taking is water-soluble, how much water you have in your body can make a difference as previously mentioned. This is more likely to occur if you are taking Diuretics. For example, if you are dehydrated, the drug concentration in your blood/serum will be higher than normal and thus could result in ototoxic side effects that you might have avoided if you were well-hydrated.[25] (Incidentally, if you have a fever it is very easy to become dehydrated.)

17. You have taken ototoxic Diuretics at the same time as other ototoxic drugs or if you have used or are using two or more ototoxic and/or nephrotoxic (toxic to the kidneys) drugs at the same time. Since various drug interactions increase the risk of ototoxicity, taking two or more ototoxic drugs at the same time sharply increases your chances of experiencing ototoxic side effects.

    Taking two or more ototoxic drugs at the same time or consecutively may cause severe permanent ototoxic side effects. The damage may occur at lower cumulative doses and much more rapidly, even when the doses of both drugs are within acceptable, published therapeutic ranges[26] as a result of potentiation (the synergistic effect of two drugs given simultaneously).

    Some drug combinations that will increase your risk of having ototoxic reactions include: Aminoglycoside antibiotics and **Indomethacin** (in newly-born babies); Aminoglycoside antibiotics and Loop diuretics; Aminoglycoside antibiotics and **Vancomycin**; **Ampicillin** or **Amphotericin B**; **Bumetanide** and **Cisplatin**; **Capreomycin** and **Kanamycin**; and **Ethacrynic acid** and some CEPHALOSPORIN antibiotics.[27 28]

LOOP DIURETICS and AMINOGLYCOSIDE antibiotics taken together are one particularly bad combination. Not only are they both ototoxic, but the LOOP DIURETICS may change the antibiotic concentration in serum and tissue, increasing the possibility of ototoxic damage. These DIURETICS also increase the chance that dehydration will develop, another risk factor for ototoxicity.[29]

18. You have had previous ear infections.

19. You are generally in poor health in the first place. This also includes having poor nutrition at the time you are taking any ototoxic drug.[30]

20. You have abnormal laboratory values such as reductions in serum albumin, serum red blood cells, hematocrit, hemoglobin or you have rising serum creatinine levels.[31]

21. You have had radiation treatments on your head or ears.[32]

22. You have either eye or proprioceptive (balance) problems. This increases the chances that vestibular ototoxicity will have a more serious impact on your life if it does occur. If ototoxic drugs destroy your vestibular system and you already have a visual or proprioceptive problem, you will not be able to maintain your balance. Therefore, if you have visual or proprioceptive problems, take great care when taking ototoxic drugs with a high risk of developing vestibular side effects, and thus only take them if you have a life-threatening condition.[33]

Here's How You Can Reduce Your Risk

You cannot do anything about certain ototoxic risk factors such as your age or your genetic makeup. However, there are still some things you (and your doctor) can do to lessen your risk of having an ototoxic reaction from taking certain drugs.

If you have any hearing or balance conditions, it is very important that you discuss them with your doctor. Here are 12 things you and your doctor can work together on to help protect your ears.

1. Be aware of the early warning signs of ototoxicity. They are (in order of frequency): you feel dizzy; you develop ataxia (staggering gait) or vertigo (spinning sensation); your ears begin ringing (tinnitus) or your existing tinnitus gets worse or you hear a new kind of tinnitus; your hearing gets

worse or begins fluctuating; you develop ear pain; or you feel pressure in your ears (unless you have a head cold or sinus congestion). Should any of these symptoms develop while taking any medication, stop the medication immediately and call your doctor.[34]

2. Tell your doctor that you are hard of hearing, especially if you have a sensorineural hearing loss and/or suffer from balance problems. Also, tell your doctor if you currently have any ringing in your ears (tinnitus). This is very important, as you may be more susceptible to drugs than the general population. Dr. Epstein cautions:

   > If you have an existing sensorineural hearing loss, regardless of the cause, when using ototoxic medications, you are more vulnerable to aggravation of that hearing loss.[35]

3. Always discuss possible side effects (including ototoxic side effects) with your doctor before you begin taking a new medication.

4. Follow your doctor's dosage instructions exactly. Make sure your doctor writes dosage information down clearly for you. Don't trust your (faulty) hearing or your (equally faulty) memory. Overdosing could certainly adversely affect your hearing.

   Also, make sure your doctor does not exceed the manufacturer's dosage instructions when he prescribes drugs for you. During the drug approval process, researchers determine the safe dose of each drug. These dosage instructions are listed in drug books such as the PDR along with warnings that drugs are not to be taken for longer than a certain number of days and/or that the dose is not to exceed a certain amount. This information is vitally important if you want to avoid adverse ototoxic side effects.

   Do doctors heed these guidelines? Not on your life! For example, a 1996 report by the FDA found that for a certain drug they had specifically warned doctors about, 85% of the prescriptions were still for longer periods than were safe![36]

   Furthermore, did you know that your doctor does not have to follow these recommended guidelines when prescribing drugs? He can prescribe as much as he wants, as often as he wants—but it is you (and your ears) that will suffer the consequences if he prescribes the wrong dose. Therefore, make sure your doctor adheres to the manufacturer's guidelines.

5. Use the same pharmacy for all your prescriptions so they know all the drugs you are taking. That way they can quickly advise you of any known dangerous drug combinations.[37]

6. Always read the labels on over-the-counter (OTC) medications and particularly watch for ototoxic side effects. You can also ask your pharmacist about potential ototoxic effects of OTC medications. Just because they are OTC drugs doesn't mean they can't damage your ears.

7. Make sure you drink plenty of fluids so you don't get dehydrated. This is especially important if you have a fever or are taking LOOP DIURETICS.

Medic Alert

If you have read this far, you likely know the ototoxic risk factors that pertain to you. Perhaps you even know your body is particularly susceptible to the ototoxic effects of certain drugs.

One way to help protect yourself is to wear a Medic Alert tag. This tag can do two important things. First, it can warn health care professionals that you have a hearing loss and/or balance problems. Second, it can warn them about specific ototoxic drugs that you know will further damage your hearing or balance.

For further information, contact Medic Alert, phone 1-800-432-5378 or visit their web site at https://www.medicalert.org.

8. If you have kidney problems, have your health care professionals carefully monitor your kidney function and report abnormalities immediately. It is most important that your doctor determine how well your kidneys are working before he prescribes various medications. This is because your body excretes many drugs through your kidneys. If they are not working properly, some drugs can quickly rise to dangerous levels of ototoxicity in your bloodstream and may result in permanent hearing loss and other ear damage.

9. Avoid using multiple ototoxic drugs at the same time (particularly AMINOGLYCOSIDE antibiotics, **Cisplatin** and LOOP DIURETICS). Also do not take nephrotoxic (kidney damaging) and other ototoxic drugs at the same time.[38]

10. Avoid noisy environments for at least 6 months after you have completed a course of an AMINOGLYCOSIDE antibiotic or a platinum compound such as **Cisplatin**. This is because your ears can still be supersensitive to noise-induced hearing loss.[39] The residual drug in your inner ears can team up with noise in a synergistic relationship to cause even more hearing damage. If you wear or obtain hearing aids during this time, you need to keep the volume down as well.[40] Tell you audiologist about this so she can program them correctly for you. (See Chapter 11 for more information on this important subject.)

11. It is most important, if you are beginning treatment with an ototoxic drug such as any of the AMINOGLYCOSIDE antibiotics, LOOP DIURETICS or platinum compounds such as **Cisplatin**, that you have a baseline **high-frequency** audiogram done **before** you begin treatment and then serial high-frequency audiograms (testing those frequencies between 8,000 Hz and the highest frequency you can hear [or up to 20,000 Hz]) during and after drug therapy. This is essential as conventional audiograms cannot catch the first indications of high-frequency hearing loss.[41] If this is done, your doctor likely can either modify or stop treatment before significant hearing loss occurs. (See Chapter 9 for more information on this important subject.)

12. If you have had vestibular (balance) problems from taking any drug, for example, **Gentamicin**, you want to be very careful not to damage your vestibular system further—unless it is so extensively damaged that you have nothing further to lose. To protect the remaining function of your vestibular system, according to Dr. Hain, you should stay away from any of the AMINOGLYCOSIDE antibiotics; ANTIHISTAMINES like **Meclizine** and **Promethazine**; TRICYCLIC ANTIDEPRESSANTS such as **Amitriptyline; Aspirin (ASA)** and other NON-STEROIDAL ANTI-INFLAMMATORY DRUGS including **Ibuprofen** and **Naproxen** (in large doses); **Cisplatin** and related anti-cancer drugs; **Erythromycin**; LOOP DIURETICS like **Furosemide** and **Ethacrynic acid**; BENZODIAZEPINES such as **Alprazolam**, **Clonazepam**, **Diazepam**, **Lorazepam** and related drugs; and **Quinine** and related drugs.[42]

    In addition, check the listing in this book for the degree of vestibular risk of any other drugs you are considering taking that are not mentioned above.

Chapter 5 Endnotes

1 Hallam, 1993. p. 45.
2 McKenna, 2010. p. 33.
3 McKenna, 2010. p. 33.
4 McKenna, 2010. p. 33.
5 McKenna, 2010. p. 33.
6 Coverstone, 2018. p. 11.
7 DiSogra, 2018. p. 8.
8 DiSogra, 2018. p. 8.
9 A Midwestern Doctor, 2023d. p. 1.
10 Troost, 1998b. p. 2.
11 Troost, 1998b. p. 3.
12 Fausti, 1993a. p. 664.
13 Haybach, 1999. p. 45.

14 Shearer, 1994.
15 Staab, 1991. p. 38.
16 Ghent, 2016. p. 1.
17 Fitzakerley, Janet, 2014. p. 1.
18 Haybach, 1999. p. 45.
19 Haybach, 1999. p. 45.
20 Haybach, 1999. pp. 48-49.
21 Haybach, 1999. p. 44.
22 Haybach, 1999. p. 50.
23 A Midwestern Doctor, 2023d. p. 1.
24 A Midwestern Doctor, 2023d. p. 1.
25 Haybach, 1998. p. 3.
26 Haybach, 1999. p. 47.
27 Haybach, 1998. p. 3.
28 Haybach, 1999. p. 47.
29 Haybach, 1999. p. 47.
30 Priuska, 1997. p. 3.
31 Haybach, 1999. p. 44.
32 Haybach, 1998. p. 3.
33 Haybach, 1999. p. 45.
34 Epstein, 1995. pp. 1-2.
35 Epstein, 1995. p. 1.
36 Freundlich, 1998. p. 2.
37 Shearer, 1994.
38 Haybach, 1998. p. 5.
39 Kalkanis, 2001. p. 3.
40 Kalkanis, 2001. pp. 8-9.
41 Kalkanis, 2001. p. 8.
42 Hain, 1999. p. 3.

Chapter 6

The Incidence of Side Effects Is Grossly Under-reported

Before you take a drug, you probably want to know how likely it will be that you will experience side effects from taking that drug. Unfortunately, when you try to look up the incidence of ototoxic (and other) side effects, you probably don't realize that the incidence of side effects occurring is grossly under-reported. Thus, you may assume a drug is much safer to take than it really is.

This is one thing that needs to be remedied in our current dysfunctional health-care system. In order to fix this gross under-reporting of drug side effects, both doctors and patients (that means you and me) need to take appropriate action because this process really begins with us since we are the first links in the side-effect-reporting process.

The system breaks down here because many people don't bother to learn which ototoxic (and other) side effects they may experience, and thus don't report them because they don't recognize them as side effects of the drug they are taking.

According to one FDA survey, 7 out of 10 patients never were told about the side effects of the drugs their doctors prescribed.[1] If your doctor or pharmacist doesn't tell you about the side effects of the drugs you are taking, you need to ask. This is **your** responsibility.

Thus, before you take a drug, learn as much as you can about the side effects of that drug, then watch for any developing side effects. Otherwise, even if you do notice a side effect, you may fail to attribute it to the drug you are taking. As a result, you won't report it to your doctor or to the FDA's database. The result is that this side effect may never be written up/published. Consequently, people will continue to damage their ears because they don't know the truth about that drug.

For example, a few years ago I was talking to a lady on the phone. She told me she had been taking **Erythromycin** for an infection. I knew it was ototoxic, so I asked her if it had bothered her ears. She didn't think so. I asked her if she had had any of the ototoxic effects you can see listed under **Erythromycin**. Right away she exclaimed, "Yes, I got that and I had that". The upshot was that she had experienced fairly severe ototoxic side effects from taking this drug and hadn't realized it was caused by this drug at all! She thought it was just some of the effects of the illness she had.

I then asked her if she had reported these side effects to her doctor. No, she hadn't. There she was—damaging her ears—and her doctor was in the dark about the whole episode. I'm afraid this happens far too often.

Incidentally, if you don't report all side effects to your doctor, how will he know to adjust your medication so it won't do further damage to your ears and body?

Therefore, if you experience any side effects, you need to report them to your doctor, and also, directly to the Food and Drug Administration's (FDA) Adverse Event Reporting System)—FAERS. This database contains voluntary reports of **drug**-related adverse events. The FDA also has a similar database called VAERS (Vaccine Adverse Event Reporting System) for reporting **vaccine** side effects/ injuries. (See pages 118-119 on how to make reports to both of these databases.)

Note: It is very important for you to report all side effects you experience as the FDA can't compile these data and take appropriate action if they don't hear from you!

Not only do you have a responsibility to report side effects to your doctor, but according to the FDA rules, doctors are also supposed to report all drug and vaccine side effects they come across for inclusion in the FAERS or VARES databases so that the FDA can accumulate accurate statistics on the incidence of drug and vaccine side effects.

Do you know whether your doctor reports to the FDA any of the side effects you have reported to him? I'll bet he doesn't!

You may find it hard to believe, but few side effects are ever reported to the FDA for inclusion in their FARES/VARES databases. Thus, the reports on ototoxicity we have to work with represent only a very small fraction of the total number of ototoxic side effects that occur in real life.

Here is a classic understatement by the FDA:

> Often the FDA only receives reports of the **most critical and severe cases**; **these numbers may therefore under-represent** the complication rate of the medication.

Just "may under-represent"? According to former FDA Commissioner, David Kessler, only about 1% of **serious** side effects are ever reported to the FDA![2] Notice that! Doctors and patients combined report to the FDA less than 1% of the **serious** side effects they come across. Since most serious side effects are never reported, at the very minimum, you need to multiply any reported statistics by a factor of 100.

To the FDA, serious refers to life threatening side effects. Thus, the FDA does not consider ear problems such as the tinnitus, hearing loss and balance problems you may experience as serious side effects! And since ototoxic side effects are not considered "serious", they are not reported even as often as the serious side effects are. Thus, only a small fraction of 1% of ototoxic side effects are actually reported. That means that you probably can multiply the figures in the FAERS database by a factor of 1,000 and **still** have very conservative results as I will show shortly.

Nor was Kessler the only one to notice this fact. Ross Lazarus reported:

> Likewise, **fewer than 1%** of vaccine adverse events are reported. Low reporting rates preclude or slow the identification of "problem" drugs and vaccines that endanger public health.[3]

Furthermore, according to Al Ozonoff, PhD, of Harvard Medical School in Boston, pharmacovigilance databases such as VigiBase and VAERS (Vaccine Adverse Event Reporting System) are:

> ...almost always **dramatically underreported** in terms of the incidence of events they report.[4]

And lest you think these people are scaremongering and blowing things out of proportion, here are some documented facts and figures.

In one study of Rhode Island doctors, researchers found that the doctors in the study had recorded in their patients' files 26,000 adverse reactions to drugs. According to FDA guidelines, these doctors should have reported all of these side effects to the FDA. Now, here's the question. How many of these 26,000 side effects in the doctor's files do you think these doctors actually reported to the FDA?

Did these doctors report all these 26,000 adverse side effects to the FDA? Or even most of them? Not on your life!

The shocking truth is that they only reported 11![5] That's only 11, not 1,100 or 11,000—just a minuscule 1/25th of 1% or 1 of every 2,364 cases in these doctor's files. Thus, the multiplication factor needs to be, not just 100 times, not just 1,000 times, but a whopping **2,363 times** for **serious** side effects.

If this study is representative of the whole country (and there is no compelling reason to believe otherwise), only 1 out of every 2,363 reports of **serious** adverse reactions ever reaches the FDA. Add to this total, the number of serious side effects that people do not report to their doctors in the first place. The result is that only a minuscule fraction of 1% of adverse side effects ever reach the FDA. Obviously, less serious and "minor" side effects such as hearing loss and tinnitus are rarely, if ever, reported. (This is why it is so important for you to help fix the system by filing such reports as you experience any side effects from taking drugs or vaccines.)

Since the multiplier for serious side effects needs to be at least 2,363, and since far fewer of "minor" ototoxic side effects such as tinnitus and hearing loss are ever reported, the true multiplication factor will be much greater still.

This would mean that if the FAERS database shows that 100 people reported tinnitus after taking a given drug, the true figure is, at a very minimum, 100 times higher—namely 10,000 people, and is likely, using the Rhode Island study multiplier, 2,363 times higher—namely 263,300 people—and that's a **lot** of people.

Now here is an example—using the drug **Pregabalin** (*Lyrica*)—showing the incidence of tinnitus, first from the original research done on this drug before it was released, and then the dismal reporting of tinnitus side effects to the FDA after it was released. This is how things often work out in real life.

Here's the tinnitus statistics for this drug. Both the CPS (Compendium of Pharmaceuticals and Specialties)—the drug reference book used in Canada and the PDR (Physicians' Desk Reference)—our USA drug book, report that in the trials for **Pregabalin**, tinnitus occurred in 2.9% of the participants. Note: The placebo figure was 0. Thus, all cases of tinnitus reported were attributed to taking **Pregabalin**.

The FMR (FactMed Report) shows that there were 397 reports to the FDA database of tinnitus side effects in the almost 9-year period between Jan 2004 and Oct 2012. Thus, the average number of tinnitus reports per year was just 44.

From this you'd quite logically think that tinnitus is not a very common side effect of taking **Pregabalin**, but if you think that, you would be just plain wrong. Here's how you can figure out a more accurate result.

The number of prescriptions for **Pregabalin** per year in the USA (for 2017) was 11,152.692.

Based on these figures, the average number of tinnitus reports per year should be 2.9% of 11,152,692 which would be a whopping 323,428 reports—not the minuscule 44 actually reported.

That is just 0.0136% or about 1/100th of 1% or only 1 report to the FDA for every 7,350 actual cases of tinnitus from this drug! (Of course this is just one drug. The ratios for other drugs vary, some are less, and others are even more.)

Thus, when you look at the figures reported to the FDA (and those used in this book), don't for one moment think that those are the true figures indicating the magnitude of the problem.

Yes, they **are** true in that those figures were actually reported, but no, they are **not** true if you think they represent **all** the incidences of those side effects.

Therefore, never assume that because there are only a few reports for hearing loss (or whatever ototoxic side effect you are interested in) for a given drug, that this reported figure represents the true number of people getting that side effect. If you did, you might erroneously consider the risk of getting this side effect as very small, when in fact the risk is much higher.

Note that in order to get the data to compile the incidences of side effects shown in this book for the various drugs, I extracted 1,700 pages of ototoxic side-effect-data from the FactMed Report website that was collected between January 2004 and October 2012. This gave me about 54,000 lines of semi-compiled ototoxic drug data to sort through and compile. You may think that this is a lot of information (and it is), but, as we have just seen, it represents only a minuscule fraction of 1% of the ototoxic side effects that actually occur in real life.

By now, you should realize that the incidence figures reported to the FAERS database are **grossly low**. They are merely the tip of the iceberg. The few adverse side effects that doctors do report are the absolute **minimum** that exist. Thus, we only know the best-case scenario. We certainly don't have a real grasp on the most likely scenario, and who knows just how bad the worst case situation is.

For example, in this book the drugs **Alprostadil**, **Cefprozil** and **Dactinomycin** each show 10 reports of hearing loss. However, if every person taking those drugs and getting a hearing loss had reported that fact to the FDA's database, the true figure could well be 3,000 times greater as we have just seen—more like 30,000 people for each drug—rather than the measly 10 cases of hearing loss actually reported.

Unfortunately, because so few side effects are reported to the FDA's database, or get into the medical literature, many doctors don't believe that the drugs they prescribe cause such "minor" side effects as tinnitus or hearing loss, not to mention all the other ototoxic side effects.

In truth, hearing loss is **not** a minor side effect at all, even though many doctors seem to treat it as such. Let's look at another real-life example. Peggy lost all the hearing in one ear and some in her other ear from taking **Atenolol**. She hurried to her doctor. Did her doctor say, "Wow, I need to get you off this medication and report this side effect now"? Absolutely not. He downplayed the seriousness of the situation and treated her as a neurotic woman instead.

He wrote on her chart that she was "just a little scared" because she had a little "reduced hearing" like it was no big deal and that she was being emotional about nothing. Losing all hearing in one ear and some in the other is not just "reduced hearing" and nothing to be concerned about! Doctors need to realize that sudden hearing loss is a medical emergency! It **is** a big deal for the person involved, not just a minor annoyance that doesn't have to be reported.

Because her doctor (and others like him) do not report these kinds of ototoxic side effects, the current PDR (and other drug books) still do not list hearing loss as a side effect for **Atenolol**. Interestingly enough, in other parts of the world, hearing loss is indeed linked to **Atenolol**.

As you will see if you look at the **Atenolol** listing in Chapter 19, there are now 511 reports of hearing loss reported to the FAERS database. If we multiply by a conservative factor of 3,000 since few of these hearing losses are ever reported, we get 1,533,000 people with hearing loss from just taking this one drug! This figure is much closer to the truth. We need to get on the ball here in the USA!

How Serious Are "Serious" Side Effects?

What ototoxic side effects should you be reporting? FDA guidelines say to report **serious** adverse events. They define serious side effects [from drugs] as those that cause death; are life-threatening; cause hospitalization; result in a significant, persistent or permanent disability; and those that require [medical] intervention to prevent permanent impairment or damage.

They further explain their definition of a disability—"a significant, persistent, or permanent change, impairment, damage or disruption in the patient's body function/structure, physical activities or quality of life".[6]

This description fits cochlear conditions such as hearing loss, hyperacusis and tinnitus, plus ataxia, dizziness, nystagmus, oscillopsia, vertigo and various other balance problems. These are significant conditions. Many times, they are permanent. Furthermore, they all can cause a very definite change in your physical activities, and they most definitely affect the quality of your life. Therefore, whether doctors and other medical professionals think of ear damage as serious or not, ototoxic damage to your ears **is** a serious adverse event and thus they (and you) need to report it!

The FDA requests you (or your doctor) report such events even if you are not absolutely certain a given drug caused the side effect you are reporting. If you are suspicious that it did so, report it.

What Does Rare Really Mean?

Pharmacists fill billions of prescriptions each year in the USA. This translates into vast amounts of drugs consumed. For example, people consume *Aspirin* (**Acetylsalicylic acid**) by the truckload. As hard as it is to believe, Americans alone consume **40 million pounds** of *Aspirin* each year![7] According to Bayer, people take more than 50 billion *Aspirin* tablets worldwide each year. These figures refer to only one drug. Add to this number the thousands of other drugs used worldwide. The total is truly monumental. As a result, "rare" ototoxic side effects can translate into enormous numbers of ears damaged.

The PDR uses the words "frequent," "infrequent" and "rare" to describe how often a given side effect occurs. In the PDR "frequent" generally means occurring in at least 1 person out of 100 (>1%). "Infrequent" side effects occur in fewer than 1 out of 100 people, but in more than 1 out of 1,000 people (0.1-1%) and "rare" side effects occur in fewer than 1 out of 1,000 (<0.1%) people taking a given drug.[8]

You will find some side effects listed as occurring only in 1 out of every 10,000 (0.01%) people taking that drug (very rare). You might consider this to be such a rare occurrence that it is not worth bothering about so let me put these figures into perspective for you.

Consider a drug that supposedly only causes hearing loss in 1 person out of every 10,000 people taking it. This would be considered very rare. Even so, this "very rare" side effect is still going to affect a lot of people. For example, the population of the United States is approximately 331,000,000. At a chance of only 1 in 10,000 (0.01%), if all the people in the USA took a certain drug that caused hearing loss, 33,100 people would end up with a hearing loss. Would you take solace in the fact that 33,100 other people now can't hear either? That is small comfort!

If the occurrence of hearing loss was rare—only 1 out of 1,000—you would be part of a third of a million people in the USA who would now be hard of hearing from taking that drug. This is certainly not a trivial number. We are talking about a **lot** of people! The comparable figures for China would be 1,200,000 people. Worldwide, the resulting hearing loss would affect over 5,000,000 people each and every year! They may call this "rare," but in reality, it is catastrophic—yet this is how many people would be affected if only one-tenth of 1% of the people taking a given drug had this side effect! Don't be fooled by the word "rare". The suffering caused by a "rare" side effect can be enormous.

The above figures assume that the incidence statistics are correct, but are they? As we have seen, only a miniscule fraction of 1% of side effects are ever reported to the FDA. Thus, the true incidence of a given side effect is likely much, much higher than the figures you see reported in the PDR.

As we have just seen, the published figures for a given side effect are grossly low. For example, a side effect that is said to occur in less than 0.01% (1 in 10,000) of the people taking it, may in fact, be occurring 2,364 times more often than reported (based on the results of the Rhode Island study). Therefore, instead of only occurring once in every 10,000 people and thus being truly a very rare side effect, this side effect theoretically might be occurring once in every four people (23.6%)! That is not rare at all!

The risk incidence figures in this book all come from reputable sources. If you see "PDR" after an incidence figure, you know that these are the figures that were reported to the FDA during the drug approval process. You can take them at face value if you want. However, now that you know how seldom side effects are really reported, you might want to factor in some constant to allow for a large margin of error in the reported figures. I think these published incidence figures warrant a healthy dose of skepticism, don't you?

Furthermore, until researchers conduct widespread studies, no one knows if the results of the specific controlled studies that are reported in the PDR and other similar drug books are reliable indicators of the true incidence of those side effects in the population at large. This is because the population at large may have different characteristics and other factors from those that prevailed during the clinical trials.

Similarly, you cannot accurately compare the cited frequencies with figures obtained from other clinical investigations involving different treatments, uses, and investigators. The cited figures just provide you with a basis for estimating the frequency of occurrence of side effects in the populations studied.[9]

In real life, the figures may vary all over the place. For this reason, you need to know the specific risk factors for your own body. (See Chapter 5 for information on risk factors.) You don't really care what the risk is to the general population. What you really want to know is how a given drug is going to affect your own body. You need to interpret any risk statistics in this book in light of the specific risk factors you know you have. Thus, a drug with a rare risk of occurrence in the general population, may really be a high-risk drug to you due to a genetic defect you might have, for example.

The upshot of all this is never let the small figures shown in this book lull you into thinking that a given side effect rarely occurs, and thus it won't happen to you. I hear from people all the time who are shocked that they now have hearing loss or tinnitus or some other ototoxic side effect after taking a given drug that they thought was very low risk or "safe" because so few side effects have been reported.

Why Side Effects Get Overlooked

Another failing in the present health-care system is that since many ototoxic (and other) side effects are never reported, they are also overlooked.

There are a variety of reasons that many ototoxic side effects often go unrecognized (and thus unreported). Here are some of them.

First, doctors are not trained to see the damage the drugs they prescribe cause. As one medical doctor explained:

> Since almost none of (pharmaceutically funded) medical training teaches you the filters for identifying pharmaceutical injuries, doctors often can't see the clear signs their patient has a pharmaceutical injury.[10]

What this means is that doctors typically deny that the negative side effects you experience from taking a drug they prescribed are due to that drug. Instead, they blame these side effects on other causes. Here are just five real-life examples of the many reported to me.

> A man reported, "I took *Humira* from September 2007 to January 2017. Since then, I've been diagnosed with tinnitus, vertigo, dizziness and ear pain. But when I brought it up to my doctors, they all dismissed the fact that *Humira* is the cause of it."

> A lady developed tinnitus and hearing loss after taking **Amlodipine**. She told her doctor and he said, "Not a side effect of **Amlodipine**," and blew her off.

> A man wrote, "My doctor prescribed **Rosuvastatin** last week and I took it for 4 days. It was like someone turned the volume of my tinnitus up as loud as it could go. I told my doctor about it and he discounted any correlation."

> A man related, "Just taking one drop of *Tobradex* made my tinnitus worse. An hour later, my head began hurting, and I immediately realized that it was because of the *Tobradex* drops. The ophthalmologist who prescribed these drops and the hearing doctor completely denied the possibility of ototoxicity from taking these eye drops."

> And finally, a lady explained, "I was put on **Citalopram**. I was fine until my doctor increased the dose to 20 mg. That's when the ringing in my right ear started. I told my doctor, but she just blew it off."

Second, ototoxic side effects go unreported because many people do not recognize the ototoxic side effects of the drugs they are taking as enunciated in Chapter 4. Few people are told what ototoxic side effects they should watch for. Therefore, they may not even recognize ototoxic side effects when they do occur. For example, a bit of hearing loss may easily go unnoticed. People may not connect dizzy spells or ringing in their ears to the medications they are taking. What it boils down to is, if you aren't aware you have a given side effect, you certainly won't report it.

Third, ototoxic side effects go unreported because when researchers and doctors are doing their studies, they may not be looking for those specific side effects. Unless those side effects reach out and grab them by the throat so to speak, it's almost certain they will miss them. There's an old adage that says, "You won't find it unless you are looking for it". This is so true in the case of the side effects of ototoxic drugs. Therefore, when drug studies are done, researchers must carefully and deliberately investigate whether any kind of ototoxic damage is being done to peoples' ears.

Unfortunately, hearing testing is not done often enough to catch many cases of drug-induced hearing loss. For example, one doctor wrote that ototoxicity from taking LOOP DIURETICS is probably under-reported because audiometric testing, which could detect early hearing loss, is seldom, if ever, done.[11]

Furthermore, recording hearing loss by subjective means is not accurate. You likely aren't even aware of having an incipient hearing loss. Without the proper testing equipment, you'll never know if an ototoxic drug has given you a mild hearing loss or not. One study revealed that only one person in 250 reported subjective hearing loss from a certain drug. However, conventional audiometric testing revealed that the true number was **ten times** higher![12] The results would have likely been much higher still if the researchers had tested for sub-clinical hearing loss by testing the frequencies between 8,000 and 20,000 Hz.

Sub-clinical hearing loss is hearing loss that only occurs in the high frequencies. It is not readily detected in an audiological clinic because few audiologists currently have the equipment to test hearing above 8 kHz. Chapter 9 reveals that many drugs cause hearing loss starting at the highest frequency you can hear. Since almost no one tests these high frequencies, a lot of drug-induced hearing loss goes undetected and thus unreported.

Fourth, another reason ototoxic side effects are often under-reported is because drugs are released to the public before they are thoroughly tested. Did you know that 51% of the approved drugs released in the past few years are now known to have had serious side effects that had **not** been detected at the time of their release to the public?[13] Some side effects only become evident after long-term drug use, yet drug trials are normally short-term affairs.

It can take years, and even decades after a drug is released, before its ototoxic properties are discovered. For example, **Erythromycin** was introduced in 1952, yet it was not until the mid-1970s that **Erythromycin** was recognized as ototoxic—a period of more than 20 years![14] In the case of *Vicodin*, it took 21 years, and in the case of **Acetaminophen**, it took an incredible 117 years!

Fifth, another reason ototoxic side effects go unreported is because some people who are being given ototoxic drugs may be unconscious, lethargic, confused, disoriented, sick or otherwise not mentally alert enough to adequately describe the side effects they feel. In these cases, they are not able to report ototoxic effects to their doctors. Then, too, some drugs are sedative in nature. Consequently, the people taking them may be less aware of some of the milder side effects. As a result, again the incidence of such side effects is likely much higher than officially reported.[15]

Sixth, yet another reason ototoxic side effects go unreported is because it is not easy to monitor a person for vestibular ototoxicity. It is both time-consuming and expensive. Drugs such as antiemetics and motion sickness drugs (e.g. **Dimenhydrinate**, **Dramamine**) may mask the nausea that frequently accompanies vestibular ototoxicity. In addition, if you are sick and confined to bed (perhaps in a hospital) you are not the most reliable person for describing side effects such as balance problems since you do not have to stand up or walk around.[16]

Finally, language can be a major barrier to reporting ototoxic side effects because if your first language is different from that of the medical staff, you may have great difficulty communicating any of the ototoxic side effects that you experience.

Increasing the Percentage of Side Effects Reported

The FDA largely relies on doctors to **voluntarily** report any side effects they come across in order to catch unreported and under-reported side effects. This is a serious weakness in the system. Doctors can report side effects if they wish but, except for certain specific serious side effects, they are not bound by law to do this. Thus, as we have seen, they only report a miniscule fraction of 1% of all side effects.

One solution would be for the government to step in and make it mandatory for doctors and pharmacists to report all adverse side effects that come to their attention. At least that way we would have a better grasp of the true frequency and severity of ototoxic side effects.

There are at least three reasons why doctors do not currently report all the side effects they come across.

The first reason is "just because they don't have to". It is human nature not to do more than you have to. Thus, typically they don't bother.

Second, doctors do not think this is important enough when looking at the overall scheme of things. Since they are pressed for time, they do only those things **they** feel are important. To them, serious heart problems may be important—ear problems apparently aren't.

Third, doctors have no economic incentive to do so. In fact, they have a big incentive **not** to do so. It takes time to fill out reports. The time spent filling out and filing such reports takes money out of their pockets! The FDA suggests it will take 30 minutes for the average person to fill out the necessary form for reporting an ototoxic side effect. Doctors may be able to shorten this time considerably. However, even if it only takes a doctor 5 to 7 minutes to fill out the form and submit it, that is the equivalent of the time many doctors take to examine a patient. This means a doctor can't see as many patients as he would otherwise. Consequently, he will not make as much money. As a result, it is the rare doctor that will take the time to report to the FDA the side effects he comes across.

Assuming the government does not change the current system any time soon, we need to encourage/urge our doctors to file ototoxic drug side-effect reports on our behalf. The FDA has made it relatively easy to file these reports.

If your doctor won't file an ototoxic side-effect report, all is not lost. According to FDA guidelines, these forms do not have to be submitted by doctors. Anybody can file such a report, including you.

Doctors (and anyone else) can use one of three methods to report ototoxic **drug** side effects. The important thing is that someone reports the occurrence of ototoxic side effects.

Phone it in: Anyone can pick up the phone and report drug side effects verbally to the FDA's MedWatch adverse-event reporting hotline (FAERS). The number to call is 1-800-332-1088. The hours are Monday to Friday 8:00 AM to 4:30 PM EST.

Report it on-line: If you want to fill out the form on-line, go to the FDA's MedWatch website at:

https://www.fda.gov/safety/medwatch-fda-safety-information-and-adverse-event-reporting-program

or use a shorter link to go to this same website by just typing in:

www.fda.gov/MedWatch.

Once there, click on the red “Report a Problem” button. This page gives you an overview and instructions. When ready, click on the “Consumer/Patient” blue box (FDA Form 3500B, then fill in the form (it is several pages long) and submit it to the FDA instantly—all from your computer/tablet/phone.

Note: If you are a Health professional, click on the “Health Professional” blue box.

Print it out and mail it in: You can download the appropriate form, print it out, fill it out manually and mail it in, or FAX it to 1-800-332-0178, or you can fill it in online, then print it out and mail it in. The address is at the bottom of the form. Download this form from:

https://www.fda.gov/safety/medical-product-safety-information/ medwatch-forms-fda-safety-reporting

When you are at this web page, click on the down arrow to the right of “MedWatch Forms for Patients and Consumers FDA Form 3500B pdf”, then click on the link that appears below it. (Note this form is in PDF format, so you will need to have Adobe’s free Acrobat Reader program (or equivalent) already installed on your computer in order to read it.)

To further encourage your doctor to report any ototoxic side effects, print a copy of this form from the FDA’s web site and take it with you to your next doctor’s appointment. If you do this, your doctor can’t say he doesn’t have a form handy!

If you want to report a vaccine side effect, you need to go to the VAERS (Vaccine Adverse Event Reporting System) website at https://vaers.hhs.gov/reportevent.html. There you can learn the requirements for vaccine reporting. When you are ready to fill out your report, click on the three-black-line icon in the blue VAERS box (upper left corner), not on the VAERS name itself, then in the drop-down menu select “Report Online” and make your report.

By simply doing this, you are helping fix our broken health-care system.

Chapter 6 Endnotes

1 Freundlich, 1998. p. 2.
2 Freundlich, 1998. p. 2.
3 Lazarus, 2010. p. 6.
4 George, 2021. p. 1.
5 Freundlich, 1998. p. 2.
6 What is a Serious Adverse Event, 2001. p. 1.
7 Haybach, 1999. p. v.

8 Physicians' Desk Reference, 2000. p. 2111.
9 Physicians' Desk Reference, 1997. p. 822.
10 A Midwestern Doctor, 2023c. p 1.
11 Shlafer, 2000. p. 10.
12 Physicians' Desk Reference, 2000. p. 2822.
13 Waltermire, 1998. p. 1.
14 Troost, 1998d. p. 3.
15 Physicians' Desk Reference, 2000. p. 2748.
16 Troost, 1998b. p. 3.

Chapter 7

Drug Research Has Been Hijacked by the Pharmaceutical Industry

We like to think that researchers, doctors, drug companies, the FDA and other government agencies all are looking out for our best interests. This is the way it should be. However, the truth is that this is not exactly the way the health-care system works anymore. Each of these entities are really looking out for themselves, not specifically for you.

As a result, drugs are damaging our ears at an alarming rate. Like me, you should find this disturbing. The systems that should be protecting us and our ears are letting us fall through the cracks. Thus, what appears to be a "minor" problem on the surface, is just the tip of an immense iceberg. The real problem (and it is enormous) is hidden below the surface where few see it or do anything about it. For better or worse, that is the way the system "works" and it is high time you learned about this so you can take steps to protect your precious ears.

All drugs have side effects. This is no secret. The United States Food and Drug Administration (FDA) is the government's watchdog on the drug industry. The FDA truthfully warns:

> When it comes to using medicine, there is no such thing as completely safe. **All** medicines have risks.[1]

In another place the FDA declares:

> **Every** prescription and over-the-counter medicine has benefits and **risks**—even such a common and familiar medicine as aspirin.[2]

Looking at it another way, and with rare insight, Dr. Aubrey Knight explains:

> A medication is a **poison** with a desirable side effect.[3]

Therefore, realize that:

> **No** drug is perfectly safe. **Every single drug** that affects our bodies will have some **adverse side effects**.[4]

Many of these drugs negatively affect our ears as this book documents.

In order to keep track of how common and severe these side effects are, this information needs to be reported to a central clearinghouse as we saw in the previous chapter. In the USA, that organization is the FDA. Here is how the system should work in an ideal world.

When people experience side effects, they report those side effects to their doctors. Their doctors, in turn, report them to the FDA, or the patient reports them to the FDA if their doctor doesn't/won't. The FDA compiles this information and reassesses whether the benefits of the drug still outweigh its side effects, and if necessary, updates the drug listings. The FDA then passes this new information on to the pharmaceutical manufacturers. The drug companies update their drug listings in books such as the *Physicians' Desk Reference* (PDR), the product information sheets included with each prescription, and their on-line websites. As a result, the health-care professionals and the general public always have access to the latest and most reliable information on the risk of side effects for each drug.

Unfortunately, our world is far from ideal, so it should be no surprise that this process breaks down all along the line. We need to change this. The first step in working to bring about change is to have a clear understanding of how the system currently "works". As we investigate the system, we begin to see where it breaks down and where things can be improved.

The place to start in fixing this broken system is in how drugs are researched and approved. We seem to have lost sight of the reason we take drugs in the first place. Is it to get healthy again, or is it to make money for the drug companies?

Obviously, we want to get and stay healthy, but the pharmaceutical industry has another objective. They want to make money whether we get well or not. And because of this, they have infiltrated and hijacked how drug knowledge is researched and disseminated.

Did you know that there have been radical changes in the way that our medical knowledge is provided? Do you realize that before 1980, most clinical research was publicly funded, but now most is funded directly by the drug and other medical industries, whose **primary** mission is to **maximize** their return on **investments** for their investors (and thus not to cure people's illnesses—or they wouldn't need their drugs any more)? Notice that the drug ads that tell you to "ask your doctor" about a particular drug have a single purpose—to sell more drugs, not primarily to improve your health.[5]

Ninety percent of clinical trials now are commercially funded—as well as seventy-five percent of published clinical research.[6] These figures, while shocking, are very likely still too conservative.

Did you know that when a pharmaceutical company sponsors a study, the odds are **five** times greater that the findings will favor its product?[7] No wonder the drug companies want to sponsor drug trials.

Furthermore, the drug and medical industries fund 70% of continuing education lectures and seminars, which are among the activities that doctors are required to attend in order to maintain their licenses to practice. Thus, wherever doctors turn for sources of information, drug companies dominate.[8]

Did you catch that? Your doctor's **primary** source of information is ultimately from the drug companies, and the drug companies are **primarily** in the business of making **money** for their investors, **not** in making you well. The drug companies have found a cash cow in making and selling drugs. This is making them billions of dollars per year. In fact, as one doctor explained,

> The pharmaceutical business model requires pharmaceuticals that are "effective" enough to somehow justify pushing them on patients but **not effective enough to fix the issue** the drug is prescribed for, thus requiring each patient to **take the drug indefinitely**. Furthermore, the larger the potential drug market is, the more aggressively the pharmaceutical industry will push to promote it to every available customer.[9]

This doctor further emphasizes:

> The pharmaceutical business model always aims to have proprietary products that only **partially** improve a chronic condition and must be taken indefinitely (as this ensures the largest amount of sales). If a product is an off-patent pharmaceutical (so it is no longer possible to make a lot of money selling it) or it effectively cures a condition (which quickly destroys its market), that is unacceptable.[10]

That is why you won't see the kind of information contained in this chapter proclaimed from every doctor's office. Yet it should be—if their aim is to help their patients become healthy and then stay healthy.

This is also why the pharmaceutical companies try to keep non-pharmaceutical treatments off the market—especially if they help people get and stay healthy. As the title of a Goldman Sachs biotech research report asked "*Is Curing Patients a Sustainable Business Model?*" This report explained:

"The potential to deliver 'one shot cures' is one of the most attractive aspects of gene therapy, genetically-engineered cell therapy and gene editing. However, such treatments offer a very different outlook with regard to recurring revenue versus chronic therapies," analyst Salveen Richter wrote in a note to clients. "While this proposition carries tremendous value for patients and society, it could represent a challenge for genome medicine developers looking for sustained cash flow.

In the case of infectious diseases such as hepatitis C, curing existing patients also decreases the number of carriers able to transmit the virus to new patients, thus the incident pool also declines."[11]

As you can now see, drug research is aimed, not a finding a cure for any disease, but finding drugs that patients have to take for the rest of their lives! In other words, the drug industry as it stands today is driven, not by altruism, but by pure greed.

That is why drug companies do the research needed to get new drugs approved by the FDA. Then they get them on the market and begin making money.

The various drug companies collectively spend billions of dollars each year advertising their products in order to get you to take their drugs. In fact, they aggressively promote their drugs to consumers and doctors to the tune of $16 billion a year. This advertising pays off handsomely for them. Business is good for the newer and most expensive drugs. For example, in its

Drug Advertising—A Disturbing Trend

A disturbing trend today is the numerous drug ads you see on TV. Even more disturbing, these ads are not primarily intended to benefit your health. They are intended to make more money for the drug companies. They are a tool to sell a product. After all, drug companies are in business like any other company and want to boost their bottom lines.

According to Nancy Chockley, President of the National Institute for Health Care Management Research and Education Foundation, you need to be wary because these ads are "presented to **influence decisions rather than truly inform**". They are "neither substantive nor objective". She cautions, "Drug ads downplay the limitations or side effects of a drug".

What this means is that these drug ads do not give you the whole story. As a result, you cannot make well-informed decisions. She warns, "Consumers need better, more balanced information in order to engage in a genuinely informed discussion with their doctors".[1]

A lot of the drugs you see regularly advertised on TV have ototoxic side effects. (You'll find these drugs and ototoxic side effects described in this book.) However, you'll seldom, if ever, see these ototoxic side effects listed in the TV ads, although ads for *Viagra* do mention hearing loss, but not its other ototoxic side effects.

Reference

[1] Chockley, 2001. p. 29.

first year on the market, *Celebrex* racked up sales of $1 billion. *Vioxx* had sales of $1.5 billion in 2000.[12]

Sales increases of the **50 most advertised drugs** made up almost half of the increase in drug spending leaving the other 9,850 drugs on the market to make up the other half.[13]

Consumers are going to their doctors and asking/demanding the drugs they see advertised. Research reveals that if 100 million Americans saw a specific drug ad, as a result, 30 million would ask their doctor about it, and doctors would prescribe it to 13.2 million of them. That quickly adds up to humongous profits for the drug companies.

This is why television ads by the pharmaceutical companies downplay the many potential side effects of the various drugs they advertise. How often have you ever seen an advertisement for a drug list hearing loss, balance problems and tinnitus as side effects that you need to watch out for? None? Nada? Zero? Zilch? Same here. If people understood all the potential side effects of a given drug, they might think twice about taking it.[14]

As I've emphasized several times already, drug companies are in the business of making money—lots of money! They only make money when they are selling drugs to you. Therefore, it should be no surprise that they are aggressive in their quest to get drugs approved so they can sell them and make even more money.

Sometimes the drug companies may push too hard and thus some of their nefarious details come to light. One researcher, Dr. Richard Deyo, wrote about "problems usually discussed only in whispers: powerful constituencies with vested financial interests are routinely intimidating investigators who point out the health risks of drugs". "This is business as usual," he says. "**Intimidation and attacks are the way business is conducted**".[15]

As wise consumers, you need to know what is going on so you can make informed decisions on the drugs you take. For example, did you know that researcher Dr. Bruce Psaty found that CALCIUM CHANNEL BLOCKERS were "associated with 60% more heart attacks than other older and cheaper forms of blood pressure medication". Another researcher, Dr. Detsky, took this one step further and published his findings on these new CALCIUM CHANNEL BLOCKERS and the glowing reports other researchers had reported. He writes, "90% of researchers who had reached positive conclusions about the drugs had economic links to their manufacturers".[16] You can draw your own conclusions as to what this could mean to your health and to your ears.

Here is another example. There are lots of men (and their wives) who are excited about the drug **Sildenafil** (*Viagra* is the most popular brand) and what it can do to

Doctors' Ties to Drug Manufacturers Result in Biased Drug Reviews

When you go to your doctor, you expect him to do what is best for you. You want his unbiased advice. You want the best (and cheapest) prescriptions with the fewest side effects to restore your health.

Is this what you get? Or is your doctor's advice skewed by drug company influence? You may never know. Here's why. The experts who write about drugs all seem to have financial ties to the drug companies. As a result, how could you expect them to give you the plain, unvarnished truth? Their reports, whether consciously or otherwise, are biased because of these financial ties.

Even the last bastion of unbiased drug reporting, *The New England Journal of Medicine* "recently loosened its guidelines regarding financial ties of experts who write for it".

Why? According to Dr. Jeffrey Drazen, the journal's editor, he couldn't find **unbiased** experts to write for him. "Everyone he found had financial ties to the firm that made the drugs they would be writing about!"

According to Dr. Ivan Oransky in his article *Ties to Drug Manufacturers Deform Medical Reviews* says, "Researchers can slant reviews in many ways: by not offering their results for publication if the data undermine a desired outcome; by writing conclusions that are contradicted by their own data, or by emphasizing certain studies while ignoring others".

He warns, "Doctors should know what's influencing the articles they read—and you should know what's influencing your doctor's decisions".[1]

It should be even more obvious now why you have to do your own research if you want to protect your ears (and the rest of your body) from the side effects of ototoxic (and other) drugs. You cannot depend on receiving unbiased professional advice.

Reference

[1] Oransky, 2002. p11A.

enrich their sex lives. However, I think few of them ever really consider the host of side effects that can result—including death! For those of you that are concerned about your ears, **Sildenafil** can cause hearing loss, tinnitus, vertigo and other bad things. You need to be aware of these things and **then** make **informed** decisions about whether or not you are prepared to accept these risks.

Pseudo-Science: Research That Is Deliberately Falsified

Not only has the pharmaceutical industry hijacked drug research and advertising, it has also developed some dirty tricks that "pull the wool over your eyes". When you are aware of what is going on behind the scenes, you have the truth on your side and thus you can expose and hopefully eliminate these shenanigans.

It used to be that you could trust scientific medical research, but not today. So much of it is falsified or twisted to make you believe the results are significant when they're not. Listen to the words of Marcia Angell, an editor of the (formerly-prestigious) *New England Journal of Medicine*. Back in 2009 she wrote:

> It is simply **no longer possible to believe much of the clinical research that is published**, or to rely on the judgment of trusted physicians or authoritative medical guidelines. I take no pleasure in this conclusion, which I reached slowly and reluctantly over my two decades as an editor of *The New England Journal of Medicine*.[17]

In 2015, Richard Horton, the then editor-in-chief of the (also formerly-prestigious) British medical journal, the *Lancet*, wrote an even more scathing assessment of the current state of scientific medical research when he reported:

> **Much of the scientific literature, perhaps half, may simply be untrue.** Afflicted by studies with small sample sizes, tiny effects, invalid exploratory analyses, and flagrant conflicts of interest, together with an obsession for pursuing fashionable trends of dubious importance, science has taken a turn towards darkness.[18]

This falsified and twisted "science" is then deliberately foisted on you using various gaslighting techniques.

Doublespeak

You don't want to believe all the hype in the advertising put out by the various drug companies. This is because advertising agencies are adept at doublespeak. Rather, you want to carefully evaluate the efficacy and potential harms of any drugs you are considering taking. Be aware that what the hype says and what it really means can be totally opposite. That's doublespeak. It is carefully designed to make you believe the opposite of the truth. In such cases, they can actually **make you believe a lie by telling you the truth**! For example:

> I can tell you the truth in such a way that you believe the opposite of what I say, but believe what I wanted you to believe, rather than the truth. Thus, you may believe that a drug really works well, when just the opposite is true.
>
> For instance, if I claim that "nothing works better than Drug A", you immediately form a picture in your mind that Drug A performs head and shoulders **above** all the other drugs. Yet what I really said was that Drug A was **no worse** (or better) that other drugs.

> Thus, the claim that "nothing works better than *Prevacid*" implies that *Prevacid* is superior to other heartburn remedies—but what the statement really means is that *Prevacid* is **no worse** than other drugs.
>
> As a result, you rush out to get Drug A, thinking you are getting the best (and putting more money in the pockets of the company that manufacturers Drug A which is exactly what the ad was designed to do) when in reality, Drugs B, C and D all work equally well (or more likely, equally poorly)—but that was not the message you got.[19]

As you can see, the drug company told you the truth, but made you believe a lie. That's how insidious doublespeak can be.

The drug companies also love to use statistics doublespeak. You've heard the old saying, "there are three kinds of falsehoods—lies, damn lies and statistics". Be aware that the drug companies are masters of manipulating statistics to make you believe their drugs give wonderful results when the truth is they are anything but.

They hide the truth by expressing the results in relative terms rather than in absolute terms. For example, suppose they are testing a new drug against a placebo. Let's assume this is a true placebo—a sugar pill—so everything seems on the up and up. They enroll 2,000 people with tinnitus in their study. Half of the people are in the placebo group and half in the drug group. The purpose of the study is to prove that their new drug gets rid of tinnitus far, far better than does the placebo.

How do they do it? At the end of the study, they analyze the results. Let's say that in the placebo group 1 person reports they no longer have tinnitus. However, in the drug group 10 people report the drug cured their tinnitus.

How do they report these results. If they report absolute results, they will say that the placebo group had only 1 person now with no tinnitus. This is 1/1,000 x 100 = 0.1%. And the drug group with 10 cured of their tinnitus would be 10/1,000 x 100 = 1%. Thus, the absolute difference in efficacy is only a miniscule 1 – 0.1 = 0.9%. This means that there is basically no real-life practical difference.

Think of it this way. If you got 0.1% on a test and your friend got 1% on the same test, you both abjectly failed. There's no real practical difference between your scores. Neither of you knows much about the subject. That's reporting the results in absolute numbers—the way results should be reported.

Now let's see how the drug companies report it. Assume they have the same above study results, but instead of using absolute results, they report relative results. Here's how they do it.

They report that their drug was 10 **times** better than the placebo since their 10 successful tinnitus cases is 10 times more than the 1 case the placebo group had. So they tout that their drug test results are wonderful—they are 10 **times** better (or if expressing it in percentages, it is 1,000% better) than the placebo.

This is absolutely true. But in practical terms it's still only 0.9% better. This is how you can turn an abject study failure (0.9% improvement) in absolute terms into a rousing success story (1,000% improvement) in relative terms, and again essentially lie by telling the truth!

Think about it. Would you take a new expensive drug that only gives less than a 1% chance of improvement (and no doubt has many offsetting serious side effects)? I wouldn't either.

So never be taken in by research studies or news releases that are reported in relative terms. Always convert study results into absolute terms to better understand what the study really found out.

Gaslighting

Another of the industry's dirty tricks is gaslighting. According to *Psychology Today*:

> Gaslighting is an insidious form of manipulation and psychological control. Victims of gaslighting are deliberately and systematically fed false information that leads them to question what they know to be true.... Over time, a gaslighter's manipulations can grow more complex and potent, making it increasingly difficult for the victim to see the truth.[20]

Unfortunately, this is exactly what has happened in the drug industry. As "A Midwestern Doctor" says:

> ...[today] this is accomplished by having medical providers all echo the same message that a patient's injury has nothing to do with the pharmaceutical...in question.[21]

As we have just seen:

> ...pharmaceuticals are inherently toxic. For example, most medications work by inhibiting enzymes (which are essential for life) and because of how interconnected the body is, this inhibition will create a variety of unintended consequences.
>
> Similarly, most vaccinations function by making the immune system (often with the aid of toxins that help provoke that response) have an unnatural and narrowly-focused response to a target substance....

> Since toxicity has always been inherent to the practice of allopathic (Western) medicine, the profession has gradually come up with a playbook to prevent its inevitable medical injuries from sabotaging business. This has essentially been accomplished by doing the following:
>
> - Telling patients the adverse events they experienced either are not occurring or are unrelated to the toxic pharmaceutical.
> - Developing an elaborate scientific apparatus that provides evidence refuting the link between these injuries and pharmaceuticals on the market, while concurrently training the population to defer to the scientific consensus rather than trusting their own observations.
> - Making competing forms of medicine that lack a similar degree of inherent toxicity illegal, therefore making the only choice within the existing medical monopoly be a toxic form of medicine (similarly consider how allopathic medicine is always considered to be the best form of medicine every other approach must find a way to measure up to).
>
> This is also why we have the doctrine in allopathic medicine that every treatment has risks and the treatments are chosen because its benefits outweigh its risk (as opposed to just exploring systems of medicine without those risks).
>
> All of this in turn results in the tragic phenomenon known as medical gaslighting, or as some like to put it "allopathic medicine gaslights you to death."[22]

This medical doctor then explains:

> I believe medical gaslighting is a natural consequence of our training. Since the therapeutic toolbox of allopathic medicine is quite limited, most doctors cannot practice their craft without administering unsafe pharmaceuticals to their patients, and thus for the sake of their self-identity, they must fully believe in their pharmaceuticals.[23]

Furthermore, since:

> ...no well-intentioned doctor wants to harm a patient, and since they often do, the reflexive psychological coping mechanism is to deny the possibility of each injury that occurs.[24]

This same doctor then explained:

> Frequently when I review a pharmaceutical injury, I hear a very similar story from the patient. They did not want to take the pharmaceutical, but since the doctor pressured them to do so, they caved in to the doctor's authority, and afterwards they deeply regretted not listening to their intuition.

He concluded:

> If prescribing pharmaceuticals were not so tied to a doctor's identity, they would be far less likely to deny that injuries occurred from the pharmaceuticals they pressed on their patients."[25]

Hundreds of people have told me the same thing—that their doctors refused to admit that the drugs they prescribed damaged their ears. Now you have a bit of insight why they do this.

Manipulating the Placebo and Nocebo Effects

You've all heard of a "placebo"—a "sugar" pill. Placebos are medications or procedures that appear to be actual medical treatments but aren't.

Typically, they are used in studies as a "control" to a drug that researchers are testing. Half the participants are given the test drug and half get the placebo—a sham treatment that they believe is the real treatment. The placebo is basically an inert substance (such as a sugar pill) that won't affect the study results. (At least, that's the way it is supposed to be.) Researchers then compare the results between the two groups—and they consider that any differences are due to the effects of the test drug.

However, there is a monkey wrench that often gets thrown into the "gear works" that upsets the outcomes. As a result of believing that the treatment they received was real, participants will sometimes/often have positive results such as feeling better or having an improvement in their symptoms. This is called the "placebo effect".

One estimate is that 1 in 3 people (33%) experience the placebo effect,[26] but the true percentage could be much higher.

Scientists have long been skeptical of the placebo effect. They have often pooh-poohed the idea that taking an inert substance (sugar pill for example) can have a positive effect on a sick person's medical condition. However, mounting evidence reveals that the placebo effect is indeed real.[27]

According to researcher Ted Kaptchuk, director of the Program in Placebo Studies at Harvard:

> The placebo effect is more than positive thinking—believing a treatment or procedure will work. It's about creating a stronger connection between the brain and body and how they work together.
>
> The placebo effect involves a complex neurobiological reaction that increases feel-good neurotransmitters like endorphins, serotonin and dopamine and

> greater activity in specific brain regions linked to mood, emotional responses, and self-awareness. Together, these can create a therapeutic effect. "The placebo effect is a way for your brain to tell your body that you can feel better."[28]

One of the interesting things about the placebo effect is that, in addition to enlisting and releasing extra brain power, you also need some degree of "ritual treatment" for it to be effective. For example:

> You must visit a clinic at certain times and be examined by medical professionals. You undergo procedures or receive special medication. All this can profoundly impact how your body perceives symptoms because you feel both consciously and unconsciously that you are getting the attention and care needed to heal.[29]

How long does the placebo effect last? In many trials, the placebo effect works for "the same duration as regular treatments, whether the study last 12 weeks, six months, or a year".

A "funny" thing is that it doesn't seem to matter whether the people in a given study know they are taking the placebo or the drug being tested. The placebo effect kicks in just the same.

You would think that the placebo effect would only work if you didn't know that you were taking a sham treatment, but the latest research shows that this is not so. You can still exhibit the placebo effect even when you know you are receiving fake treatments (known as open-label placebos).

This begs the question, "How can the placebo effect work if you know your treatment is not real?" Kaptchuk explains:

> People associate the routine of taking medicine with a positive healing effect. Even if they know it's not medicine, the action itself can stimulate the brain into thinking the body is being healed. And the more ritualized the treatment, the more serious and important it feels.[30]

How significant is the improvement due to the placebo effect? The truth is, the percentage due to the placebo effect ranges all over the place. For example, in randomized medical trials, the placebo cure rates ranged from a low of 15% to a high of 79%.[31] In fact, I've read that some drug trials are called off because the placebo effect is so prominent that it obscures any (dubious) benefits the drug under study may have!

As I previously mentioned, the placebo effect results can range all over the place. For example, in some opioid trials, the placebo effect was relatively low and ranged between 5% and 17%. In some mental health trials using antidepressants, the test participants experienced a 53% improvement, which sounds great until you learn that the participants receiving the placebo experienced a 42.3% improvement. Thus, the real improvement due to the drug was an unimpressive 10.7%.

In other cases, the placebo effect results are very high. For example, in a 2014 study using the trial results for antidepressant drugs filed with the FDA, psychotherapist, Irving Kirsch reported that the placebo effect accounted for a whopping 82% of the beneficial responses to antidepressants. In other words, the drugs were only efficacious to any degree 18% of the time. This means that 4 out of every 5 people that take antidepressant drugs are not being helped at all by the drugs according to the drug company's own drug trial results as filed with the FDA.[32]

Here's some more evidence of how the placebo effect messes with study results. In a trial of people with asthma, those taking **Albuterol** experienced an impressive subjective improvement of 50%. However, those taking the placebo experienced a somewhat similar subjective improvement of 45%. Thus, the actual improvement due to the drug was only a measly 5%. However, in this study, when they used objective breathing tests, the results were much lower. The figures were a 20.1% improvement in breathing for the people who received **Albuterol** vs. 7.5% for those taking the placebo. The improvement due to the **Albuterol** was still only a very modest 12.6%.[33]

Therefore, if a study reveals a new drug shows improvements of less than 5% to 15% or so, the change could well be due entirely to the placebo effect, and as we have just seen, those percentages could range up to an incredible 82%. Thus, high positive scores may not have anything to do with the efficacy of the drug being tested.

Note: One of the fraudulent dirty tricks drug researchers sometimes use to get around the placebo effect and "prove" the efficacy of a new drug is to not use a true (inert) placebo. Rather, they compare the test drug to another already-approved drug (which they call a "placebo" in the study) in order to lower the apparent incidence of certain side effects.

This is particularly true when in comes to vaccines in order to prove that they are safer than they really are. Dr. Suzanne Humphries, an expert in vaccine safety explains:

> Part of the fraud is using another vaccine as the control in lieu of a true placebo. You simply cannot prove a vaccine is safe by comparing it to another, most likely unsafe, vaccine.
>
> Yet that's how it's done. By using a toxic "control," many of the adverse effects are automatically hidden as people in the control group end up suffering similar adverse events, and at a similar rate.[34]

For example, if a new drug has at 10% rate of tinnitus, if they used another drug that had a 7% rate of tinnitus as the "placebo" instead of a true inert substance, then the difference between the new drug and the "so-called placebo" is only 3%, not the 10% true rate. Thus the new drug appears to have a risk of tinnitus 70% lower than it actually does.

Another dirty trick is to not publish the results of any drug trials that do not show the drug is effective, thus keeping the true results secret. For example, the FDA requires drug companies to provide data on all clinical trials they've sponsored, **including** unpublished trials. In one study, it turned out that nearly half of all clinical trials on antidepressants remained unpublished because they didn't show positive results. However, when both published and unpublished trials were included, a whopping 57% of the trials showed the antidepressant drugs under study had **no** clinical benefits over the placebos.[35]

Yet another dirty trick is to choose the people for the placebo component of a new drug study who have been on a psychotropic drug (typically Selective Serotonin Reuptake Inhibitors or SSRIs) for some months and have built up a dependence on that drug. Then, before the drug trial starts, they take them off the drug cold turkey. This causes them to experience all sorts of nasty side effects—but these people are technically "placebo people" because they are not currently on an SSRI drug—even though they are still experiencing the nasty withdrawal side effects of that drug.

Then, they compare the side effects experienced by these "placebo people" to those taking a new SSRI that **causes** the same kinds of side effects the "placebo people" are experiencing.

Now, since both groups are experiencing the same effects, they don't have to count them as side effects of the new drug because these side effects are no different from the placebo side effects. As a result, the new drug seems to have few and mild side effects when in reality, the new drug has many, major side effects. Ultimately, they write up the results of the study making those taking the new drug look "better" than the "placebo people"[36] and again the wool is pulled over the eyes of doctors and an unsuspecting public.

You now know about the "Placebo Effect", however, I doubt you are aware of its counterpart called the "Nocebo Effect".

Simply put, the "Nocebo Effect", also known as the "Nocebo Response", is the phenomenon in which inert substances (placebos) or even the mere suggestion of such substances causes you to experience negative side effects because of your negative expectations of that treatment. In other words, being informed of a pill or procedure's potential side effects is enough to bring on real-life symptoms. The result is that you now feel worse, not better.

An example of a nocebo effect would be if I tell you that taking a certain medication will result in a negative side effect such as tinnitus. You take the medication (really an inert placebo ["sugar pill"], but you don't know that) and sure enough, you begin to experience tinnitus. If I had not told you about tinnitus being a side effect, you wouldn't have experienced any tinnitus.

Obviously, no company is going to hint or suggest that one of their drugs will cause a side effect if they don't have to in order to keep the nocebo effect from occurring. However, they may do the opposite and suggest that if you don't take their drug, you will experience certain symptoms, thus scaring you into taking their drug.

Researchers and Doctors Make Too Many Assumptions

Another problem with the current health-care system is that doctors and researchers may assume drugs only affect certain bodily systems. For example, consider **Montelukast** (*Singulair*). **Montelukast** is a drug prescribed for severe cases of asthma. It's labeling clearly indicates that **Montelukast** has only "minimal distribution across the blood-brain barrier" and that it only inhibits "airway" receptors.[37]

Thus, when Laura's son suddenly and dramatically began suffering from depression, anxiety, panic attacks, paranoia, insomnia, nightmares and both auditory and visual hallucinations after he stopped taking this drug due to developing severe depression, doctor after doctor, rejected her idea that suddenly stopping taking **Montelukast** could possibly have caused his sudden onset of severe, debilitating neuropsychiatric symptoms.[38] These doctors did not believe that **Montelukast** could cause these side effects because they assumed it only affected airway receptors.

Thus, these medical doctors, even though they should have known that this type of reaction typically only occurs with the abrupt discontinuation of centrally acting medications such as antidepressants and benzodiazepines should have stopped and said, "Hey! Wait a minute. What's going on?" and investigated further, rather than brushing Laura off because they assumed these side effects could not be related to **Montelukast**.

Despite their indifference, Laura "determined to understand how an asthma/ allergy medication acting only on the respiratory system could have such severe, potentially irreversible effects on the brain". She connected with doctors, researchers, drug safety advocates and thousands of other affected individuals. Together, they found numbers of studies evaluating the effects of **Montelukast** on the brain.[39]

These studies revealed that a substantial amount of **Montelukast** reaches the brain where it causes structural and functional effects. The effects are mediated, not through the receptor that **Montelukast** was known to inhibit, but through a completely different receptor action, the GPR17 receptor. This receptor is recognized as a regulator of cells with evidence linking their disruption across most psychiatric conditions."[40]

Thus, the assumptions of the medical community were wrong! These wrong beliefs are likely the reason why doctors sometimes are so adamant that the drugs they prescribe do not, and cannot, affect your ears, and thus typically relegate all the ototoxic side effects you suffer to coincidence and other causes.

This is just **one** example of **one** drug where doctors assumed it only acted on one receptor. There are probably hundreds, if not thousands, of other drugs where doctors have made the same assumptions. Maybe, in the future, like in the case of **Montelukast**, the truth will finally come out and vindicate all the ototoxic side effects documented in this book that doctors today so cavalierly dismiss.

The truth is that drugs can have numerous side effects—up to 300 or more different side effects. Thus, when you take a drug—say for a stomach ailment—it could cause many side effects elsewhere in your body. It may act on hundreds of different receptors and thus cause all sorts of untoward medical conditions as we just saw in the case of **Montelukast**.

The question is why do drugs have so many seemingly-unrelated side effects? The short answer is that drugs bind to various receptors throughout your body. Doctors want them to bind to a specific receptor to fix the specific problem at hand. However, since they may bind to numerous different receptors, many unexpected side effects can occur.

Take **Vitamin D_3** as an example. **Vitamin D_3** is a very important substance to your body's proper functioning. Your body converts **Vitamin D_3** into a steroid hormone.[41] When you have enough **Vitamin D_3** in your body, it binds to Vitamin D receptors located throughout your body, thereby acting like a key that opens various doors.[42]

Now here's the problem. **Vitamin D_3** is a powerful epigenetic regulator[43] of not just one gene, but of a whopping 2,700 genes.[44] An epigenetic regulator can either turn genes on (making them active) or turn genes off (making them inactive).[45] Because it affects more than 2,700 different genes, it regulates more than 1,000 different physiological processes in your body and thus controls at least 5% of the human genome.[46]

What this means is that if you are deficient in **Vitamin D_3**, this deficiency can be responsible for causing hundreds of seemingly-unrelated conditions to appear.

What is true for **Vitamin D_3** is also true for drugs to some degree or other. That is why taking drugs that affect your kidneys, e.g. LOOP DIURETICS, can also cause you to develop a hearing loss—two seemingly-unrelated conditions.

Furthermore, researchers like Dr. Peter Lurie think that using newer genetic engineering technologies "can make highly targeted changes in animals at the base-pair level"—one specific rung on the DNA ladder—thus enhancing precision and reducing the likelihood of "off-target effects" in which the base pairs are unintentionally added to or deleted from the genome.

However, while it is true that targeted genetic engineering is indeed possible, and modern technology lowers the likelihood of unintentional additions or deletions, this precision does not guarantee there won't be adverse effects. One of the reasons for this is because many genes are multifunctional as we have just seen, and thus can have multiple downstream effects.

Therefore, by altering a single gene, researchers can inadvertently and unknowingly affect the expression of hundreds of other genes. What's more, the multifunctionality of genes is rarely intuitive. As a result, for example, while it may seem convenient to genetically engineer cows without horns to prevent injury to other cows and farmhands, as suggested by Dr. Lurie, there's no telling what that tweak might do to internal organs or biological pathways.[47] The same applies to tinkering with human genes. Thus, any genetic drug therapy can result in hundreds of untoward side effects including ones that affect your ears.

Chapter 7 Endnotes

1 Be an Active Member of Your Health Care Team, 2016. p. 1.
2 Aspirin for Reducing Your Risk of Heart Attack and Stroke: Know the Facts, 2019. p. 1.
3 Mercola, 2022a, p. 4.
4 Questions about CDER, 2001. p. 3.
5 Are You Taking Too Many Medications, 2007.
6 Are You Taking Too Many Medications, 2007.
7 Are You Taking Too Many Medications, 2007.
8 Are You Taking Too Many Medications, 2007.
9 A Midwestern Doctor, 2023b. p. 2.
10 A Midwestern Doctor, 2023b. p. 19.
11 A Midwestern Doctor, 2023b. pp. 19-20.
12 Goodman, 2002. p. 17.
13 Barry, 2002. pp. 3, 17-18.
14 Waltermire, 1998. p. 1.
15 O'Hara, 1998. p. 67.
16 O'Hara, 1998. p. 67.
17 Lena, 2023. p. 1.
18 Lena, 2023. p. 1.
19 Drug Advertising Errors, 2014. p. 1.
20 Gaslighting, 2023. p. 1.

21 "A Midwestern Doctor", 2023a. p. 2.
22 "A Midwestern Doctor", 2023a. p. 4.
23 "A Midwestern Doctor", 2023a. p. 5.
24 "A Midwestern Doctor", 2023a. p. 5.
25 Mercola, 2023b. p. 1.
26 Seladi-Schulman, 2020. p. 1.
27 Kaptchuk, 2022. p. 3.
28 Kaptchuk, 2022. p. 3.
29 Kaptchuk, 2022. p. 3.
30 Kaptchuk, 2022. p. 3.
31 Zuckerman, 2020. p. 1.
32 Mercola, 2023a. p. 1.
33 Zuckerman, 2020. p. 1.
34 Humphries, 2024. p. 1.
35 Mercola, 2023a. p. 1.
36 A Midwestern Doctor, 2023e. p. 1.
37 Moratta, 2020. p. 3.
38 Moratta, 2020. p. 3.
39 Moratta, 2020. p. 3.
40 Moratta, 2020. p. 3.
41 Mercola, 2023d. p. 1.
42 Mercola, 2023d. p. 1.
43 Mercola, 2023c. p. 1.
44 Mercola, 2023e. p. 1.
45 Mercola, 2023d. p. 1.
46 Mercola, 2023d. p. 1.
47 Mercola, 2023e. p. 1.

Chapter 8

The Drug Approval Process

Very briefly, here is how drug testing is done. As a new drug is being developed, the drug manufacturer is supposed to follow certain specific steps. Initially, they accumulate tissue cultures and animal safety data. The proposed new drug (called the Investigational New Drug or IND) is tested on animals to determine how toxic it is, to see if it does what it is supposed to do and to watch for any side effects. Obviously, not all side effects are caught because animals cannot tell you if they are experiencing tinnitus or the feeling their ears are blocked.

If the initial testing is favorable, the FDA approves the results of the animal studies. The drug manufacturer then moves on to the first of four phases of human testing.

Phase 1. In Phase 1, approximately 20 to 80 healthy male volunteers between the age of 18 and 45 sequentially take the test drug in small doses until the first signs of toxicity appear. Researchers also watch to see how the drug is metabolized, how quickly it is eliminated from the body and what side effects show up.

Phase 2. In Phase 2 researchers evaluate approximately 80 to 100 people who have the same disorder this drug is intended to treat. During this phase, researchers look for the optimal dose that has the fewest side effects. They closely monitor for adverse drug reactions.

Phase 3. Phase 3 is a full clinical trial where many physicians test the drug on hundreds or even thousands of patients. They compare the test drug results with the results of other drugs to see how "good" it is. If there are no other drugs to use as controls, they do a double-blind study where neither the researchers nor the patients know which patients are given the drug and which patients are given a placebo until after the study is over. The analysis of these data shows whether those getting the drug do better than those that get the placebo. (Note that using other drugs rather than a true placebo just "cooks the books" and hides lots of side effects they'd otherwise have to report.) During this phase, the patients are closely monitored to detect any side effects that were not identified in the earlier phases.

Unfortunately, it appears that often drug manufacturers select only the lowest-risk or "best-case" patients on whom to conduct trials. These are the people with little or no history of adverse side effects and/or those with the less severe illnesses.[1] Naturally they have fewer side effects, which helps "prove" that the drug is safer than it really is.

Phase 4. During Phase 4, the test drug is evaluated on specific groups of people such as children, pregnant women, and seniors. Side effects are reported to the FDA at prescribed intervals throughout this process.[2]

In the past few years, it seems that too many drugs are being rushed through these phases without full testing being done, and/or the studies are only being done on a few people, not the hundreds or thousands needed to ensure patient safety.

Records are kept of the benefits and the adverse side effects observed over the course of the trials. When the study is over, the drug company compiles these adverse side effects and sends this information together with other descriptive, warning and prescribing information to the FDA for approval. The FDA reviews this information, and if all is to its liking, approves the drug for use by doctors. This approved product information then becomes the official data sheet that is released by the drug company for that product.

New is Not Always Better!

Psychiatrist Dr. Harold McPheeters spent a lifetime practicing medicine. He wrote:

"Be cautious of the newer medications that have recently been introduced and are being heavily marketed by the drug companies. Most drugs are systematically tested only for life threatening conditions such as heart damage, liver and kidney damage and **not** for other toxic effects such as ototoxicity, neurotoxicity, etc.

Conditions such as ototoxicity will only be reported **if they are noticed** as side effects on the initial life-safety tests, but otherwise drugs go to market without systematic investigation for other forms of toxicity. Those conditions are then supposed to be reported as they are observed by physicians and pharmacists in the course of using the drugs on their patients.

Many of the newer medications are very powerful and are inclined to have more serious toxic effects than some of the older medications that were previously used for the same conditions. This seems to be especially true in the field of psychiatry in which the newer psychotropic medications may have many serious side effects—especially on the nervous system".[1]

Reference

[1] McPheeters, 2001. p. 1.

The drug approval process, like anything else involved with statistics, has some inherent weaknesses. It is very easy to manipulate statistics whether intentionally or not. "Hard" data such as is reported by the drug companies are really only "estimates of reality". For most drugs, only a comparatively small number of doses have been given in the pre-marketing phase. Many (most) of these data are derived from administering a given drug under carefully controlled conditions. Unfortunately, the same conditions do not prevail in real life.

Once a drug is approved and is in the hands of doctors, the process of reporting side effects becomes unreliable. Many ototoxic side effects just don't get reported—even if they are detected as we have already seen! The problem is further compounded because many people take more than one drug at a time. Furthermore, they may have more than one medical condition that predisposes them to developing an ototoxic side effect. Finally, they may be taking higher doses than what is recommended. All of these factors may render supposedly "hard" data "soft".[3]

Each drug company is solely responsible for any information they include on the product information sheets they release about the drugs they manufacture, although the FDA may insist that they include certain specific information.

This begs the question, "What happens when more information is discovered about a drug—maybe months or years after it has been released?" If it is good—new benefits and such—the drug company will naturally approach the FDA with a revised product information sheet for approval. However, if the new information is negative, for example if more adverse side effects are discovered, the drug companies have no incentive to make this information public. Why should we even expect a company to "bad mouth" its own "cash cow" products?

Therefore, unless the FDA receives enough information on adverse side effects from other sources (meaning you, me and our doctors), and insists that it be included in the next product information sheet for that drug, these new side effects may never see the light of day. Who knows how many adverse side effects never appear in the PDR and CPS because of this?

If the PDR, CPS and on-line drug sites such as Drugs.com do not list all adverse side effects, neither you, as a consumer, nor your doctors have any easy way of knowing the truth about any given drug. This is a very serious flaw in the current system that needs fixing.

I again emphasize that until doctors are required to report **all** side effects, and the FDA requires the drug companies to **compile and report all these side effects** on product information sheets (and subsequently added to the PDR) and on-line, how will people ever be able to make truly informed decisions and thus avoid needlessly damaging their ears or losing their precious hearing, for example, as the following story attests.

The Story of Vicodin

Vicodin, a narcotic painkiller, is a brand name for the combination drug **Hydrocodone** and **Acetaminophen**. (There are also other brands by other manufacturers containing these same two drugs such as *Lortab*, *Norco* and *Zydone*.) Originally, during the pre-approval trials, apparently no sign of hearing loss was found. As far as anyone knew, it was not ototoxic. Since its release (around 1982), neither the PDR nor the CPS mentioned any ototoxic side effects. For 17 years everything went well. Sales were booming. By the year 2000, *Vicodin* had climbed to become the most prescribed drug in America.[4] Then it happened.

On April 26, 1999, House Ear Institute physicians reported a previously unknown and devastating side effect of *Vicodin*—rapid, profound, bilateral, irreversible hearing loss after overuse of this drug.[5]

According to Dr. John W. House:

> Some patients have retained some hearing if they stopped using the painkillers immediately, but for most, the damage was already done. Once the process starts, it seems irreversible.[6]

Although *Vicodin* had been on the market since 1982, hearing loss attributed to *Vicodin* did not begin showing up until 17 years later, in 1999.[7] This was likely because no one was looking for a link between sudden hearing loss and *Vicodin*.

In one report, a man was taking 20 to 30 *Vicodin* pills a day for pain. One day he noticed his ears were ringing. From the time he first noticed his ears ringing until he was completely deaf was only 4 weeks.[8]

After the House report was published, two audiologists called the journal that published this study to report that each of them had had a patient who experienced sudden and significant hearing loss after taking *Vicodin*.

Soon other stories began to surface. Since the House Ear Institute report came out, and while I was writing the first edition of this book, several people wrote to me telling how they too had lost their hearing from taking *Vicodin*. I have anecdotal reports of two women who took *Vicodin* for several months. During that time both noticed a definite drop in their hearing.

Furthermore, I have corresponded with a lady who totally lost her hearing from taking *Vicodin*. Here is her story. Jodi had back surgery, so her doctor put her on *Vicodin* for the pain. She built up a tolerance to it and had to take more and more. The pain persisted, and she ended up taking high doses of *Vicodin* for several years. Then one day she noticed her ears were ringing and she couldn't hear things she used to hear. In a matter of months her hearing dropped from normal to so bad that even hearing aids couldn't help her. Now she has a cochlear implant to help her hear.

Note that *Vicodin* is supposed to be prescribed for short-term use of 2 to 3 weeks at most. A typical dose is one pill every 6 hours. So far, hearing loss has not been reported when taking *Vicodin* at recommended dosages and time frames. However, trouble to your ears develops when you take much higher doses such as 20 or more pills a day for 2 months or longer.[9]

You should be aware that *Vicodin* is addictive and thus subject to abuse. As a result, it has a staggering potential for severe hearing loss when used wrongly.

Because the potential for severe hearing loss is enormous, you would have thought that both the FDA and the drug companies would scramble to amend their product information sheets on drugs using the **Acetaminophen/Hydrocodone** combination and get that information widely distributed. This was not the case. Neither the 2000 PDR nor the 2001 PDR gave any indication that such drugs can cause hearing loss.

According to a news report, the doctors at the House Ear Institute reported hearing loss incidents to the FDA in 1999 (and again in August 2001). To their credit, in 2000 the firm that manufactures *Vicodin* added a warning about the potential for hearing loss to the drug's label. However, it seems that the label change was largely unnoticed, even among top hearing specialists.[10]

In September 2001, another article blowing the whistle on *Vicodin* appeared in the papers.[11] Finally, in the 2002 edition of the PDR things begin to change. Under the brands containing the **Hydrocodone/Acetaminophen** combination such as *Lortab*, *Norco* and *Vicodin*, it warns, "Very rare cases of hearing loss have been reported in patients predominantly receiving very high doses of **Hydrocodone/ Acetaminophen** for long periods of time".[12]

What I want to know is why in this same PDR the other drugs that contain both **Acetaminophen** and **Hydrocodone** do not have this same warning? For example, in the 2003 edition of the PDR, there are three different brands of drugs containing **Acetaminophen** and **Hydrocodone** that do not have any warning about hearing loss whatsoever.[13]

Is this side effect all that rare? Officially, there were only 48 cases of hearing loss reported as of September 2001, although there have been millions of prescriptions written for *Vicodin*. Since many of these prescriptions were for refills, not for new patients, the incidence is not really as rare as it first appears.

On top of that, hearing loss may be "much more prevalent than we think" according to Dr. Akira Ishiyama, an assistant professor of otolaryngology at UCLA Medical School. According to him, some doctors have not drawn a connection between *Vicodin* use and sudden hearing loss in their patients because they haven't been looking for it.[14]

Apparently, the FDA isn't ordering the drug companies to include this new information in future editions of the PDR. As a result, unless doctors know of this information from some other source, they will continue to prescribe *Vicodin* to their patients and will not warn them that they could lose much of their hearing because of it.

This is the way the present system "works". How many more people have to lose their hearing before an effective warning is distributed to doctors and consumers alike?

It's about time things changed. Instead of worrying about politics and the almighty dollar, governments and companies need to concern themselves with people and their well-being. At the same time, people have to take responsibility for their own health and carefully follow the dosage guidelines for taking drugs and not insist their doctors prescribe them drugs for longer than the guidelines recommend.

The Role of the PDR and Other Drug Books

Many people are not clear exactly how the PDR (and CPS and other drug books) fit into the present "system". There are several misconceptions I'd like to address.

First, the PDR is not a complete listing of all the drugs that are available in the USA. (The same is true for the CPS in Canada.) It only contains the relatively few drugs that the drug companies want listed there in that particular edition. Thus, if a drug company wants a new (or existing) drug included in the next edition of the PDR, it forwards the official product information sheets to the PDR Network, LLC, the publisher of the PDR. (In Canada, these product information sheets go to the Canadian Pharmacists Association for inclusion in the Canadian counterpart to the PDR, the *Compendium of Pharmaceuticals and Specialties*, commonly called the CPS.)

The decision whether a drug is included in the PDR or not appears to be entirely up to the company that manufactures the drug. For whatever reason, a pharmaceutical company can choose **not** to send this information to be included in the next edition of the PDR. Thus, a given drug can be listed there one year and not the next. You can be sure that some older, less profitable, but equally effective drugs are dropped in favor of new, high-profit medications. This is just how it is.

Second, the PDR only lists the information about each drug that the drug companies send it. After the FDA approves the wording on the product information sheets, it is basically set in stone. This—and only this—information is printed in the PDR. The PDR Network, LLC (the publisher of the PDR) publishes the product information sheets in the PDR exactly as they come from the drug manufacturers. They do not edit or change in any way the official product information sheets they receive.

They are not a clearinghouse for such information, nor do they compile drug information from various sources. They do not verify the accuracy or completeness of the information contained on the product information sheets they receive. They act solely as a compiler and publisher of this information whether it is right or wrong, complete or incomplete. If new information comes to light on a given drug, unless the drug company includes this new information in a revised product information sheet and sends it to the publisher, that information will never be printed in the PDR. Also, be aware that recalled, discontinued, experimental and foreign drugs are not included in the PDR. Again, this is just how it is.

Third, not all the drugs in the PDR have complete drug listings. Some are quite abbreviated, and others basically only give the names of the drug. Again, it seems to be up to the drug companies whether it will be a brief listing, a complete monograph for that drug or something somewhere in between that is included in the PDR.

Abbreviated drug listings obviously cannot contain as much information as full listings. Thus, the adverse side effects section is greatly abbreviated too. As a result, ototoxic side effects may not even be listed.

Fourth, the drug companies only need to list the side effects the FDA requires. As a result, the PDR listings are not necessarily complete records of all known side effects of any listed drugs. Thus, be aware that only a subset of the side effects of any given drug is included in the PDR.

Fifth, when independent labs, researchers or doctors find other adverse side effects, and even after these side effects are documented in one of the respected medical journals, this information is not updated in the PDR, **unless** the drug company sends updated product information sheets to the PDR. Since there is no incentive for drug companies to bad-mouth their own drugs, they often leave well enough alone unless the FDA directs them to include this new information. Otherwise, these new side effects stay safely buried and you, a hard-of-hearing consumer, lose out.

Sometimes the information for a given drug is identical in both the CPS and PDR. Other times this information is quite different. You should be aware of this. For example, the CPS lists hearing loss as a side effect of **Itraconazole**, but the

PDR doesn't. With **Lorazepam**, the situation is reversed, and hearing loss is listed in the PDR but not in the CPS.

At times, the ototoxic side effects listed can be very different. For example, the CPS lists hearing loss, tinnitus, dizziness and vertigo as side effects of **Cephalexin**, yet the PDR only lists dizziness. For **Quetiapine** the PDR lists hearing loss, tinnitus, ataxia, dizziness, vertigo and earache, yet the CPS only lists dizziness and earache for the identical brand of this same drug.

These discrepancies exist because the drug companies and drug regulatory bodies in each country decide which side effects are to be included and which may be left off the official product information sheets. What this means is that you cannot get the whole truth from any given drug source. Some sources list some side effects while other sources may list different side effects.

Furthermore, notice how few side effects are listed in the CPS and PDR (and other drug books) as compared to the many different ototoxic side effects that are reported to the FDA's FAERS database for the same drugs. This shows how grossly incomplete the published ototoxic drug side effect listings really are.

Therefore, do not be surprised if your doctor or pharmacist doesn't know that a given drug can damage your ears. Your doctor might prescribe **Itraconazole** for you. You ask him to see if it can cause hearing loss. He looks it up in his PDR and assures you it does not cause hearing loss. He is telling you the truth as he knows it since the PDR doesn't list hearing loss as a side effect. However, he will still be wrong, and your ears may suffer for it!

Now you can see why you need to be extremely careful of the drugs you take so you don't inadvertently damage your ears by taking a drug that you and your doctor did not know was ototoxic.

Unfortunately, you can't expect to come close to finding all the published information about the ototoxic side effects of drugs unless you take the time to research **all** the drug lists, books and databases in the world and that could take you years. That is why this book can be so valuable to you. I have scoured the literature for the past 30+ years, searching for all reported ototoxic drug side effects. This book contains the information I have gleaned, not only from various issues of the PDR, CPS and BNF, but also from other reliable drug books and on-line drug sources from around the world as well.

This book is as complete as I can make it given the sources available to me, but you need to remember that it does not include every ototoxic drug and ototoxic side effect because I do not have access to all the repositories of ototoxic drug information on the planet. Nor is it possible for one person to find and compile all this information. Thus, I likely have missed valuable ototoxic information I would have included had I known about it.

The Role of the Food & Drug Administration (FDA)

In the USA, the Food and Drug Administration (FDA) plays a critical role in the present drug system. You may be surprised to learn exactly what they do and do not do.

The FDA is the government body that approves and regulates drug use in the USA. Here is a shocking statistic. "The FDA regulates fewer than 1% of the drugs [chemicals] brought into the marketplace".[15] These unregulated drugs (chemicals) are used in all sorts of things like cosmetics and cleaners and on and on.

When the FDA approves a drug, it doesn't mean that drug is "safe". It just means that the supposed benefits outweigh the known risks that are outlined on the drug's label. The FDA website itself explains:

> FDA approval of a drug simply means that the benefits outweigh the known risks.[16]

Note the words "known risks". If hearing wasn't checked during the drug trials, then hearing loss is not considered as one of the "known risks". Likewise, if a study wasn't continued long enough to bring to light certain side effects, then those side effects are not part of the "known risks". You need to understand that the risks listed in any FDA-approved materials are the **minimum** risks you will encounter. The real-life risks typically are much, much higher.

The FDA may approve a drug following clinical trials of a few months, involving controlled populations of a handful to several hundred people. But later, surprises can occur. To detect these problems, the FDA relies on doctors submitting **voluntary** reports. Thus, many side effects only show up later when the general population begins taking that drug. This is a big mistake. Unfortunately, as we saw previously, once a drug is released for public consumption, the data about side effects does not pour into the FDA from the doctors like it is supposed to. As a result, the incidence of side effects of drugs continue to be grossly under-reported.

Although the FDA regulates drugs, you should know that the FDA neither develops or tests drugs. That is left up to the drug manufacturers. They do the studies and submit them to the FDA. The FDA then evaluates the data and assesses the benefit-to-risk relationship based solely on the data submitted. Then, they either approve or reject that drug without doing any independent testing to verify the accuracy and efficacy of the drug they are approving![17]

Unfortunately, the FDA seems more concerned about claims of how good a drug is (you can't say a drug will cure a certain condition without proper proof) than it is with listing all the bad side effects that could result. The FDA only evaluates the information given to them. If the studies they receive are flawed, less than thorough, do not list every side effect they have found or know about, or is biased, how would they ever know? The system breaks down here too. There needs to be independent corroboration.

You also should be aware that the FDA has extremely limited resources to monitor the safety of all the thousands of drugs on the market today. Around the year 2000 only 52 employees were dedicated to monitoring drug safety. Their Department of Pharmacovigilance and Epidemiology (DPE) comprised only 8 physicians and 1 Ph.D. The DPE has the task of "protecting the American public from the health risks of marketed drugs". How can we expect this minuscule staff to do an effective job for us?[18]

The FDA needs to allocate more resources to monitoring drug safety. They are already stretched much too thinly to effectively monitor all the new drugs coming on the market each year.

In fact, things are going from bad to worse. In order to keep up with the volume of new drugs, the FDA even created a new "fast-track" system where the drug manufacturers can pay a fee to accelerate the release of their new drugs. This translates into a system that approves more and more drugs with less and less information documenting their efficacy and safety![19]

Is this what you want? Do you like being the guinea pig and risking your health and your precious ears? If not, you have to speak up and do something to change this inadequate system.

The FDA Sits on an Enormous Database of Drug Side Effects

Here's another thing that needs to change. The FDA sits on an enormous database of largely inaccessible, yet vitally-important information on drug side effects that have surfaced since the drugs were approved and put on the market. If the FDA had your best interests at heart, why don't they make this information readily available to the public in an easy-to-understand format as fast as it comes in?

This information could be invaluable to people wondering about the side effects of any given drug—information that is not otherwise available—that is, the millions of reports of side effects collected by the FDA that are not included in drug books such as the PDR like you think they would be.

Let me give you one small example that I happened to run across serendipitously. This report by the FDA concerns the drug **Omeprazole.**[20] Between September 14, 1989, when **Omeprazole** was approved to be released to the public, and March 31, 2000, when this report was compiled (a period of about 10½ years), the FDA had accumulated 10,005 reports of side effects of **Omeprazole** (and they consider this pile of reports to be **"low"** compared to other drugs). As I read this report, I realized that some of the ototoxic side effects contained in this report had not been listed in the PDR when this drug first came out, and they **still** are **not** mentioned in the latest edition of the PDR. This leads the public to believe that this drug is safer that it really is.

In spite of all its shortcomings, the FDA could help right things if it would make available to the public the enormous amount of information on drug side effects it has buried in its humongous database. As a minimum, they could list all the side effects reported to it for each drug in this database, together with the number of reports of each side effect.

Let's look at this information on **Omeprazole**. First, here's what's readily available. The PDR (after 10 years of reporting on **Omeprazole**) lists tinnitus, dizziness and vertigo as the only ototoxic side effects of this drug. However, in this FDA report we find that in addition to these side effects, the FDA also had reports on hearing loss, ear pain and ototoxicity.

If you had been prescribed **Omeprazole**, wouldn't you have liked to know **before** you started taking it that taking it could cause hearing loss? Wouldn't you have liked to know how many people had lost their hearing due to taking this drug, so you could estimate your chances of having the same side effect?

You won't find those pieces of information in the PDR or on-line databases such as Drugs.com. And if you were one of the unfortunate people to lose their hearing from taking **Omeprazole**, wouldn't you wish to know what the chances are of your hearing loss being permanent or temporary? All the above information is contained in the FDA's database.

I've only listed 6 ototoxic side effects above related to **Omeprazole**. Yet this edition of Ototoxic Drugs Exposed lists 27 different ototoxic side effects extracted from this database that was reported between January 2004 and October 2012.

For example, the above report explains that 35% of the 17 people who experienced hearing loss from taking **Omeprazole** had permanent loss. In the remaining 65% of the cases, the hearing loss was either temporary, or at least some degree of hearing returned. Only 17 people with hearing loss? You've got to be kidding! As you'll see in the listing under **Omeprazole** in this book, you'll see that between January 2004 and October 2012 alone there were a total of 903 reported cases of hearing loss. Thus, even this "detailed" report on **Omeprazole** is still grossly low in reporting the true extent of ototoxic side effects.

Fortunately, this above report contains the kind of anecdotal reports I have included in this book. As an example, it mentions the case of a 42-year-old man who was prescribed **Omeprazole**. Seven days later he experienced hearing loss in one ear and stopped taking this drug. Since that time his hearing has only improved slightly.[21]

This is the kind of information that could be extracted from this database for every drug it contains. I'd love to include all the ototoxic information it contains for every drug in this book, but I don't have easy access to this kind information. Neither do you. This too needs to change.

Here's something else that needs to change. The FDA needs to give timely reports of the information it has in its database—not sit on it and hide this information from the public while people die from the side effects of taking various drugs.

For example, think of **Rofecoxib** (*Vioxx*). This popular drug was only on the market for about 5 years. It was withdrawn on September 30, 2004 because of concerns that it was causing heart attacks. Yet this information had been available (but hidden from the public) for some years at that point. The prestigious medical journal, *The Lancet*, published an article on November 5, 2004 where the authors concluded that "owing to the known cardiovascular risk, **Rofecoxib** should have been withdrawn several years earlier". If this had been done thousands of people would still be alive that died due to heart attacks from taking **Rofecoxib**.

How bad was it? In the 5 years **Rofecoxib** was on the market, the FDA estimated that between 88,000 and 139,000 people had experienced heart attacks from taking **Rofecoxib**, and of this number an estimated 26,400 to 55,600 people died.[22] That's scary!

If you had been prescribed **Rofecoxib**, wouldn't you have wanted to know this information regarding heart problems, as well as its ototoxic properties, as this information was being reported to the FDA? Wouldn't you have wanted to learn this information promptly, rather than having to wait for 5 years until tens of thousands of people had died from taking this drug? I know I would have.

This is one reason that Dr. Wolfe of *Worst Pills, Best Pills* typically recommends waiting for 7 years after a new drug comes out before you begin taking it. In that time, many of the "missed" side effects come to light, and the worst drug offenders are often removed from the market in that time frame—as was the case with **Rofecoxib**.[23]

Your Role

You, as the consumer, are the final link in this drug-system chain. You are now aware of how the system works. Since you are the consumer and have the most to lose, you need to be constantly alert to the unexpected damage drugs can do to your body.

Warning! Drugs Are Not a Panacea.

Dr. Harold McPheeters, MD, who was himself hard of hearing, was concerned about the indiscriminate use of drugs today. Listen to him as we warned:

> I get concerned at how many folks, influenced by all the drug advertising and promotions, are seeking medications for the most inconsequential and trivial ailments.
>
> I continue to be dismayed at how frequently folks with hearing losses seem to be searching for some new medications that will solve some relatively-minor problem they have. They would be much better advised to avoid medications whenever possible because of the very good chance that such medicines and combinations of medications will cause further assaults to their hearing.
>
> The risks of toxic and allergic reactions are just too great to take unnecessary chances, especially when medications are combined.
>
> The pharmaceutical industry has been remarkably successful in convincing Americans that they should never suffer any discomfort—that there is a medication that will solve or relieve any distress. Too often, those medications have serious side effects that are likely to include ototoxicity.[1]

Doctors need to help their patients understand that often they really need to change their lifestyles, rather than putting their faith in yet another prescription for the latest "miracle" drug.[2]

References

[1] McPheeters, 2001. p. 1.

[2] Waltermire, 1998. p. 4

Here are some words of warning from a medical doctor.

> The most highly promoted and advertised drugs are the very ones that have not yet been fully tested for all kinds of toxic reactions. They are the newer drugs that are still under patent, but the main safety testing has been on the heart and vital functions—not "minor" effects such as ototoxicity, neurotoxicity or toxic effects on the skin, digestion, muscles, etc. These effects are reported as

> they are discovered in various patients, in part, during the original drug evaluations, but primarily after the drug is already on the market.[24]

According to Dr. McPheeters, if you already have a hearing loss, it is important that you know which drugs most likely have ototoxic effects. If your doctor prescribes one of these for you, you need to ask him to choose another medication with less risk if possible. You should also avoid neurotoxic drugs whenever possible since the hair cells in the cochlea are basically part of your nervous system and are likely to be similarly affected. Also, avoid taking combinations of medications as much as possible.

Furthermore, Dr. McPheeters warns that if you are hard of hearing, you should choose well-established medications that are known to be relatively free from ototoxic effects over newly-introduced medications that have not been fully evaluated for possible ototoxic effects.[25]

Since new drugs are more powerful and have far greater potential for serious toxic side effects, if you have sensorineural hearing loss or Meniere's disease, you should be very cautious about using them. Only use drugs if there is a very definite need. Take them only as prescribed, for as long as prescribed and then stop. Do not take additional medications that will only compound the possibility of trouble.[26]

Always tell your doctor about your hearing loss. Emphasize that you want to avoid ototoxic medications if possible. At the same time, be on your guard. Some doctors really don't have a clue about hearing loss and how ototoxic drugs can affect our ears.

Once when Malisa Rh.D. had a case of viral flu, she went to her doctor. He prescribed a medication for her condition. When she asked him if it was ototoxic both he and his nurse said, "Oh, no problem with this drug". To be sure, Malisa took out the list of ototoxic drugs she carried with her and said, "Look!" Right there at the top of her list was the drug he was prescribing for her!

Malisa severely admonished them:

> I take this very seriously. One physician has already cost me most of my hearing and I won't give up what tiny bit of hearing I still have because a physician and nurse won't look things up![27]

You have to learn to speak up for yourself. If Malisa's physician—bright and knowledgeable in other areas—will try that stunt with her (and she is **very** assertive when it comes to her health), imagine what happens to all the shy and timid folk who are afraid to confront their physicians. They lose more of their precious hearing without so much as a whimper.

Malisa isn't alone in losing her hearing because a doctor was too busy/lazy to check whether a drug was ototoxic before prescribing it to a patient. One man wrote me:

> I was deafened by a doctor who didn't have time to look up the potential side effects of an antibiotic he prescribed for me. I trusted this doctor implicitly, so I never looked it up myself.

This is a mistake so many people make. Don't trust your doctor. Check things out for yourself! It's your ears—not your doctor's ears—that will be damaged.

This man continued:

> I resent apologists for doctors who invalidate the "first do no harm" aspect of the Hippocratic Oath and the system that protects them. If more doctors were made accountable and responsible for their medical "mistakes" in courts of law, they would not take the cavalier attitude that they do. In my state, a doctor is not required by law to inform patients of adverse events of any medications they prescribe.[28]

Therefore, you need to take responsibility for yourself. The FDA urges you to put together a health care team consisting of your doctor/physician, nurse, pharmacist and yourself. You have to play an active role on this team if you want to reduce your risk to drug-related side effects while, at the same time, getting the maximum benefit from taking those drugs.

The FDA has an excellent short article entitled "Be an Active Member of Your Health Care Team" at:

https://www.fda.gov/drugs/resources-drugs/be-active-member-your-health-care-team-article

Before you fill a prescription or purchase an over-the-counter (OTC) medicine, learn as much about it as you can, including any adverse side effects that could harm your ears.

After you have learned all you can about the proposed drug treatment and have discussed it thoroughly with your health-care team, then weigh your options. You and your health-care team need to decide if the supposed benefit from taking any drug far outweighs the risk of damage to **you**. However, the final choice is always **yours**.

If you choose to go ahead, but later experience an adverse side effect, let your health-care team know immediately! If the side effect is ototoxic, you do not want to wait and risk permanent damage to your ears.

For better or for worse, this is how the system works. Now it is up to you. You are free to believe what you wish from whatever sources you choose to trust. You are free to take the drugs you choose to take and are free to avoid those you choose not to take. Use the information in this book however you want. Most importantly, whatever you do, consult with a knowledgeable doctor or other health-care professional. Never take more than the recommended dose, at the recommended times/intervals. Never, never fall into the trap of thinking that "if one 'pill' is good, more is even better". The health of your ears is **your** responsibility. If you won't watch out for them, who will?

Chapter 8 Endnotes

1 Waltermire, 1998. p. 2.
2 DiSogra, 2001. pp. 4-5.
3 Shlafer, 2000. p. 3.
4 Top 200 Prescriptions, 2001. p. 1.
5 PRNewswire, April 26, 1999.
6 Jaeger, 2001. p. 5.
7 Jaeger, 2001. p. 4.
8 Jaeger, 2001. p. 4.
9 Jaeger, 2001. p. 3.
10 Jaeger, 2001. p. 3.
11 Jaeger, 2001. p. 1.
12 Physicians' Desk Reference, 2002, p. 518.
13 Physicians' Desk Reference, 2003. pp. 1308-9. 3302 and 3327-8.
14 Jaeger, 2001. p. 3.
15 Carmen, 1999. p. 37.
16 Be An Active Member Of Your Health Care Team, 2016. p. 1.
17 Questions About CDER, 2001. p. 3.
18 Waltermire, 1998. p. 2.
19 Waltermire, 1998. p. 4.
20 Omeprazole (Prilosec) OPDA Post-marketing Safety Review, 2000. pp. 24-25.
21 Omeprazole (Prilosec) OPDA Post-marketing Safety Review, 2000. pp. 24-25.
22 Rofecoxib. 2010. "Withdrawal".
23 Wolfe, 2010a.
24 McPheeters, 2000-2001. p. 1.
25 McPheeters, 2000-2001. p. 1.
26 McPheeters, 1999. p. 1.
27 Janes, 2000. p. 1.
28 Personal communication, 2000.

Chapter 9

The Shocking Truth About Hearing Testing and Ototoxic Drugs

How Bad Is It?

Years ago in one of the Hearing Loss Coping Skills classes I used to teach, I was shocked to find that about one-quarter of the people in that class had ear damage from taking ototoxic drugs. Unlike what doctors would have you believe; this is not an isolated case. One hard of hearing doctor wrote to me concerning the members of his HLAA[1] group. "It seems to me that nearly half of our members with severe hearing loss developed their loss from ototoxic drugs". Another doctor asserted that we know some drugs cause hearing/balance problems in up to 92% of the people taking them.[2]

Cisplatin is very likely the most ototoxic drug used in medicine today. According to one study, **Cisplatin** caused hearing loss in 86% of those studied.[3] Another study revealed that approximately 40% ended up with hearing loss from taking it.[4] The PDR reports an incidence of 31%.

In actual fact, the results reported in the literature range all over the place. Some researchers report that this drug only produces ototoxic side effects in 3% of the people taking it,[5] that it "occasionally causes ototoxicity"[6] and that this ototoxicity is "seldom permanent". Other researchers just as authoritatively assert that not a single person escapes its ravages—that 100% of the people taking **Cisplatin** damage their ears[7]—and that the resulting hearing loss "is usually irreversible (permanent)".[8]

Why the enormous difference in opinion? Who is right? What are we to believe? If the former researchers are right, then ototoxic drugs are probably few and the damage they cause is minimal—nothing to worry about at all. However, if the latter researchers are correct, then there are likely lots of ototoxic drugs out there that can seriously damage our ears.

As I see it, there are two main factors for this enormous variation. First, in real life, people only report a small fraction of 1% of all ototoxic side effects as we saw in Chapter 6. Therefore, if a researcher is really looking for ototoxic side effects, he will likely find far more of them than another researcher who only reports ototoxic side effects if he happens to stumble over them. This alone could account for much of the difference between the 3% and the 100% results.

Second, there are no set standards for determining ototoxicity—specifically for reporting how much hearing has to be lost before saying a given drug is ototoxic.

The Need for Standards

There are several definitions of ototoxicity in regard to hearing loss and several different ways of monitoring for it. As a result, one researcher decides whether a drug is ototoxic by using one set of rules and another uses completely different criteria.

Thus, there is a real need for standardized guidelines so research results will be consistent.[9] Some researchers consider there must be a resulting 10 dB hearing loss at any frequency in both ears (or 15 dB in one ear) before they will classify the drug as being ototoxic. Others use 15 dB or 20 dB at any given frequency.[10] Still others use a decrease of hearing of at least 15 dB over two or more adjacent test frequencies. Some researchers say that for the purposes of determining ototoxicity, the results have to be repeated for a minimum of two consecutive test sessions,[11] and on it goes.[12]

This means that while some researchers will say a given drug is ototoxic, other researchers—using different criteria—will give it a clean bill of health. Some researchers base their conclusions on objective test results. Others reach more nebulous, subjective conclusions. Still others are so sloppy that they don't even report the basis for their findings.

Back in 1994, the American Speech-Language-Hearing Association (ASHA) proposed some guidelines to clear up this confusion. Let's hope doctors and researchers finally adopt these (or similar) guidelines and bring some semblance of order to this mess.

Here is ASHA's six-step program regarding hearing loss from taking ototoxic drugs.

1. **Specific criteria for identifying ototoxicity.** For example, they suggest that a drug be considered ototoxic if hearing loss drops 20 dB or more at any one test frequency, or if it drops 10 dB or more at two or more consecutive (adjacent) test frequencies, or if there is no response at three consecutive test frequencies where there was a response before.[13]

2. **Timely identification of at-risk patients.** Generally, people are at greater risk if they are either very young or old; if they have a pre-existing hearing loss; if they have kidney problems; or if they have had previous ototoxic reactions to drugs. (See Chapter 5 for further information on numerous ototoxic risk factors.)

3. **Pre-treatment counseling regarding potential ototoxic side effects.** Prior to ototoxic drug treatment, doctors should counsel their patients regarding the potential ototoxic side effects of the drugs they will be taking. Doctors should carefully and completely explain the risks and benefits of such drug therapy. Counseling should include the ototoxic signs and symptoms to watch for (such as hearing loss, tinnitus, loss of balance, etc.) and what to do if such signs or symptoms occur. (Chapter 4 describes in detail many of the ototoxic side effects that may occur.) Furthermore, counseling needs to cover how the potential side effects can affect a person's ability to communicate effectively. In addition, people need to know how noise and certain drugs can team up to cause even more ear damage than would normally be expected. (Chapter 11 explains this very important topic in detail.)

4. **Have valid baseline measures.** This means that a person needs to have a complete audiological evaluation **before** starting drug treatment. The purpose of baseline testing is to document the status of hearing prior to drug treatment. At the very minimum, this testing needs to include pure-tone hearing testing and word recognition (discrimination) scores.

5. **Monitor hearing at sufficient intervals to document the progression of hearing loss** (or fluctuations in hearing sensitivity). The monitoring intervals need to be such that they will detect the first signs of ototoxic effects. For people receiving AMINOGLYCOSIDE antibiotics, this monitoring interval may be as short as every 2 or 3 days.

6. **Follow-up evaluations to determine and document the permanent ototoxic effects of this drug treatment.** Such follow-up evaluations should be done immediately after the end of the drug treatment and 3 and 6 months later.[14]

This six-step program is an excellent start to consistent care for people receiving drugs known to cause hearing loss. However, it has one serious flaw. It fails to mention the range of frequencies that must be tested during audiometric evaluation—specifically those frequencies above the conventional testing range where most drug-induced hearing loss first occurs.

High-frequency Hearing Testing Needed

One of the reasons doctors and researchers do not know the true incidence of hearing loss in the ototoxic drugs they prescribe is because the initial damage to the hearing system typically occurs in those frequencies of sound well outside the standard speech test frequencies that lie between 250 Hz and 8,000 Hz. The way it stands today, the frequencies above 8,000 Hz are almost never tested for hearing loss.

Incidentally, this same problem also occurs in the vestibular (balance) system. Initial ototoxic damage in the vestibular system occurs well outside the normal active and passive head movement range.[15] This means that a lot of damage can be done to both your cochlear and vestibular systems **before** ear specialists can detect it using the methods in common use today.

Research on how ototoxic drugs affect high-frequency hearing began back in the early 1980s and was reported in the mid-1980s.

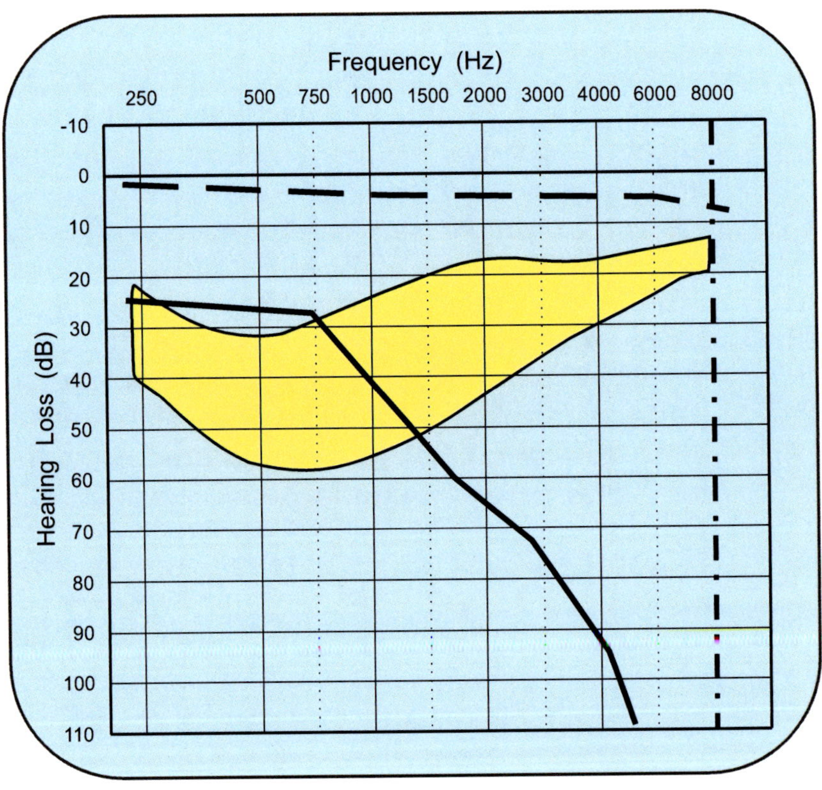

Fig. 9-1. An audiogram in the conventional frequencies. The yellow area is the "speech banana". It shows the frequencies and loudness covered by normal speech sounds. The horizontal dashed line represents normal hearing. The solid sloping line indicates a ski-slope-shaped hearing loss in the conventional frequencies.

Researchers are now beginning to realize just how important it is to detect high-frequency hearing loss as early as possible. For example, did you know that high-frequency audiometry can reveal the early effects of an ototoxic drug long before tinnitus typically appears, or actual damage is visible, on a conventional audiogram?

Here are some things you should know. People with normal hearing can typically hear up to 18,000 or 20,000 Hz or even higher. The frequencies you use for speech generally lie between 500 and 6000 Hz. Therefore, when you take a hearing test, your audiologist will test your hearing between 250 and 8000 Hz. This is the normal or "conventional" testing range (Fig. 9-1).

Now comes the insidious part. Many ototoxic drugs begin their nefarious work in the highest frequencies you can hear where you seldom notice it (and where audiologists do not test), and then work their way down the frequency spectrum. This high-frequency hearing loss is typically undetectable since most audiometers are only calibrated to test frequencies between 250 and 8,000 Hz.

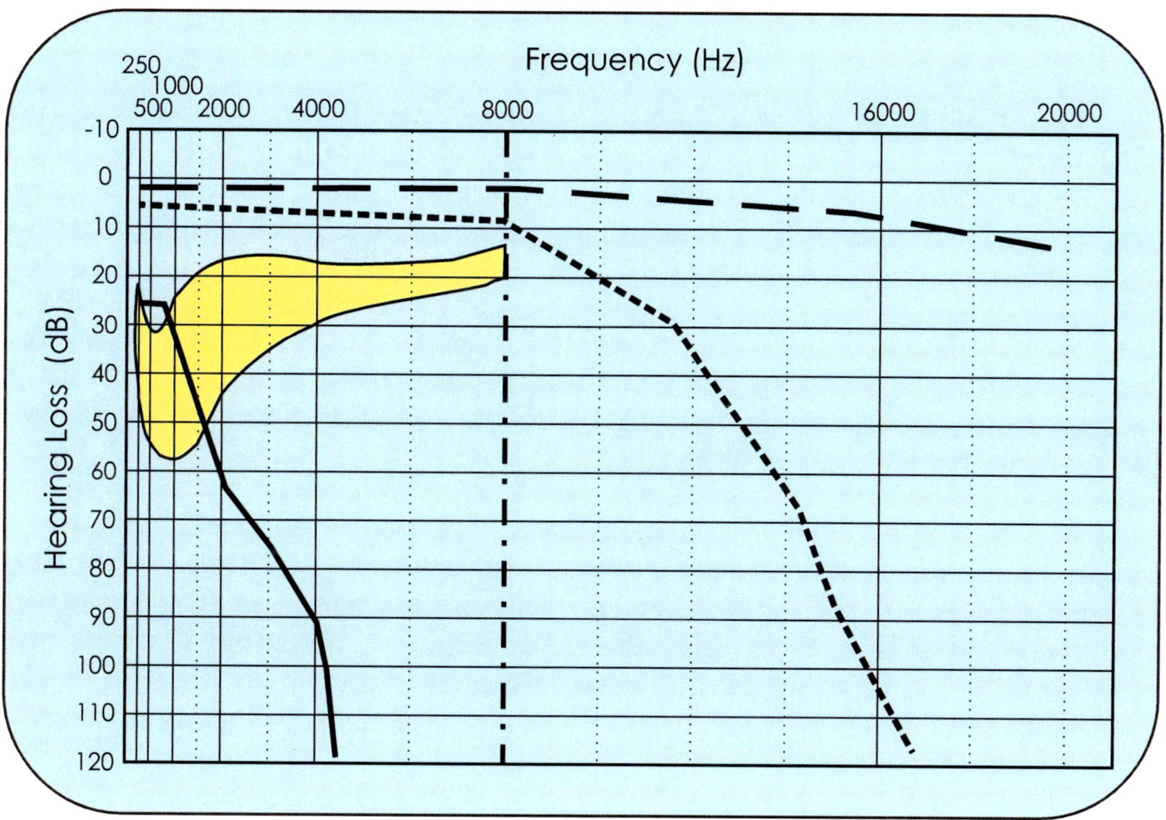

Fig. 9-2. An audiogram showing both the conventional frequencies (below 8,000 Hz) and the high frequencies. The horizontal dashed line represents normal hearing. The dotted line shows a ski-slope hearing loss only noticeable when testing in the high frequencies. Note: hearing is completely normal in the conventional test frequencies yet ranges to a profound loss in the high frequencies. The solid line indicates a ski-slope hearing loss in the conventional frequencies. (This line is identical to the solid line in Fig. 9.1 but looks different because of differences in the horizontal scale. Likewise, the speech banana is really identical, but looks different in the two graphs.)

In studies done on **Cisplatin**, the first indications of hearing loss always showed up between 10,000 and 16,000 Hz. These frequencies are well above those shown on conventional audiograms.[16]

This means that even with complete standard audiometric testing, your ears could test at normal—indicating that a certain drug is not ototoxic—yet you could have lost some/much/all of your hearing between 9,000 and 20,000 Hz and no one would know. In fact, you could lose 60% of your hearing spectrum, yet the drug would get a clean bill of health as far as ototoxicity goes (Fig 9-2)!

Ototoxic chemicals have this same characteristic as do ototoxic drugs, namely, affecting the high frequencies first. For example, high-frequency hearing testing revealed that workers exposed to low concentrations of **Styrene** fumes for 5 years had hearing losses in the high frequencies even though their hearing tests in the conventional frequencies were normal. If high-frequency hearing testing hadn't been done, **Styrene** could have been given a clean bill of health even though it is ototoxic.

Breathing **Styrene** fumes is now known to cause a reduction in the upper limit of hearing. (The upper limit of hearing is the highest frequency that you can hear.) Researchers have concluded that the upper limit of hearing is a sensitive indicator for early detection of ototoxicity in workers exposed to **Styrene**[17] and indeed, probably for most drugs and chemicals.

Therefore, if you want to know the truth about your hearing and whether drugs or chemicals are insidiously stealing your hearing from you without your being aware of it, your audiologist needs to **test your hearing right up to the highest frequency you can hear**.

As we have already seen, when researchers document hearing loss, they typically limit their testing to the conventional frequencies between 250 Hz and 8,000 Hz.[18] When they do this, they miss all the hearing loss that shows up in the high frequencies, even though one study demonstrated that testing only the conventional hearing range is the **least effective** method to determine **initial** hearing loss.[19] Because of this, the real incidence of hearing loss is much higher than is commonly reported.

It's not that doctors and audiologists can't readily test these high-frequency sounds. They can—if they had the desire to do so. All it takes is an audiometer designed and calibrated to test hearing loss in the higher frequencies. Such audiometers are available. It's just that most doctors and audiologists don't think such extended testing is necessary. How wrong can they be?

Since hearing loss typically begins at the highest frequency you can hear and progresses to the lower frequencies, it is essential that doctors and audiologists monitor the highest frequencies people with pre-existing hearing loss can hear in order to provide the earliest possible warning of any incipient hearing loss.

Early detection does not, by itself, prevent further damage to your ears. However, it does give doctors time to adjust the dose or stop the medication altogether before hearing loss spreads into the conventional test frequencies.[20] If monitoring is restricted to frequencies below 8,000 Hz, by the time doctors detect any hearing loss, it is already too late to effectively treat it. Hearing loss will have already affected those frequencies necessary for hearing speech.[21]

High-frequency testing is even more important in young people because they likely still have more residual high-frequency hearing than older people, therefore they have more high-frequency hearing to lose.

How good is high-frequency testing? When researchers compared testing the high frequencies with testing the conventional frequencies only, here is what one study revealed. In the high frequencies only, 45% had initial hearing loss. However, just 29% showed initial hearing loss in the conventional frequencies only, while 26% showed initial hearing loss in both frequency ranges at the same time. Thus, if only the high frequencies had been tested, 71% of the ears tested would have revealed the initial hearing loss.[22]

In a study on the ototoxic effects of AMINOGLYCOSIDES and **Cisplatin**, 70% of the ears tested showed hearing loss due to ototoxicity. (Note that 70% is a far cry from the 3% some researchers have reported when testing these drugs.) Of the ears with drug-induced hearing loss, 52% were first detected in the high-frequency range only.

This study again shows that more than half of the people with drug-induced hearing loss have hearing loss that was **not** detected by conventional means. In this case, if only high-frequency hearing testing had been done, 67% of all the ears demonstrating initial hearing loss due to ototoxicity would have been found.[23]

Another study revealed that only 13.5% of the people (ears) studied had initial drug-related hearing loss in the conventional frequencies. An additional 24% had initial detectable hearing loss in the conventional frequencies as well as the high frequencies. This means that if you suspect you have drug-induced hearing loss, your audiologist only has a 37.5% chance of catching it. Thus, a whopping 62.5% of drug-induced hearing loss likely goes undetected because it initially **only** occurs in the high frequencies![24] However, if only the high frequencies had been tested, audiologists would have detected 86% of all cases of drug-induced hearing loss.

The Five-frequency Hearing Testing Process

It is now clear that doctors and audiologists need to test the entire hearing frequency spectrum if they want accurate results. However, there are a couple of problems to overcome.

First, testing all the frequencies between 125 Hz and 20,000 Hz is both time consuming and tiring, especially to the person being tested. Furthermore, if the people being tested are already sick, they may not have the stamina to get through a complete audiometric test.

Second, as people age, their hearing deteriorates especially at the high frequencies. Thus, researchers need to factor this in when testing the higher frequencies of older people. Some people may not have any hearing at all above 10,000 Hz, for example.

In one study, although the average age of the subjects was 55 years, 93% of the ears tested had measurable baseline hearing up to 12,500 Hz, while 48% had responses up to 16,000 Hz. This means that even if older people cannot hear anything at 20,000 Hz, there is still plenty of usable high-frequency spectrum left to test.

Fortunately for us, a few researchers have been concerned about drug-induced high-frequency hearing loss. They have been searching for the most effective and accurate way to test for the ototoxic effects of drugs in any given person without the draining and time-consuming process of testing all test frequencies below 20,000 Hz.

Audiometric Test Frequencies

Audiologists test your hearing at selected intervals. They do not test every frequency in your hearing range. That would take "forever". For the conventional frequencies, they normally test in whole "octaves". An octave is exactly double the frequency of the preceding frequency tested. Therefore, they test at 125, 250, 500, 1000, 2000, 4000 and 8000 Hz.

Notice that as the frequency goes up, the interval between adjacent octaves increases. Therefore, they may test fractional octaves like half-octaves between 1000 and 8,000 Hz. These intermediate test frequencies would be close to 1600, 3150, and 6300 Hz.

For the purposes of high-frequency testing, Dr. Fausti recommends that testing should be at one-sixth octave spacing.[1] Above 8,000 Hz, the one-sixth octave testing frequencies are 9000, 10,000, 11,200, 12,500, 14,000, 16,000, 18,000 and 20,000 Hz.

Reference

1 Fausti, 1999. p. 1.

One of their goals was to determine where drugs first affect hearing. They discovered that there is a five-frequency range that is very sensitive to the ravages of ototoxic drugs. This is the frequency range they recommend be tested.

The beauty of the five-frequency range testing is that it is highly sensitive to **initial** ototoxic hearing loss. This range varies depending on each person's pre-existing hearing loss, and thus is unique to each person. These five frequencies are generally separated by 1/6 octave. For example, a person with pre-existing hearing loss might have a five-frequency range consisting of 8, 9, 10, 11.2 and 12.5 kHz.[25]

Since each person's hearing loss is unique, audiologists can't just test for five specific frequencies. They have to tailor the testing process for each individual person. Here is how they can do this easily and accurately.

First, using an audiometer calibrated to accurately test up to 20,000 Hz, the audiologist determines the highest frequency a person can hear. (Note: the hearing loss at this frequency must be 100 dB or less. The reason for the 100 dB cut-off is because researchers noticed that at hearing losses greater than 100 dB, they saw fewer changes in ototoxic activity. After all, at that point, there isn't much hearing left to lose!)

Second, they test both this frequency and the next four lower consecutive audiometric test frequencies. They call this the five-frequency slope range.[26]

Depending on your particular hearing loss, this five-frequency slope may all lie within the extended high-frequency range, it may straddle the 8,000 Hz boundary between the conventional and high frequencies, or it may only reside in the conventional frequencies (Fig. 9-3). It doesn't matter where this slope is, as long as your audiologist finds it and carefully tests you in that range.

The worse your high-frequency hearing is, the greater the chance that conventional testing will reveal any ototoxic drug damage. Therefore, when testing older people or people with severe losses, there may be no need for high-frequency testing. In contrast, if children or people with normal hearing are being tested, almost all of them will likely fall into the high-frequency only range. However, a good number of adults will fall into the range that straddles the 8,000 Hz line. Therefore, apart from people with obvious ski-slope losses entirely in the conventional frequencies, everyone else needs base-line high-frequency testing.

Just how effective is this five-frequency slope in detecting hearing loss from ototoxic drugs? The results may surprise you!

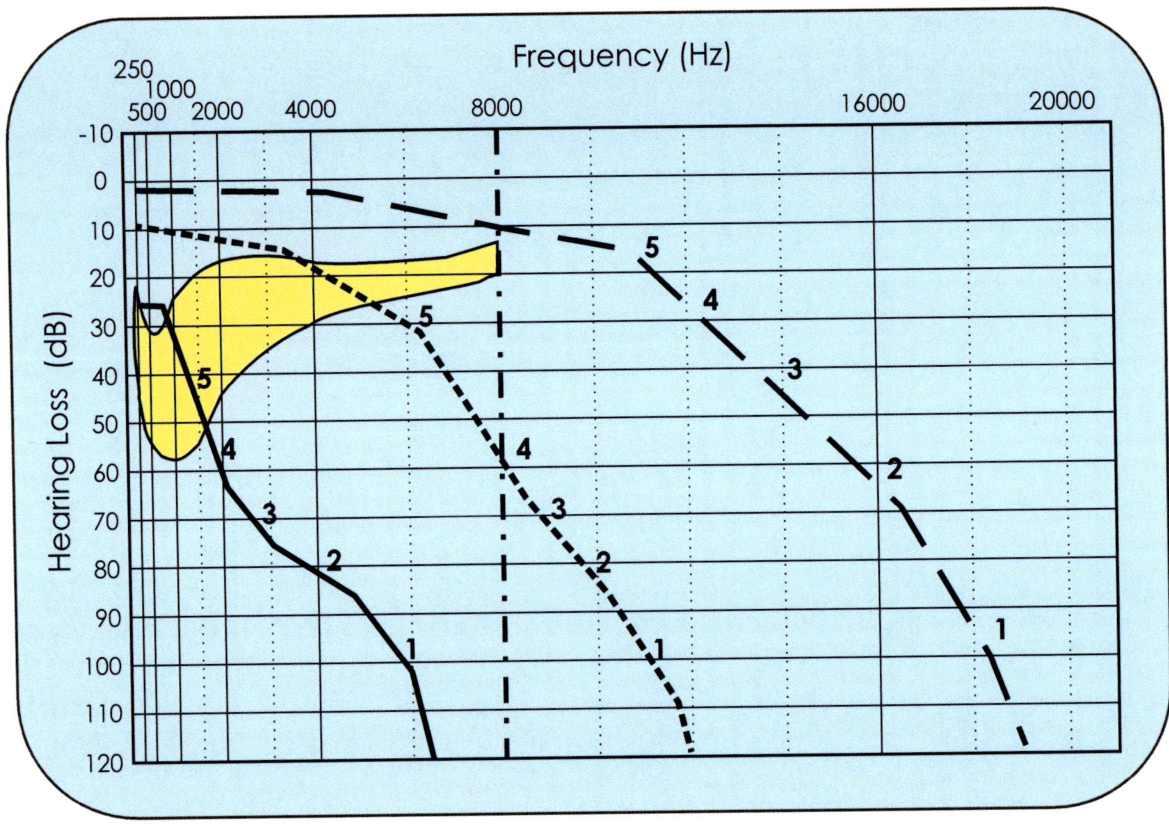

Fig. 9-3. An audiogram showing the five-frequency slope testing profile. Hearing loss from ototoxic drugs will normally be the most noticeable and be the most sensitive in this five-frequency slope range. The dashed line shows hearing loss only in the high frequencies. The dotted line indicates hearing loss straddling the 8,000 Hz boundary between the conventional frequencies normally tested and the high frequencies. The solid line reveals hearing loss exclusively in the conventional test frequencies (no high-frequency hearing remaining). It is here that any change in hearing loss becomes obvious to conventional testing. The numbers on the lines indicate the location of each of the five frequencies of the five-frequency test protocol.

In one study on the ototoxic effects of **Cisplatin**, if only the five frequencies in the five-frequency slope had been tested, 93% of the people with ototoxic drug-induced hearing loss would have been detected.[27] This is in sharp contrast to the 39% detected in this same study using only the conventional frequencies.

Other studies have yielded similar results. For example, in one case, researchers found that if only the five-frequency slope frequencies had been tested, initial hearing loss would have been detected in 82%, instead of just 42% using only the conventional frequencies.[28]

Another study reported that if only the five-frequency slope values were tested, hearing loss due to Aminoglycoside antibiotics would be detected 84% of the time, and for **Cisplatin**, the results would be even higher at 94%.[29]

Yet, another study revealed that initial hearing loss would have been detected in 89% of the people with hearing loss if only the five-frequency slope had been tested. Testing only the conventional frequencies caught just 37%.

This means that conventional audiometric testing would miss five people with drug-induced hearing loss for every two people it detects. This is just not acceptable![30]

In all these cases, if they had tested **both** the conventional frequencies and any portion of the five-frequency slope values above the conventional frequencies, they would, of course, have detected 100% of the cases of ototoxic drug induced hearing loss.

I think it is about time you insist that your ears get tested at those frequencies that will best detect the initial effects of ototoxic drugs. The routine use of high-frequency audiometry is not just "nice," it is essential.[31]

Many doctors reject high-frequency monitoring of hearing loss for two reasons. First, they think that many of their patients being given massive doses of ototoxic drugs will die (of cancer) anyway, so there is no need to worry about their hearing. Second, they think that middle-aged and older people with pre-existing hearing losses have no useful high-frequency hearing left to monitor.

Both assumptions are wrong. Many people are now surviving drug therapy (for cancer) and need their hearing to facilitate their recovery and for their emotional and mental well-being. Also, as studies have shown, doctors can obtain high-frequency thresholds in people with pre-existing hearing loss.[32] True, they may not hear up to 20,000 Hz like they used to, but many can still hear up to 10,000 or 12,000 Hz.

There are several advantages to using the five-frequency protocol. First, of course, is that it is much more accurate in detecting initial hearing loss. Second, the testing procedure is significantly shorter.

However, for those in hospitals that have to undergo drug therapy with ototoxic drugs, having audiograms can be a problem, especially if they are unconscious, semi-conscious or very sick. In that case, instead of doing the hearing testing using a conventional audiometer, it can be done reliably using auditory brainstem response (ABR) techniques modified to work in the higher frequencies. In one such study, high-frequency tone-burst-evoked ABRs alone identified 93% of the initial changes in hearing loss.[33]

Note that it is critical to have base-line high-frequency audiometry done **before** you begin taking a drug so subsequent audiometry can reveal whether the drug(s) you are taking are stealing your hearing, or whether you are simply losing hearing as you age.

The five-frequency slope protocol is fast. It has been proven effective in providing early warning of hearing loss. The critical missing link to this process is the final step—getting your doctors and audiologists to use this five-frequency slope audiometric testing procedure in their everyday practices and help us save your precious hearing from the insidious ravages of ototoxic drugs.

Chapter 9 Endnotes

1 HLAA—Hearing Loss Association of America—a national organization for hard of hearing people headquartered in Rockville, MD, USA.
2 Tange, 1985. p. 77.
3 Fausti, 1993a. p. 663.
4 Tange, 1985. p. 77.
5 Guidelines for the Audiologic Management of Individuals Receiving Cochleotoxic Drug Therapy, 1994. p. 4.
6 Shlafer, 2000. p. 12.
7 Guidelines for the Audiologic Management of Individuals Receiving Cochleotoxic Drug Therapy, 1994. p. 4.
8 Kalkanis, 2001. p. 1.
9 Fausti, 1993a. p. 662.
10 Troost, 1998a. p. 1.
11 Fausti, 1993a. p. 662.
12 Guidelines for the Audiologic Management of Individuals Receiving Cochleotoxic Drug Therapy, 1994. p. 4.
13 Guidelines for the Audiologic Management of Individuals Receiving Cochleotoxic Drug Therapy, 1994. p. 5.
14 Guidelines for the Audiologic Management of Individuals Receiving Cochleotoxic Drug Therapy, 1994. pp. 5-7.
15 Troost, 1998b. p. 1.
16 Tange, 1985. pp. 77-80.
17 Morioka, 1999. pp. 1-5.
18 Guidelines for the Audiologic Management of Individuals Receiving Cochleotoxic Drug Therapy, 1994. p. 4.
19 Fausti, 1992, p. 1031.
20 Fausti, 1993a. p. 661.
21 Fausti, 1993a. p. 664.
22 Fausti, 1993a. p. 663.
23 Fausti, 1993b. p. 4.
24 Fausti, 1994. pp. 232-9.
25 Fausti, 1999. p. 1.
26 Fausti, 1993a. p. 663.
27 Fausti, 1993a. pp. 663-664.
28 Fausti, 1993b. p. 5.
29 Fausti, 1999. p. 1.
30 Fausti, 1994. p. 1.
31 Kalkanis, 2001. p. 8.
32 Fausti, 1993b. p. 6.
33 Fausti, 1993b. p. 1.

Chapter 10

We "Hear" with Our Eyes

Ototoxic drugs aren't the only drugs for which hard of hearing people have to be wary. You also need to watch out for drugs that can damage your eyes. This is critical because so often your eyes have to take over to help out your damaged ears.

Vision Is Vitally Important

Your eyes fill in for your ears in several capacities. For example, if you have a severe hearing loss, your eyes become the primary means of warning you of impending danger. Furthermore, your eyes help you to communicate, whether it be by speechreading, thus supplementing what your faulty ears hear, or by reading captions and the written word. Thus, in a very real sense, you, as a hard of hearing person "hear" with your eyes.

Your eyes have another critical function. Along with your proprioceptive system, they help you maintain your balance. (See Chapter 4 for information about how your eyes and your proprioceptive system work together to maintain your balance.) If you already have poor vestibular function, possibly from taking ototoxic drugs, then you **need** your eyes. Thus you must protect your vision at all costs.

Very few people, doctors included, realize the immense importance of this. You need to emphasize to your doctor that you don't want any drugs that will damage either your ears **or** your eyes.

Sharon knows what it is like to have both her eyes and her ears damaged by drugs. She wrote:

> One thing that bugs me is doctors that seem to think because I already have a hearing loss, it doesn't matter if they give me more ototoxic drugs. They load me up with ototoxic antibiotics at the slightest sign of an infection.

Another of Sharon's pet peeves is:

> ... doctors that disregard the concerns of a hard of hearing or deaf patient about being given a drug that has a high risk of both cataracts and glaucoma.

She specifically singled out **Prednisone** "which frequently results in people developing both cataracts and glaucoma with the resultant blindness". She laments, "Doctors don't understand that my eyes are my ears".

This is a most serious concern. Imagine for a moment that you are now both deaf and blind. Think of the enormous changes that will bring to your lifestyle. This is nothing to take lightly. The psychological impact will be enormous! Would you want to live under such conditions?

Sharon has already lost much of her hearing. and some of her vision. She explained:

> If I become blind, I'm afraid I would lose my will to live because my eyes are my connection to the world around me. I already have severe visual difficulties due to the **Prednisone**. I have cataracts in both eyes and the pain in my eyes from glaucoma is really bad. I tapered myself off the **Prednisone** on my own. My doctor just did not understand my concerns about blindness and what my eyes mean to me. This kind of attitude towards the drugs given to us really bothers me.[1]

You have been warned folks. Sharon has been there—is still there—and tells it like it is.

You Need to Watch Out for Yourself

Since this book only deals with ototoxic drugs and their side effects, it is up to you to check out the visual side effects of any drugs you take. While you are busy protecting your remaining hearing, you also need to be protecting your precious vision.

Here's another thing. Don't let your guard down—even when visiting your eye doctor. The truth is that your eye doctor may be unwittingly prescribing drugs that could damage your ears because the "drug bible" he uses, the *Physicians' Desk Reference for Ophthalmic Medicines* does a poor job (in my opinion) of listing ototoxic side effects for the drugs it describes.

The 2002 edition of the *Physicians' Desk Reference for Ophthalmic Medicines* lists about 108 different generic drugs used in treating eye problems. As you would expect, it has a reasonably comprehensive list of side effects reflecting various eye conditions. However, when it comes to listing the side effects affecting the rest of the body, particularly the ears, that's a different story.

For example, of the 108 drugs mentioned above, 42 (that I knew about back then) can be ototoxic, yet only 11 of these drugs had even one ototoxic side effect listed.[2] Three of these eleven only report dizziness although the *Physicians' Desk Reference* lists several other ototoxic side effects in addition to dizziness. Now comes the scary part. Thirty-one of these forty-two ototoxic drugs (including extremely ototoxic drugs such as **Gentamicin**, **Neomycin** and **Tobramycin**) didn't have even one ototoxic side effect listed!

The 2010 edition of the *Physicians' Desk Reference for Ophthalmic Medicines* is even worse. It lists about 71 different generic drugs of which 58 (a whopping 82%) can be ototoxic, yet it only lists side effects for 2 of these drugs! This is why you have to do your homework before it is too late.

Drugs That Can Damage Our Eyes

In the back of the book, *Essential Guide to Prescription Drugs 2006,* Table 4 lists many of the drugs that can adversely affect your vision. The opening preamble to this table states, "A significant number of all medicine-related problems (adverse drug effects) involve visual changes or eye damage". This is something you need to know!

This table lists 152 specific drugs that can damage your eyes.[3,4] The scary thing is that of these 152 drugs, 123 (81%) of them not only can damage your eyes, but at the same time, they can damage your ears, and thus seriously compromise your balance, make it difficult or impossible to speechread or read captions!

Table 10-1 lists drugs that can damage your eyes but are not known to be ototoxic. This list is probably nowhere near complete. However, at

Table 10-1: Drugs That Can Have Adverse Side Effects on Your Eyes (But Not Your Ears)

Amodiaquine
Amyl nitrite
Atacurium
Carbachol
Cephaloglycin
Ergot
Ethchlorvynol
Guanethidine
Hydrochloroquine
Mephenesin
Mephenytoin
Methotrimeprazine
Monamine oxidase
Nialamide
Oxyphenbutazone
Paramethadione
Pargyline
Pentylenetetrazol
Phenacetin
Phenmetrazine
Phensuximide
Terfenadine
Triflupromazine
Trimethadione[1]

Reference

[1] Rybacki, 2006. pp. 1219-1221.

Table 10-2: Drugs That Can Have Adverse Side Effects on Both Your Eyes and Your Ears

Abobotulinum toxin A	Digitoxin	Nicotine
Acetaminophen	Digoxin	Nitrofurantoin
Acetazolamide	Dimetindene	Nitroglycerin
Acetylsalicylic acid	Diphenhydramine	Norfloxacin
Allopurinol	Disulfiram	Orphenadrine
Amantadine	Doxepin	Penicillamine
Amiodarone	Ephedrine	Pentazocine
Atropine	Epinephrine	Perphenazine
Belladonna	Ergotamine	Phenelzine
Brompheniramine	Erythromycin	Phentermine
Bupivacaine	Ethambutol	Phenylbutazone
Busulfan	Ethionamide	Phenytoin
Carbamazepine	Ethosuximide	Pilocarpine
Carbinoxamine	Etretinate	Pregabalin
Carisoprodol	Fenfluramine	Primidone
Cephalexin	Fenoprofen	Prochlorperazine
Chloramphenicol	Fluphenazine	Promazine
Chlordiazepoxide	Furosemide	Promethazine
Chloroquine	Gabapentin	Propranolol
Chlorpheniramine	Griseofulvin	Quinacrine
Chlorpromazine	Haloperidol	Quinidine
Chlorpropamide	Hydroxychloroquine	Quinine
Chlorprothixene	Ibuprofen	Rabies vaccine
Chlortetracycline	Imatinib	Reserpine
Chlorthalidone	Indomethacin	Sildenafil
Cimetidine	Interferon alpha-N3	Sodium salicylate
Ciprofloxacin	Isocarboxazid	Spironolactone
Cisplatin	Isoniazid	Streptomycin
Clomiphene	Isosorbide	Tacrolimus
Clonidine	Latanoprost	Tadalafil
Codeine	Levodopa	Tetracycline
Colchicine	Lisinopril	Thioridazine
Colistin	Lithium	Thiothixene
Cyclizine	Mefenamic acid	Tolbutamide
Cycloserine	Memantine	Tranylcypromine
Cyproheptadine	Mesoridazine	Travoprost
Dapsone	Methocarbamol	Trifluoperazine
Dexbrompheniramine	Methsuximide	Trimeprazine
Dexchlorpheniramine	Methysergide	Tripelennamine
Dicloxacillin	Morphine	Vardenafil
Diethylstibestrol	Nalidixic acid	Ziconotide[1,2]

References

1 Rybacki, 2001. pp. 1200-1202.

2 Rybacki, 2006. pp. 1219-1221.

least you can watch out for these drugs. The drugs in this table are not otherwise listed in this book.

Table 10-2 lists drugs that can damage **both** your eyes and your ears, thus they can zap you with a "double whammy". All the drugs in this table are included in this book, but I only list their ototoxic side effects. I do not mention any of their visual side effects.

These two tables are not necessarily up to date nor exhaustive, but they give you an idea of the many drugs that can damage your eyes or damage your ears and ears at the same time. However, they serve as warnings that you need to check all drug side effects out for yourself if you want to protect **both** your eyes and your ears.

In addition to the above individual drugs, there are a number of drug classes where the drugs in that class can affect both your eyes and your ears. Some of these clearly-defined drug classes include:

Amphetamine-like drugs (see section 53.44.1 in Table 19-1)
Antidepressants (see section 60.1 in Table 19-1)
Antidiabetic drugs (see section 40.8 in Table 19-1)
Barbiturates (see section 60.12.4 in Table 19-1)
Benzodiazepines (see section 60.12.8 in Table 19-1)
Cortisone-like drugs (see section 40.1.4 in Table 19-1)
Monoamine oxidase (MAO) inhibitors (see section 60.1.1 in Table 19-1)
Oral contraceptives (see section 40.12 in Table 19-1)
Phenothiazines (see section 60.8.1 in Table 19-1)
Sulfonamides (see section 7.4.56 in Table 19-1)
Tetracyclines (see section 7.4.60 in Table 19-1)
Thiazide diuretics (see section 30.5.12 in Table 19-1)
Tricyclic antidepressants (see section 60.1.8 in Table 19-1)

Furthermore, there are some more-general classes of drugs including anti-arthritic/anti-inflammatory drugs, antihistamines, atropine-like drugs, bromides, organophosphates, sedatives/sleep-inducers and tranquilizers that also can affect both your eyes and your ears.[5]

Chapter 10 Endnotes

1 Cohen, 2000. p.,1.
2 Physicians' Desk Reference for Ophthalmic Medicines, 2002. pp. VIII-XII.
3 Rybacki, 2001. pp. 1099-1202
4 Rybacki, 2006. pp. 1219-1221.
5 Rybacki, 2006. pp. 1219-1221.

Chapter 11

The Sinister Partnership Between Ototoxic Agents and Noise

It is no secret that noise damages your ears. Since you are reading this book, you know that many drugs and chemicals also can damage your ears. Studies are now revealing there is often a sinister partnership between ototoxic agents and noise. In a review of some studies, researchers observed that the incidence of sensorineural hearing loss was higher than expected in those workers who were exposed to both noise and organic solvents at the same time.

This had puzzled researchers. Why could some people working in noisy places not seem to suffer any hearing loss, while others working in quieter places end up with severe hearing loss and other ear damage? What factor was increasing the risk of ototoxic damage? They know now. Being exposed to certain ototoxic agents and noise at the same time can make all the difference.

Unfortunately, two of the more common ototoxic hazards that occur in many work environments are exposure to noise and to organic solvents. Researchers have found that taking an ototoxic drug, or being exposed to an ototoxic industrial solvent, might not cause noticeable damage to your ears if you are in a relatively quiet place. However, if you take the same dose, and at the same time are exposed to loud noise for any length of time (say at work on a construction site or in a factory), the result could be significant ear damage. In fact, the combination of noise and drugs/chemicals can increase the risk of hearing damage many times over!

In a 20-year study of hearing sensitivity in 319 employees, a remarkably large proportion (23%) of the workers in the chemical sector showed pronounced hearing loss as compared with employees in non-chemical environments (5-8%). These results were found in spite of the fact that the noise levels in the chemical sector (80-90 dB) were less than those in other divisions (95-100 dB).[1]

Not only can hearing loss be worse in the presence of both noise and chemicals, but so can be your ability to understand speech. By comparing pure tone audiometry results to speech audiometry results, researchers determined that the chemical solvents not only caused hearing loss in the cochlea, but also damaged the auditory circuits in the brain so that speech was not processed as clearly as before. This gives rise to lower than expected word recognition (discrimination) scores.[2]

Researchers are just beginning to understand how noise and ototoxic chemicals team up to damage your ears. In some cases, it appears that the noise changes the rate of blood flow and thus allows the ototoxic agent to reach a higher level of penetration than it otherwise would. In other cases, the noise apparently increases hair cell activity to such an extent that it leads to their injury. Also, researchers think that both noise and ototoxic chemicals can upset intracellular energy production, which could compound the effects of each.[3]

Additive vs. Synergistic Effects

When noise and ototoxic drugs or chemicals get together in your ears, the resulting damage can either be "additive" or "synergistic".

Adding Decibels Looks Weird

The results of adding decibels together look weird. This is because decibels are logarithmic units. Thus, 23 dB is twice as loud as 20 dB. If sound levels were measured in linear units rather than in logarithmic units then the result would have been the familiar 20 units plus 20 units = 40 units.

For example, if you were exposed to an ototoxic chemical (or drug) that caused you to lose 20 dB of hearing and at the same time you were exposed to noise that caused you to also lose 20 dB of hearing, the total effect would be a 20 dB + 20 dB = 23 dB of hearing loss. This is the additive effect—the total is **equal to** the sum of its parts.

However, let's say you were exposed to exactly the same situation above and your resulting hearing loss was 33 dB instead of the expected 23 dB. This loss would be 10 **times** worse than expected. This extra loss above the expected additive effect is called the synergistic effect—where the result is **greater** than the sum of the individual parts.

Think of it this way. To get the additive effect, you **add** the two separate effects together. However, you "**multiply**" the two effects together to get the synergistic effect.

Just how pronounced is this synergistic effect? In one study, workers were grouped into one of four groups—those exposed to both noise and **Toluene**, those exposed to **Toluene** alone, those exposed to noise alone, and those not exposed to either **Toluene** or noise (the control group). The hearing loss of those exposed to noise alone was 4 times greater than the control group; the hearing loss of those exposed to **Toluene** alone was 5 times greater; and the hearing loss of those exposed to both noise and **Toluene** was 11 times greater![4]

Decibels and Powers of Ten

Since decibels are logarithmic units, if one number is 10 dB greater than another, it is one order of magnitude greater (10 times greater). If one sound level is 20 dB greater than another, then the second sound is 2 orders of magnitude greater (100 times greater) and so forth.

Sometimes the results can be dramatic! In a study of Brazilian workers, those exposed to both noise and **Toluene** had a 53% incidence of hearing loss. In contrast, those exposed to noise alone had a 26% incidence rate while the control group had an incidence rate of only 8%. When these results were adjusted for age, they showed that noise exposure increased the risk of hearing loss by 4.6 times. When the noise was combined with exposure to **Toluene**, the risk jumped to a whopping 27.5 times![5]

One very interesting thing that has come out of animal studies is that the order of exposure seems to determine how bad the resulting hearing loss will be. If the noise exposure comes **before** the drug/chemical exposure, the effect is **additive** at best. However, if the noise exposure comes **after** exposure to the drug/chemical, the effect is **synergistic**.[6]

For example, in a **Toluene** study using rats, **Toluene** alone and noise alone each caused considerable hearing loss, particularly in the high frequencies. However, the hearing loss of rats exposed to **Toluene** followed by noise was greater than the sum of the effects of **Toluene** and noise alone.

Who Are the Guilty Parties?

Not all drugs and chemicals work together to wreck your ears, but certain classes of drugs and chemicals are definitely part of this unholy alliance. Unfortunately, not much is known about many of the ototoxic agents and the damage they cause to your ears in the presence of noise. Here are the ones we know to be guilty at the present time.

Drugs

Noise is often a co-factor in medication type ototoxicity, especially when combined with antibiotics. For example, if you get a hearing loss from taking an ototoxic antibiotic, you may, at the same time, also be at much greater risk of additional hearing loss from exposure to noise.[7]

The AMINOGLYCOSIDE class of antibiotics appears to exacerbate the damaging effects of noise exposure on your hearing. This means that if you are taking any of these antibiotics and are exposed to loud noise at the same time, the effects on your hearing may be considerably worse than either one by itself (the synergistic effect).[8]

For example, exposing your ears to loud noise while you are taking **Gentamicin** can make the ototoxic effects worse than if you are not around loud noise when taking this drug.[9] Numerous studies of people taking **Kanamycin** plus being exposed to noise at the same time have revealed both additive and synergistic effects.[10]

In addition to the AMINOGLYCOSIDE antibiotics, **Nicotine** and the anti-cancer drug **Cisplatin** can act together with noise to cause even greater damage to your hearing.[11] This is also true of over-the-counter drugs such as **Aspirin**. Studies have shown that taking higher doses of SALICYLATES like **Aspirin** in the presence of noise causes a greater temporary hearing loss. Furthermore, it takes longer for hearing to return to normal if you take **Aspirin** in the presence of noise than it does if you take **Aspirin** without the noise component.[12]

When **Chloramphenicol**, a common microbial antibiotic, is taken alone, it typically is not very ototoxic. However, in the presence of noise, the synergistic effect of this drug and noise shoots the risk way up![13]

One "recreational" drug that apparently also has this effect is 3,4-methylenedioxy-N-methamphetamine, commonly known as MDMA or Ecstasy. Although MDMA is not thought to cause hearing loss by itself, an animal study showed that taking MDMA in the presence of loud noise caused significantly greater hearing loss to occur than noise exposure alone caused.[14] This is another good reason not to "do" recreational drugs such as Ecstasy.

Caffeine Prevents Full Hearing Loss Recovery

Not only do some drugs have a synergistic effect when combined with noise, a surprising discovery has revealed another nefarious trait of some drugs, specifically **Caffeine**. If you have exposed your ears to loud sounds that has resulted in a temporary threshold shift (temporary hearing loss), caffeine can stop your hearing recovery in its tracks and turn what would have been a temporary hearing loss into a permanent one.[15]

For example, let's say you were out for a good time at your favorite night-club. Due to the loud music being played, by the end of the evening, you notice everything sounds muffled. This has happened to you in the past and you are not worried. You head for home and bed to sleep it off and let you ears recover.

The next morning you down a strong cup (or two) of coffee to combat your hangover and get you going again. This is a typical scenario for thousands of people. But without realizing it, your cup of joe has likely just permanently cost you some of your precious hearing.

Remember that caffeine is found not only in coffee, but also in tea, soft drinks, chocolate and a number of drugs.

Chemicals and Heavy Metals

Until recently, not much was known or done about identifying the high-risk chemicals, especially those that have synergistic effects in relation to hearing loss.

So far, the high-risk chemicals seem to be the organic solvents. Ototoxic organic solvents known to cause even greater damage to your ears in the presence of noise include **Carbon disulfide**, **Dinitrobenzene**, **Styrene**, **Trichloroethylene**, **Toluene** and **Xylene**. In addition, both **Carbon monoxide** (an asphyxiant) and **Lead** (a heavy metal) have this same nefarious characteristic.[16,17,18,19]

Further research adds chemicals such as **Arsenic**, **Butyl alcohol**, **Butyl nitrite**, **Heptane**, **Hexane**, **Manganese**, **Mercury** and **Trimethyltin** to this list.[20]

Apparently, this is just the tip of the iceberg. Suspicion is already cast on **Carbon tetrachloride**, various other metals and other asphyxiants.[21,22] Strange as it may seem, there is even some evidence that heavy salt eaters are more susceptible to damage from noise.[23] Who knows what other chemicals will be implicated in the future?

A review of studies suggested that organic solvents such as those present in oil-based paints interact synergistically with noise to cause increased hearing loss in humans.[24]

In one study almost half of the workers exposed to synthetic varnishes and noise were found to have permanent hearing losses ranging from 10 dB to 60 dB. These varnishes contained organic solvents such as **Benzene**, Butyl acetate, **Styrene**, **Toluene** and **Xylene.**[25]

A **Carbon disulfide** study revealed that the incidence of hearing loss was higher than expected among workers exposed to both noise and **Carbon disulfide** at the same time. In addition, researchers also found that the hearing losses were more severe and began sooner than in those workers only exposed to noise and not to **Carbon disulfide**.[26]

In a 1989 study of 258 workers in a viscose rayon factory, the incidence of hearing loss increased with the duration of exposure from 47% in the group exposed for up to 2 years as compared to 71% having hearing loss in the group exposed for 3 years or longer. Not only did the incidence of hearing loss increase with time, but also so did the severity of the resulting hearing losses. These findings help show the synergistic relationship that exists between **Carbon disulfide** exposure and noise.[27]

Carbon monoxide in the presence of noise also has a synergistic effect and makes threshold shifts (hearing loss) worse and causes more hair cell damage, particularly in the outer hair cells.[28]

Manganese is a heavy metal that interacts synergistically with noise exposure to cause increased hearing loss. Workers exposed to both noise and **Manganese** had accelerated hearing loss compared to those exposed to **Manganese** alone.[29]

Furthermore,

> A study on the effect of noise and **Cadmium** fumes on the hearing of metallurgical workers found that these workers had worse hearing at 4,000 and 6,000 Hz compared with a group of workers exposed only to noise.[30]

A study of Korean workers revealed that workers exposed to both certain metals and noise had 64% greater odds of hearing loss at 500 Hz to 6,000 Hz compared with those exposed only to noise.[31]

One study of shipyard workers found that workers exposed to a combination of high metal concentrations (including **Lead**, **Cadmium** and **Arsenic**) and solvents (including **Toluene** and **Xylene**) combined with high levels of noise increased their odds of developing significantly-reduced hearing at 2,000, 3,000, and 4,000 Hz by nearly 2.5 times as compared to workers who were not exposed to noise levels greater than 85 dB.[32]

In another shipyard investigation, workers exposed to a combination of noise and high concentrations of **Lead**, **Cadmium**, **Arsenic**, **Toluene** and **Xylene** were found to have significantly worse hearing between 1,000 Hz and 4000 Hz when compared to a group of workers exposed only to high levels of noise.[33]

It seems that ototoxic metals and chemicals decrease hearing most in the middle, high and very high frequencies depending on the specific ototoxic substance.[34]

New Standards Needed

Researchers were surprised to discover that when noise and ototoxic agents team up to damage your ears, this damage can occur even though exposure to both noise and chemicals are within currently acceptable limits![35] For example, you may work in an environment where exposure to ototoxic chemicals is kept in what is generally considered the "safe" range for those chemicals.

At the same time, you may also work in an environment where the noise level is kept below the level considered at risk for noise. Your ears are thus safe, right?

Wrong! You may still be damaging your ears. Therefore, the government needs to set more stringent standards. That way, people exposed to both ototoxic chemicals **and** noise will not inadvertently lose their hearing while their companies are complying with all current government standards.

Much more work needs to be done in this field. Unfortunately, even now, the association between occupational exposure to solvents and hearing loss is rarely evaluated. Since noise is often present in most occupational settings where solvent exposures occur, the hearing losses observed in these situations are often attributed to noise alone. Even studying audiograms is of little help. This is because the pure tone audiogram can look identical whether the hearing loss was caused by noise or by ototoxic chemicals or drugs.[36]

Watch Out for Noise for a Long Time

One of the treacherous effects of ototoxic drugs teaming up with noise is something you'd probably never suspect. This is the length of time your ears are susceptible to damage after taking certain ototoxic drugs.

When you are warned not to take certain drugs at the same time as you are exposed to noise, you might think this is referring to just the days you are actually taking the drug therapy and maybe a few more days for the drug to leave you body. Surprise! Not true! You have to avoid noise for much, much longer.

When you take Aminoglycoside antibiotics or platinum anti-cancer drugs, such as **Cisplatin**, they are quickly transported to your inner ears. The problem is that, once there, they persist in your inner-ear fluids, not just for a few days, but in can be for several weeks to several months, and up to a year!

During this time, your ears are still susceptible to the synergistic effects of loud noise.[37] This means that if you have taken an Aminoglycoside antibiotic or **Cisplatin** and are now finished with this drug therapy, your ears are still in danger of even more hearing loss if you expose them to loud noise any time in the next few months or more, depending on your specific body chemistry. Heed this warning if you want to protect your ears from additional hearing loss!

Here is something else you should know as I don't think many audiologists are aware of this. If you are getting a hearing aid, instruct your audiologist to set the gain and maximum power output to a lower level than optimum in order to protect your ears during this critical time when your ears are still very sensitive to the effects of noise. If you already wear hearing aids, keep the volume down during this time.[38]

Avoiding noise is important, but even here the story is complicated. Research indicates that moderate amounts of noise may protect your ears from extreme amounts of noise. Therefore, you don't need to try to live in silence. Your ears need sound, just not too much sound!

Now for the Good News

Here's some good news. Research now shows that anti-oxidants help protect your ears from noise.[39]

For example, the glutamate receptor antagonist MK-801 appears to block the ototoxic effects of **Trimethyltin** in rats. The aim is for researchers to develop new drugs that can prevent or reverse ototoxicity caused by exposure to chemicals and drugs.

In the past, researchers have been working more or less randomly identifying those chemicals that are ototoxic. Now, however, they are beginning to understand the fundamental mechanisms of how these chemicals damage your ears. This should allow them to more effectively predict in the future which new chemicals and drugs are likely to be ototoxic, and to develop ways to protect your ears from damage due to such ototoxic agents.[40]

Here's some more good news. Researchers have recently discovered that antioxidants can help prevent noise-induced hearing loss. This may also work for drugs that cause hearing loss.

Here's how this works. When hair cells are overstressed by loud noise, free radicals—unstable oxygen atoms that are short an electron—are produced. The free radicals steal electrons from nearby molecules, like the hair cell's fatty walls. Enough of this thievery will kill the hair cell and with it more of your hearing.

Think of these free radicals as tiny enemy bullets. If they "zap" and fatally damage a cell, the cell goes into a process called **apoptosis**—in which it systematically shuts itself down and dies. If those cells are the hair cells in your inner ears, then you lose hearing when those hair cells die. Thus, it is important to zap the free radicals before they do their dastardly deeds.

The antioxidants are the "good guys". They act as tiny missiles that shoot down the free radicals before they can cause any damage.

Researchers have discovered that if enough powerful antioxidants are supplied before and/or shortly after noise exposure, these antioxidants in your inner ears can largely prevent much of the resulting noise damage that usually occurs.[41]

Glutathione is considered to be the most powerful natural antioxidant in your body. Your body makes this antioxidant naturally from compounds such as **N-acetyl-cysteine** and D-methionine which in turn. are made from three amino acids–cysteine, glycine and glutamic acid.

When your ears need extra help, taking **N-acetyl-cysteine** and D-methionine helps your body to quickly make more glutathione. You can buy both D-metin and **N-acetyl-cysteine** in health food stores or on-line.

Note that you don't want to overdose on **N-acetyl-cysteine**, as it can actually work against you and cause even more ear damage. I've seen figures that if you take more than 2,800 mg of **N-acetyl-cysteine** a day it can reverse its activity and become a pro-oxidant rather than the beneficial antioxidant. Your ears need some **N-acetyl-cysteine**, but too much can be dangerous.

In addition, researchers now know that the mineral **magnesium** plays an important part in hearing. Scientists have found that a magnesium deficiency increases susceptibility to noise damage. One of the things that happens is that a lack of magnesium causes the tiny blood vessels in your ears to constrict, thus depriving them of an adequate supply of oxygen. At the same time, loud noise depletes your ears of magnesium–so loud noise causes a double-whammy. There is evidence that high doses of **Magnesium** taken soon after a sudden hearing loss from loud noise can sometimes help restore hearing.[42]

There are other mechanisms by which we can also help protect our ears from the side effects of ototoxic drugs.

One person once asked me:

> I was wondering if you had an opinion on a drug called STS (sodium thiosulfate). It's being developed to protect chemotherapy patients taking platinum-based anti-cancer drugs from hearing loss. Is this (STS) something that could be more broadly applied to the numerous drugs that can cause ototoxicity?

I explained:

> The research looks promising so far. It's certainly possible that STS will help protect against hearing loss from **some** ototoxic drugs. Because different

ototoxic drugs have different mechanisms of damage, the trick is to find an "antidote" that interacts specifically with each ototoxic drug.

I think more likely, that there will be different drugs found to protect hearing against specific classes of ototoxic drugs. For example, sodium thiosulfate may work best for the platinum-based drugs such as **Cisplatin**, **Carboplatin** and **Oxaliplatin**.

For the AMINOGLYCOSIDE antibiotics, maybe iron chelators such as **Deferoxamine** will prove to be the ticket. Unlike how **Cisplatin** affects our ears, preliminary research indicates that AMINOGLYCOSIDES such as **Gentamicin** are only ototoxic when they react with iron found in the bloodstream. Thus, if this proves to be the case, iron chelators that "soak up" excess iron in the bloodstream may prove to be the route to go. Another possibility is **Aspirin** taken with **Gentamicin** to do the same job.

Unfortunately, few drugs are specifically studied to determine their ototoxic mechanisms. The notable exceptions are the platinum drugs and the AMINOGLYCOSIDE antibiotics. The rest mostly get the short end of the stick, so it may be a long time before anyone finds a specific antidote for them. However, in general, powerful antioxidants currently look like the most promising line of protection against ototoxicity.[43]

Chapter 11 Endnotes

1 Morata, 1994. pp. 359-366.
2 Morata, 1994. pp. 359-366.
3 Niall, 1998. p. 3.
4 Morata, 1994. pp. 359-366.
5 Rybak, 1992. p. 679.
6 Rybak, 1992. pp. 679-680.
7 Hain, 2001b. p. 6.
8 *Noise And Hearing Loss*, 1990. p. 8.
9 Hain, 2001a. p. 3.
10 Suter, 1991. p. 17.
11 Soh, 1999. p. 2.
12 Rosen, 2001. p. 5.
13 Carmen, 1999. p. 37.
14 Church, 2013. pp. 96-106.
15 Zawawi, 2016. pp. 383-388.
16 Cary, 1997. pp. 455-465.
17 WorkPro, 1999. p. 1.
18 Forge, 1999. p. 1250.
19 Morata, 1994. pp. 359-366.
20 Niall, 1998. p. 3.
21 Morata, 1994. pp. 359-366.
22 Rosen, 2001. p. 6.
23 Hain, 2001b. p. 6.
24 Bisesi, 1994. p. 4.

25 Rybak, 1992. p. 677.
26 Morata, 1994. pp. 359-366.
27 Rybak, 1992. p. 678.
28 Rybak, 1992. p. 680.
29 Rybak, 1992. p. 684.
30 Schaal, 2018. p. 9.
31 Schaal, 2018. p. 9.
32 Schaal, 2018. p. 9.
33 Schaal, 2018. pp. 9-10.
34 Schaal, 2018. p. 10.
35 Forge, 1999. p. 1250.
36 Morata, 1994. pp. 359-366.
37 Kalkanis, 2001. p. 2.
38 Kalkanis, 2001. pp. 8-9.
39 Hain, 2001b. p. 6.
40 Environmental Impact on Hearing: Is Anyone Listening, 1994. p. 4.
41 Shachtman, 2003. pp. 1-3.
42 Bauman, 2005. p. 1.
43 Bauman, 2009. p. 1.

Chapter 12

Aminoglycoside Antibiotics Are the Ototoxic "Bad Boys"

What Are Aminoglycosides?

The AMINOGLYCOSIDE antibiotics are probably the most ototoxic of all the classes of drugs. Taken as a whole, these drugs are the "bad boys" as far as your ears are concerned. Every doctor, nurse and pharmacist should know this well. Unfortunately, some either never learned this, don't believe it, or have forgotten it. As a result, your ears may have to pay the penalty.

Be wary of the AMINOGLYCOSIDES. They are "high-powered" antibiotics and are normally reserved for life and death situations, or for bacteria that just won't respond to other antibiotics.

There are a bunch of AMINOGLYCOSIDE antibiotics in existence and new ones are being produced all the time. Here in North America, some of the more common ones include **Amikacin**, **Gentamicin**, **Kanamycin**, **Neomycin** (**Fradiomycin**), **Netilmicin**, **Streptomycin** (**Dihydrostreptomycin**) and **Tobramycin**.

In Europe, Japan and the Far East, they use a number of others including **Arbekacin**++, **Astromicin**, **Betanamycin**++ (**Aminodeoxy-kanamycin**), **Capreomycin**, **Dibekacin**, **Framycetin**, **Hygromycin B**, **Isepamicin**, **Lividomycin**++, **Micronomicin**, **Paromomycin** (**Aminosidine**), **Ribostamycin**, **Sisomicin**, **Spectinomycin** and **Viomycin**.[1]

Some AMINOGLYCOSIDES like **Hygromycin** are just too dangerous and are not used on people.

Note: Drugs marked with a "++" do not have separate listings in this book simply because. I do not have any ototoxic information on these foreign AMINOGLYCOSIDES. Others have very sketchy listings. However, you can assume that they are all ototoxic, just like the other AMINOGLYCOSIDES for which I have information.

Before you take any AMINOGLYCOSIDES, both you and your doctor should carefully weigh the potential risks to your ears (and to other parts of your body) against the expected benefits you hope to obtain from taking one of these drugs. Depending on your situation, the risk of hearing loss may be largely insignificant compared to the situation you face. For example, if you have a life-threatening infection from a particularly virulent bacteria, an AMINOGLYCOSIDE may be your only option. Your choice may be simple—be deaf or be dead!

However, there are often alternatives that would allow you to continue with effective treatment while minimizing the risk to your ears. For example, you might ask your doctor to substitute another drug that is just as effective yet is not as ototoxic. You could ask him to try a less effective drug that has fewer ototoxic risks. You could also have your doctor adjust the dose to minimize the side effects to your ears. Finally, you could suggest he combine the AMINOGLYCOSIDE with another antibiotic that would reduce the overall dose of the AMINOGLYCOSIDE.[2] If you fail to consider these alternatives, or if you fail to optimize treatment based on them, you can greatly increase your risk of hearing loss and other damage to your ears.

In the past, some AMINOGLYCOSIDES such as **Streptomycin** had largely been replaced by less ototoxic drugs. Unfortunately, in recent years, AMINOGLYCOSIDE use has been increasing again. This is due to the increasing number of tuberculosis infections and because organisms resistant to other drugs are becoming more prevalent.[3]

What's the Damage?

One of the interesting things about AMINOGLYCOSIDE antibiotics is how some of them mainly damage the cochlear (hearing) system while others mainly attack the vestibular (balance) system. Of course, a few of them attack both systems equally. However, make no mistake about it, **all** the AMINOGLYCOSIDE antibiotics can damage **both** systems to a greater or lesser degree.

Those AMINOGLYCOSIDES that have a decided preference for attacking the cochlear system include **Amikacin**, **Dihydrostreptomycin**, **Kanamycin** and **Neomycin**.[4] Those that tend to mainly cause damage to the vestibular system include **Netilmicin** and **Streptomycin**. In contrast, **Gentamicin** and **Tobramycin** attack both systems equally, although **Gentamicin** tends more towards vestibular damage.[5, 6]

Here is something important that few people know about AMINOGLYCOSIDE antibiotics. When you take them, they head straight for your inner ear fluids—the endolymph and perilymph. They dive in there quickly and easily. The problem is that they persist in your inner ear fluids for a long time after they disappear from your bloodstream[7]—from several weeks to several months[8] and even up to a year. During all the time that AMINOGLYCOSIDES are present in your inner ear fluids, they can be damaging your ears. Also, during this time, your ears are especially susceptible to noise-induced hearing loss. (See Chapter 11 for more information on this.)

Since AMINOGLYCOSIDES persist in your ears for such a long time, hearing loss (and other ear damage) may occur any time up to a year after you stop taking them. As a result, even after you have detected a hearing loss, your hearing can continue to deteriorate for up to 12 months.[9] In extreme cases, AMINOGLYCOSIDE ototoxicity may not show up for many months or not until years later.[10]

However, don't get the idea that you always have to wait a long time for AMINOGLYCOSIDE damage to show up. There is a lot of variation. The first symptoms you experience may be sudden, or they may appear slowly during the time you are taking the AMINOGLYCOSIDE, or they may not even appear until sometime after you have stopped the treatment. Watch for any early symptoms of ototoxicity. One problem is that you may not recognize the early symptoms of ototoxicity, or you may not even be looking for them until it is too late. By then, you may have suffered irreversible ear damage.

Hearing loss from AMINOGLYCOSIDE damage begins at the base of the cochlea and progresses to the tip. Since the high-frequency hair cells are at the base of the cochlea and the low frequency ones are at the tip, hearing loss begins at the very high frequencies and progresses to the lower frequencies as the damage increases.

Damage also begins with the outer rows of hair cells and ultimately progresses to the row of inner hair cells. The inner row of the outer rows of hair cells is affected first, followed by the other two rows of outer hair cells. Finally, it affects the inner hair cells.[11]

One of the more insidious things about hearing loss due to AMINOGLYCOSIDE antibiotics is that because hearing loss begins in the very high frequencies, you don't notice it until it works its way down to the speech frequencies where it eventually becomes apparent. The problem is, testing high-frequency hearing loss needs specially calibrated audiometers to detect it as we saw in Chapter 9. Since audiologists currently only measure the speech frequencies, hearing loss can go totally unnoticed for a considerable period of time.[12] In fact, because of the insidious nature of these ototoxic effects and the minimal symptoms at first, significant hearing loss and vestibular dysfunction may occur before ototoxicity is even detected.

Therefore, if you have any warning symptoms, you need to immediately contact your doctor and stop taking the drug, if possible, before it is too late. Typically, ototoxic damage first manifests itself as high-pitched tinnitus. It then progresses to high-frequency hearing loss and vestibular problems. Early detection of these ototoxic side effects provides critical information that can allow your doctor to implement alternate treatment strategies in order to minimize the risk of further damage to your ears.[13]

If you are taking an Aminoglycoside antibiotic, you should receive a complete baseline audiometric evaluation consisting of the frequencies between 250 Hz and the highest frequency you can hear (or up to 20,000 Hz). Ideally, you should have your hearing tested at these same frequencies every 2 to 3 days during treatment in order to detect the first indications of hearing loss.[14]

After you stop taking an Aminoglycoside, you may continue to notice progressive hearing loss over the next several weeks and months. That is why audiometric testing, particularly in the high-frequency range, is so important. You need audiograms done before, during and for several months after taking any Aminoglycoside antibiotic.[15]

If you stop audiometric testing at the same time you stop taking an Aminoglycoside, you will miss any hearing loss that shows up later. In one study, 61% of the people tested showed initial hearing loss during or immediately after treatment. However, 78% showed change one month after treatment stopped.[16] Thus, if follow-up testing had not been done, doctors would have missed this 17% of delayed hearing loss.[17]

If you lose your hearing or balance from taking an Aminoglycoside, you probably want to know what chance you have of getting your hearing (and/or balance) back. If you recognized the early warning symptoms in time and stopped the drug treatment, your chances are much better. In these cases, the damage is typically not total. Therefore, your chances for improvement are about 10 to 15% depending on the drugs involved and your particular risk factors. The tinnitus normally goes away in a week or two.

However, if you are unlucky or the resulting damage is severe, there is little chance of recovery. Any damage is likely permanent.[18] However, rarely, recovery does occur, so don't completely give up hope.

How you take an Aminoglycoside is also important. Studies are now showing that giving the total daily dose at one time, rather than spreading it throughout the day, does not result in higher rates of ototoxicity. In fact, it may decrease the incidence.[19]

> **Overweight?**
>
> If you are overweight and are taking an AMINOGLYCOSIDE antibiotic, it is most important that your doctor calculates your dose based on your lean muscle mass, not on your total body weight including fat. Otherwise, you may receive an overdose that can cause severe permanent ototoxic damage.[1]
>
> **Reference**
>
> [1] Haybach, 1999. p. 50

Furthermore, if you are taking another ototoxic drug and an AMINOGLYCOSIDE at the same time, the **order** you take them is most important. Animal studies have shown that giving a LOOP DIURETIC followed by an AMINOGLYCOSIDE does not affect cochlear toxicity (hearing loss) any more than these drugs taken singly. However, reverse the order and wham—the two drugs act synergistically to really damage your ears.[20] So the secret is, never take an AMINOGLYCOSIDE antibiotic at the same time as other ototoxic drugs if you can avoid it. However, if you must take another ototoxic drug and an AMINOGLYCOSIDE, if possible, **take the other drug first**. Then, when you have completed that prescription, begin the AMINOGLYCOSIDE antibiotic. Your ears will thank you for doing this.

Genetics and Aminoglycoside Ototoxicity

Researchers have puzzled over why there is extreme variability in the resulting hearing loss from taking an AMINOGLYCOSIDE.[21] For example, some people can take an AMINOGLYCOSIDE with seeming impunity, while other people taking the same dose end up with severe hearing loss and/or no balance. Furthermore, studies have revealed that some families have a higher incidence of hearing loss than others.[22] This implicates genetics in any resulting AMINOGLYCOSIDE ototoxicity.

Researchers now know that you can inherit a genetic susceptibility to hearing loss via mitochondrial DNA. This is an example of the way medications and genes can interact.[23]

Mitochondria have their own genome. The genome is passed down from mother to child (maternal inheritance) and contains 37 genes, one of which is the MT-RNR1 gene (mitochondrially encoded 12S RNA).[24] The most common MT-RNR1 variant is a single nucleotide substitution of a guanine at position 1555 for an adenine (m.1555A>G).[25]

You are much more likely to have a resulting hearing loss from taking an AMINOGLYCOSIDE if you have this particular variant present.[26] Note that the prevalence of this m.1555A>G variant varies among different populations. For example, the prevalence of this m.1555A>G variant is thought to be 1 in 385 Caucasians.[27] Now, since 76% of Americans are Caucasians, that translates into about 654,000 Americans carrying this particular genetic variant and therefore if you fall into this group, you should probably never take AMINOGLYCOSIDE antibiotics if you want to preserve your hearing.

If you have this variant, you are likely to be very sensitive to AMINOGLYCOSIDE-induced hearing loss. This hearing loss typically will be moderate to profound, bilateral, irreversible, and have a rapid onset.[28]

Furthermore, if you have this variant, for some reason it appears that only your cochlea—but not your vestibular system—is the part of your inner ears that is extremely susceptible to AMINOGLYCOSIDES. In contrast, if you do not have this variant, then dose-dependent ototoxicity can occur after you take AMINOGLYCOSIDE therapy, but in this case, ototoxicity involves both your cochlear and vestibular systems.[29]

Another interesting thing about AMINOGLYCOSIDES is the relationship between the 12S rRNA gene and the resulting hearing loss caused by AMINOGLYCOSIDE antibiotics. Here is how it works. AMINOGLYCOSIDE antibiotics kill bacteria by interfering with the normal operation of certain proteins in the bacteria. Fortunately for us, these proteins are either unimportant or not present in humans. This is why AMINOGLYCOSIDES do not kill us.

However, the 1555A>G variant of the 12S rRNA gene changes this balance. The 1555A>G variant "looks" similar to a protein in the bacteria the AMINOGLYCOSIDE is targeting. When this variant is present in humans, an AMINOGLYCOSIDE can interfere with the function of this variant protein. For reasons still unknown, this leads to loss of hearing.[30]

For example, even a single injection of **Gentamicin** may cause hearing loss in people who have this m.1555A>G variant. Furthermore, in genetically-susceptible people this occurs—even in cases where drug levels remain within the therapeutic range.[31]

Note that this effect is distinct from "dose-dependent ototoxicity" (damage to the inner ear), which can affect any person, typically occurring after 5-7 days of AMINOGLYCOSIDE therapy.[32]

Incidentally, people carrying the 1555A>G variant are also more likely to develop hearing loss over time even if they never take AMINOGLYCOSIDE antibiotics.[33]

In the past, genetic testing for the MT-RNR1 gene was slow—taking up to 3 days for hospital laboratories to provide the results. This is much too long to wait if you have a septic condition requiring immediate treatment such as is the case with newborns.

Dr John McDermott, from the Manchester Centre for Genomic Medicine, Manchester, UK explains, "This is inadequate, considering that life-saving antibiotics need to be given in the first **hour** of admission."

In June 2018, together with another Manchester-based company, he developed a simple bedside test that uses a cheek swab that can produce results in around 40 minutes.[34] This permits tailored prescribing. The result? "We are thus able to avoid the antibiotic-related deafness that can occur in infants with this genetic mutation."[35]

As this new test protocol becomes widely available, all children admitted can be tested for this genetic variant and the antibiotics they are given can be tailored accordingly.[36]

According to Dr. McDermott, "This represents the first example of a point-of-care genetic test being used in the acute setting."[37] This can prevent a lot of babies with sepsis losing their hearing due to being prescribed **Gentamicin** or other Aminoglycoside antibiotics.

How Ototoxic Are the Aminoglycosides?

All the Aminoglycoside antibiotics can cause auditory (hearing loss) and vestibular (balance) toxicity. These symptoms occur more frequently in people with a present or past history of kidney impairment, in people treated with other ototoxic or nephrotoxic (kidney-damaging) drugs, and in people treated for longer periods and/or with higher doses than recommended.

Exactly how common is Aminoglycoside ototoxicity? According to one study, you have a 25% chance of incurring a hearing loss from taking any of the Aminoglycoside antibiotics.[38] However, these figures may be too low. This is because many people receiving Aminoglycosides are not tested for high-frequency hearing loss as we saw in Chapter 9.

Researchers estimate that between one and four million Americans receive Aminoglycoside antibiotics each year.[39] Thus, up to four million people each year are potentially at risk for hearing loss associated with taking Aminoglycosides.[40] Based on the above 25% incidence figure, between 250,000 and 1,000,000 people a year in the United States end up with hearing losses from taking these drugs. That is a staggering number of people with hearing loss! Many more millions are at potential risk of getting tinnitus and a whole host of balance problems related to taking Aminoglycoside antibiotics.

Other studies show that even this figure is much too low and is only the tip of the iceberg. One researcher reports that, depending on the specific AMINOGLYCOSIDE and the dose, one-third of the people taking an AMINOGLYCOSIDE antibiotic have a resulting hearing loss as confirmed by (conventional) audiometric testing.[41] This figure would be even higher if high-frequency audiometric testing was done.

According to research published in the Journal of Infectious Diseases in 1992, audiological monitoring revealed that aminoglycoside-induced ototoxicity occurred in up to 47% of people treated with an aminoglycoside.[42]

Another researcher reveals that a staggering percentage of the people taking AMINOGLYCOSIDE antibiotics experience ototoxic side effects.[43] For example, of 53 people treated with AMINOGLYCOSIDE antibiotics (4 with **Amikacin**, 47 with **Gentamicin** and 2 with **Tobramycin**), 63% had resulting ototoxic hearing loss.

Furthermore, as we saw in Chapter 9, it is critical to do high-frequency audiometric testing in order to know whether you are losing hearing due to taking an AMINOGLYCOSIDE. In one study of those with hearing loss, 62% revealed initial hearing loss in the high-frequency range, 29% showed initial hearing loss in the conventional frequencies, while 9% showed initial hearing loss in both frequency ranges at the same time.[44] This is why it is critical to have your hearing checked at the highest frequencies you can hear. When only the conventional frequencies are tested, most hearing loss (62%) is missed!

Here are some more shocking statistics from around the world. "Up to two-thirds of all cases of hearing loss in many parts of the developing world are caused by the indiscriminate use of AMINOGLYCOSIDE antibiotics such as **Streptomycin** and **Gentamicin**."[45] It is bad in Canada and the United States, but it is horrible in many third world countries.

Part of the problem is that in certain countries, antibiotics are prescribed freely, or are available without a prescription. In these areas, AMINOGLYCOSIDE antibiotics account for up to 66% of the deaf people found there.[46] According to Dr. Dinesh Kumar, deafness from ototoxic drugs is "becoming quite common in India" since many of the people there believe in self-medication. The drugs causing much of the hearing losses there include the AMINOGLYCOSIDE **Gentamicin**, and other ototoxic drugs such as **Erythromycin**, **Chloroquine** and **Furosemide**.[47]

In China, up to two-thirds of the cases of deafness may be caused by AMINOGLYCOSIDE antibiotics, which are frequently given to children for upper respiratory tract infections.[48] One study of hard of hearing children in China revealed that 80% (123 of the 154 studied) had lost their hearing from taking antibiotics. Of these 123 children, 60 (49%) of them had hearing problems due to taking **Gentamicin**.[49]

There are three prime reasons for this needless carnage. First, AMINOGLYCOSIDE antibiotics are relatively cheap. Second, people are ignorant of the devastating effects on these drugs on their ears. Third, far too many people have as their philosophy "a pill for every ill" and even worse, "for each infection, an injection".[50] Thus, sadly, millions of people around the world continue to needlessly lose their hearing from these drugs and few seem to know or care.

No matter what doctors may say to the contrary, using AMINOGLYCOSIDE eardrops to fight middle-ear infections is not without risk. Many doctors will tell you that there is no risk unless you have a hole in your eardrum. Even then, they don't seem to take the risk of hearing loss and other ototoxic effects seriously. This needs to change.

Bad things do indeed happen to our ears from taking eardrops. It must be much more common than the doctors think. For example, in one study, seven people with middle ear infections and eardrum "defects" were given AMINOGLYCOSIDE eardrops. Guess what? Surprise! **Every single one** ended up with ototoxic effects like hearing loss, tinnitus, vertigo, ataxia, and oscillopsia. In fact **all** were **severely** affected and some incapacitated![51] Does this sound harmless to you?

Wobble, Wobble, Wobble

When an AMINOGLYCOSIDE antibiotic attacks your balance system, it can turn your life upside down. Such occurrences are not as rare as you might be led to believe. You can read a number of tragic stories in the notes section under the generic drug **Gentamicin.** These are the stories of people who now wobble and stagger around instead of walking normally due to **Gentamicin** damaging their vestibular (balance) system.

Furthermore, these people were carefully monitored. What happens to the masses of people who are given eardrops and never closely monitored? Do the doctors just assume that there is no ototoxic damage? Bet they do—if they give it any thought at all—but they are wrong.

According to one researcher, the incidence and prevalence of ototoxicity may be higher than reported because of the difficulty in distinguishing between the natural course of the inner ear infections and the ototoxic drugs. Since hearing loss typically first occurs far above the speech frequencies, people don't notice this loss right away. At the same time, doctors often miss the vestibular toxicity or blame it on labyrinthitis. Since hearing loss and vestibular damage are generally permanent, both you and your doctor need to carefully monitor what is happening to your ears whenever you are taking ear drops.[52]

Neomycin, besides being used in ear drops, has proven to be ototoxic whether injected, taken orally or used externally on a wound. Yes, when just used for cleaning and sterilizing wounds, **Neomycin** has caused deafness in a number of people.[53]

When you are around Aminoglycosides remember, they are the ototoxic "bad boys" and you always need to treat them with respect.

Preventing Aminoglycoside Ototoxicity

There is some exciting news coming out concerning Aminoglycoside antibiotics. Researchers are studying iron chelators, antioxidants and gene therapy as possible ways of preventing hearing loss as a result of taking Aminoglycosides.[54]

Current research indicates that it is not the Aminoglycoside antibiotics themselves that destroy the hair cells in your hearing and balance systems. Rather, the by-products of these drugs cause free radicals to be formed. It is these free radicals that cause the ototoxicity. Here is how it works.

In 1995, Dr. Jochen Schacht and his colleagues discovered a surprising fact. **Gentamicin** is not ototoxic until it combines with iron in the bloodstream and becomes "activated". As **Gentamicin**-iron molecules form, they trigger production of free radicals—unstable molecules that rip apart and damage cells. Unfortunately, the thousands of tiny hair cells in the cochlea are particularly vulnerable to free radical attacks. When these hair cells are damaged or die, you don't hear. It's that simple.

To prevent the iron binding with the **Gentamicin**, Schacht decided to try iron chelators to "soak up" the excess iron in the bloodstream. The iron chelators he used were **Deferoxamine** (DFO) and 2,3-Dihydroxybenzoate (DHB). He also tried the antioxidant **Mannitol**.

In low doses, **Deferoxamine** helps to protect against this type of Aminoglycoside ototoxicity.[55] In addition, laboratory test animals injected with **Gentamicin** as well as Dihydroxybenzoate and **Mannitol** had complete protection at all measured hearing frequencies. Equally important, this treatment did not affect the antibiotic properties of **Gentamicin**. This is the good news. Now this needs to be tested on people to see if it will prevent hearing loss in humans like it did in the animal studies.[56]

The bad news is that this medical advance may never see the light of day. More research needs to be done to confirm preliminary studies, but funds are not forthcoming. Apparently, the big pharmaceutical companies do not want to invest their research dollars in "old" drugs whose patents have expired.[57]

Other researchers have recently discovered that **Acetylsalicylic acid** (**ASA** or **Aspirin**) is also a good chelator and thus may also help protect our ears from the damaging effects of taking Aminoglycoside antibiotics. **ASA** quickly breaks down in our bodies to produce Salicylate, a compound that soaks up any extra iron and thereby prevents the Aminoglycosides from forming free radicals.

Again, the results in animal studies are impressive. Guinea pigs receiving **Gentamicin** alone had severe hearing loss of up to 70 dB and almost complete destruction of the outer hair cells in the cochlea. In contrast, guinea pigs given both **Gentamicin** and **Aspirin** only had minor hearing loss of less than 20 dB and minimal hair-cell damage.[58] Current research is now determining if **Aspirin** affords the same protection in humans. Let's hope it does!

Still other researchers have discovered that when glial cell line-derived neurotrophic factor (GDNF) is present, it helps protect inner-ear hair cell degeneration from the effects of both loud noise and ototoxic drugs. This is good news for our ears. Now researchers are looking into whether GDNF can still provide this protection if given shortly after a person has taken an Aminoglycoside antibiotic. Preliminary results suggest that this is the case and hair cell destruction is not as great when GDNF is given following an ototoxic antibiotic.[59]

And if you want a totally natural solution, you could use garlic since among its other beneficial properties, garlic is also an antioxidant.

Researchers from Turkey tested garlic to see if it would reduce oxidative stress on laboratory rats that had ototoxic reactions to **Gentamicin**. They divided the rats into three groups. The first group was given **Gentamicin** only. The second group was given **Gentamicin** and garlic. The third group was the control group. After the 16-day trial, they tested the hearing of the rats using auditory brainstem response testing in response to sudden loud noise. The results of their research revealed that none of the rats in the **Gentamicin** only group had any response (they were now deaf), while the rats in the **Gentamicin** and garlic group had normal responses.

The researchers concluded that a garlic-supplemented diet holds promise in preventing or ameliorating Aminoglycoside antibiotic-induced hearing loss.[60] Therefore, if you have an infection that needs to be treated with **Gentamicin**, it seems wise to supplement your diet with sufficient garlic to preserve your hearing.

Perhaps the day will come when doctors will give an Aminoglycoside antidote at the same time they give the Aminoglycoside antibiotic. If that ever happens, one of the biggest ototoxic threats to our ears will have been eliminated!

Chapter 12 Endnotes

1 Antibiotics Index, 2001. p. 4.
2 Fausti, 1992. p. 1026.
3 Kalkanis, 2001. p. 2.
4 Kalkanis, 2001. p. 2.
5 Shlafer, 2000. p. 6.
6 Guidelines for the Audiologic Management of Individuals Receiving Cochleotoxic Drug Therapy, 1994. pp. 2-3.
7 Guidelines for the Audiologic Management of Individuals Receiving Cochleotoxic Drug Therapy, 1994. p. 3.
8 Kalkanis, 2001. p. 2.
9 Haybach, 1999. p. 35.
10 Oghalai, 1996. p. 1.
11 Lyos, 1992. p. 1.
12 Troost, 1998d. p. 3.
13 Fausti, 1992. p. 1026.
14 Fausti, 1992. p. 1030.
15 Shlafer, 2000. p. 7.
16 Fausti, 1992. p. 1030.
17 Shlafer, 2000. p. 7.
18 Troost, 1998b. p. 3.
19 Haybach, 1999. p. 50.
20 Troost, 1998a. p. 1.
21 Fausti, 1992. p. 1029.
22 Haybach, 1999. p. 44.
23 WebMDHealth, 2001. p.3.
24 Dean, 2015. p. 2.
25 Dean, 2015. p. 3.
26 WebMDHealth, 2001. p.2.
27 Dean, 2015. p. 3.
28 Dean, 2015. p. 3.
29 Dean, 2015. p. 3.
30 WebMDHealth, 2001. p.5.
31 Dean, 2015. p.1.
32 Dean, 2015. p. 1.
33 Snow & Wackym, 2008. p.276
34 New Rapid Genetic Test May Prevent Sepsis-Related Hearing Loss, 2018. p. 1.
35 New Rapid Genetic Test May Prevent Sepsis-Related Hearing Loss, 2018. p. 1.
36 New Rapid Genetic Test May Prevent Sepsis-Related Hearing Loss, 2018. p. 1.
37 New Rapid Genetic Test May Prevent Sepsis-Related Hearing Loss, 2018. p. 1.
38 Shlafer, 2000. p. 7.
39 Haybach, 1999. p. 19.
40 Guidelines for the Audiologic Management of Individuals Receiving Cochleotoxic Drug Therapy, 1994. p. 2.
41 Kalkanis, 2001. p. 2.
42 Steyger, 2012. p. 13.
43 Guidelines for the Audiologic Management of Individuals Receiving Cochleotoxic Drug Therapy, 1994. p. 4.
44 Fausti, 1992. p. 1028.
45 Abdulla, 1996. p. 648.
46 Kalkanis, 2001. p. 2.
47 Kumar, 1998. p. 1.
48 Priuska, 1997. p. 2.
49 Shearer, 1991. pp. 74-75.

50 Abdulla, 1996. p. 648.
51 Helal, 1997. pp. 1056-59.
52 Helal, 1997. pp. 1056-59.
53 Suss, 1993. p. 183.
54 Kalkanis, 2001. p. 3.
55 Priuska, 1997. p. 5.
56 Schacht, 1997. pp. 1-2.
57 Abdulla, 1996. p. 648.
58 Aspirin Component Prevents Antibiotic-induced Deafness, 1999. pp. 1-2.
59 Yagi, 1999. p. 1.
60 Keate, 2013. p. 1.

Chapter 13

Beware of the Benzodiazepines—Nasty Time Bombs

Another class of "nasty" ototoxic drugs is the BENZODIAZEPINES (pronounced ben-zoe-die-AZ-eh-peens). This class of drugs can blindside you with its nasty "time bomb". Hence you are typically better off never taking them in the first place. As Dr. Stephen Nagler explained:

> All things being equal (and they never are), in general, you are better off not taking BENZODIAZEPINES such as **Alprazolam** (*Xanax*) than taking them.[1]

The BENZODIAZEPINES are a class of drugs commonly known as tranquilizers and sleeping pills. They are predominantly prescribed for anything associated with anxiety or sleeping problems.

As a class of drugs, the BENZODIAZEPINES are moderately ototoxic, and thousands upon thousands of people have experienced ototoxic side effects from taking them.

The BENZODIAZEPINES are "nasty" drugs because they are dependence-forming. As a result, any ototoxic side effects they may cause—including hearing loss, tinnitus, hyperacusis and balance problems—are very difficult to bring under control once they get started.

There are at least 30 different BENZODIAZEPINES and BENZODIAZEPINE derivatives (see Section 60.12.8 in Table 19-1). Their generic names (with four exceptions) either end in "lam" or "pam" so that's an easy way to identify them.

Some of the more common BENZODIAZEPINES used as anti-anxiety medications are **Alprazolam** (*Xanax*), **Clonazepam** (*Klonopin & Rivotril*), **Diazepam** (*Valium*), **Lorazepam** (*Ativan*) and **Triazolam** (*Halcion*). These drugs are quick-acting and may be beneficial (to some degree) on a very **short-term** basis (two weeks or less) for acute anxiety.[2]

In addition to the BENZODIAZEPINES, there are three other drugs that, although not BENZODIAZEPINES, have similar effects including the same horrible dependence and withdrawal problems. They are **Zaleplon** (*Sonata*), **Zolpidem** (*Ambien*) and **Zopiclone** (*Imovane*). Thus, what I say about the BENZODIAZEPINES largely applies to these three drugs too.

How Benzodiazepine Dependence All Begins

When people go to their doctors with problems sleeping or feeling anxious, and are prescribed one of the BENZODIAZEPINES, the last thing on their minds is that weeks, months or years later they will find themselves "hooked" on a horror drug.

BENZODIAZEPINES are only meant to be taken for short periods of time. They are **temporary** solutions to problems such as severe anxiety and sleeplessness. Used responsibly and taken in the short term to tide you over a rough spot, BENZODIAZEPINES sometimes can do some good. Relatively safe and appropriate use of BENZODIAZEPINES is for **no longer** than 2 weeks or so if taken daily.[3]

However, so often people abuse these drugs. They were **never** meant to be long-term solutions to these problems. Unfortunately, doctors allow multitudes of people to stay on these drugs for months, and in many cases, years. For example, according to one estimate, one person in every 50 people has been taking a BENZODIAZEPINE **for longer than 6 months**![4]

When you stay on a BENZODIAZEPINE for too long, the less good they do you. Eventually, bad things begin to happen. For example, the longer you take a BENZODIAZEPINE, the less effective it becomes and your anxiety starts getting worse. For problems sleeping, BENZODIAZEPINES are only effective for about 1 to 2 weeks. When your symptoms begin to get worse, doctors typically increase your dose. This works for a few more weeks, then the nastiness begins and you begin to feel worse and worse.[5] Then, when you try to taper off them, you anxiety gets worse yet.

This is because if you take BENZODIAZEPINES for longer periods of time, not only does the drug become less and less effective, but it also induces drug dependency. When this happens, your body comes to depend on the drug to function. Thus, you are "hooked" much as a person becomes addicted to certain drugs. (Note that technically, BENZODIAZEPINES cause dependency, not addiction, but the end result is similar.)

Thus, in order to prevent either psychological or physiological dependence, only take Benzodiazepines if you do **not** have a history of substance abuse, and only in the short term (two weeks or less).

Research indicates that 30% to 50% of regular Benzodiazepine users will develop a dependency to these drugs. I can't emphasize this enough—the longer you take a Benzodiazepine, the greater your risk is of becoming dependent on that drug.[6]

Benzodiazepine "Addiction" Warning

"The biggest drug-addiction problem in the world doesn't involve heroin, cocaine or marijuana. In fact, it doesn't involve an illegal drug at all. The world's biggest drug-addiction problem is posed by a group of drugs, the Benzodiazepines, which are widely prescribed by doctors and taken by countless millions of perfectly ordinary people around the world."

"Drug-addiction experts claim that getting people off the Benzodiazepines is more difficult than getting addicts off heroin. The only genuine long-term solution is to be aware of these drugs and to avoid them like the plague."

"It seems that the dependency is so ingrained, and the withdrawal symptoms you get are so intolerable, that people have a great deal of problem coming off Benzodiazepines. The other aspect is that with heroin, usually the withdrawal is over within a week or so. With Benzodiazepines, a proportion of patients go on to long term withdrawal. These people have very unpleasant symptoms month after month, and this can go on for two years or more. Some of the tranquilizer groups document people who still have symptoms ten years after stopping."[1]

Reference

[1] Benzodiazepine Addiction, Withdrawal & Recovery, 2006.

Dependence makes it very difficult to get off Benzodiazepines. In fact, researchers estimate that between 50% and 80% of the people who have taken Benzodiazepines continually for 6 months or longer will experience withdrawal symptoms when reducing the dose or stopping completely.[7] Therefore, you need to exercise extreme caution if you are considering taking Benzodiazepines.

Here's What It's Like When You Are in the Grip of Benzodiazepines

After you have been on Benzodiazepines for some weeks or months, you become dependent on this psychotropic drug. This is when things can become really nasty and can make your original symptoms worse. For example, if you are taking

BENZODIAZEPINES for insomnia, eventually they can make your sleep problems even **worse** than they were before you began taking these drugs.

The same thing happens with anxiety. Initially, the BENZODIAZEPINES help you, but if you continue to take them for extended periods, the resulting physical dependency typically **increases** your anxiety—even while taking the same dose![8]

You continue to feel worse and worse, yet increasing the dose no longer helps. Your ears may begin to experience a number of cochlear side effects such as hearing loss, auditory hallucinations, hyperacusis and tinnitus. Add to these the side effects that affect your vestibular (balance) system such as dizziness, ataxia, loss of balance, vertigo and nystagmus.

In addition to messing up your ears, taking BENZODIAZEPINES can cause a number of other scary side effects such as anxiety, fears, feelings of unreality, hypersensitivity to light, insomnia, lack of concentration, loss of memory, nightmares, panic attacks, rapid mood changes, shaking, sweating, depersonalization (a feeling of not knowing who you are), outbursts of rage or aggression, paranoia, persistent unpleasant memories, feeling of pins and needles, rapid changes in body temperature, blackouts and a host of other symptoms. Ultimately, you no longer feel like yourself. You determine to get off the drug, but that makes you feel even worse, if that were possible.

When I mentioned to one lady that she likely would be shocked to learn that almost all of her symptoms, both ear-related and otherwise, were known side effects of taking the BENZODIAZEPINES she replied, "I'm scared. Everything you have said about the drugs I take really hit home".

Thus, again I can't stress this enough—BENZODIAZEPINES and similar drugs are not for long-term use. If you use them long-term be prepared for nasty problems to arise. For example, one man cautioned:

> **Alprazolam** (*Xanax*) [one of the more commonly-prescribed BENZODIAZEPINES] is a really dangerous drug, physically and mentally. My wife lost hearing permanently while on it, and I lost my wife permanently while she was on it. I would rank it on a par with heroin and crack, and worse than coke. Do not use it!

To be sure, some people seem to be able to take BENZODIAZEPINES with seeming impunity, however many people have such bad experiences they sincerely wish they had never taken the first pill. Here is one such example. A lady explained:

> About 15 years ago I started having panic attacks and began taking **Alprazolam** (*Xanax*) at 1.5 mg/day and have been on it ever since. Two years ago I had some really bad panic attacks so my doctor doubled my *Xanax* medication to 3 mg/day.

> Now everything is out of control for some reason. In the past year or two, in spite of the increased dose, things have been getting much worse to the point I don't feel normal any more.
>
> My hearing is a lot worse, I have vertigo and balance problems. I feel unsteady on my feet. My ears are ringing. They are also supersensitive to sounds [loudness hyperacusis]. As a result, I can't wear a hearing aid in one ear anymore.
>
> I feel like I am only 50% here—kind of like a bad head cold feeling or living in a dream state. I feel shaky and out of sorts and panicky. I feel weird and feel like I am going to pass out. I can be fine one minute, then bam—all of a sudden, I feel this odd feeling coming on as if my hearing gets very quiet. I feel as if I am chilled. I get a tingly feeling in my head, and then I feel a sort of darkness and closed-in feeling about to happen. I start to shake and sweat, and I just feel as if I am drifting away.
>
> I have always thought that my medications could be hurting me more than helping me. Why did the doctor do this to me? My neurologist feels I won't be able to stop taking the *Xanax* as my body is now dependent on it. If I would go off this drug, he feels I would spin out of control—but I'm already out of control!
>
> For some time I have wanted to try to taper down, or get off the *Xanax*, but I am scared I will feel worse. How am I going to live my life without the *Xanax*? I want to be able to get through the day, but not like this! I would love to be **free** and be **me** again!

Unfortunately, this lady is not alone. I have heard numbers of similar stories from people who have been taking Benzodiazepines for a number of months or years. Eventually, like this lady, they finally decide the Benzodiazepines (and SSRIs) aren't doing them any good, and indeed are causing them much more harm than good. At this point they try to go off them. Yet when they try to go off them, the nasty time-bomb hidden in these drugs ambushes their ears.

When you reach this point, the range and severity of the resulting withdrawal side effects will likely take you by surprise. This is when you discover to your horror that when you try to go off them, your existing symptoms intensify and still other side effects appear.

Some people, for example, get hyperacusis when they try to go off Benzodiazepines. In one study of 22 people, 4 (18%) had hyperacusis. Fortunately, by 3 months, only 1 person of the 4 still had hyperacusis.[9]

Other people end up with protracted tinnitus when they try to go off a Benzodiazepine. For example, one man who had taken **Diazepam** for 8 years for anxiety, got obnoxious tinnitus just 4 days after discontinuing **Diazepam**. His tinnitus persisted for 3 months. Fortunately, after 6 months, his tinnitus was only occasional and of short duration, and by 1 year it had completely disappeared.[10]

Another man began to hear high-pitched ringing tinnitus in both his ears for the first time in his life as he reduced his **Diazepam** dose to a low level. Unfortunately, in his case, he still had tinnitus 1 year later, but was learning to cope with it.

The withdrawal side effects can be so incapacitating that some people choose to stay on these drugs because they cannot cope with the horrible side effects they experience when they try to stop taking BENZODIAZEPINES (or SSRIs for that matter—see the next chapter). By doing so, they condemn themselves to a miserable existence for the rest of their lives.

For example, one man, after taking **Diazepam** for 12 years for anxiety had severe tinnitus upon discontinuing **Diazepam**. In his case, he discovered he couldn't stop taking the **Diazepam** because of his incapacitating high-pitched intense tinnitus in both his ears which began each time he reduced his dose of **Diazepam**.[11] Like him, you may find the intensity of psychotropic drug withdrawal is overwhelming—it flips your life upside down and leaves you worried about your ability to function in the future.

Some Other Nasty Side Effects of Taking Benzodiazepines

According to psychiatrist Dr. Amen, taking BENZODIAZEPINES have a number of drawbacks. Brain SPECT imaging studies show that "benzos" reduce overall blood flow and activity in your brain and are harmful to your brain function. They can cause memory problems, daytime drowsiness, confusion and addiction. In short, they mess up your brain. This is in addition to your experiencing severe withdrawal syndrome if you abruptly discontinue taking a benzo.[12]

Dependence/Withdrawal Hell

If you take BENZODIAZEPINES for longer than two weeks or so, you risk becoming dependent on them, but side effects can show up even sooner, so beware. You may discover that BENZODIAZEPINES can be very "addicting" when you try to **go off** them after taking them for a period of time. You may find yourself dealing with some horrible side effects—the very conditions you often were trying to eliminate in the first place.[13] This can be **really** tough to deal with. One person with this problem wrote,

> I am currently in BENZODIAZEPINE withdrawal hell, which, for me, includes **extreme tinnitus** and other symptoms.

According to Dr. Nagler, the challenge of coming off BENZODIAZEPINES lies in the fact that your anxiety level is apt to increase considerably as you try to come off BENZODIAZEPINES such as **Alprazolam** (*Xanax*).[14] It's ironic that trying to get off these drugs can greatly increase your anxiety so that it is much worse than it was before you started taking the medication.

This is because 1) the drug tends to be habit-forming; 2) the drug tamps down your emotions, so you don't feel as anxious (or feel anything else for that matter); and 3) the drug decreases your distress from conditions such as tinnitus without effectively addressing the underlying cause of the distress so it surfaces with a vengeance when you try to go off the drug.[15]

Can't Habituate to Tinnitus

A number of people get hooked on BENZODIAZEPINES because their tinnitus is driving them buggy. They are then blindsided when they not only discover that the BENZODIAZEPINES do not fundamentally help their tinnitus, but that they do the opposite. Not only that, but they now find it difficult or impossible to habituate to their tinnitus. This is another nasty result of taking any benzos.[16] As Dr. Jastreboff explains:

> The neural plasticity of the brain is essential in the habituation process. In my experience, doses of **Alprazolam** (*Xanax*) greater than 1.5 mg per day basically block the habituation process, thus preventing successful outcome of the treatment. Moreover, withdrawal from BENZODIAZEPINES may increase or even create the tinnitus perception. Therefore, while it is possible to achieve habituation over a longer period of time when patients are on relatively small doses of BENZODIAZEPINES, larger doses of BENZODIAZEPINES prevent habituation from occurring.[17]

Thus, if you suffer from tinnitus and take large doses of BENZODIAZEPINES, you are just shooting yourself in the foot because you are making it almost impossible to habituate to your tinnitus. Furthermore, since BENZODIAZEPINES reduce the plasticity of your brain, this makes it very difficult for your brain to change and undo the tinnitus connections it has already made.[18]

Dr. Jastreboff further explains:

> A third of my patients take BENZODIAZEPINES, because 70% of patients who suffer from tinnitus have sleep problems, and ENT doctors prescribe them as if they were sleeping pills.
>
> When patients are on doses of 1 to 1.5 mg per day, I try to convince them to stop taking them altogether in the second phase of Tinnitus Retraining Therapy. But if they take 2 mg or more, I know it is very difficult for TRT to work.[19]

The Benzodiazepines Are Also Killers

Not only are the BENZODIAZEPINES nasty, but they are also killers. If I asked you which side effect was most commonly reported to the Food and Drug Administration (FDA) in the USA for many of the BENZODIAZEPINE class of drugs, what would you answer? I'll give you a clue—it's not related to ears, yet it makes your ears totally stop working. Sounds serious, doesn't it?

Well, it is. You see, the shocking truth is that the most commonly-reported side effect to the FDA of seven of the BENZODIAZEPINES is death (completed suicide)! Another six BENZODIAZEPINES list attempted suicide as the 1st, 2nd or 3rd most commonly- reported side effect. In addition, another three BENZODIAZEPINES list drug overdose (which is another way of saying "attempted suicide" as the 1st or 2nd most common side effect reported to the FDA.

You don't find this kind of information in all the "sanitized" drug books published including the Physicians' Desk Reference (PDR). However, if you go to the website that reports what real people report to the FDA as side effects they've experienced (or that of a loved one in the case of suicide/death), you'll see a much different story. I used the DrugCite website (http://www.drugcite.com) to get the above statistics. (Unfortunately, this website no longer works to give this information, effectively hiding this important information.)

What you can take away from all this is that the drugs you are taking for one problem or other can mess up your head so much that they can cause you to take, or attempt to take, your own life. Furthermore, many of the people involved in mass shootings in the USA had been taking drugs such as the BENZODIAZEPINES or the SELECTIVE SEROTONIN REUPTAKE INHIBITORS (see the next chapter) before they went on their killing sprees.

This is why you always need to do your own "due diligence" and satisfy yourself that the potential good a given drug can do is not far outweighed by the bad it actually does. Therefore, beware of the BENZODIAZEPINES.

Chapter 13 Endnotes

1 Nagler, 2018b. p. 24.
2 Amen, 2020. p. 1.
3 About Benzodiazepines, 2005. p. 5.
4 About Benzodiazepines, 2005. p. 3.
5 About Benzodiazepines, 2005. p. 4.
6 About Benzodiazepines, 2005. p. 6.
7 About Benzodiazepines, 2005. p. 7.
8 About Benzodiazepines, 2005. p. 4.

9 Busto, 1988. p. 4.
10 Busto, 1988. p. 3.
11 Busto, 1988. p. 3.
12 Amen, 2020. p. 1.
13 Busto, 1988. p. 1.
14 Nagler, 2018b. p. 24.
15 Nagler, 2018b. p. 24.
16 Bauman, 2022. p. 570.
17 Robb, 2015. p. 17.
18 "'We Cannot Do Anything About Your Tinnitus.' This Is Simply Not True", 2016. p. 6.
19 "'We Cannot Do Anything About Your Tinnitus.' This Is Simply Not True", 2016. p. 6.

Chapter 14

Selective Serotonin Reuptake Inhibitors (SSRIs)—Also Nasty Drugs

The SELECTIVE SEROTONIN REUPTAKE INHIBITORS (SSRIs) and their close cousins, the SELECTIVE SEROTONIN & NOREPINEPHRINE REUPTAKE INHIBITORS (SSNRIs) have nasty side effects that can also blindside you, just like the BENZODIAZEPINES can. Furthermore, given the right conditions, they also can be killers. As one doctor explained, "The SSRI antidepressants are some of the most harmful medications on the market, but also some of the most profitable."[1] That is why the drug companies push their use.

SELECTIVE SEROTONIN REUPTAKE INHIBITORS include such drugs as **Citalopram** (*Celexa*), **Escitalopram** (*Lexapro*), **Fluoxetine** (*Prozac*), **Fluvoxamine** (*Luvox*), **Paroxetine** (*Paxil*), **Sertraline** (*Zoloft*), **Vilazodone** (*Viibryd*) and **Zimeldine** (*Zelmid*).

SELECTIVE SEROTONIN & NOREPINEPHRINE REUPTAKE INHIBITORS include drugs such as **Desvenlafaxine** (*Pristiq*), **Duloxetine** (*Cymbalta*), **Milnacipran** (*Savella*) and **Venlafaxine** (*Effexor*).

You have likely heard that serotonin—also known as 5-hydroxytryptamine or 5-HT—is the "happiness hormone" and that these antidepressant drugs supposedly attempt to alleviate symptoms of depression and anxiety by increasing the level of serotonin in your brain.

It is common knowledge that if you are depressed, you are low on serotonin. That is why depression is routinely treated with selective serotonin reuptake inhibitors (SSRIs) that raise serotonin levels in your brain.

However, this is just the opposite of the truth. The truth is that serotonin is **not** responsible for depression, and that raising your serotonin levels is the last thing you want to do.[2] In reality, high levels of serotonin mess up your brain, not low levels. However, the drug industry has a strong incentive to suppress any information saying otherwise since most antidepressants on the market today capitalize on this idea that low serotonin in your brain is responsible for depression.[3]

According to one knowledgeable doctor:

> When SSRIs were discovered, the industry created the mythology that they worked by fixing a serotonin deficiency in the brain. As the years went by, that was gradually disproven.[4]

Even so, this myth continues to be perpetuated by the drug companies and the press, most likely due to an attempt to preserve the status of serotonin as the "happiness hormone,", and no doubt as well as to delay/prevent the avalanche of lawsuits from all the people that have been hurt from taking SSRIs.[5]

Originally, pharmaceutical companies developed the class of antidepressant drugs known as SELECTIVE SEROTONIN REUPTAKE INHIBITORS (SSRIs) to treat depression, anxiety, and other mood disorders.[6,7] This is because serotonin seems to have a positive effect on mood, and because low levels of serotonin are thought to be central to feelings of depression.

Now researchers have concluded that SSRIs work:

> ...by rewiring your brain (which is why psychiatrists tell you to keep taking an SSRI even if it doesn't initially work as they want a few weeks for that "beneficial" rewiring to take place).[8]

A recent study found that it is **not** low levels of serotonin, but low levels of the serotonin transporter (SERT) that makes all the difference. (Be careful not to confuse serotonin with SERT.) In simple terms, the study discovered that having low levels of SERT is linked to problems with memory and thinking skills.[9] This is because low SERT levels lead to having too much serotonin hanging around where it shouldn't be, and that's what's deteriorating brain health.

Here's why. SERT is like a "clean-up crew" in your brain. It helps **remove** excess serotonin, which is a chemical messenger in your brain. When there's not enough SERT around to do its job, serotonin levels outside of your brain cells can rise too high. It is this excess serotonin floating around that causes all the trouble.[10]

Serotonin's job is to help ensure that cellular resources are used efficiently during times of stress without causing long-term harm to your body. However, when vital enzymes involved in cellular metabolism are persistently suppressed, it prompts your body to conserve energy by scaling back on non-critical physiological functions such as mood-related processes.

Thus, contrary to popular belief, elevated serotonin levels can have devastating psychological effects, including depression.[11]

Multiple studies have demonstrated that serotonin is basically a lobotomizing chemical when it comes to emotions. It doesn't make you feel happy. In fact, it doesn't make you feel anything. So yes, it will numb your depression, but at the same time, it will also numb your other emotions.[12]

Did you know that various studies, even a court case, recently agreed that serotonin destroys empathy, love and wisdom. This is because the role of serotonin is probably for numbing pain when you're under stress. It turns off your pain reaction, even your grief reaction, but at the expense of turning off your other (positive) emotions as well.[13]

Considering these adverse effects, you'd be wise to keep your serotonin level as low as possible. One way to do that is by increasing your levels of Gamma-Aminobutyric Acid (GABA), which is available as a supplement. Since GABA increases the breakdown of serotonin, you cannot have high levels of both.[14] Thus, people who have high GABA levels usually have low serotonin levels and vice-versa.

As a result, "GABA is a more effective solution for conditions typically treated with SSRIs, such as depression and anxiety, without the adverse effects associated with elevated serotonin."[15]

The result? People with high levels of GABA and low levels of serotonin are typically calm and gregarious, whereas those with high levels of serotonin and low levels of GABA typically exhibit anxiety, fear, depression, short temper, phobias, impulsiveness and disorganization.[16]

Here's some more good news. GABA is readily available at health food stores and on-line. You do not need a prescription to get it. But because it is inexpensive, the drug companies want you to take their high-priced SSRI drugs, not the inexpensive GABA.

Furthermore, you need to understand that anti-depressant drugs are a fickle lot. You take a drug to fix one problem such as depression—only to find it causes another, and often worse, problem such as severe tinnitus.

Doctors often prescribe Selective serotonin reuptake inhibitors as an off label use for treating people with tinnitus. The idea is that the SSRI will reduce your depression and thus make your tinnitus less noticeable. Consequently, many people take SSRIs and temporarily find these drugs give them some degree of help for their tinnitus because it numbs their emotions, so their tinnitus doesn't bother them as much.

This help does not last, however. This is where the fickleness of such drugs comes into play. A recent study revealed that taking SSRIs can be a two-edged sword—instead of working to ease symptoms of depression and thus making things better, they can (and do) eventually make tinnitus worse.[17]

Note that SSRIs do not (and cannot) create serotonin, as many people believe. Rather, the way this class of drugs works is that they prevent the reuptake of serotonin (essentially preventing the serotonin from being recycled) so it remains active in the synapses between neurons longer than it otherwise would.[18] This is why, doctors prescribe one of these drugs in an effort to improve the mood of the person and reduce the level of their depression.

Reducing the depression people experience typically has a seemingly beneficial effect on their tinnitus. For example, one man took **Sertraline** and found a resultant 40% reduction in the perceived level of his tinnitus.[19] That's the good news.

However, the other side of the coin is that every one of the above-mentioned drugs can cause tinnitus (and other) ototoxic side effects. Thus, for many people with depression, this increased level of serotonin affects their tinnitus alright—but in a negative way. They are often blindsided by the resulting severe tinnitus they experience from taking these antidepressants, and as a result, their anxiety and depression increases, not decreases.

This is why if you have depression, taking SSRI drugs can lead to your depression becoming even more of a recurring condition and thus make your condition worse.[20] Researcher Zheng-Quan Tang, Ph.D., noted that:

> ... a review of existing scientific literature indicated that many patients reported an **increase** in tinnitus soon after they began taking SSRIs.[21]

Obviously, you don't want this to happen, but it occurs more than you might think. For example, over the past number of years, I've received more anecdotal reports of tinnitus resulting from taking the SSRI drug **Citalopram** (*Celexa*) than for any other drug.

Numerous people get tinnitus from taking this drug and numbers of people are left in worse condition than they were before they started taking the drug. Here are some of their real-life stories. As "Rick" explained:

> The irony is that the **Citalopram** I was taking for stress has caused me to have tinnitus which is now triggering **more** stress than was there before I started the drug.

In a similar manner, "Ben" explained:

> This is so ironic. I started on **Citalopram** to reduce my depression and now I'm depressed over the side effects of using it.

"Josh" lamented:

> Because of my physical limitations, my depression is terrible. I started taking **Citalopram** but stopped 17 days later because of severe ringing and hissing in both my ears—actually through my whole head. It's unbearable. My depression is only more-so now.

And finally, "Cindy" observed:

> I took **Citalopram** 20 mg for 2 days and my very mild tinnitus became much worse. Now it is two months later, and it has still not improved, and I am **very** depressed.[22]

Did you get that? Notice that taking these SSRIs **caused** depression or made existing tinnitus **worse**! Therefore, if you are being treated for depression, especially if you also have hearing loss or tinnitus, you need to be extra careful about taking a drug that compounds your feelings of anxiety. Be aware that SSRIs (or other psychotropic drugs) you are taking can cause or exacerbate the very condition you're trying to fix![23] A man explained:

> My doctor prescribed **Citalopram** 20 mg to help my irritable bowel syndrome. After 11 days, my ears started ringing. It began in my right ear which sounded like water rushing through a pipe, then my left and then became a constant, high-pitched squeal—every minute of every day. No warning of this side effect from my doctor. To be honest, **this is so much worse than the problem the pills were prescribed for**. Tapered down to 10 mg and now been off them for 8 days. Ringing is just as bad as when it started.

Medical researchers at the Oregon Health and Science University recently discovered why these SSRI antidepressants can make tinnitus so much worse. Their study focused on serotonin, otherwise known as 5-HT, an important brain neuromodulator[24] and the dorsal cochlear nucleus (DCN), a part of your brain where auditory and multisensory integration and tinnitus occur. They discovered that fusiform neurons in your DCN become **hyperactive** and **hypersensitive** to sound when exposed to serotonin.[25]

In short, "the activity of the affected neurons went through the roof", according to Laurence Trussell, Ph.D. Therefore, based on the results of this and other studies, the rise in serotonin that occurs when you take SSRIs apparently makes your tinnitus (and loudness hyperacusis) worse.[26]

That's not the only thing that taking SSRIs upsets. Since SSRI drugs block the normal uptake of serotonin, with long-term use of SSRIs, your brain is fooled into thinking that there is plenty of serotonin available.[27] Your brain's response is to dramatically decrease serotonin synthesis. One study on rat brains revealed that SSRI drugs reduced serotonin levels by an average of 60%.[28]

What this means is that without realizing it, you are hooked on such drugs. Then, when you try to stop taking these medications, you can have serious withdrawal problems. Consequently, many people who use SSRI antidepressants for a number of years are completely unable to stop using them and thus, are effectively sentenced to antidepressant use for the rest of their lives.[29] This makes the drug companies happy since these drugs are some of the most widely used, and thus profitable, medications on the market today.[30] It's just you and others like you that are left to suffer.

When you think of getting hooked on drugs you probably immediately think of narcotics where you become addicted to them. But there are other classes of drugs, and the SELECTIVE SEROTONIN REUPTAKE INHIBITORS (SSRIs) are one of these classes of drugs, that, while you do not become addicted to them, you build up a physical dependence to them. Thus, it becomes very hard to get off them as we just saw. In fact, depending on your make-up, it can be harder to get off such commonly-prescribed drugs as the SSRIs and BENZODIAZEPINES than it is to get off narcotics.

Building up dependence to psychotropic drugs is insidious. It sneaks up on you without your even being aware of it—often until it is too late. This is why you want to be very careful when taking drugs that can cause dependence.

It is often the better part of valor not to take them in the first place, then you won't have to worry about becoming hooked on them. This will save you from the horrible side effects they can have on your body and mind, and the even worse withdrawal side effects, when you finally decide to get off them. This is particularly true of the ANTIDEPRESSANT classes of drugs of which the SSRIs are one.

For example, a study in 2022 found that ANTIDEPRESSANTS caused more reports of withdrawal symptoms than any other drugs in the study. Overall, ANTIDEPRESSANTS, and particularly those classified as SSRIs, were more likely to cause withdrawal symptoms than all other classes of drugs.[31]

The ANTIDEPRESSANTS that are disproportionately associated with more reports of withdrawal side effects than others include the SSRI **Paroxetine** (*Paxil*) and the SELECTIVE SEROTONIN NOREPINEPHRINE REUPTAKE INHIBITORS SSNRIs **Duloxetine** (*Cymbalta*), **Venlafaxine** (*Effexor*) and **Desvenlafaxine** (*Pristiq*).[32] Based on my experience, I'd add the SSRI **Citalopram** (*Celexa*) to this list as well.

Furthermore, it is well-known in the SSRI recovery community that the risk of experiencing withdrawal varies greatly depending on the particular drug. For example, **Paroxetine** (*Paxil*) is notorious for this. **Duloxetine** (*Cymbalta*) is also a common offender).[33]

Experiencing withdrawal side effects is very common. A recent meta-analysis found that 56% of patients who stop using SSRIs experience withdrawals, that 46% who discontinue an SSRI experience severe withdrawals, and that these withdrawals last for weeks to months.[34]

When you stop taking such drugs, withdrawal/discontinuation side effects can cause a range of symptoms such as dizziness, nausea, frequent electrical brain "zaps", paresthesia (tingling sensations), headaches, anxiety, feeling abnormal, suicidal thoughts, insomnia and depression.[35]

Unfortunately, when people suffer such SSRI withdrawal side effects, doctors typically interpret it as a relapse and a sign that the withdrawn medication had been "working" (hence the person needs to continue taking the drug) and they increase the dose. To be fair, some doctors do recognize the above symptoms are, in fact, withdrawal side effects, but only know to "treat" it by resuming the offending drug.[36]

Regrettably, there are no predictors for who will likely suffer severe withdrawal, and who will just have a mild withdrawal experience.[37] As one doctor lamented:

> For the roughly 50% of people who experience SSRI withdrawals, one of the most challenging things is how incredibly slowly they have to stop taking them.[38] Very few people appreciate just how difficult it can be to get off an SSRI (even after only a brief course of the drugs), or that there is absolutely no support within the conventional medical field for people wishing to get off these drugs. This is particularly tragic because many of the SSRI suicides and murders are preceded by someone having their SSRI dose changed (e.g., increased, decreased or changed to a different medication).[39]

Withdrawal side effects are more common if you have been taking ANTIDEPRESSANTS for longer than 4 to 6 weeks and then abruptly stop taking these medications or do not slowly decrease the dosage. For most people, symptoms usually last a few weeks, but for others, symptoms are so severe that they permanently impact the quality of their lives.[40]

You have an even higher risk of experiencing severe withdrawal symptoms if you have taken ANTIDEPRESSANTS for more than two years or are taking two or more psychotropic medications at the same time. Note that your risk of experiencing serious side effects increases the more medications you are taking at the same time.

For example, if you were prescribed an antipsychotic medication in addition to an ANTIDEPRESSANT, you are more than three times as likely to report withdrawal symptoms. Furthermore, if you were also taking BENZODIAZEPINES (tranquilizers) and mood stabilizers, you risk is almost double.[41]

What is the take-home message? Simply this. Be very careful when considering taking antidepressant drugs if you want to avoid tinnitus in the first place, or if you want to avoid having your existing tinnitus become worse. You need to carefully weigh the expected benefits against the known adverse side effects.

Ultimately, it's much better to treat depression with natural, non-ototoxic solutions. This is because most people are just struggling with natural, normal, temporary human conditions such as sadness, grief, anxiety, "the blues" and depression. In many ways, these are a part of your body's communication system, revealing nutritional or sunlight deficiencies and/or a spiritual disconnect.[42] Therefore, it is better to treat them with proper diet, exercise, counseling, GABA supplements and if necessary, a herbal such as St. John's Wort, which a number of studies have shown to be just as effective as prescription antidepressants, but without their many nasty symptoms listed below.

Some Nasty Symptoms of Taking SSRI Drugs

The side effects from taking SSRI drugs can fluctuate. Thus, sometimes you will feel better and sometimes you will feel terrible. This is true while you are on these drugs, and/or when you try to get off them. Here are a number of these wretched side effects:

- Psychotic violence such as suicide and murder. (These side effects can be triggered simply by increasing or decreasing the dose of a SSRI or changing to another SSRI—which sadly is a common story in many of the SSRI homicides or suicides.)[43]
- A feeling of inner restlessness and inability to stay still. (This is known as akathisia and often precedes psychotic SSRI violence).
- Suicidal thoughts. (Known as "suicide ideation".)
- Rapidly changing moods. (e.g., spontaneous weeping spells, attacks of sheer terror, or sudden plunges into unprecedented contentless black holes of pure dread.)
- Feeling "electric shocks" in your arms, legs, or head. (The horrible "electric shocks" to your head are commonly called "brain zaps".)
- Feeling that things are not real. (Referred to as "derealization".) SSRIs cause over half of the users to no longer feel like themselves and in many cases as though they were losing their own minds.[44]

- Developing bipolar disorder. Did you know that taking SSRIs causes 7.7% of the users each year to develop bipolar disorder (ultimately affecting between 20-40% of SSRI users)? For many, bipolar disorder is a permanently debilitating disorder which significantly impacts their quality of life.[45]
- Causing sexual dysfunction in 59% to 62% of users. Note: Sexual dysfunction is one of the fastest ways to make someone depressed.[46]
- Low mood, feeling unable to be interested in, or enjoy things. SSRIs emotionally anesthetize 60% of users. This numbness frequently results in you losing your will to leave a toxic relationship or work situation (often for years if not decades), to stop emotionally reacting to things you should react to (e.g., someone being mean to you or violating your boundaries), and to no longer experience the joy and vibrancy of life.[47]
- Anxiety that comes and goes—sometimes in intense surges.
- Difficulty in getting to sleep and experiencing vivid or frightening dreams.
- Experiencing a large number of sensitivities (e.g., to light, heat, a supplement or food).
- A sense of being physically unwell.
- Crippling muscle pain or spasms.
- Anger, sleeplessness, tiredness, loss of co-ordination and headache.
- Visual problems.
- Dizziness (mild to severe).
- Queasiness or indigestion.
- Difficulty in concentrating.[48]

The SSRIs Are Also Killers

Few people realize this, but just like the benzos, the SSRIs can be killers. In fact, they carry a black box warning that these drugs can cause suicidal and homicidal ideation,[49] that is, thinking about killing yourself and/others. The truth is antidepressants figure prominently in many mass shootings. For example, research shows:

- 31 drugs, including 11 antidepressants, six sedatives and three ADHD medications, account for 78.8% of all cases of violence toward others reported to the FDA.

- A 2021 analysis of the Violence Project database, which is funded by the U.S. Justice Department, revealed 23% of mass shooters were on psychiatric drugs.

- According to CDC Surveillance for Violent Deaths data, 35.3% of those who committed suicide in 2013 tested positive for antidepressants at the time of death.[50]

Mass shootings that make the headlines are not the only result of taking SSRIs. They also are a cause of a great number of suicides that never reach the press.

> Consider for instance that one study found 10% of mentally healthy volunteers on an SSRI became suicidal, while a much larger survey of SSRI users found 39% had experienced suicidal ideation while on the drugs. Additionally, SSRIs have been repeatedly shown to significantly increase the incidence of hostile (but not yet psychotic) behavior.[51]

As you can see, a long-standing problem with SSRI drugs is that a certain portion of people who take them become violently psychotic and then either kill themselves or others (e.g., in a school or workplace shootings).[52]

Why is it that the SSRIs and BENZODIAZEPINES are so deadly? What makes otherwise "normal" people turn psychotic when they take SSRIs?

Researchers have discovered one common thread in those that turn psychotic (violent) is that they have genetically-reduced P450 function, yet doctors seldom test for this when prescribing SSRIs.

Here's how it develops. The cytochrome P450 family of enzymes (CYP450) are a group of enzymes encoded by the P450 genes and responsible for the metabolism of most prescription drugs.

When doctors prescribe a drug, they assume you have the normal levels of CYP450 enzymes. Since these enzymes break down the drug in your digestive process, not much of the drug is absorbed into your bloodstream. Thus, you are only getting a small fraction of the therapeutic drug dose you need. For example, if only 10% of a given drug is absorbed, your doctor prescribes a dose that is 10 **times** greater than you need so you end up with correct level—and if that happens, all is well.

However, if your body only produces 10% of the normal level of CYP450, then only 10% is broken down and you absorb basically 10 **times** the desired dose.

That is like taking 10 pills instead of 1 and you get a massive overdose. (You'll learn more about this in Chapter 16.)

This is very important because very few physicians who prescribe SSRIs are even aware of this CYP450 issue. As a result, they don't screen you for CYP450 function when they prescribe you an SSRI. Furthermore, once you start developing early psychotic symptoms, it is rare for the physician to attribute that to the SSRI they prescribed. Rather, they often assume the dose they prescribed is too low, and thus increase your dose. This just exacerbates the problem and you become violently psychotic.

Therefore, if you have low CYP450 function and are taking SSRIs, this results in your having dangerously-high levels of the SSRI in your bloodstream and these high levels of an SSRI can cause you to exhibit violent behavior. For example, in one study evaluating 10 people suspected to have this issue (due to them becoming violent after starting an SSRI), all ten were found to have a genetically-altered P450 function, and all ten became normal once they stopped taking the offending SSRI.[53]

Antidepressant Treatments That Actually Work

If you are interested in following science-based recommendations for depression, instead of taking a prescription antidepressant, you'd place antidepressants at the very bottom of your list of treatment options.[54] Rather, you'd opt for far more effective (and natural) treatments for your depression such as:

Exercise—A number of studies have shown exercise outperforms antidepressant drug treatment. Exercise helps create new GABA-producing neurons that help induce a natural state of calm, and boost serotonin, dopamine and norepinephrine, which, in turn, help you better deal with the effects of stress. In fact, there is a strong correlation between improved mood and aerobic capacity, but even gentle forms of exercise such as walking can be effective.[55] If you are low in GABA, also consider taking GABA supplements.

Good Nutrition—Keeping inflammation in check is an important part of any effective treatment plan. For example, if you're gluten-sensitive, you should remove all gluten from your diet. A food sensitivity test can help ascertain this. As a general guideline, eating a whole food diet can go a long way toward lowering your inflammation and thus your depression. Certain nutritional deficiencies are also notorious contributors to depression, especially:[56]

Omega-3 fats—You want to increase your intake of omega-3 fats and cut way down on your omega-6 fats.[57] And ideal ratio is 1:1.

B vitamins—This includes Vitamin B_1 (Thiamine), Vitamin B_2 (Riboflavin), Vitamin B_3 (Niacinamide), Vitamin B_6 (Pyridoxine), Vitamin B_8 (Inositol/Biotin), Vitamin B_9 (Folate) and Vitamin B_{12} (Methylcobalamin). Most people with depression are low on the "B" vitamins. For example, if you are low on dietary folate (Vitamin B_9), this can raise your risk of depression by as much as 300%. One of the most recent studies showing the importance of vitamin deficiencies in depression involved suicidal teens. Most turned out to be deficient in cerebral folate.[58]

Vitamin D_3—Studies have shown that a vitamin D_3 deficiency can predispose you to depression (and attempted suicide) and concluded that depression can respond favorably when you optimize your vitamin D_3 levels. Ideally, you'd do this by getting sensible sun exposure. If you can't get enough sun exposure to bring your Vitamin D_3 up to optimal levels, take Vitamin D_3 supplements.

In one study, people with a Vitamin D_3 level below 20 nanograms per milliliter (ng/mL) had an 85% increased risk of depression compared to those with a level greater than 30 ng/mL.[59] However, for optimal health, make sure your vitamin D_3 level is at least 40 mg/mL and ideally between 60 and 80 ng/mL year-round.

Probiotics—Keeping your gut microbiome healthy has a significant effect on your moods, emotions and brain. If you are like most people, when it comes to mental health, you assume your brain is in charge. However, in reality, often it is mostly your gut that is calling the shots. This is because your state of mind is influenced, if not largely directed, by the microflora in your gut. Furthermore, a number of studies have confirmed that gastrointestinal inflammation can play a critical role in your developing depression. Thus, healthy, beneficial bacteria (probiotics) in your gut play a role not only in the successful treatment of inflammation, but also act as natural antidepressants.[60]

Chapter 14 Endnotes

1 A Midwestern Doctor, 2023g. p. 1.
2 Mercola, 2024d. p. 1.
3 Mercola, 2024c. p. 1.
4 A Midwestern Doctor, 2023e. p. 1.
5 Mercola, 2024c. p. 1.
6 Salters-Pedneault, 2021. p. 2.
7 Keate, 2021a. p. 4.
8 A Midwestern Doctor, 2023e. p. 1.
9 Mercola, 2024c. p. 1.
10 Mercola, 2024c. p. 1.
11 Mercola, 2024c. p. 1.
12 Mercola, 2024c. p. 1.
13 Mercola, 2024c. p. 1.

14 Mercola, 2024c. p. 1.
15 Mercola, 2024d. p. 1.
16 Mercola, 2024c. p. 1.
17 Whiteman, 2017. p. 1.
18 The Serotonin/Melatonin Correction, 2011. p. 1.
19 Hogan, 1998. pp. 121-122.
20 Cohn, 2017. p. 1.
21 Robinson, 2017. p. 1.
22 Bauman, 2017b. p. 2.
23 Cohn, 2017. p. 1.
24 Tang, 2017. p. 1.
25 Robinson, 2017. p. 1.
26 Whiteman, 2017. p. 1.
27 Keate, 2020. p. 5.
28 The Serotonin/Melatonin Correction, 2011. p. 1.
29 Keate, 2020. p. 5.
30 Keate, 2021a. p. 4.
31 Carome, 2023. p. 1.
32 Carome, 2023. p. 1.
33 A Midwestern Doctor, 2023e. p. 1.
34 A Midwestern Doctor, 2023e. p. 1.
35 Carome, 2023. p. 1.
36 A Midwestern Doctor, 2023e. p. 1.
37 About Benzodiazepines, 2005. p. 8.
38 A Midwestern Doctor, 2023e. p. 1.
39 A Midwestern Doctor, 2023g. p. 1.
40 Carome, 2023. p. 1.
41 Carome, 2023. p. 1.
42 Mercola, 2024a, p. 1.
43 A Midwestern Doctor, 2023e. p. 1.
44 A Midwestern Doctor, 2023g. p. 1.
45 A Midwestern Doctor, 2023g. p. 1.
46 A Midwestern Doctor, 2023g. p. 1.
47 A Midwestern Doctor, 2023g. p. 1.
48 A Midwestern Doctor, 2023e. p. 1.
49 Mercola, 2023f. p. 1.
50 Mercola, 2023f. p. 1.
51 A Midwestern Doctor, 2023g. p. 1.
52 A Midwestern Doctor, 2023d. p. 1.
53 A Midwestern Doctor, 2023d. p. 1.
54 Mercola, 2024a, p. 1.
55 Mercola, 2024a, p. 1.
56 Mercola, 2024a, p. 1.
57 Mercola, 2024a, p. 1.
58 Mercola, 2024a, p. 1.
59 Mercola, 2024a, p. 1.
60 Mercola, 2024b. p. 1.

Chapter 15

Safely Tapering Off the Benzodiazepines, SSRIs and Other Psychotropic Drugs

Getting on psychotropic drugs such as the BENZODIAZEPINES and SELECTIVE SEROTONIN REUPTAKE INHIBITORS is easy. You see your doctor, typically he writes you a prescription and you pick up your medications at your local pharmacy. It's that easy.

However, getting off these drugs once your body has built up a dependence to them is another story. For some people it is hard, and for other people it is next to impossible.

Since the side effects of BENZODIAZEPINES and SSRIs can be so insidious, your first line of defense is knowledge. If you have read the previous two chapters, you now know that BENZODIAZEPINES and SSRIs are only supposed to be used for short periods of time—2 to 3 weeks at the most, and for some people, even that is too long! This is because it is extremely difficult to stop using them after you have built up a dependence on them, and frequently that can start after using them for just a month.[1]

Any doctor who prescribes these drugs for longer than two weeks or so is ultimately doing you a disservice and may be harming you. Yet in one study, about one-quarter of those who had taken an antidepressant in the past month reported being on them for 10 years or more![2] No wonder so many people have a horrible time getting off these drugs. Thus, absolutely refuse to take any BENZODIAZEPINES or SSRIs for longer than 2 or 3 weeks. By doing so, hopefully you will avoid most withdrawal problems, but this is by no means guaranteed.

Once you have been on a psychotropic drug and want to get off it, the trick is to taper off these drugs **very slowly**. But so often doctors don't realize just how slowly you need to taper. Their idea of "slow" is typically much too fast. The result? Horrible withdrawal side effects. For example, as one lady reported:

> I've been on 20 mg **Citalopram** for 4 years. My doctor told me to drop to 10 mg for 3 weeks, then stop. This resulted in my getting headaches, tinnitus, electric shocks and the most horrendous anxiety.

Even a 6-month taper can be much too fast. One lady explained:

> I was given **Lorazepam** [a BENZODIAZEPINE] from my doctor to help me sleep. Not researching right away, it already did its damage short term. I tapered off from start to finish 6 months—maybe a total of 85 pills. I am still suffering **6 years later** and never touched that evil medication again. **I have yearly setbacks that are worse than withdrawal and they last months**. They include every symptom in the book. Right now, I'm in an absolutely hellish, evil, tortuous setback (4 months long so far).

One of the nasty things is that withdrawal side effects don't necessarily start right away. It can be days, weeks or months later that these horrible side effects begin to appear. Here is one lady's experience with the SSRI **Paroxetine** (*Paxil*).

> I had only been taking *Paxil* for 3 months and ran out of medicine. After 2 weeks I started to get a very strange pressure in my ears and tinnitus. The pressure was so horrible I thought there had to be something wrong—maybe an infection. I went multiple times to the specialist for it and I had no issues he could see in my ears.
>
> Two weeks later (still having the issue) dizziness started. This dizziness was so bad I could hardly walk. More issues kept arising. I had been off the medicine for more than a month when I went to the neurologist. I had an MRI and x-ray on my head and neck to look for issues.
>
> The doctor put me back on the *Paxil* thinking it would help and it did, but I had already stopped the medicine for 6 weeks at this time and the symptoms only progressed until I started taking the *Paxil* again. Now I am afraid I will never be able to change medicines. Even tapering off, I start all the same side effects that progress the longer I am not taking *Paxil.*"

Unfortunately, even with a relatively slow taper, you can still experience withdrawal side effects a year or more later, so ultimately you are left worse off that you were before you began to take such drugs.

For example, a lady took the anticonvulsant **Gabapentin**. Here is her story.

> I took **Gabapentin** for 10 months, then tapered off the drug. Within a month of completing the taper, I developed terrible hyperacusis, and mild tinnitus. I had become much worse. After 1 year, my hyperacusis is much better, but still not gone, and my tinnitus is somewhat better but still worse than prior to my taking the **Gabapentin**.

That's how easy it is to get hooked on these psychotropic drugs and how hard it is to get off them.

Make Haste Slowly

In order to **safely** go off any of the BENZODIAZEPINES, SELECTIVE SEROTONIN REUPTAKE INHIBITORS (SSRIs) and their close cousins, the SELECTIVE SEROTONIN & NOREPINEPHRINE REUPTAKE INHIBITORS (SSNRIs), it is important not to do so abruptly. You need to gradually (this means **extremely slowly**) reduce the dosage under medical supervision to minimize nasty withdrawal side-effects. Unfortunately, you may experience withdrawal symptoms even if you gradually decrease the dosage.[3]

In addition to the above classes of drugs, this also applies to the "Z" drugs such as **Zaleplon** (*Sonata*), **Zolpidem** (*Ambien*) and **Zopiclone** (*Imovane*) and its close relative **Eszopiclone** (*Lunesta*) as these drugs work in similar ways to the BENZODIAZEPINE drugs inside your brain.[4] This also may apply to any other psychotropic drugs to which you have formed a dependence.

The reason for this is that reducing the dose of the drug very slowly minimizes the severity of the withdrawal symptoms you will experience. One lady that that had built up a drug dependence explained,

> The secret to getting off these drugs is to do it **very** slowly. You may or may not know this, but the medical community is in the dark ages about tapering off anti-psychotic medications. There is a significant minority, including me, who have trouble big time, if we were to taper by their protocol which is very fast. (Actually, I suspect we are far more than a minority.)
>
> One psychiatrist told me that anti-psychotic medicine should not be tapered any faster than 10% of the current dose every 4 weeks. Yes, it is a slow process, but here is the proof. I have had minimal side effects and can hold down a full-time job. The people who taper off too quickly have a totally different experience, and it is **not** pleasant!

A doctor explained the reason for this slow 10% taper in more detail. He wrote:

> To "cure" an SSRI dependency, you need to let your brain slowly rewire itself back to normal. Until that happens, your brain will continue to behave in an abnormal fashion (e.g., its ability to adapt to outside stressors in a healthy way is dramatically reduced). This is often a very slow process....
>
> A major reason for this extremely slow taper is due to the non-linear relationship between an SSRI dose and its binding to the brain. What this essentially means is that to reduce a SSRI, you have to decrease your dose by a progressively slower rate (once a month reducing last month's dose by 10% is commonly recommended). This process thus often takes a long time (e.g., people

> often stop at 2.5% of their original dose, which requires reducing the dose by 10% **thirty-five times**). Note: In the best-case scenario, they find antidepressants can be withdrawn from in 6 months. Typically, it takes years.[5]

Furthermore, this doctor explains that:

> **Paroxetine** (*Paxil*) is particularly difficult to withdraw from because it inhibits its own metabolism, so as you lower the dose, it gets metabolized faster, and you become more likely to suffer withdrawals. Additionally, *Paxil* can cause alcohol cravings and lower your resistance to those cravings which can become a huge problem.[6]

Here is another tip from the above-mentioned lady. She explained that you should only slowly taper off **one** drug at a time. Since she was on several drugs, at her safe taper rate, it was going to still take her another **six years** to be drug free at the time she contacted me. This is the way to do it if you don't want unpleasant side effects cropping up because of tapering off too fast. It also gives your brain a chance to get its brain chemistry working properly again without the help of drugs. A doctor reinforced this opinion. He explained:

> Since, at most, people can tolerate withdrawing from one SSRI (or antipsychotic) at a time, the withdrawal process becomes much more challenging when patients are on multiple drugs (which sadly is very common in psychiatry).[7]

Furthermore, since SSRIs are given at a much higher dose than is typically appropriate, this makes them extremely dependence-forming and thus extremely difficult from which to taper off.[8]

As you can see, overcoming the withdrawal side effects of psychotropic drugs can take many weeks, months or years. Usually, the length of time someone has been taking a psychotropic drug, and the size of the dose they have been taking, will have the most impact on how long it takes for their withdrawal symptoms to pass.

If you are on any of the Benzodiazepines and want to stop taking them, you would do well to download and read the excellent manual *Benzodiazepines: How They Work and How to Withdraw* (sometimes called *The Ashton Manual*) by Dr. Heather Ashton (now retired), one of the foremost authorities on the planet on how to break free from these drugs. She developed this manual after working one-on-one for twelve years in a clinic with physically-dependent Benzodiazepine patients wishing to withdraw.[9] Not only is this manual free, it's easy to read and packed with the information you need to help you.[10] You can download it from http://www.benzo.org.uk/manual/contents.htm.

Your goal should be to become healthy and drug free. Then you won't have to worry about ototoxic (or other) adverse side effects. The good news is that Dr.

Ashton reports a 90% success rate for her stepwise, gradual, patient-controlled taper plan.[11] Thus, if you persist through the agonies of the withdrawal stage—no matter how long it takes—in the end, as the lady in the above story expressed it, "I will be free and be 'me' again"! That makes it all worth it.

How to Calculate the Dosage for a "Safe" 10% Taper

Once you have developed a dependence on a psychotropic drug, (about 56% of those taking a psychotropic drug do), you want to taper off such drugs very slowly if you want to avoid as much as possible nasty withdrawal side effects.

A good starting point is to taper your dose by **10% per month** on the **descending balance**. This means that you reduce your dose by 10% per month, calculated on the **last** dosage you took, not the **initial** dosage. This 10% taper rate is a "harm reduction" approach to going off psychotropic drugs. It causes the least harm to the greatest number of people that are hooked on psychotropic drugs. Unfortunately, a few people will still experience side effects, even at this slow rate.

Therefore, "if you are very sensitive to dosage reductions, you may have to reduce by very, very small amounts, less than 10% per month, or hold for even longer than a month at a time."[12] For example, you may need to do a 5% taper, or take longer intervals between each step—such as 6 weeks instead of 4 weeks per step. Do whatever works for you so that you don't experience withdrawal side effects, or only experience very mild side effects, as you taper off a drug.

I want to emphasize that you do **not** want to do a straight taper off the initial dose. This is the **wrong** way. For example, say you were on a high dose of 40 mg per day. A straight 10% taper would be to reduce your dose by 4 mg each month (10% of 40=4). Thus, after 10 months you'd be off the drug. This is too fast a taper for most people. As a result, you will likely find that negative withdrawal side effects crop up.

The **right** way is to do a 10% taper off the **last** dose you took. For example, again say you were on a dose of 40 mg per day. To do a correct 10% taper, you'd do the same as the above for the first month. 10% of 40 is 4 mg. So for the first month you'd take 40 – 4 = 36 mg/day. Then for the second month, you'd reduce this 36 mg dose by 10%. So the second month you'd take 36 – 3.6 mg = 32.4 mg/day. For the third month you'd reduce the 32.4 mg dose by 10% and thus take 32.4 – 3.24 mg = 29.16 mg/day and so on.

So that you don't have to do all the figuring each time you reduce the dose, Table 15-1 gives the correct 10% taper on the reducing balance for starting daily doses of 40, 20, 15 and 10 mg.

Table 15-1: The 10% "Harm-Reduction" Taper for Doses of 40, 20, 15 and 10 mg in 40 Steps

40 mg pill Dose (mg)	20 mg pill Dose (mg)	15 mg pill Dose (mg)	10 mg pill Dose (mg)	Drink (ml)	Pour out (ml)
40.0	20.0	15.0	10.0	100.0	0.0
36.0	18.0	13.5	9.0	90.0	10.0
32.4	16.2	12.2	8.1	81.0	19.0
29.2	14.6	10.9	7.3	72.9	27.1
26.2	13.1	9.8	6.6	65.6	34.4
23.6	11.8	8.9	5.9	59.0	41.0
21.3	10.6	8.0	5.3	53.1	46.9
19.1	9.6	7.2	4.8	47.8	52.2
17.2	8.6	6.5	4.3	43.0	57.0
15.5	7.7	5.8	3.9	38.7	61.3
13.9	7.0	5.2	3.5	34.9	65.1
12.6	6.3	4.7	3.1	31.4	68.6
11.3	5.6	4.2	2.8	28.2	71.8
10.2	5.1	3.8	2.5	25.4	74.6
9.2	4.6	3.4	2.3	22.9	77.1
8.2	4.1	3.1	2.1	20.6	79.4
7.4	3.7	2.8	1.9	18.5	81.5
6.7	3.3	2.5	1.7	16.7	83.3
6.0	3.0	2.3	1.5	15.0	85.0
5.4	2.7	2.0	1.4	13.5	86.5
4.9	2.4	1.8	1.2	12.2	87.8
4.4	2.2	1.6	1.1	10.9	89.1
3.9	2.0	1.5	1.0	9.8	90.2
3.5	1.8	1.3	0.9	8.9	91.1
3.2	1.6	1.2	0.8	8.0	92.0
2.9	1.4	1.1	0.7	7.2	92.8
2.6	1.3	1.0	0.6	6.5	93.5
2.3	1.2	0.9	0.6	5.8	94.2
2.1	1.0	0.8	0.5	5.2	94.8
1.9	0.9	0.7	0.5	4.7	95.3
1.7	0.8	0.6	0.4	4.2	95.8
1.5	0.8	0.6	0.4	3.8	96.2
1.4	0.7	0.5	0.3	3.4	96.6
1.2	0.6	0.5	0.3	3.1	96.9
1.1	0.6	0.4	0.3	2.8	97.2
1.0	0.5	0.4	0.3	2.5	97.5
0.9	0.5	0.3	0.2	2.3	97.7
0.8	0.4	0.3	0.2	2.0	98.0
0.7	0.4	0.3	0.2	1.8	98.2
0.7	0.3	0.2	0.2	1.6	98.4
0.6	0.3	0.2	0.1	1.5	98.5

Tapering like this—10% on the reducing balance—will go on "forever" with ever smaller quantities. Thus, at some point you need to simply stop taking the drug and "jump off".

A safe jumping off point for the average person would be when you have reduced the dose to somewhere around 2.5% of the original dose which will take you 3 years.

The length of time you stay on your taper depends on what you consider a "safe jumping off" point. People may choose considerably different "jumping off" points. In practical terms, your safe "jumping off" point is that point where, when you stop taking the drug, you don't experience any (or minimal) withdrawal side effects.

However, don't be in too great a hurry and "jump off" too soon if you are particularly sensitive to the drug you are on. The truth is, as you get to a smaller and smaller dose, you need to taper **extra** slow, not faster as the last bit of the drug to leave your brain is the hardest for you to get through.[13] That is why as you near your "jumping off" point, you are taking almost minute quantities of the drug This has to do with the percentage of receptors in your brain that the drug is occupying. So, for the few months just before you decide to "jump off", it is wise to go extra slow on your taper. For example, you could take longer than a month between these last few tapers—extending the time for say 6 weeks or more instead of the usual 4 weeks. Let how you feel be your guide as to how fast (or slow) you taper off the drug.

Feel free to modify the taper to fit your body. You don't have to slavishly follow the above taper schedule. As far as I know, there is no exact science to the taper rate. Therefore, if you find this "harm-reduction" protocol too slow and you feel you can taper faster depending on which drug you are taking, you can always speed things up by making the 10% reductions more often—for example, every 3 weeks or every 2 weeks—whatever interval works for your body.

If you used the above taper rate, you would normally "jump off" after 3 years. However, if you used a faster taper (semi-monthly), using the same table, it would take you 18 months to get off the drug.

Just be sure you don't go too fast. The risk of withdrawal side effects appearing increases as you increase the taper rate. Therefore, if you do a faster taper and begin to experience withdrawal symptoms, this is your body's way of telling you that you are tapering too fast, so stop the taper at the level you are at until the side effects settle down, then resume your taper but at a slower rate.[14]

If you find the 10% taper is too fast for your body, slow it down. You could change the taper rate from the standard 10% to any smaller amount such as 5% and/or you could increase the interval between the taper steps.

How long it takes you to taper off a drug is not important. Remember, this is not a race to see how fast you can get off the drug—I know you want to get of the drug as fast as possible—but rather this is a way to safely get off the drug. The important thing is that you slowly progress towards your goal at a speed that doesn't cause you any major/severe withdrawal reactions no matter how long it takes.

Now, I can hear you asking, "However do I split a 40 mg pill into precise pieces such as 12.6 mg or 2.3 mg?" Don't worry. There is an easy way to get a precise taper using hard pills (not capsules). Here's how you can do it.

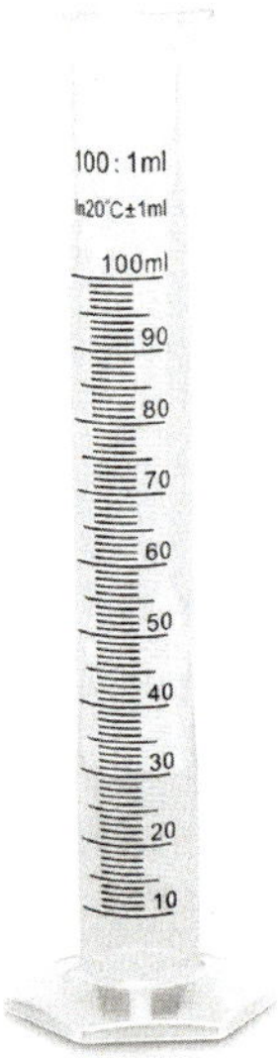

First you need to get yourself two or three things—a 100 ml beaker, a mortar and pestle, and if you need it, a graduated dropper/pipette to measure tiny precise amounts as you near the end of your taper.

Fig. 15-1. 100 ml beaker.

The beaker needs to be tall and about 1″ in diameter and marked for each individual ml. You can get a nice one on Amazon at https://www.amazon.com/100ml-Plastic-Graduated-Cylinder-Beaker/dp/B0728C224F for about $9.00. See Fig. 15-1.

A nice mortar and pestle set is on Amazon at https://www.amazon.com/Best-Mortar-and-Pestle-Set/dp/B01DJBY1LA for around $22.00. See Fig. 15-2.

Fig. 15-2. Mortar and pestle.

You probably also want a 10 ml pipette marked in tenths of ml to precisely measure the correct dose. Amazon has a nice set of two 10 ml glass graduated dropper/lab pipettes for about $9.00 at https://www.amazon.com/Graduated-Droppers-Pipettes-Dropper-Pipette/dp/B07XX3P1TJ/. See Fig. 15-3.

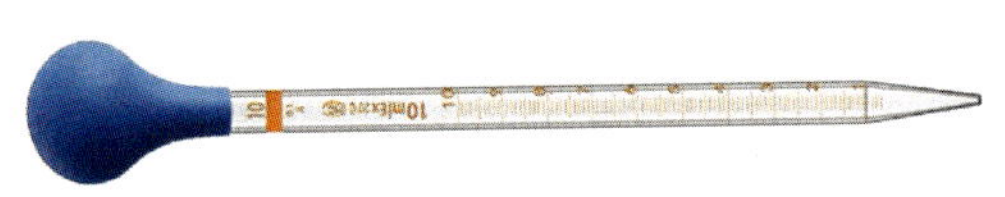

Fig. 15-3. 10 ml pipette.

In order to precisely measure the amount of the drug you need at each step of the taper process, you simply place your daily pill in the mortar and crush and grind it to a fine powder using the pestle. Second, scrape the powdered pill into your beaker. Third fill your beaker with water to exactly the 100 ml mark. Fourth, cover the top of the beaker with the palm of your hand and vigorously shake it until the pill is completely dissolved. (Note that using warm water [not hot water] will make the pill powder dissolve faster.

Now using the last column in Table 15-1 and the appropriate step in your taper, pour out the amount indicated and drink the rest.

That works for the early stages in your taper, but when you get down to the smaller amounts, it's hard to pour out the precise amount shown in the table. This is where a micro-pipette comes in.

In this case, using the second last column (labeled "Drink ml" insert the pipette into the beaker until the water reaches the precise level you are supposed to drink, put your finger over the end and let it drain into your mouth or glass if it's easier to drink from a glass.

Does this slow taper really work? Here is one lady's experience. She wrote:

> Hallelujah, I have a success story for you. Thanks for your direction on how to taper off **Citalopram**, I am now free and clear of this horrible drug. I had been on 10 mg for over 10 years and finally decided it wasn't working for me but when I tried to "get off" I suffered many side effects. This led me to find you. After your recommendations, (I was able to speed up the process a tad), I'm now off the drug with no intention of **ever** going back to this type of drug again. This drug was devastating to my body. My physician did me a huge disservice by prescribing it to me for "hot flashes". The only symptom I have left after these many years of being on this drug is a little bit of a ringing in my ears, but I'll take that over the many other symptoms while trying to taper off this drug. In time, I hope the ringing in my ears will dissipate as well. I just wanted to let your readers know to stay the course and don't give up. Even if you feel like it is hopeless you **will** get better. You can possibly speed the process up as I did but listen to your body as it will tell you, and all you do is just go back to your schedule and keep going.

This slow taper worked for her. It will most likely work for you too!

Stay Away from Drug and Alcohol Detox Centers

When you have formed a strong dependence on doctor-prescribed benzos, SSRIs, SSNRIs, the "Z" drugs and related psychotropic drugs, you may need help to get off them. Quite logically, you'd think the obvious place to go would be to a drug and alcohol detoxification or rehabilitation center. However, if you think that, you'd be wrong!

Here are four reasons why such facilities are inappropriate for weaning yourself off these drugs.

1. They Treat Drug Addiction, Not Physical Drug Dependence

First, it is important to understand that physical dependence on a drug and addiction to a drug are not the same thing at all. Thus, they need different treatments. Drug and alcohol detoxification or rehabilitation centers are set up to treat addictions, **not** drug dependence issues, and are thus inappropriate if you have a dependence on a given drug.

Physical or physiological dependence to one of these drugs means that your body now **relies** on this drug to **prevent** withdrawal symptoms. Further, realize that physical dependence is a normal and predictable outcome of taking such drugs. Thus, you should **expect** you will form a dependence on these tolerance-forming drugs if you take them for any length of time,[15] and that could be as short as two weeks to a month.

In contrast, addiction to a drug is a set of destructive behaviors, often driven by your uncontrollable cravings, including compulsive drug use, drug-seeking, and your inability to control your drug use in spite of the resulting harms it causes to yourself and to others.

Note that, depending on the drug, you can be both physically dependent on the drug **and** addicted to the drug at the same time. Again, depending on the drug, you can be physically dependent on the drug but **not** addicted to it. Thus, physical dependence in and of itself does not constitute addiction, although it can accompany addiction. As a general rule, if you take your medications as prescribed by your doctor, you may become physically dependent on that drug, but not addicted to it.[16]

Once you become dependent on a drug, you may often find that intolerable withdrawal side effects appear when you try to get off the drug. At that point, many doctors try to solve this problem by prescribing this drug permanently, telling you that you'll not be able to quit taking this drug. Instead, they increase the dose to try to hold these side effects in check, but ultimately this does not work.

As a result, they may assume you are addicted to the drug and "pass the buck" and pawn you off to a rehab or detox center. The problem is that nearly all these centers use a 12-step model patterned after Alcoholics Anonymous. This model focuses on the compulsive use and behavioral problems of addiction, not on the specific treatment needed for drug dependence. That is, they focus on maintaining abstinence through fellowship and completing "the 12 steps"—admitting that one cannot control one's compulsion; recognizing a higher power; examining past errors; making amends for these errors; learning to live a new life with a new code of behavior; and helping others with addiction.

This doesn't work because if you are dependent on a drug, neither these 12-step programs nor detoxification safely addresses and reverses the physiological changes in the GABA receptors. This is because the GABA receptors now won't react to host GABA, but only to the dependent drug you are physically dependent on. That is why you can only do a very slow taper to address the underlying problem and gradually restore proper GABA receptor function.[17]

2. The Treatment Time Is Far Too Short

Not only is the 12-step program used in detox facilities the wrong treatment for drug dependence, but the program is also much too short for resolving drug dependence, not to mention is very expensive.

This is because detox facilities usually do not offer programs or stays lasting any longer than 7-90 days. In contrast, to safely taper off psychotropic drugs after dependence is established takes a number of months to several years for a large percentage of the people who struggle to discontinue psychotropic drugs.[18]

3. Their Wrong Treatments Leads to Poor and Dangerous Outcomes

Rehab/detox facilities that accept people with drug-dependence often will abruptly stop the person's psychotropic drug (which is asking for horrible and sometimes permanent withdrawal side effects). They then replace the drug "with a short (one week or so) **Phenobarbital** or **Chlordiazepoxide** "taper," sometimes followed by medications such as **Gabapentin**, **Pregabalin**, BETA BLOCKERS, ANTIDEPRESSANTS and ANTIPSYCHOTICS (which are the very drugs classes from which they are trying to stop taking), etc. to "manage" the withdrawal. In such cases, the person can be admitted to the facility on one drug—a BENZODIAZEPINE for example—and are then discharged home on prescribed multiple drugs, including drugs which carry their own similar risk of physical dependence and withdrawal and requirements for taper.[19] This is totally the wrong approach.

After a rapid "taper" or cold-turkey withdrawal, is it any wonder that some people develop severe, delayed symptoms of withdrawal that may not fully manifest themselves until after a few months? These people have been discharged from their rehab centers with little or no support or aftercare, only to go on to develop psychosis, seizures, suicidality at home a few weeks or months later.

At this point, due directly to the rapid detox from BENZODIAZEPINES, these people may find themselves in an even more treacherous position. Dr. Heather Ashton in her manual explains:

> Many BENZODIAZEPINE users who find themselves in this position have withdrawn too quickly; some have undergone "cold turkey". They think that if they go back on the BENZODIAZEPINES and start over again on a slower schedule, they will be more successful.
>
> Unfortunately, things are not so simple. For reasons that are not clear, (but perhaps because the original experience of withdrawal has already sensitized

> the nervous system and heightened the level of anxiety), the original BENZODIAZEPINE dose often does not work the second time round. Some may find that only a higher dose partially alleviates their symptoms, and then they still have to go through a long withdrawal process again, which again may not be symptom-free.[20]

4. Their "One Size Fits All" Doesn't Work for Drug Dependence

Since each person is unique, each person's experience of withdrawing from psychotropic drugs will vary in severity and duration. For example, in the case of the BENZODIAZEPINES some people, even those who took high doses of prescribed BENZODIAZEPINES long-term, will experience only minor or, in some cases, no withdrawal symptoms, others will experience extreme reactions. Again, according to Dr. Heather Ashton,

> Some people can stop their BENZODIAZEPINES with no symptoms at all. According to some authorities, this figure may be as high as 50% even after a year of chronic usage. Even if this figure is correct (which is arguable) it is unwise to stop BENZODIAZEPINES suddenly". Dr. Malcolm Lader states, "I estimate about 20-30% of people who are on a BENZODIAZEPINE like **Diazepam** have trouble coming off and of those about a third have very distressing symptoms." His figures are conservative, as Reconnexion, a nonprofit organization in Australia offering counseling and support for BENZODIAZEPINE-dependent patients, states: "It is estimated that between 50-80% of people who have taken BENZODIAZEPINES continually for six months or longer will experience withdrawal symptoms when reducing the dose."[21]

Unfortunately, there is no way to know in advance which people will experience withdrawal symptoms when they try to go off these drugs. Nor is it possible to know in advance which people will go on to develop severe or protracted withdrawal problems, or which patients could quit "cold turkey" or taper rapidly with next to no symptoms. Therefore, you should not play "Russian roulette" when it comes to coming off BENZODIAZEPINES as it puts you at unnecessary risk for the sometimes-devastating outcomes[22]

Thus, using slow person-controlled tapers are safer, more successful and have better outcomes for getting off psychotropic drugs such as BENZODIAZEPINES, SSRIs and related drugs.

Chapter 15 Endnotes

1 A Midwestern Doctor, 2023e. p. 1.
2 Mercola, 2024, p. 1.
3 Carome, 2023. p. 1.
4 Lamberson, 2019. p. 1.
5 A Midwestern Doctor, 2023e. p. 1.

6 A Midwestern Doctor, 2023e. p. 1.
7 A Midwestern Doctor, 2023e. p. 1.
8 A Midwestern Doctor, 2023e. p. 1.
9 Lamberson, 2019. p. 1.
10 Ashton, 2002.
11 Lamberson, 2019. p. 1.
12 Altostrata, 2011. p. 1.
13 Altostrata, 2011. p. 1.
14 Altostrata, 2011. p. 1.
15 Lamberson, 2019. p. 1.
16 Lamberson, 2019. p. 1.
17 Lamberson, 2019. p. 1.
18 Lamberson, 2019. p. 1.
19 Lamberson, 2019. p. 1.
20 Lamberson, 2019. p. 1.
21 Lamberson, 2019. p. 1.
22 Lamberson, 2019. p. 1.

Chapter 16

Grapefruit Juice and Ototoxic Drugs

Drinking grapefruit juice could be hazardous to your ears. Surprised? Here's the scoop. It's not that grapefruit juice isn't good for you—it is. The problem is that grapefruit juice also contains a substance that can greatly increase the potency of some drugs.[1]

You probably know that mixing medications can be dangerous to your health. This is because certain drugs can enhance the effects of other drugs leaving you with a dangerously-high level of a given drug in your body. Your doctor and your pharmacist normally watch out for such interactions and prescribe accordingly.

However, downing certain drugs with a drink of grapefruit juice can be just as harmful. Researchers stumbled on to this effect in 1991.[2]

Some of the other citrus fruits may contain limited amounts of these chemicals called furanocoumarins such as Seville oranges, limes, pomelos[3] tangelos and Minneolas.[4] However, furanocoumarins are particularly abundant in grapefruit.

Mary Anne Hochadel, a pharmacist, warns that while many doctors know that grapefruit juice can be a problem, they might not understand that all parts of the grapefruit, whether fresh, juiced or concentrated in any quantity has the same effect. Earlier studies implicated the concentrated forms, but newer studies have shown that all parts of the grapefruit have this effect.[5]

Here is how it all works. When you drink a glass of grapefruit juice, these furanocoumarins chemically bond to the Cytochrome P-450 3A4 (CYP 3A4 for short) enzymes located in the lining of your intestines. This prevents these enzymes from doing their work.[6]

One of the things these enzymes do is to break down certain compounds before they are absorbed into your bloodstream. This is what God designed them to do.

The trick is to get your body to absorb the medication compounds before the CYP 3A4 enzymes break them down and render them useless. If the medication doesn't break down at the "normal" rate, a problem arises because this changes the effective dose.

Your Body Does Not Absorb All the Medications You Take

Surprising as it may seem, your body does **not** normally absorb much of the medications you take. According to Dr. Paul Watkins, "For many medications that are taken orally in pill form, the majority of the drug is not absorbed from the digestive tract but instead passes out of the body and is, in effect, wasted".[1]

Reference

[1] It's Not Pulp Fiction: Taking Medications with Grapefruit Juice May Increase Their Potency, 1996. p. 1.

What normally happens is that, for instance, maybe 10% of a given drug is absorbed into your bloodstream before these enzymes break it down. As a result, doctors prescribe pills that in this hypothetical example would contain ten times the amount they want to be absorbed—knowing that 90% will be destroyed by these enzymes.

However, if you drink grapefruit juice, these enzymes can no longer do their normal work of breaking down such drugs. When that happens, your body absorbs all (or almost all) of the drug into your bloodstream, possibly giving you a horrendous overdose that your doctor never intended. This overdose could wreak havoc in your body or even kill you. If those drugs were ototoxic, this dose could result in various kinds of damage to your ears.

This grapefruit juice effect may last only a few hours. However, taking some drugs as much as 1 to 3 days after drinking some grapefruit juice will result in higher drug levels in your blood than would normally occur.

Studies Show Significant Blood Drug Level Increases

Studies report that **Felodipine** concentrations increased an average of 300% (with peak concentrations as high as 600%) when taken with grapefruit juice. Similarly, **Nisoldipine** levels increased 500% with peak concentrations increasing to 900%.[1]

Other studies report levels of **Lovastatin** increasing by a whopping 1,500% and **Simvastatin** increasing by 1,513%! These are the largest effects of grapefruit juice reported so far.[2]

References

[1] The Grapefruit Juice Effect, 1997. p. 3.

[2] Elbe, 1999c. pp. 1-2.

Furthermore, the effects of drinking grapefruit juice are cumulative. This means that if you drink a glass of grapefruit juice daily for a week, the drug interaction would be stronger than if you only occasionally drink some grapefruit juice.[7] Mixing grapefruit juice with certain medications causes the body to react as if up to 15

times the recommended drug dose had been taken. As you can imagine, that could be dangerous to your health!

For older people, the difference in drug levels in the blood can be higher than for younger people. One study reported that older people had a given drug blood level 3.5 times higher than normal after taking grapefruit juice. Other studies have shown that younger people had drug blood levels between 2 and 2.5 times higher than did those who took their medications with water instead of grapefruit juice.[8]

I am not aware of the literature reporting anyone having specific ototoxic side effects from drinking grapefruit juice while taking certain drugs, but it may have happened since such things few people are even aware that this can occur and thus, such results are seldom reported. Doctors are currently more worried about "serious" side effects like severe heart problems and death than they are with damage to your ears.

There are a good number of drugs that "interact" with grapefruit juice.

Table 16-1: Ototoxic Drugs Known to Interact with Grapefruit Juice

Albendazole	**Erlotinib**	**Pazopanib**
Aliskiren	**Erythromycin**	**Pimozide**
Alprazolam	**Everolimus**	**Praziquantel**
Amiodarone	**Felodipine**	**Primaquine**
Amitriptyline	**Fentanyl**	**Propafenone**
Amlodipine	**Fesoterodine**	**Quazepam**
Amprenavir	**Fexofenadine**	**Quetiapine**
Apixaban	**Fluvoxamine**	**Quinidine**
Atorvastatin	**Imipramine**	**Quinine**
Budesonide	**Indinavir**	**Ranolazine**
Buprenorphine	**Isradipine**	**Repaglinide**
Buspirone	**Itraconazole**	**Ritonavir**
Carbamazepine	**Ivabradine**	**Rivaroxaban**
Carvedilol	**Ketamine**	**Saquinavir**
Cerivastatin	**Ketoconazole**	**Sertraline**
Cilostazol	**Lapatinib**	**Sildenafil**
Cisapride	**Loratadine**	**Silodosin**
Clarithromycin	**Losartan**	**Simvastatin**
Clomipramine	**Lovastatin**	**Sirolimus**
Clonazepam	**Lurasidone**	**Solifenacin**
Clopidogrel	**Maraviroc**	**Sunitinib**
Colchicine	**Mercaptopurine**	**Tacrolimus**
Crizotinib	**Methadone**	**Tadalafil**
Cyclosporine	**Midazolam**	**Tamsulosin**
Darifenacin	**Nefazodone**	**Ticagrelor**
Dasatinib	**Nelfinavir**	**Trazodone**
Dextromethorphan	**Nicardipine**	**Triazolam**
Diazepam	**Nifedipine**	**Vandetanib**
Digoxin	**Nilotinib**	**Vardenafil**
Diphenhydramine	**Nimodipine**	**Vemurafenib**
Disopyramide	**Nisoldipine**	**Verapamil**
Dofetilide	**Nitrazepam**	**Vinblastine**
Domperidone	**Nitrendipine**	**Warfarin**
Dronedarone	**Omeprazole**	**Zaleplon**
Eplerenone	**Oxycodone**	**Ziprasidone**
Ergotamine		

> Affected drugs possess 3 essential characteristics: they have an oral route of administration [they are taken by mouth], they have very low to intermediate intrinsic oral bioavailability, and they are metabolized by CYP 3A4....The lower the innate oral bioavailability of the drug, the greater the possible increase in systemic drug concentration.... Drugs with very low bioavailability are the most likely to interact with grapefruit in a way that substantially alters their pharmacokinetics (i.e., analogous to consuming many doses of the drug alone).[9]

One source reports that taking grapefruit juice increases the blood level of more than 85 different medications[10] but there are even more than that. I list 106 different ototoxic medications in alphabetical order in Table 16-1 for your easy reference. This listing is not necessarily exhaustive but was reasonably complete at the time I wrote this. Note that this table only includes drugs that have known ototoxic properties **and** are known to interact with grapefruit juice.

Ototoxic Drugs Known to Interact with Grapefruit Juice by Class

This section lists the various drugs by their classes and gives you a good idea of the kinds of drugs for which you have to watch. If you are in doubt, have your pharmacist look up the specific information on grapefruit juice/drug interactions for that drug.

Note that the percentages in square brackets (if any) after a drug name are the increase over normal in drug blood levels for that drug after taking grapefruit juice according to a specific study.

ALPHA-ADRENERGIC BLOCKING DRUGS such as **Silodosin** (*Rapaflo*).[11]

ANGIOTENSIN-2-RECEPTOR BLOCKERS such as **Losartan** (*Cozaar, Hyzaar*).[12]

ANTI-ANGINALS such as **Ranolazine** (*Ranexa*).[13]

ANTI-ARRHYTHMICS such as **Amiodarone** (*Cordarone*) [84%],[14, 15] **Disopyramide** (*Norpace*),[16] **Dofetilide** (*Tikosyn*), **Dronedarone** (*Multaq*)[17], **Propafenone** (*Rythmol*),[18] and **Quinidine** (*Cardioquin, Quinidex*).[19]

ANTI-CLOTTING DRUGS such as **Warfarin** (*Coumadin*).[20]

ANTI-CONVULSANT DRUGS such as **Carbamazepine** (*Tegretol*) [40%].[21, 22]

ANTIDEPRESSANT DRUGS (MISC.) such as **Nefazodone** (*Serzone*).[23]

ANTI-DIABETIC DRUGS such as **Repaglinide** (*Prandin*).[24]

ANTI-GOUT AGENTS such as **Colchicine** (*Colcrys*).[25]

ANTIFUNGAL ANTIBIOTICS such as **Itraconazole** (*Sporanox*)[26, 27] and **Ketoconazole** (*Nizoral*).[28]

ANTHELMINTIC DRUGS such as **Albendazole** (*Albenza*)[29] and **Praziquantel** (*Biltricide*).[30]

ANTIHISTAMINES (H_1 RECEPTOR ANTAGONISTS) such as **Diphenhydramine** (*Benadryl, Tylenol*),[31] **Fexofenadine** (*Allegra*)[32] and **Loratadine** (*Claritin*).[33] (Note that for **Fexofenadine**, blood concentrations are decreased rather than increased when taking grapefruit juice.)[34]

ANTI-HYPERTENSIVE DRUGS (MISC.) such as **Ivabradine** (*Corlanor*).[35]

ANTI-MALARIAL DRUGS such as **Primaquine**[36] and **Quinine** (*Legatrin*).[37]

ANTI-NEOPLASTICS such as **Erlotinib** (*Tarceva*),[38] **Mercaptopurine** (*Purixan*),[39] and **Vinblastine** (*Velban*).[40]

ANTIPSYCHOTIC DRUGS such as **Lurasidone** (*Latuda*),[41] **Pimozide** (*Orap*),[42] **Quetiapine** (*Seroquel*)[43] and **Ziprasidone** (*Geodon*)[44].

ANTI-RETROVIRAL CC CHEMOKINE RECEPTOR 5 ANTAGONISTS such as **Maraviroc** (*Celsentri*).[45]

ANTI-RETROVIRAL PROTEASE INHIBITORS such as **Indinavir** (*Crixivan*),[46] **Ritonavir** (*Norvir*), **Nelfinavir** (*Viracept*),[47] **Saquinavir** (*Fortovase, Invirase*) [200%].[48, 49, 50]

ANTI-SPASMODICS such as **Darifenacin** (*Emselex, Enablex*) and **Solifenacin** (*VESIcare*).[51]

ANTI-THROMBOTIC DRUGS such as **Apixaban** (*Eliquis*) and **Rivaroxaban** (*Xarelto*).[52]

ANTITUSSIVE DRUGS such as **Dextromethorphan**.[53]

ANXIOLYTICS such as **Buspirone** (*Buspar*) [920%].[54]

BENZODIAZEPINES such as **Alprazolam** (*Xanax*),[55] **Amprenavir** (*Agenerase*),[56] **Clonazepam** (*Klonopin*),[57] **Diazepam** (*Valium*) [320%],[58] **Midazolam** (*Versed*) [240%],[59, 60, 61] **Nitrazepam** (*Mogadon*), **Quazepam** (*Doral*)[62] and **Triazolam** (*Halcion*) [48%].[63, 64]

BETA-ADRENERGIC BLOCKERS such as **Carvedilol** (*Coreg*) [16%].[65]

CALCIUM CHANNEL BLOCKERS such as **Amlodipine** (*Lotrel, Norvasc*) [16%],[66] **Felodipine** (*Plendil*) [600%],[67, 68, 69] **Isradipine** (*DynaCirc*), **Nicardipine** (*Cardene*),[70] **Nifedipine** (*Adalat, Procardia*)[200%],[71] **Nimodipine** (*Nimotop*),[72] **Nisoldipine** (*Sular*) [900%],[73, 74] **Nitrendipine** (*Bayotensin*)[75] and **Verapamil** (*Calan, Isoptin*)[43%].[76, 77]

CARDIAC GLYCOSIDES such as **Digoxin** (*Lanoxin*).[78]

Cholesterol lowering drugs (HMG-CoA REDUCTASE INHIBITORS) such as **Atorvastatin** (*Lipitor*) [250%],[79] **Cerivastatin** (*Baycol*),[80] **Lovastatin** (*Mevacor*) [1,500%][81, 82]and **Simvastatin** (*Zocor*) [1,513%].[83, 84]

DIURETICS—POTASSIUM-SPARING such as **Eplerenone** (*Inspra*).[85]

DOPAMINE ANTAGONISTS such as **Domperidone** (*Domstal, Peridone*).[86]

EPIDERMAL GROWTH FACTOR RECEPTOR INHIBITORS such as **Lapatinib** (*Tykerb*).[87]

ERGOT ALKALOIDS such as **Ergotamine** (*Cafergot*).[88]

GENITOURINARY TRACK DRUGS such as **Fesoterodine** (*Toviaz*).[89]

GLUCOCORTICOIDS such as **Budesonide** (*Budecort*).[90]

HETEROCYCLIC ANTI-DEPRESSANTS such as **Trazodone** (*Desyrel*).[91]

IMMUNOSUPPRESSANT DRUGS such as **Cyclosporine** (*Sandimune, Neoral*)[300%][92, 93, 94] **Sirolimus** (*Rapamune*),[95] and **Tacrolimus** (*Prograf*) [400%].[96, 97]

MACROLIDE ANTIBIOTICS such as **Clarithromycin** (*Biaxin*)[98] and **Erythromycin** (*Ery-Tab*) [84%].[99, 100, 101]

MTOR INHIBITORS such as **Everolimus** (*Afinitor*).[102]

MULTIKINASE INHIBITORS such as **Crizotinib** (*Xalkori*) and **Vemurafenib** (*Zelbora*).[103]

NEUROLOGICAL/NERVOUS SYSTEM DRUGS such as **Ketamine** (*Kentan*) [200%].[104, 105]

OPIATE AGONIST DRUGS such as **Buprenorphine** (*Buprenex*),[106] **Fentanyl** (*Actiq*),[107] **Methadone** (*Metadon*),[108] and **Oxycodone** (*OxyContin*).[109]

PHOSPHODIESTERASE TYPE 5 INHIBITORS such as **Sildenafil** (*Viagra*), **Tadalafil** (*Cialis*) and **Vardenafil** (*Levitra*).[110]

PLATELET INHIBITOR DRUGS such as **Cilostazol** (*Pletal*),[111] **Clopidogrel** (*Plavix*) and **Ticagrelor** (*Brilinta*).[112]

PROKINETIC DRUGS such as **Cisapride** (*Prepulsid, Propulsid*) [39%].[113, 114]

PROTON PUMP INHIBITORS such as **Omeprazole** (*Prilosec*).[115]

PYRAZOLOPYRIMIDINES such as **Zaleplon** (*Sonata*).[116]

RENIN INHIBITORS such as **Aliskiren** (*Tekturna*).[117]

SELECTIVE SEROTONIN REUPTAKE INHIBITORS such as **Fluvoxamine** (*Luvox*)[118] and **Sertraline** (*Zoloft*).[119]

TRICYCLIC ANTI-DEPRESSANTS such as **Amitriptyline** (*Elavil*),[120] **Clomipramine** (*Anafranil*) [300%][121] and **Imipramine**.[122]

TYROSINE KINASE INHIBITORS such as **Dasatinib** (*Sprycel*), **Nilotinib** (*Tasigna*) and **Pazopanib** (*Vorient*).[123]

Note also that there have been several reports that **Caffeine** is affected by grapefruit juice. This is not true. Further research shows that **Caffeine** is metabolized by the 1A2 isoenzyme, not the 3A4 isoenzyme found in grapefruit juice.[124]

A Reasonable Solution

It is important for you to know that people differ greatly in their ability to absorb varying amounts of many medications. Thus, it is very difficult for researchers to predict exactly how much drinking grapefruit juice is going to affect blood drug levels in any given person. Your body might absorb only one-tenth of a pill, or it might absorb five times more.[125] Thus, a dose that does not hurt your ears could cause hearing loss in another person and vice versa.

The reason for this is because people have widely varying levels of the CYP 3A4 enzymes in their intestinal tract.[126] Dr. Paul Watkins, a professor of medicine, explains:

> The amount of the enzyme in the intestinal wall varies greatly among people, which explains why the grapefruit juice effect may be serious for some people and unimportant for others.[127]

He adds:

> It probably makes very little difference if people with relatively low levels of the intestinal enzyme take their medicine with grapefruit juice or with water. But for others with a great deal of the enzyme, an unaccustomed glass of juice in the morning may send enzyme levels plummeting and drug levels soaring as much as nine-fold.[128]

Dean Elbe, a pharmacist, suggests that a reasonable guideline is simply this. If you are not currently taking your medications with grapefruit juice regularly, don't start. If you are already taking your medications with grapefruit juice regularly and are not experiencing any adverse side effects, don't stop.[129]

CYP 3A4 Stabilizes Drug Absorption

One most interesting finding in the studies with which Dr. Watkins was associated is that after taking grapefruit juice, CYP 3A4 levels were virtually the same for everyone in the study instead of the large differences normally found between people.[1]

This means that adding the active ingredient in grapefruit juice (furanocoumarin) to drugs that are affected by the CYP 3A4 enzyme could ensure that much more of the drug would be absorbed and less wasted. At the same time, it would produce nearly the same effect in each person. Research is continuing on this.

Reference

[1] The Grapefruit Juice Effect, 1997. p. 5.

If you are unsure about your medications and how grapefruit juice will affect their absorption in your body, you can prevent any negative reactions by simply bypassing grapefruit altogether and drink water instead. It's that simple!

Chapter 16 Endnotes

1 Grapefruit Juice Can Interact with Medications, 1999. p. 1.
2 Grapefruit Juice Can Interact with Medications, 1999. p. 1.
3 Bailey, 2013. p. 1.

4 Thorpe, 2023. p. 1.
5 Grapefruit Interferes with Select Medications, 2000. p. 1.
6 Grapefruit Juice Can Interact with Medications, 1999. p. 1.
7 Grapefruit and Serious Drug Interactions, 2000. p. 1.
8 New Grapefruit Juice—Drug Interactions Found, 1998. p. 1.
9 Bailey, 2013. p. 1.
10 Bailey, 2013. p. 1.
11 Thorpe, 2023. p. 1.
12 Be Careful When Mixing Grapefruit Juice with Your RX, 1999. p.1.
13 Anderson, 2022. p. 1.
14 Grapefruit—Drug Interactions, 2023. p. 6.
15 Thorpe, 2023. p. 1.
16 Grapefruit—Drug Interactions, 2023. p. 7.
17 Grapefruit—Drug Interactions, 2023. p. 9.
18 The Grapefruit Juice Effect, 1997. p.3.
19 Grapefruit—Drug Interactions, 2023. p. 7.
20 Grapefruit—Drug Interactions, 2023. p. 8.
21 Elbe, 1999e. p. 2.
22 New Grapefruit Juice—Drug Interactions Found, 1998. p. 1.
23 Grapefruit—Drug Interactions, 2023. p. 9.
24 Grapefruit—Drug Interactions, 2023. p. 8.
25 Anderson, 2022. p. 1.
26 Grapefruit Juice and Medications, 1997. p. 1.
27 The Grapefruit Juice Effect, 1997. p.2.
28 Grapefruit Juice and Medications, 1997. p. 1.
29 Thorpe, 2023. p. 1.
30 Grapefruit—Drug Interactions, 2023. p. 7.
31 Food and Medication Interactions Can Be Very Harmful, 1999. p. 1.
32 Be Careful When Mixing Grapefruit Juice with Your RX, 1999. p.1.
33 Food and Medication Interactions Can Be Very Harmful, 1999. p. 1.
34 Grapefruit—Drug Interactions, 2023. p. 8.
35 Grapefruit—Drug Interactions, 2023. p. 9.
36 Thorpe, 2023. p. 1.
37 Bailey, 2013. p. 1.
38 Grapefruit—Drug Interactions, 2023. p. 8.
39 Grapefruit—Drug Interactions, 2023. p. 9.
40 Be Careful When Mixing Grapefruit Juice with Your RX, 1999. p.1.
41 Thorpe, 2023. p. 1.
42 Bailey, 2013. p. 1.
43 Grapefruit—Drug Interactions, 2023. p. 9.
44 Thorpe, 2023. p. 1.
45 Bailey, 2013. p. 1.
46 Food and Medication Interactions Can Be Very Harmful, 1999. p. 1.
47 Grapefruit—Drug Interactions, 2023. p. 9.
48 Elbe, 1999e. p. 3.
49 Zuger, 1997. p. 1.
50 Be Careful When Mixing Grapefruit Juice with Your RX, 1999. p.1.
51 Bailey, 2013. p. 1.
52 Thorpe, 2023. p. 1.
53 Grapefruit—Drug Interactions, 2023. p. 9.
54 Grapefruit—Drug Interactions, 2023. p. 9.
55 Grapefruit Juice and Drugs, 2000. p. 2.

56 Grapefruit—Drug Interactions, 2023. p. 9.
57 Grapefruit—Drug Interactions, 2023. p. 9.
58 Elbe, 1999a. p. 1.
59 Elbe, 1999a. p. 1.
60 Grapefruit Juice and Drugs, 2000. p. 2.
61 Grapefruit Juice and Medications, 1997. p. 1.
62 Grapefruit—Drug Interactions, 2023. p. 6.
63 Elbe, 1999a. p. 1.
64 Grapefruit Juice Can Interact with Medications, 1999. p. 1.
65 Elbe, 1999e. p. 3.
66 Elbe, 1999b. p. 1.
67 Zuger, 1997. p. 1.
68 Be Careful When Mixing Grapefruit Juice with Your RX, 1999. p.1.
69 The Grapefruit Juice Effect, 1997. p.3.
70 Grapefruit—Drug Interactions, 2023. p. 9.
71 Procardia (Nifedipine) Capsules, 2002. p. 1.
72 Grapefruit Juice Can Interact with Medications, 1999. p. 1.
73 The Grapefruit Juice Effect, 1997. p.1.
74 Elbe, 1999b. p. 1.
75 Grapefruit—Drug Interactions, 2023. p. 8.
76 Elbe, 1999b. p. 1.
77 Grapefruit Juice and Drugs, 2000. p. 2.
78 Be Careful When Mixing Grapefruit Juice with Your RX, 1999. p.1.
79 Elbe, 1999c. p. 2.
80 Elbe, 1999c. p. 1.
81 Elbe, 1999c. p. 1.
82 Grapefruit Juice and Medications, 1997. p. 1.
83 Elbe, 1999c. p. 2.
84 Grapefruit Juice and Drugs, 2000. p. 3.
85 Thorpe, 2023. p. 1.
86 Bailey, 2013. p. 1.
87 Bailey, 2013. p. 1.
88 Grapefruit—Drug Interactions, 2023. p. 7.
89 Bailey, 2013. p. 1.
90 Anderson, 2022. p. 1.
91 Grapefruit—Drug Interactions, 2023. p. 9.
92 Elbe, 1999d. p. 1.
93 Be Careful When Mixing Grapefruit Juice with Your RX, 1999. p. 1.
94 Grapefruit Juice and Medications, 1997. p. 1.
95 Grapefruit—Drug Interactions, 2023. p. 9.
96 Elbe, 1999d. p. 1.
97 Grapefruit Juice and Drugs, 2000. p. 3.
98 Anderson, 2022. p. 1.
99 Grapefruit Juice and Medications, 1997. p. 1.
100 The Grapefruit Juice Effect, 1997. p.2.
101 Thorpe, 2023. p. 1.
102 Bailey, 2013. p. 1.
103 Bailey, 2013. p. 1.
104 Grapefruit—Drug Interactions, 2023. p. 9.
105 Grapefruit—Drug Interactions, 2023. p. 8.
106 Grapefruit—Drug Interactions, 2023. p. 7.
107 Thorpe, 2023. p. 1.

108 Grapefruit—Drug Interactions, 2023. p. 8.
109 Grapefruit—Drug Interactions, 2023. p. 8.
110 Grapefruit—Drug Interactions, 2023. p. 9.
111 Anderson, 2022. p. 1.
112 Thorpe, 2023. p. 1.
113 Grapefruit—Drug Interactions, 2023. p. 9.
114 Elbe, 1999e. p. 1.
115 Grapefruit—Drug Interactions, 2023. p. 8.
116 Grapefruit—Drug Interactions, 2023. p. 9.
117 Anderson, 2022. p. 1.
118 Grapefruit—Drug Interactions, 2023. p. 9.
119 Grapefruit—Drug Interactions, 2023. p. 6.
120 Grapefruit—Drug Interactions, 2023. p. 7.
121 Elbe, 1999e. p. 1.
122 Grapefruit and Serious Drug Interactions, 2000. p. 1.
123 Bailey, 2013. p. 1.
124 Elbe, 1999f. p. 1.
125 It's Not Pulp Fiction: Taking Medications with Grapefruit Juice May Increase Their Potency, 1996. p. 1.
126 Grapefruit Juice Can Interact with Medications, 1999. p. 2.
127 Zuger, 1997. p. 2.
128 Zuger, 1997. p. 2.
129 Elbe, 1999b. p. 1.

Chapter 17

Potpourri

When Ototoxic Drugs Team Up, They Can Further Assault Your Ears

Not only can ototoxic drugs team up with noise to destroy your ears as we saw in Chapter 11, but they also can team up with other ototoxic drugs to continue their assault on your ears. The sad fact is that there are thousands of drugs on the market, yet very little hard data exists on what taking these drugs in various combinations can do to your ears.

Furthermore, Americans are a nation of pill poppers as I've mentioned previously. It is the rare person that doesn't take any drugs at all. Did you know that by the time they are 65, about half of all Americans are taking 5 or more drugs a day, while about one quarter of Americans over the age of 65 take between 10 and 20 medications each day.[1]

Since 100% of the most prescribed drugs can have ototoxic side effects (see page 395, this means that most seniors are taking several potentially ototoxic drugs each day, and no one knows what these various combinations of ototoxic drugs have on our ears.

When you take two or more drugs at the same time, there can be (and often will be) interactions between these drugs. These interactions can produce one of the following results.

1. The effect of each drug is unchanged. It would be wonderful if this was always the case.

2. The drug will be less effective. In other words, it is not doing what your doctor intended.

3. The drug may be more effective. This means you are essentially receiving an overdose. If the drug is ototoxic, the enhanced effects may damage your ears more than you would have expected this drug to do.

4. There may be unexpected side effects. If these side effects are ototoxic, you could damage your ears whereas taking each drug separately would not have done so.

If you are only taking one drug at a time, there won't be interactions with other drugs, but you still have to be careful as any given drug may interact with the food you eat or the beverages you drink. The result of this could be to increase the ototoxicity of the drug you are taking. For example, one such interaction is taking certain drugs with grapefruit juice as we just saw in the previous chapter. This could result in your body receiving an overdose of that drug. If that drug is ototoxic, you could inadvertently damage your ears.

The United States Food and Drug Administration (FDA), has a lot of good information on their web site for you to study. Check out their web page called "Drug Interactions: What You Should Know" at: https://www.fda.gov/drugs/resources-drugs/drug-interactions-what-you-should-know.

Which drug combinations are particularly dangerous to your ears? One of the worst combinations is taking LOOP DIURETICS (**Ethacrynic acid**, **Furosemide** or **Torsemide**) and AMINOGLYCOSIDE antibiotics (**Gentamicin**, **Kanamycin**, **Neomycin**, **Streptomycin** or **Tobramycin**) at the same time. In fact, taking drugs of these two classes together greatly increases your chance of having permanent ototoxic results[2] as the ototoxic effects are synergistic.

Another nasty combination is **Cisplatin** when used in combination with an AMINOGLYCOSIDE antibiotic and a LOOP DIURETIC such as **Furosemide**—a typical combination used to treat cancer.[3]

LOOP DIURETICS can also team up with other antibiotics such as **Polymyxin B**,[4] which can greatly increase the risk of ototoxicity.

This is just scratching the surface of drug combinations. When taking several different drugs at the same time, you need to practice your ABCs—Always Be Careful!

Non-steroidal Anti-inflammatory Drugs (NSAIDs) Can Cause Meningitis and Hearing Loss!

One little-known side effect of taking NON-STEROIDAL ANTI-INFLAMMATORY DRUGS (NSAIDs) is aseptic meningitis. Aseptic meningitis can, in turn, cause hearing loss and tinnitus. The signs and symptoms of NSAID-induced meningitis are similar to those of viral or bacterial meningitis.

One of the symptoms of aseptic meningitis can be a bilateral, sudden, sensorineural hearing loss while you are on NSAIDs.

Doctors are not sure why NSAIDs can cause aseptic meningitis. Some think it is a hypersensitivity reaction to the drug. They are also unclear how it causes the hearing loss—whether in the cochlea or in the brain. One theory is that the endolymphatic sac is irritated, which may account for the predominantly low-tone pattern of the resulting hearing loss.

Types of Meningitis

Meningitis may be caused by a virus (viral meningitis), or by bacteria (bacterial meningitis). If it is not caused by either of these pathogens, doctors call it aseptic meningitis. Drug-induced meningitis is a type of aseptic meningitis.

The NSAIDs most frequently associated with this disorder include **Ibuprofen**, **Sulindac**, **Naproxen** and **Tolmetin**. Other ototoxic drugs that may cause aseptic meningitis are the ANTIBIOTIC drugs **Trimethoprim** and **Sulfamethoxazole**,[5] the ACETIC ACIDS **Diclofenac**[6] and **Ketorolac**,[7] the PROPIONIC ACID **Ketoprofen**,[8] the COX-2 INHIBITOR **Rofecoxib**,[9] the ANTI-CONVULSANT drug **Carbamazepine**,[10] and the **Mumps vaccine**.[11]

The risk factors discovered so far that appear to be associated with NSAID-induced aseptic meningitis include heavy use of drugs, systemic lupus erythematosus and mixed connective tissue disease.

Fortunately, with the cases studied so far, when NSAID use is stopped, hearing returns to normal within a few months and tinnitus subsides.[12]

Watch Out for Your Pet's Ears Too

If you are hard of hearing, you probably rely to a certain extent on your dog to be your ears like I did with the various dogs I have had over the years. Dogs make excellent "furry ears" to help us hear. In fact, many deaf and hard of hearing people have specially-trained service dogs (called "hearing ear dogs" in Canada and "hearing dogs" in the USA) to alert them to all kinds of things they can't hear. This is wonderful!

However, all may not be well in doggy-land. Your faithful Fido can get sick. Perhaps you notice he is scratching his ear. You take him to the veterinarian. The vet looks into his ears and prescribes an antibiotic to clear up an ear infection.

After a few days of faithfully applying the eardrops, the infection clears up. Both of you are now happy—until a few days later you discover to your horror that Fido is now deaf! He can't hear you yelling right by his head. Whatever happened to his hearing?

Surprise! Dog's ears are very susceptible to the ototoxic effects of drugs just like your own ears are. I know. It happened to our dog Riley. It happened to this lady's dog too. She wrote to me about her pet going deaf from taking ototoxic drugs:

> It is an eye opening experience to realize that drugs specifically prescribed for treatment of the ear could damage it!

Make no mistake. This stuff happens. Even though our vet said Riley's hearing loss was the only case he had seen in his 25 years of practice as a veterinarian, it must occur much more frequently than is commonly thought. Just 4 or 5 weeks later, I was talking to a phone repairman. I mentioned to him that our dog was still pretty deaf from taking a course of eardrops to clear up an ear infection so he might not let me know if anyone was knocking on my door. Imagine my surprise when this repairman exclaimed:

> That happened to my dog too! He had an ear infection, so the vet gave me some drops for him. Within a week he was totally deaf. Fortunately, most of his hearing came back about 3 weeks later.

I further questioned him about whether his dog's hearing all returned, and he said it was not back to what it was before. This is the same experience we had with Riley. He could not hear as well as he used to—but at least he could hear some sounds! I think he ended up with a moderate hearing loss.

Certainly not every pet taking an ototoxic medication loses his hearing any more than this happens to every person that takes an antibiotic. Just as in humans, some dogs are more susceptible to ototoxic side effects than others. There are a lot of factors that put your pet at higher risk of ototoxic damage. These include such things as age, concurrent infections, anesthesia, pre-existing cochlear damage and repeated courses of antibiotics.[13]

Unfortunately, by the time you notice that your pet is losing his hearing, it is likely already too late, and the ototoxic effects may be permanent. The Aminoglycoside antibiotics are very ototoxic to dogs, just as they are to humans. The two most commonly-used Aminoglycosides in veterinary practice are **Gentamicin** and **Neomycin**. They often come in the form of ear drops or topical creams.[14]

For example, the drug compound we used on Riley's ears was sold under the trade name of *Otomax*. *Otomax* is an ointment used for ear infections. Notice that it is a combination of three drugs: **Gentamicin**, **Betamethasone** and **Clotrimazole**. All three are known to be ototoxic, but **Gentamicin** is by far the worst.

You may be staggered to discover just how many of the drugs your veterinarian prescribes are ototoxic! I wonder how many vets know this. One article I read stated that there are more than 180 ototoxic compounds. The author then listed 57 of the more common ones likely to be seen in veterinary practice.[15]

In my research, I came across a reasonably comprehensive data base of veterinary drugs used in the United States, Britain, France, Germany and Holland that listed 687 different drugs.[16] Other lists yield additional veterinary drugs.[17] In one list, I recognized well over 220 drugs used by veterinarians that are ototoxic to humans. In addition, I'm positive there are drugs only used in veterinary medicine that are also ototoxic. If pets are affected by the same drugs as humans, it would appear that at least 50% of veterinary medicines have the potential to damage your pet's ears.

Table 17-1 lists 303 of the more-commonly-used veterinary drugs that are known to be ototoxic to humans. Your pet may have the same ototoxic reactions to these drugs as you do.

The next time your veterinarian prescribes a drug for your dog, check it out. If it is ototoxic to humans, there is a good chance it will also be ototoxic to your pooch. Watch him closely for any signs of ototoxic side effects since he can't tell you if his ears are ringing or that he is going deaf. He looks out for you. The least you can do is watch out for him!

Table 17-1: A Sampling of Drugs Used in Veterinary Practice That Are Known to be Ototoxic to Humans and Thus May Damage Your Pets Ears Too

Acebutolol	**Aminophylline**	**Albuterol**
Acepromazine	**Aminosalicylic acid**	**Alclofenac**
Acetazolamide	**Amiodarone**	**Allopurinol**
Acetylsalicylic acid	**Amitriptyline**	**Alprazolam**
Albendazole	**Amlodipine**	**Amantadine**
Albuterol	**Amobarbital**	**Amikacin**
Alclofenac	**Amoxicillin**	**Amiloride**
Allopurinol	**Acebutolol**	**Aminophylline**
Alprazolam	**Acepromazine**	**Aminosalicylic acid**
Amantadine	**Acetazolamide**	**Amiodarone**
Amikacin	**Acetylsalicylic acid**	**Amitriptyline**
Amiloride	**Albendazole**	**Amlodipine**

Table 17-1: **A Sampling of Drugs Used in Veterinary Practice That Are Known to be Ototoxic to Humans and Thus May Damage Your Pets Ears Too (Cont'd.)**

Amobarbital
Amoxicillin
Amphotericin B
Ampicillin
Apomorphine
Arsenic trioxide
Atenolol
Atropine
Auranofin
Bacitracin
Baclofen
Benazepril
Benzalkonium
Benzethonium
Benzocaine
Betamethasone
Bethanechol
Bismuth subsalicylate
Bretylium
Bromocriptine
Bumetanide
Bupivacaine
Buprenorphine
Buspirone
Butorphanol
Cabergoline
Caffeine
Calcitonin
Calcitriol
Captopril
Carbamazepine
Carprofen
Cefazolin
Cefpodoxime
Cephalexin
Chloral hydrate
Chlorambucil
Chloramphenicol
Chlordiazepoxide
Chlorhexidine
Chloroquine
Chlorothiazide
Chlorpheniramine
Chlorthalidone
Chlortetracycline
Cholecalciferol
Cholestyramine
Ciprofloxacin
Cisapride
Cisplatin
Clemastine
Clindamycin
Clomiphene
Clomipramine
Clonazepam
Clonidine
Codeine
Colistin
Cortisone
Cyanocobalamin
Cyclizine
Cyclophosphamide
Cyclosporine
Cyproheptadine
Cyproterone
Cytarabine
Dactinomycin
Danazol
Dapsone
Deferoxamine
Dexamethasone
Dexmedetomidine
Diazepam
Diazoxide
Dibekacin
Dichlorphenamide
Diclofenac
Digoxin
Diltiazem
Diphenhydramine
Diphenylhydrazine
Dipyridamole
Disopyramide
Doxepin
Doxorubicin
Doxycycline
Doxylamine
Enalapril
Ephedrine
Epinephrine
Ergonovine
Erythromycin
Estradiol
Ethacrynic acid
Ethosuximide
Etodolac
Etretinate
Famotidine
Fenoprofen
Fentanyl
Flavoxate
Flecainide
Fluconazole
Flucytosine
Fludrocortisone
Flumazenil
Fluorouracil
Fluoxetine
Flurazepam
Framycetin
Frusemide
Furosemide
Gabapentin
Gemfibrozil
Gentamicin
Glipizide
Glyburide
Glycopyrrolate
Griseofulvin
Guaifenesin
Haloperidol
Hydrochlorothiazide
Hydrocodone
Hydrocortisone
Hydromorphone
Hydroxyzine
Hygromycin B
Hyoscyamine
Ibuprofen
Imipenem
Imipramine
Indomethacin

Table 17-1: A Sampling of Drugs Used in Veterinary Practice That Are Known to be Ototoxic to Humans and Thus May Damage Your Pets Ears Too (Cont'd.)

Ipratropium
Isoflurane
Isoniazid
Isosorbide
Isotretinoin
Isoxsuprine
Itraconazole
Ivermectin
Kanamycin
Ketamine
Ketoconazole
Ketoprofen
Ketorolac
Levamisole
Levetiracetam
Levothyroxine
Lidocaine
Lincomycin
Lisinopril
Lithium
Lorazepam
Magnesium salicylate
Mannitol
Mechlorethamine
Meclizine
Medroxyprogesterone
Mefenamic acid
Megestrol
Meloxicam
Meperidine
Meprobamate
Methazolamide
Methenamine
Methimazole
Methocarbamol
Methotrexate
Methylprednisolone
Metoclopramide
Metoprolol
Metronidazole
Mexiletine
Midazolam
Minocycline
Mirtazapine
Misoprostol
Mitotane
Morphine
Moxifloxacin
Nadolol
Nalbuphine
Nalidixic acid
Naltrexone
Naproxen
Neomycin
Netilmicin
Nifedipine
Nimesulide
Nitroglycerin
Norethindrone
Nortriptyline
Nystatin
Octreotide
Ofloxacin
Omeprazole
Oxazepam
Oxymorphone
Papaverine
Paroxetine
Penicillamine
Penicillin
Pentazocine
Pentobarbital
Pentoxifylline
Pergolide
Perphenazine
Phenobarbital
Phenylbutazone
Phenylephrine
Phenylpropanolamine
Phenytoin
Pilocarpine
Pimozide
Pindolol
Piperazine
Piroxicam
Polymyxin B
Praziquantel
Prazosin
Prednisolone
Prednisone
Pregabalin
Primidone
Procainamide
Procarbazine
Progesterone
Promethazine
Propafenone
Propofol
Propranolol
Propylene glycol
Propylthiouracil
Protriptyline
Pseudoephedrine
Pyrantel
Pyridostigmine
Quinidine
Quinine
Ranitidine
Ribavirin
Rifampin
Scopolamine
Secobarbital
Sertraline
Sevoflurane
Sisomicin
Sodium salicylate
Sotalol
Spironolactone
Streptomycin
Sucralfate
Sulfamethazine
Sulfasalazine
Suramin
Tamoxifen
Tenoxicam
Terbutaline
Testosterone
Tetracycline
Theophylline
Thiabendazole
Thiopental
Thioridazine

Table 17-1: **A Sampling of Drugs Used in Veterinary Practice That Are Known to be Ototoxic to Humans and Thus May Damage Your Pets Ears Too (Cont'd.)**

Timolol
Tobramycin
Tocainide
Tolbutamide
Tramadol
Tranylcypromine
Trazodone
Triamcinolone
Triamterene
Triazolam
Trimeprazine
Trimethoprim
Tripelennamine
Ursodeoxycholic acid
Valproic acid
Vancomycin
Vasopressin
Verapamil
Vinblastine
Vincristine
Zidovudine
Zonisamide [1 2 3, 4, 5]

References

1 VetBase: List of Drugs, 2000. pp. 1-7.
2 Strain, 1996. pp. 2-4.
3 Veterinary Formulary, 2001. pp. 2-3.
4 Pharmacology: Commonly Used Drugs, 2018. p. 1.
5 Veterinary Pharmaceutical Drugs, 2023. p. 1.

Chapter 17 Endnotes

1 Dangers of Polypharmacy, 2011. p. 1.
2 Haybach, 1998. p. 6.
3 Audiological Aspects of Ototoxicity, 1996. p. 1.
4 Guidelines for the Audiologic Management of Individuals Receiving Cochleotoxic Drug Therapy, 1994. p. 3.
5 Physicians' Desk Reference, 2003. p. 2184.
6 Physicians' Desk Reference, 2003. p. 2236.
7 Physicians' Desk Reference, 2003. p. 2945.
8 Physicians' Desk Reference, 2002. p. 3550.
9 Physicians' Desk Reference, 2003. p. 2124.
10 Physicians' Desk Reference, 2003. p. 3145.
11 Physicians' Desk Reference, 2003. p. 2046.
12 Davison, 1998. p. 820.
13 Strain, 1996. p. 2.
14 Strain, 1996. p. 2.
15 Strain, 1996. pp. 2-4.
16 VetBase: List of Drugs, 2000. pp. 1-7.
17 Veterinary Formulary, 2001. pp. 2-3.

Chapter 18

Keep Yourself Healthy While Taking Few or No Drugs

People often ask me how they can protect their ears from the ravages of ototoxic drugs. They want to know about safer alternatives. In fact, one man took me to task. He wrote:

> You keep saying what drugs are ototoxic and should not be used if we want to protect our ears and hearing. However, you don't tell us what we should be taking. It would enlighten us all if you explained some of the safer treatments we can use.

With this in mind, I have added this chapter. The information in this chapter is not intended to be comprehensive as that alone would be a major book. Rather, here are examples of a number of things you should consider in order to help protect yourself from the side effects of ototoxic drugs.

Educational, Not Medical Advice

Again, let me reiterate that this information is not intended to be taken as medical advice. I am not a medical doctor, and therefore I do not diagnose conditions and prescribe treatments. However, I do provide educational information that you and your doctor can use to help prevent drugs from damaging your ears.

Take Responsibility for Your Own Health

"If it's to be, it's up to me." This was one of the slogans I heard repeatedly in one company with which I was once associated. The meaning is clear. If you want something to happen, you have to make it happen yourself. Don't expect someone else to do it.

What does this have to do with ototoxic drugs? Simply this. If you want to protect your ears from the ravages of ototoxic drugs, you have to be eternally vigilant. This means you have to become **informed** on the side effects of drugs **before** you take them.

If you don't know much or anything about ototoxic drugs, this book is a good place to obtain this information. Take the time to look up any drugs your doctor wants to prescribe for you. This way you will know the risks to your ears from taking that drug before you take it. Then you and your doctor can mutually decide what drugs may work for you while still protecting your ears. If your doctor brushes you off, maybe it's time to find another doctor—one that is willing to work with you to save your ears.

Part of taking responsibility for your own health is that you need to learn how to become and stay healthy. Therefore, you need to research any proposed treatments, especially drug therapy, in light of good health before you begin them.

For example, my experience reveals that many prescription drugs cause unnecessary damage to our bodies. Thus, I use other means in order to stay healthy. There are many alternative ways of achieving health without taking drugs. Talk to various alternative medicine practitioners—for example, naturopathic doctors, herbalists, chiropractors, acupuncturists, massage therapists, natural food nutritionists and so on. These practitioners have a wealth of knowledge about good health, and the wisdom to help you become, and stay, healthy.

When you do this, not only will you save the money that you now spend on drugs, but you will also likely feel ever so much better. Furthermore, you'll never have to worry about drugs damaging your ears either!

It takes time and effort to maintain good health. It doesn't just happen by itself. You must be involved. Remember, "If it's to be, it's up to me!"

Choose a Health Care Professional Who Knows About Health, Not Just About Sickness

If you want to stay healthy, you need to choose your health care professionals wisely. If you are sick, who would you rather go to—a doctor who is an expert in health and can teach you how to become and stay healthy, or a doctor who is an expert in sickness and treats the symptoms of your condition with drugs and/or surgery, but never treats the fundamental cause, so you are never really cured?

You might be shocked to know that in medical school the typical medical doctor (MD) gets extremely limited training in good health. He spends the bulk of his time learning about sickness. In contrast the typical naturopathic doctor (ND) spends much of his time learning about health and how to keep the body healthy.

Check out the various health care professionals that practice alternative medicine and therapies. For example, some medical doctors have learned a lot about good health and practice some alternative therapies. Naturopathic doctors are trained in how to restore you to health and use natural means to accomplish that. Sometimes what your body needs is not a medical doctor, but the skills of a chiropractor. Other conditions respond best to an acupuncturist. Other times, a herbalist may be the person to see, or a massage therapist. No one health care professional knows it all.

Since doctors practice what they learn, no wonder the typical MD treats you with drugs and surgery, while the typical ND talks to you about health and nutrition, and the typical chiropractor uses manipulation to help restore you to health.

Here's an easy way to separate the medical doctors who are truly trying to help you from the doctors that just run "patient mills". It's based on the astute observation of J. Apley who, back in 1978, wrote:

> Doctors who treat the **symptoms** tend to give a prescription.
>
> Doctors who treat the **patient** are more likely to offer guidance.

No matter what condition you have–whether its hearing loss, balance problems, tinnitus, or anything else wrong with your body, if you want to get better, you and your doctor need to root out the **source** of the problem, not just suppress the **symptoms** with drugs.

Take Prescription Drugs as a Last Resort, Not as Your First Line of Attack

If you want to stay as healthy as possible, only take drugs when they are absolutely necessary. Instead of taking drugs, seek to fix any underlying health problems. Most drugs do not do that. Typically, they just mask symptoms. Thus, you end up taking the drug "forever," because when you stop, the symptoms reappear. If you dig down to the root cause of your health problems and fix them, you'll seldom need drugs.

Not only do drugs typically not cure diseases, but they also introduce a whole host of side effects, often referred to as adverse drug events (ADE). These adverse drug events crop up all over the place.

Therefore, if you experience new adverse symptoms, especially if you are an older person, consider them drug-related until proven otherwise, according to Dr. Paula Rochon.[1]

Americans take a **lot** of prescription drugs. Any way you look at it, Americans are a nation of pill poppers. I think the motto of many Americans is "A pill for every ill". It is the rare person who doesn't take any drugs at all. It's no wonder that prescription drug use is at record highs.

In 2022, doctors in the USA prescribed a total of 1,621,396,427 prescriptions **for just the 50 top prescription drugs**.[2] The retail value of these 1.6 billion prescriptions was more than $53,000,000,000.00![3]

Each year more and more people are damaging their ears from taking ototoxic drugs. Why? Simply this. People are taking more and more drugs, and the law of averages says that the more drugs you take, the greater your chances of having adverse side effects.

The scary thing is that **all** the top 50 prescription drugs[4] (and the top 200 drugs—see sidebar) can be ototoxic and damage your ears in some way (and all of them also have numerous other side effects).

Top 200 Prescription Drugs for 2020 All Ototoxic

Here's a shocking statistic. Of the top 200 prescriptions written in America in the year 2020 (representing more than 2.45 billion prescriptions), **all** (100%) of these drugs had ototoxic side effects listed! There are currently more than 6.3 billion prescriptions filled every year just in the USA![1] That works out to about 19 prescriptions filled every year for every American in 2020. You'll find all these drugs detailed in this book. That's scary. Thus, the trick now is not trying to find a drug that is not ototoxic, but finding the drug that is the least ototoxic.

Reference

1 Ho, 2023. p. 1

Dr. John Abramson of the Harvard Medical School, when asked, "Are most Americans overmedicated?" replied, "They sure are!" He further explained, "It is no secret that **Americans take many drugs unnecessarily**, and when drugs are needed, people often take the wrong ones".[5] The late Dr. Sidney Wolfe, the Health Research Group founder and the former senior advisor of Public Citizen's Worst Pills, Best Pills News, which can be found at www.citizen.org echoed the same sentiment. He lamented:

> So often, drugs are prescribed unnecessarily, especially to older adults. The result is that what might have been minor problems becomes major problems.

So, who's to blame—patients? doctors? or the drug industry? They all are! Here's why.

People: People want the magic pill that instantly gets rid of their physical problems, so they buy into the idea of "an injection for every infection", "a pill for every ill" and "a drug for every bug". They don't want to change their lifestyle, eating habits or exercise habits to get (and stay) well.

Doctors: Most doctors prescribe drugs because they think it's in their patients' best interest to do so because that is what they have been taught to believe. Where did they get this idea? From the drug companies, of course. Doctors need to quit believing everything the drug companies tell them and investigate all the different methods for healing people apart from drugs.

Drug Companies: Drug companies want to make money by selling you drugs that don't cure your condition but make insane amounts of money for themselves by selling you drugs that you have to take for the rest of your life.

So where does that leave you? If you want to get healthy, you need to do your homework **before** you decide whether to take a drug for a given condition, or whether you should look for an alternate solution that is not harmful to your ears (and the rest of your body) and has the potential to make you truly healthy again.

You need to ask yourself, "Are natural therapies a better alternative to some drugs?" If you look at the data rather than listen to the drug ads, you will see that natural alternatives, such as improved diet and routine exercise, often are **far more effective** than drugs at achieving real health improvements such as less heart disease and longer life.[6]

Now, here comes the kicker. Many patients prefer pills because they're easier. In other words, people are **lazy** when it comes to protecting their health. There is no question that many people would rather take a pill than change their lifestyle.

If the pills worked, it would simply be a question of how you want to spend your money. The problem is that the "magic" of the pills often is empowered by your cultural beliefs but without a genuine scientific basis. **About two-thirds of your health is determined by the way you live your life**, and—for better or worse—no pills can change that.[7]

Therefore, you want to be sure that any drug you take is **absolutely necessary** before you take it, if you truly value your health. Drugs should always be your **last** resort, not your first line of attack.

Instead of worrying whether a certain drug is ototoxic or not, you should be questioning whether that drug is really necessary or not, and whether it can cure you or not. When the answer is "no", you should be actively looking for better alternatives.

In my own life I have always followed this principle. I keep my drug usage to an absolute minimum. For example, in my adult life until recently, I can only remember getting two prescriptions—one was an antibiotic for an infection that I couldn't kill using natural methods, and the other was for a bad case of sciatic pain. Even then, I only took two of the pills, not the whole bottle. Apart from that, the only drug I take occasionally is the painkiller the dentist injects before working on a live tooth. I **never** touch over-the-counter medications either.

It's tragic that people typically ignore the basic things that will help them the most to stay healthy such as getting adequate exercise, eating a healthy diet, watching their weight and getting plenty of rest. People typically refuse to do these things because they take effort, and they want effortless health—hence they pop pills instead of doing those things that really make a difference.

Get Off the Drug Treadmill

When you take a drug, often you get side effects. When you complain to your doctor about the side effects, instead of taking you off the drug, he often just prescribes another drug to suppress the side effects of the first drug. Unfortunately, this second drug then produces even more side effects, so you have to take a third drug. Soon you are popping a handful of drugs 3 or 4 times a day—and your health steadily deteriorates.

Here is a fictitious (yet still true to life) example. Let's say you are depressed so you go to your doctor. He prescribes **Quetiapine** (*Seroquel*). That works for your depression (at least to some extent), but it gives you hyperglycemia (high blood sugar and you start to develop diabetes). Your doctor then puts you on **Rosiglitazone** (*Avandia*) for your diabetes. One of the side effects of **Rosiglitazone** is increased LDL cholesterol (the bad kind of cholesterol), which in turn increases your blood pressure, and thus your risk for heart attacks. As a result, your doctor puts you on **Diltiazem** (*Cardizem*), a CALCIUM CHANNEL BLOCKER, to bring down your blood pressure. But **Diltiazem** increases your high blood sugar even more, so your doctor puts you on **Olmesartan** (*Benicar*) to try to bring down your high blood sugar. The **Olmesartan** increases the risk that you will die of a heart attack or stroke. At the same time, the **Diltiazem** you are now taking causes you to have GastroEsophageal Reflux Disease (GERD), so your doctor prescribes **Esomeprazole** (*Nexium*) a PROTON-PUMP INHIBITOR to try to control your acid reflux.

By now, these drugs have also affected your ears. You suffer from horrible bilateral tinnitus which exacerbates your initial depression. You now feel like a zombie, you look like a walking cadaver, and you hope for an early death to put you out of your misery. This is what can happen when you get on the drug treadmill and blindly take one drug after another.

At some point you have to say, "Enough is enough!" You need to stop popping pills and get off this drug treadmill if you ever hope to regain your health.

Although this example is fictitious, it is representative of the miseries multitudes of people go through as one drug is added to another drug as their health deteriorates. When they can't stand it anymore and want to do something about it, they may contact me to see if I can help them.

In case you think this scenario is far-fetched, guess again. Each of these drugs do indeed cause such side effects.

One of the side effects of both **Quetiapine** and **Diltiazem** is hyperglycemia—they cause high blood sugar where none existed before—according to the PDR.

Rosiglitazone substantially increases your bad, low-density LDL cholesterol levels resulting in increased heart attacks. In fact, studies have revealed that the risk for heart attacks among people taking **Rosiglitazone** was 40% higher than for those taking other diabetes medications—yet it is still on the market (although restricted) at this time.[8] In fact, **Rosiglitazone** is now believed to have caused more than 83,000 heart attacks between 1999 and 2007![9]

Olmesartan also increases your risk of heart attacks and strokes. Here is more background on this drug. The:

> ...FDA is evaluating data from two clinical trials in which patients with Type 2 diabetes taking the blood pressure medication, **Olmesartan** (*Benicar*), an ANGIOTENSIN-2-RECEPTOR BLOCKER, had a **higher rate of death** from a cardiovascular cause compared to patients taking a placebo.[10]

Notice that! **Olmesartan**, a high-blood pressure medication, causes death more often in those taking it, than in those who have high blood pressure but don't take it!

This report admits, "An unexpected finding observed in both trials was a greater number of deaths from a cardiovascular cause (heart attack, sudden death, or stroke) in the *Benicar*-treated patients compared to placebo".[11]

Now the reason you supposedly take a high blood pressure medication is to **prevent** heart attacks, strokes and sudden death—yet this drug apparently actually **causes** them—based on the results of not just one, but two, long-term studies.

After hearing this, any normal person would conclude that taking the drug could be dangerous to their health and quit taking it, yet does the FDA reach the same conclusion? Not on your life (and it is **your life** they are talking about)!

Here's what they say. The "FDA's review is ongoing, and the Agency has **not** concluded that *Benicar* increases the risk of death". (Yet the two studies they reviewed showed just the opposite.)

So what is their recommendation? You're not going to believe it. The "FDA currently believes that the benefits of *Benicar* in patients with high blood pressure **continue to outweigh its potential risks**".[12]

What I want to know is what **benefits** are they talking about—since the supposed benefits of high-blood pressure medication are to **reduce** the risk of heart attacks, strokes and sudden death—and these studies clearly show that taking this drug results in **more** heart attacks, **more** strokes and **more** sudden death! Why would you ever want to take such a drug? Yet 1.2 million people (representing 4.6 million prescriptions) here in the USA take this killer drug each year.

Diltiazem, and indeed all the CALCIUM CHANNEL BLOCKERS have a different nefarious side effect. They can cause GastroEsophageal Reflux Disease (GERD), and that "requires" still another drug for treatment.

Drugs that can result in GERD include not only the CALCIUM CHANNEL BLOCKERS (**Amlodipine**, **Diltiazem**, **Felodipine**, **Nicardipine**, etc.) but also the BETA BLOCKERS (**Acebutolol**, **Atenolol**, **Betaxolol**, **Carteolol**, etc.), some ANTIDEPRESSANTS and some ANTI-ANXIETY DRUGS.

Thus, when doctors prescribe drugs to treat conditions such as high blood pressure, heart disease, depression and anxiety, the drugs they prescribe can cause GERD where none existed before.

The statistics are alarming. "The number of people hospitalized for conditions related to GastroEsophageal Reflux Disease (GERD) doubled between 1998 and 2005." At the present time, "more than 20 million Americans have GERD".[13] Burgeoning drug use in the above classes of drugs no doubt is largely responsible for this enormous increase in GERD.

Here's how these drugs cause GERD. "When you eat or drink, food and liquid move from your mouth to your esophagus where a valve, called the lower esophageal sphincter (LES), relaxes to allow the food and liquid to pass into your stomach. The lower esophageal sphincter then squeezes shut to keep stomach contents from backing up (a process known as reflux) into your esophagus."[14]

As long as this valve stays tightly shut, you don't have a problem. However, if you take any of the above drugs, you need to be aware that these (and other) drugs reduce lower esophageal sphincter (LES) pressure (that is, they relax this muscle located at the top of your stomach). As a result, the contents of your stomach can then back up into your esophagus, eventually resulting in GERD.

When this happens, your doctor prescribes yet another drug such as the PROTON PUMP INHIBITOR **Esomeprazole** (*Nexium*) to try to control your GERD. Surprise, **Esomeprazole**—the little purple pill—has a number of side effects, including ototoxic side effects such as ataxia, dizziness, ear pain, tinnitus and vertigo.

Thus, when you use even more drugs to "cure" the side effects of other drugs, you can end up increasing the risk of damage to your ears (not to mention the rest of your body).

The way to prevent this is to find a health care professional who will treat your original underlying problem without causing all these other escalating side effects and health problems.

Enough is enough. Get off the drug treadmill while you still can.

Don't Take Drugs for Minor Ailments—Tough It Out Instead

Americans have become a nation of wimps. For every little ache and pain, they either turn to the medicine cabinet, or they run to the doctor for some drug or pain killer. The problem is, these drugs and pain killers can damage your ears and the rest of your body too.

Often, all you need to do is just let nature take its course. The problem will heal itself naturally in a day or two, or a week or two. Perhaps you just need to get extra rest, or take it easy, or have a massage, or put ice on it, or heat on it—things like that—rather than take drugs.

For example, don't be like so many women who take hormone replacement therapy (HRT) for their hot flashes—and later find out that the drugs they took caused unexpected nasty side effects. One lady, with the wisdom of hindsight, after she had lost most of her hearing to HRT, wrote:

> [In retrospect] my life would have been much easier if I'd just withstood the hot flashes and not medicated them away!

So often people take drugs for essentially minor problems. However, the side effects of the drugs cause major problems. Having trouble sleeping at times is a minor problem. Breaking your hip is a major problem. So don't let ototoxic drugs break your hips. I'm serious. Each year 32,000 older adults suffer hip fractures that are **attributable to drug-induced falls** that result in in more than 1,500 deaths. That's a **lot** of broken hips each year just from taking ototoxic drugs.[15]

In one study, the main categories of drugs responsible for the falls leading to hip fractures were sleeping pills and minor tranquilizers (30%), anti-psychotic drugs (52%) and antidepressants (17%). All these drugs are often prescribed unnecessarily, especially in older adults.[16]

Specifically notice the above sentence. Doctors commonly **unnecessarily** prescribe these drugs for what are essentially minor problems. The result is major problems such as hip fractures and death.

Therefore, if you want to keep your "pins" under you as you age, go easy on the drugs! Herbals may work just as well or better, and won't compromise your balance.

Make Your Doctor Prove That the Benefits Will Far Outweigh the Side Effects

A new poll in Consumer Reports Magazine revealed that one in six Americans who have ever taken a prescription drug experienced a side effect that was serious enough to send them to the hospital![17] One in six! Considering the percentage of people in this country who are on some form of daily prescription medication (remember, it's over 50 percent now), this is a stunning statistic. That's 16 percent of the people who've ever taken a prescription medicine!

Since there are around 331 million people in the USA, and since 90% or more of the population have taken a prescription drug at some time in their lives, that works out to around 49 million people in the USA that have been hospitalized at one time or another by serious side effects from taking prescription drugs!

Remember, this poll is only talking about the "serious" side effects. Added to this are all the side effects that were not considered serious enough to go to the hospital. These side effects include many of the ototoxic side effects people also experience.

Thus, it appears that taking drugs ultimately may do more harm to your body than good (Fig. 18-1). Therefore, **before** you take any drugs, make your doctor justify to you how the supposed benefits of taking the prescription will **far** outweigh the negative side effects (Fig. 18-2). If he can't do

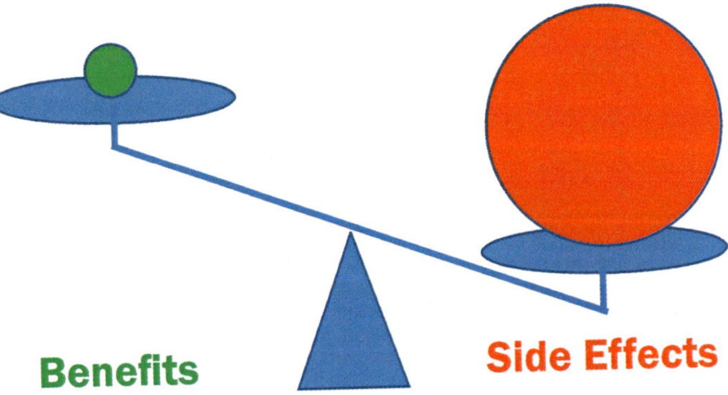

Fig. 18-1: What often actually happens—you experience many/big side effects and few/small benefits.

that, you'll just be exchanging one problem for another, or more likely just adding more health issues to those you already have. As the cases mentioned throughout this book so powerfully testify, your doctor may be hard-pressed to do this and your results may look more like those in Fig. 18-1 than those in Fig. 18-2 like you want.

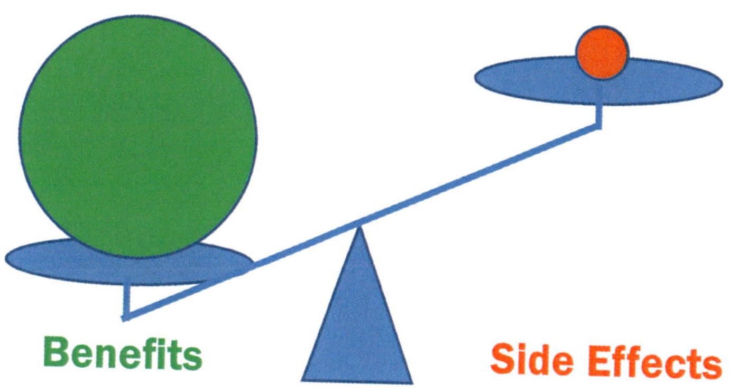

Fig. 18-2: What you and your doctor want/expect a drug will do for you—have many/big benefits and few/small side effects.

Choose the Least Ototoxic Drug That Will Do the Job

If you want to avoid all ototoxic side effects of drugs, the obvious answer is, "Don't take ototoxic drugs in the first place". Use alternative medicine therapies instead.

However, if you do choose to use drugs that have ototoxic side effects, the wise solution is to choose the least ototoxic drug that will do the job.

The way to do this is to ask your doctor for a list of the drugs you could take for your condition that he feels will do the job. Then look up each of these drugs in Chapter 19 to see what their ototoxic side effects are, how likely they are to occur and how severe these side effects might be. Next, list the drugs in order from the least ototoxic to the most ototoxic. From this list, choose the drug that has the fewest side effects.

Also, choose a drug that has side effects with which you are prepared to live (if you should be unlucky enough to get them). For example, if you already have bad tinnitus, you may decide not to take any drugs that have tinnitus as a side effect, but you are prepared to live with a drug that has some dizziness as a side effect. If you want to preserve your remaining hearing, you may choose to stay away from any drugs that have hearing loss as a side effect.

Important: While you are looking at the ototoxic side effects of the various drugs on your list, you must **not** neglect to look up in some authoritative drug book, or on-line drug website (such as Drugs.com), **all** the other side effects of that drug. This book only deals with your ears, but you must consider your **whole** body, not just your ears. What is the ultimate benefit if you protect your ears, but severely damage your heart in the process. If your body dies, your ears won't hear anything either!

Take the Lowest Dose for the Shortest Possible Time

Once you have decided on which drug or drugs you are prepared to take, ask your doctor to prescribe the **lowest** dose that will treat your condition. This is because many drugs do not exhibit ototoxic side effects at very low doses, but such side effects may become apparent at higher doses. Thus, by keeping the dose low, you can often fly under the ototoxic drug radar so to speak and thus protect your ears from ototoxic side effects.

Numbers of people have told me that the original dose their doctor put them on did not affect their ears in any way, but when their doctor increased their dose, they soon noticed problems with their ears.

For example, one lady explained that her existing tinnitus became noticeably louder when her doctor put her on a higher dose of **Irbesartan**. When she complained to her doctor, he reduced the dose to its old level again, and her tinnitus returned to its previous level.

Flying Under the Ototoxic Drug Radar

If you have to (or choose to) take drugs, here are my four rules of thumb to prevent most ototoxic side effects from appearing.

1. Take the least ototoxic drug that will do the job.
2. Take the lowest dose that will do the job.
3. Take the drug for the shortest time that will do the job.
4. Take as few drugs at the same time (ideally just one at a time so you can avoid synergistic side effects from occurring.

By following these four rules of thumb, you can often fly under the ototoxic drug radar and not experience any obvious ototoxic side effects. Your ears will love you for it.

Furthermore, ask your doctor to prescribe any drug for the **shortest** effective time possible. This is because some ototoxic drugs do not damage your ears in the short term, but the longer you take the drug, the more likely it is to damage your ears. Thus, by taking a given drug for only two weeks, for example, you may avoid all ototoxic side effects, whereas taking the same drug for several months may cause serious damage to your ears.

Use Herbals Instead of Prescription Drugs

In order to protect your ears (and the rest of your body) from drug side effects, you need to use the mildest medication that will do the job, not a harsh medication that stomps rough-shod over your body.

For example, a lady asked me:

> Do you have an opinion on which antidepressants are the safest for our ears—e.g. *Pamelor, Zoloft, Lexapro, Celexa*, etc. Is there one that is significantly less ototoxic than the others?

In my reply to her, I explained that personally I wouldn't use any of the above drugs. Why? Because there is a much safer alternative—the herbal, **St. John's Wort**.

You see, numerous studies have shown that **St. John's Wort** is at least as effective as prescription drugs in treating mild to moderate cases of depression, but it does not have the harsh action on your body that prescription anti-depressants have.

Here's some more good news. **St. John's Wort** is only very mildly ototoxic. Thus, at normal doses, you can take it for as long as you need to without unduly worrying of causing hearing loss, aggravating your tinnitus, making your hyperacusis worse or wrecking your balance. In addition, it doesn't have many other bad side effects like the above drugs have.

St. John's Wort really works. "Jane" takes it as needed and has never had any ototoxic (or other) side effects like she had with prescription drugs. I know other people that have had the same experience.

If you do decide to try **St. John's Wor**t, first run it by your doctor or pharmacist because **St. John's Wort** is known to interact with various medications. You don't want to cause problems due to interactions between **St. John's Wort** and any other drugs you might be taking.

Also, be sure it says on the bottle that it is standardized to 0.3% to 0.7% hypericin. (Hypericin is the active ingredient.) When you use a standardized formulation, you know exactly how much of the active ingredient you are getting. Otherwise, the active ingredient may vary all over the place, and you don't want that.

Here is another example of how you can substitute a herbal for a more ototoxic drug. This time it is a safer alternative to anti-anxiety drugs.

A lady explained:

> I have been suffering from tinnitus for several years, and it drives me crazy when I'm trying to get to sleep. I have been to an ear, nose and throat specialist, and to my local doctor and I have been told I will just have to live with it. I was on *Prozac* for a few years. I ended up on just half a tablet, but I found it made me feel flat and I didn't like it so I went off it. Is there anything I could

> take to stop me feeling anxious, especially when I'm trying to go to sleep? It seems *Prozac* could have made my tinnitus worse, is this correct? Does *Effexor* make tinnitus worse?

This lady is caught in the drug trap. This is because doctors often prescribe drugs such as **Fluoxetine** (*Prozac*) and **Venlafaxine** (*Effexor*) to help you reduce the anxiety you feel towards your tinnitus. These drugs can work for some people, but for others, they actually make their tinnitus worse.

For example, **Fluoxetine** can cause tinnitus in about 2% of the people taking it. Since multitudes of people take *Prozac*, this is a pretty significant number of people. **Venlafaxine** is no better. In fact, it causes tinnitus in about 3% of the people taking it.

There are safer alternatives to taking these prescription drugs. For example, if I were anxious about my tinnitus and had trouble sleeping because of it, I'd choose a herbal that has a relaxing, calming effect.

There are a number of herbs that have been used for hundreds of years—long before drugs hit the market—to reduce anxiety and promote sleep, and they did (and still do) work. You seldom hear about them, but if you are concerned about ototoxic (and other) side effects, they are a good place to start.

My choice of a herb that reduces anxiety, calms you down and helps you sleep is Valerian (***Valeriana officinalis***). You can get it at health food stores, or from a herbalist or a naturopathic doctor (ND).

Caution: as with **St. John's Wort** and other herbals, you should not mix herbals and prescription drugs without first talking to your doctor or pharmacist about any drug interactions. For example, in this case you wouldn't want to take *Prozac* and Valerian (***Valeriana officinalis***) at the same time since the combined action of both may be too much for your body.

Build Up Your Body So You Won't Need to Take Drugs

Practice living a healthy life-style so you don't get sick in the first place, or build up your health, if you are already "sick". By building up your body, you'll discover that you no longer will need to take drugs. This advice is so obvious, but many people seem to miss it, or choose not to practice it because it means changing their diet and lifestyle, and that is just too much effort.

There are a number of ways you can build up and keep your body healthy. Diet and exercise are two very important ones. You also need to ensure that you keep your immune system robust, so it can fight off any infections before they can take hold.

Diet

As most people know, but few practice, eating the right foods goes a long ways towards keeping your body healthy, whereas eating too much junk food causes all sorts of problems. That is why diet and nutrition should be at the top of your list of things you do to keep yourself healthy so you won't have to take any drugs and medications.

Here's an example of how this can work out in practice. Millions of people take anti-inflammatory drugs (typically Non-Steroidal Anti-Inflammatory Drugs [NSAIDS]) to reduce pain and inflammation in their bodies. Unfortunately, these drugs have numerous side effects, and can also damage their ears.

Non-steroidal anti-inflammatory drugs include the:

- Acetic acids such as **Diclofenac** (*Voltaren*) and **Ketorolac** (*Toradol*).
- Cox-2 inhibitors such as **Celecoxib** (*Celebrex*) and **Valdecoxib** (*Bextra*).
- Fenamates such as **Mefenamic acid** (*Ponstel*).
- Oxicams such as **Meloxicam** (*Mobic*).
- Propionic acids such as **Ibuprofen** (*Advil*) and **Naproxen** (*Aleve*).
- Salicylates such as **Acetylsalicylic acid** (*Aspirin*) and **Mesalamine** (*Asacol*).

The above list is just a small representative sample of the drugs in these classes. For a more complete listing, see Sections 1.1-1.1.16 in Table 19.1. These drugs can have numerous ototoxic side effects. Some of the more common ototoxic side effects of NSAIDs include ear pain, hearing loss, tinnitus, and vestibular (balance) side effects such as ataxia, dizziness and vertigo.

People have asked me how they can both control the pain/inflammation they experience, and yet not suffer from these ototoxic side effects. The good news is that changes in diet go a long way towards reducing inflammation (and thus the need for such drugs).

Note: inflammation is not a "minor" problem but is a "well-known contributor to chronic health conditions such as heart disease, diabetes, cancer and dementia".[18]

In order to reduce inflammation, you need to greatly reduce your intake of foods that cause inflammation. According to nutrition expert Dr. Andrew Rubman, ND, the 10 worst inflammatory foods include:[19]

1. Desserts made with lots of sugar (cookies, candy, ice cream and so on).

2. Sweetened cereals.

3. "White" carbohydrates (white bread, white rice, white potatoes, English muffins, etc.).

4. Non-diet soft drinks.

5. Anything containing high-fructose corn syrup.

6. Processed meats (bologna, salami, hotdogs, sausage and others made with preservatives and additives).

7. French fries, potato chips and other fried snack foods.

8. Fast foods, most specifically the ones that are high-fat, high-calorie, high simple carbohydrate—which describes most of the inexpensive offerings at quick-serve restaurants.

9. Margarine, because it contains processed sterols called stanols that have been implicated in both atherosclerosis and various fatty-deposit diseases.

10. Organ meats such as liver, because these often contain undesirable products including antibiotics, fertilizer and other unwanted residues (unless they are certified organic).

11. In addition, you definitely want to eliminate as much as possible foods high in linoleic acid (omega-6) This particularly means cooking (seed) oils—especially safflower, sunflower, corn, cottonseed and soybean oils due to their high linoleic acid (omega-6) content.

At the same time, you want to include (or greatly increase) your intake of the 10 best anti-inflammatory foods. Dr. Rubman's choices include:

1. Wild Alaskan salmon, mackerel and other omega-3-fatty-acid-rich fish.

2. Berries, especially dark blue ones.

3. Green, leafy vegetables (e.g., spinach and kale).

4. Cruciferous vegetables (broccoli, Brussels sprouts, cabbage, etc.).

5. Deeply pigmented produce, such as sweet potatoes, eggplant and pomegranates...along with carrots, plums, oranges, peppers, peas and red grapes.

6. Nuts—low linoleic acid nuts/seeds such as: macadamia nuts, cashews, hazelnuts, pistachios, flaxseeds, almonds and chia seeds.

7. Tea—specifically black, green and white teas.

8. Cold-pressed fresh oils, including avocado, flaxseed and olive oils in particular.

9. Spices (specifically, garlic, ginger, turmeric, saffron).

10. Whole grains. (Note: Dr. Mercola says that even whole grains can cause inflammation and suggests eliminating all grains from your diet if you suffer from inflammation.)

11. Also, and this is most important, replace high linoleic acid (omega-6) seed oils with low-linoleic acid healthy fats such as organic butter, coconut oil and tallow (beef fat).

Incidentally, wolfing your food down also increases the inflammation index of the foods you eat, so slow down and chew your food completely before swallowing.

Since making drastic lifestyle changes is difficult and prone to failure for many people, start by consciously choosing to replace **one** of the foods in the "worst" list with **one** of the foods in the "best" list. As you continue to do this, over time you will realize you have almost eliminated the worst inflammatory foods from your diet—and surprise—you'll notice you feel ever so much better in the process, and thus likely won't need to take anti-inflammatory drugs anymore. (And likely a lot of your other health problems will have improved too.)

Boost Your Immune System

Millions of people take antibiotics each year to kill infections in their bodies. The truth is your body's immune system can handle most of these infectious agents if it is working properly.

Recurrent infections are a sign that your immune system is not functioning properly. Therefore, if you get infections easily, you need to boost your immune system. If you boost your immune system, you will likely find that your susceptibility to infections will drop dramatically. Two herbal preparations that help boost your immune system are **Echinacea** and Astragalus.

Echinacea (*Echinacea angustifolia, E. purpurea, E. pallida*) is a powerful immune-system booster. A typical dosage is up to nine 300 to 400 mg capsules per day. (If you are allergic to asters and ragweeds, you may also be allergic to **Echinacea**. Also, don't use if you have an autoimmune disease.)[20] Astragalus

(*Astragalus membranaceus*) is a herbal you can take long-term if you are prone to recurrent infections. A typical dosage is eight or nine 400 to 500 mg capsules a day.[21]

Take probiotics—bacterial cultures—such as *Lactobacillus acidophilus*. Some naturopathic doctors explain that your intestinal tract comprises almost **half** of the functionality of your immune system. So having healthy intestinal flora helps keep you healthy, and your immune system robust.

It is important that every time you take an antibiotic, you also take more probiotic cultures since antibiotics kill off the "good guys" in your intestinal tract, thus shooting down your immune system, and thus leaving you open to further (opportunistic) infections.

Just be sure any product you buy contains a minimum of 2.5 billion live organisms per gram. Even better, you can eat live-culture yogurt or kefir to get the same benefits.

Boost Your Intake of Vitamins, Minerals and Enzymes

In Chapter 11 and the section "Now the Good News" you learned that loud noise produces free radicals that can zap the hair cells in your inner ears and cause them to die. With the death of each hair cell, a bit more of your hearing dies too.

Various ototoxic drugs also produce free radicals in your inner ears. You can fight these free radicals the same way you do when loud noise produces them.

The above-mentioned section in Chapter 11 shows you how to fight this free radical assault on your inner ears by taking the powerful antioxidant **N-acetyl-cysteine** (NAC) which your body converts to glutathione. You also learned your inner ears need adequate supplies of **Vitamins A, C** and **E** and the minerals **Magnesium** and **Zinc** to maintain good ear health.

While you are at it, make sure you supplement your diet with all the other vitamins and minerals you need to maintain your whole body in good health.

Exercise

In order to be healthy, your body needs exercise (movement)—the more the better. Few people get enough exercise for optimal health. Far too many people have sedentary jobs, and they are "couch potatoes" at home. This leads to poor health, and before you know it, your doctor is prescribing more drugs for whatever ails you.

Therefore, build some exercise into your daily routine. For example, before he died, each afternoon I'd take my dog and we'd go for a brisk walk in the fresh air in the country. (Fortunately, a mile in any direction from where I lived was "in the country". This is one advantage to deliberately choosing to live in a small town.) We typically walked for a mile or two. It didn't take us long—about half an hour. That got the blood circulating again before I returned to my desk.

Furthermore, I was the only one on my street that used a walk-behind lawnmower. The rest relax on their riding mowers while I worked up a sweat mowing my grass. In order to get even more exercise, I deliberately mowed up and down my hilly property rather than mow across the slope.

Exercise can also help cut down on your need for anti-anxiety drugs and sleeping pills. If you are anxious, instead of taking anti-anxiety drugs, why not try a moderate to vigorous exercise program. Such exercise will work off that extra nervous energy and make you healthily tired, resulting in a good night's sleep without the need for taking sleeping pills or anti-anxiety drugs.

These are just some of the many things you can do to help protect yourself from the ototoxic, and other, side effects of drugs. Keep your eyes and mind open for other strategies you can implement that also will help restore your body to health without drugs. I look forward to the day you too will have a spring in your step, a glow on your cheeks and a song in your heart.

Chapter 18 Endnotes

1 Rochon, 2018. p. 1.
2 Lewis, 2022. p. 1.
3 AARP Bulletin, October, 2009.
4 Lewis, 2022. p. 1.
5 Are You Taking Too Many Medications, 2007.
6 Are You Taking Too Many Medications, 2007.
7 Are You Taking Too Many Medications, 2007.
8 Avandia—How Dangerous Is It Really? 2010.
9 Diabetes Health Warning, 2010.
10 FDA MedWatch – Benicar (Olmesartan) Ongoing Safety Review. June 11, 2010.
11 FDA MedWatch – Benicar (Olmesartan) Ongoing Safety Review. June 11, 2010.
12 FDA MedWatch – Benicar (Olmesartan) Ongoing Safety Review. June 11, 2010.
13 Minocha, 2010.
14 Minocha, 2010.
15 Dancer, 2007. Quoting an article in the American Family Physician.
16 Worst Pills Best Pills News, September 2007.
17 Don't be a silent victim of a drug's side effects. 2008.
18 10 Best and Worst Foods for You. 2010.
19 10 Best and Worst Foods for You. 2010.
20 White, 2000. p. 221.
21 White, 2000. p. 221.

Section III

Detailed Ototoxic Drug, Herbal & Chemical Listings

Index to the Ototoxic Drugs, Herbals & Chemicals Mentioned in This Section

This index lists the generic names and many of the brand names of the drugs, together with the scientific and common names of the herbals and the chemical and trade names of the chemicals that are mentioned in this book—a whopping total of 6,546 names of ototoxic substances!

Note that some chemicals are used in industrial processes as well as used as medications so it is hard to know whether to list them as drugs or as chemicals. The same holds true for herbals and drugs as numbers of drugs are derived from herbals.

Thus, in this index, rather than having you look at three different indices, I have arranged these three classes of ototoxic substances in one combined alphabetical listing. After each name is either a C, D or H in parentheses—indicating whether it is listed in the drugs (D), herbals (H) or chemicals (C) sections in this book and the page number where you will find the ototoxic information on this substance.

Chapter 19

Ototoxic Drugs

Abacavir

Pronunciation guide: ah-BAH-kah-veer

Drug classification: ANTI-RETROVIRAL PROTEASE INHIBITORS (see section 7.17.1.1 in Table 19-1)

Brand names: *Epzicom*[1], *Kivexa*, *Ziagen*

Ototoxic effects:
  Cochlear:
    Auditory hallucinations: (8 cases reported to FDA [FMR])
    Hearing loss: (27 cases reported to FDA [EHM])
    Tinnitus: (13 cases reported to FDA [EHM])
  Vestibular:
    Ataxia/Gait disturbance: (56 cases reported to FDA [FMR])
    Balance disorder: (7 cases reported to FDA [FMR])
    Dizziness: (240 cases reported to FDA [FMR])
    Vertigo: (24 cases reported to FDA [FMR])
  Outer/Middle Ear:
    Ear discomfort/Ear pain: (6 cases reported to FDA [FMR])
    Otitis media: (4 cases reported to FDA [FMR])

Risk assessment: Class 1

Notes:

[1] *Epzicom* is a combination of **Abacavir** and **Lamivudine**. (See the generic drug **Lamivudine** for its specific ototoxic properties.)

Abatacept

Pronunciation guide: ah-BAY-tah-sept

Drug classification: TUMOR NECROSIS FACTOR MODIFIERS (see section 14.36 in Table 19-1)

Brand names: *Orencia*

Ototoxic effects:
- Cochlear:
  - Hearing loss: <1% (CPS) (17 cases reported to FDA [FMR])
  - Tinnitus: <1% (CPS) (13 cases reported to FDA [FMR])
- Vestibular:
  - Ataxia/Gait disturbance: (45 cases reported to FDA [FMR])
  - Balance disorder: (10 cases reported to FDA [FMR])
  - Dizziness: 2.6-4.6% [0.9% above placebo results] (CPS) (134 cases reported to FDA [FMR])
  - Vertigo: <1% (CPS) (17 cases reported to FDA [FMR])
- Outer/Middle Ear:
  - Ear blocked: <1% (CPS)
  - Ear discomfort/Ear pain: (9 cases reported to FDA [FMR])
  - Ear infection: (25 cases reported to FDA [FMR])
  - Otitis externa: 1.7% [placebo 0] (CPS)
  - Otitis media: 1.1-1.3% (CPS) (5 cases reported to FDA [FMR])
- Outer/Middle Ear:
  - Ear disorder: <1% (CPS)

Risk assessment: Class 1.5

Abciximab

Pronunciation guide: ab-SIK-sih-mab

Drug classification: PLATELET INHIBITOR DRUGS (see section 36.24 in Table 19-1)

Brand names: *ReoPro*

Ototoxic effects:
- Vestibular:
  - Dizziness: (39 cases reported to FDA [FMR])
  - Vertigo: (3 cases reported to FDA [FMR])
- Outer/Middle Ear:
  - Otorrhagia: (4 cases reported to FDA [FMR])

Risk assessment: Class 0.5

Abiraterone

Pronunciation guide: AH-bih-RAH-teh-rone

Drug classification: ANTI-NEOPLASTICS (ANTI-CANCER DRUGS) (see section 14 in Table 19-1)

Brand names: *Zytiga*

Ototoxic effects:
  Cochlear:
    Hearing loss: (6 cases reported to FDA [FMR])
    Tinnitus: (6 cases reported to FDA [FMR])
  Vestibular:
    Ataxia/Gait disturbance: (24 cases reported to FDA [FMR])
    Balance disorder: (15 cases reported to FDA [FMR])
    Dizziness: (44 cases reported to FDA [FMR])

Risk assessment: Class 0.5

Abobotulinum Toxin A

Pronunciation guide: a-boe-BOT-yoo-line-um TOKS-in

Drug classification: Neurotoxins (see section 53.40 in Table 19-1)

Brand names: *Dysport*

Ototoxic effects:
  Cochlear:
    Hearing loss: (6 cases reported to FDA [FMR])
    Hyperacusis: (5 cases reported to FDA [FMR])
    Tinnitus: (6 cases reported to FDA [FMR])
  Vestibular:
    Ataxia/Gait disturbance: (9 cases reported to FDA [FMR])
    Balance disorder: (9 cases reported to FDA [FMR])
    Dizziness: (PDR) (54 cases reported to FDA [FMR])
    Nystagmus: (3 cases reported to FDA [FMR])
    Vertigo: (PDR) (11 cases reported to FDA [FMR])
  Outer/Middle Ear:
    Ear discomfort/Ear pain: (3 cases reported to FDA [FMR])

Risk assessment: Class 1.5

Anecdotal Reports:

A lady reported, "I had *Dysport* in my forehead and crow's feet and developed tinnitus in both ears 2 weeks after."

A young man wrote, "I had 25 units of *Dysport* in my forehead/between my eyebrows. The next day I had loss of hearing in my right ear. Now I have a big problem."

A lady explained, "I tried *Dysport* and within one hour, I got severe tinnitus for three months which finally went away."

Acamprosate

Pronunciation guide: ah-KAM-proe-sate

Drug classification: Miscellaneous drugs (see section 46 in Table 19-1)

Brand names: *Campral*

Ototoxic effects:
  Cochlear:
    Auditory hallucinations: (4 cases reported to FDA [FMR])
    Hearing loss: 0.1-1% (CPS, PDR) (4 cases reported to FDA [FMR])
    Tinnitus: 0.1-1% (CPS, PDR) (14 cases reported to FDA [FMR])
  Vestibular:
    Ataxia/Gait disturbance: (11 cases reported to FDA [FMR])
    Dizziness: 3-4% [<1% above placebo results] (CPS, PDR) (36 cases reported to FDA [FMR])
    Vertigo: 0.1-1% (CPS, PDR)

Risk assessment: Class 1

Notes:

This drug is being tested as a treatment for tinnitus. One early study shows promise, but it still does have adverse side effects as noted above.

Acarbose

Pronunciation guide: ah-KAR-bose

Drug classification: Alpha-glucosidase inhibitors (see section 40.8.2 in Table 19-1)

Brand names: *Glucobay*, *Glucor*, *Kaboping*, *Precose*

Ototoxic effects:
  Cochlear:
    Hearing loss: (7 cases reported to FDA [EHM])
    Tinnitus: (11 cases reported to FDA [EHM])
  Vestibular:
    Ataxia/Gait disturbance: (29 cases reported to FDA [FMR])
    Balance disorder: (3 cases reported to FDA [FMR])
    Dizziness:(101 cases reported to FDA [FMR])
    Labyrinthitis:(3 cases reported to FDA [FMR])
    Vertigo: (20 cases reported to FDA [FMR])

Risk assessment: Class 1

Acebutolol

Pronunciation guide: ah-see-BYOO-toe-lawl

Drug classification: BETA-ADRENERGIC BLOCKING DRUGS (BETA BLOCKERS) (see section 20.8.12 in Table 19-1)

Brand names: *Acetanol, Apo-Acebutolol, Monitan, Rhotral, Sectral*

Ototoxic effects:
 Cochlear:
  Auditory hallucinations: (3 cases reported to FDA [FMR])
  Hearing loss: (17 cases reported to FDA [FMR])
  Tinnitus: (CPS) (6 cases reported to FDA [EHM])
 Vestibular:
  Ataxia/Gait disturbance: (27 cases reported to FDA [FMR])
  Balance disorder: (19 cases reported to FDA [FMR])
  Dizziness: 2-4% (CPS, PDR) (84 cases reported to FDA [FMR])
  Vertigo: (CPS) (22 cases reported to FDA [FMR])
 Unspecified/General Ear Conditions:
  Ear disorder: [1] (7 cases reported to FDA [DCC])
  Ototoxicity: (3 cases reported to FDA [FMR])

Risk assessment: Class 0.5

Notes:

[1] Ear disorders include 3 cases of external auditory canal atresia (ear canals missing), 2 cases of unspecified ear malformations and 2 cases of microtia (tiny external ears).

Aceclofenac

Pronunciation guide: ah-SEE-kloe-fen-ack

Drug classification: ACETIC ACIDS (see section 1.1.1 in Table 19-1)

Brand names: *Acecol, Aclon, Preservex*

Ototoxic effects:
 Cochlear:
  Tinnitus: <0.01% (BNF, GIP)
 Vestibular:
  Ataxia/Gait disturbance: (14 cases reported to FDA [FMR])
  Balance disorder: (5 cases reported to FDA [FMR])
  Dizziness: [1] (BNF) (15 cases reported to FDA [FMR])
  Vertigo: <0.01% (BNF, GIP)

Risk assessment: Class 0.5

Acemetacin

Pronunciation guide: ah-see-MET-ah-sin

Drug classification: ACETIC ACIDS (see section 1.1.1 in Table 19-1)

Brand names: *Emflex, Rantudil Retard, Tilur*

Ototoxic effects:
  Cochlear:
    Hearing disorder: [2]
    Tinnitus: [3] (San, She)
  Vestibular:
    Ataxia/Gait disturbance: (4 cases reported to FDA [FMR])
    Dizziness: (BNF) (5 cases reported to FDA [FMR])
    Vertigo: (BNF) (3 cases reported to FDA [FMR])

Risk assessment: Class 0.5

Notes:

Acemetacin is a prodrug of **Indomethacin**. Your body converts **Acemetacin** into **Indomethacin**. As such you could expect it to have similar ototoxic side effects as **Indomethacin**. (See the generic drug **Indomethacin** for its specific ototoxic properties.)

Acenocoumarol

Pronunciation guide: ah-see-noe-KOOM-ah-rol

Drug classification: ANTI-CLOTTING DRUGS (see section 36.1 in Table 19-1)

Brand names: *Sintrom*

Ototoxic effects:
  Cochlear:
    Hearing loss: (16 cases reported to FDA [FMR])
    Tinnitus: (7 cases reported to FDA [FMR])
  Vestibular:
    Ataxia/Gait disturbance: (45 cases reported to FDA [FMR])
    Dizziness: (112 cases reported to FDA [FMR])
    Nystagmus: (3 cases reported to FDA [FMR])
    Vertigo: (23 cases reported to FDA [FMR])
    Vestibular disorder: (8 cases reported to FDA [FMR])
  Outer/Middle Ear:
    Ear discomfort/Ear pain: (5 cases reported to FDA [FMR])
  Unspecified/General Ear Conditions:
    Ototoxicity: (3 cases reported to FDA [FMR])

Risk assessment: Class 1

Acepromazine

Pronunciation guide: ah-see-PROM-ah-zeen

Drug classification: PHENOTHIAZINES (see section 60.8.1 in Table 19-1)

Brand names: *Noctran*

Ototoxic effects:
  Cochlear:
    Hearing loss: (3 cases reported to FDA [FMR])
  Vestibular:
    Ataxia/Gait disturbance: (3 cases reported to FDA [FMR])
    Balance disorder: (10 cases reported to FDA [FMR])
    Vertigo: (6 cases reported to FDA [FMR])

Risk assessment: Class 0.5

Acetaminophen (Paracetamol, APAP)

Pronunciation guide: ah-seet-ah-MIN-oh-fen (pah-rah-SEE-tah-mol)

Drug classification: ANALGESIC DRUGS (PAINKILLERS) (see section 1 in Table 19-1)

Brand names: *Acephen, Alvedon, Anhiba, Calonal, Cetamol, Children's Tylenol* [1], *Citodon*[2], *Cocarl, Co-codamol*[2], *Co-Dydramol*[3], *Concentrated Tylenol Infant Drops, Co-proxamol*[4], *Dafalgan, Darvocet* [5], *Di-Antalvic*[6], *Di-Gesic*[2], *Doliprane, Dolko, Duradrin*[7], *Ed-Flex*[8], *Efferalagan, Equate, FeverAll, Flexar, Geluprane, Goody's Extra Strength Headache Powder*[9], *Ixprim, Lamaline*[10], *Midrid*[11], *Midrin*[7], *Migraleve*[2], *Norel SR*[12], *NyQuil*[13], *Pamol, Panadol, Panamax, Paradex*[4], *Propacet 100*[5], *Propofan*[14], *Propo-N/Apap*[5], *Propoxy* [5], *Theraflu*[15], *Tylenol, Tylenol Aches & Strains*[16], *Tylenol Flu Medication*[17], *Tylox, Tyl-Sinus*[18], *Wygesic*[5], *Zaldiar*

Ototoxic effects:
  Cochlear:
    Auditory hallucinations: (271 cases reported to FDA [FMR])
    Hearing disorder: (11 cases reported to FDA [FMR])
    Hearing loss: [19] (1,583 cases reported to FDA [FMR])
    Hyperacusis: (21 cases reported to FDA [FMR])
    Phonophobia: (22 cases reported to FDA [FMR])
    Tinnitus: (GIP) (709 cases reported to FDA [FMR])
  Vestibular:
    Ataxia/Gait disturbance: (3,444 cases reported to FDA [FMR])
    Balance disorder: (1,470 cases reported to FDA [FMR])
    Dizziness: (7,689 cases reported to FDA [FMR])
    Labyrinthitis: (117 cases reported to FDA [FMR])

Nystagmus: (112 cases reported to FDA [FMR])
Vertigo: (GIP) (1,363 cases reported to FDA [FMR])
Vestibular disorder: (54 cases reported to FDA [FMR])

Outer/Middle Ear:

Ceruminosis: (150 cases reported to FDA [FMR])
Cholesteatoma: (17 cases reported to FDA [FMR])
Ear blocked: (91 cases reported to FDA [FMR])
Ear discomfort/Ear pain: (916 cases reported to FDA [FMR])
Ear infection: (521 cases reported to FDA [FMR])
Eustachian tube dysfunction: (97 cases reported to FDA [FMR])
Otitis externa: (142 cases reported to FDA [FMR])
Otitis media: (488 cases reported to FDA [FMR])
Otorrhagia: (62 cases reported to FDA [FMR])
Otorrhea: (90 cases reported to FDA [FMR])
Perforated eardrum: (34 cases reported to FDA [FMR])

Unspecified/General Ear Conditions:

Ear disorder: (81 cases reported to FDA [FMR])
Meniere's disease: (40 cases reported to FDA [FMR])
Ototoxicity: (12 cases reported to FDA [FMR])

Risk assessment: Class 5 when taken in large doses for long periods of time.
Class 3.5 when taken regularly at normal doses for more than 1 year.

Notes:

[1] *Children's Tylenol* is a combination of **Acetaminophen** and **Pseudoephedrine**. (See the generic drug **Pseudoephedrine** for its specific ototoxic properties.)

[2] *Citodon*, *Co-codamol*, *Di-Gesic* and *Migraleve* are combinations of **Acetaminophen** and **Codeine**. (See the generic drug **Codeine** for its specific ototoxic properties.)

[3] *Co-Dydramol* is a combination of **Acetaminophen** and **Dihydrocodeine**. (See the generic drug **Dihydrocodeine** for its specific ototoxic properties.)

[4] *Co-proxamol* and *Paradex* are combinations of **Acetaminophen** and **Dextropropoxyphene**. (See the generic drug **Dextropropoxyphene** for its specific ototoxic properties.)

[5] *Darvocet*, *Propacet 100*, *Propo-N/Apap*, *Propoxy* and *Wygesic* are combinations of **Acetaminophen** and **Propoxyphene**. (See the generic drug **Propoxyphene** for its specific ototoxic properties.)

[6] *Di-Antalvic* is a combination of **Acetaminophen** and **Codeine**. (See the generic drug **Codeine** for its specific ototoxic properties.)

[7] *Duradrin* and *Midrin* are combinations of **Acetaminophen**, Isometheptene and Dichloralphenazone. (**Acetaminophen** is the ototoxic agent.)

[8] *Ed-Flex* is a combination of **Acetaminophen**, **Hydroxybenzamide** (**Salicylamide**) and Phenyltoloxamine. (See the generic drugs **Hydroxybenzamide** for its specific ototoxic properties.)

[9] *Goody's Extra Strength Headache Powder* is a combination of **Acetaminophen** and **Caffeine**. (See the generic drug **Caffeine** for its specific ototoxic properties.)

[10] *Lamaline* is a combination of **Acetaminophen**, **Caffeine** and **Morphine** (**Opium**). (See the generic drugs **Caffeine** and **Morphine** [**Opium**] for their specific ototoxic properties.)

[11] *Midrid* is a combination of **Acetaminophen** and Isometheptene. (**Acetaminophen** is the ototoxic agent.)

[12] *Norel SR* is a combination of **Acetaminophen**, **Chlorpheniramine**, **Phenylephrine** and Phenyltoloxamine. (See the generic drugs **Chlorpheniramine** and **Phenylephrine** for their specific ototoxic properties.)

[13] *NyQuil* is a combination of **Acetaminophen**, **Dextromethorphan** and **Doxylamine**. (See the generic drugs **Dextromethorphan** and **Doxylamine** for their specific ototoxic properties.)

[14] *Propofan* is a combination of **Acetaminophen**, **Caffeine** and **Dextropropoxyphene**. (See the generic drugs **Caffeine** and **Dextropropoxyphene** for their specific ototoxic properties.)

[15] *Theraflu* is a combination of **Acetaminophen**, **Chlorpheniramine**, **Dextromethorphan** and **Pseudoephedrine**. (See the generic drugs **Chlorpheniramine**, **Dextromethorphan** and **Pseudoephedrine** for their specific ototoxic properties.)

[16] *Tylenol Aches & Strains* is a combination of **Acetaminophen** and **Chlorzoxazone**. (See the generic drug **Chlorzoxazone** for its specific ototoxic properties.)

[17] *Tylenol Flu Medication* is a combination of **Acetaminophen**, **Diphenhydramine** and **Pseudoephedrine**. (See the generic drugs **Diphenhydramine** and **Pseudoephedrine** for their specific ototoxic properties.)

[18] *Tyl-Sinus* is a combination of **Acetaminophen** and **Phenylephrine**. (See the generic drug **Phenylephrine** for its specific ototoxic properties.)

[19] A recent study revealed that **Acetaminophen** is very ototoxic. Cochlear cultures exposed to **Acetaminophen** began dying after about 24 hours, and by 96 hours, 100% of the hair cells had died. That's how ototoxic **Acetaminophen** really is![4]

Acetaminophen is one of the ingredients in a number of compound drugs. As always, check the labels and then look up each drug listed to see its ototoxic properties.

Acetaminophen is better known in Europe as **Paracetamol** or **APAP** (N-acetyl-para-amino-phenol).

People can develop progressive, irreversible hearing loss from taking "extremely high doses of **Acetaminophen** for a little as 2 months, or after taking clinically acceptable doses for as long as 10 years".[5] At regular dosages (e.g.: up to 4 pills a day), when taken two or more times a week for more than a year, **Acetaminophen** can cause hearing loss. For example, in a study of 26,917 men between the ages of 40 and 75 at the beginning of the study, men that used **Acetaminophen** at least twice a week had a 22% increased risk of hearing loss. However, when only men under the age of 50 were considered, the risk factor skyrocketed to 99%.[6]

In just 9 years, the FDA received 18,308 reports of ototoxicity from this drug (see listing above).

Doctors have discovered that **Acetaminophen** depletes your body's stores of glutathione, a powerful natural antioxidant that helps protect your hearing from the effects of free radicals that are produced when your ears are exposed to loud noise,[7] to prescription drugs and to various chemicals. When glutathione levels are reduced, the free radicals floating around in the cochlea zap (kill) the hair cells, resulting in some degree of sensorineural hearing loss.

Since **Acetaminophen** depletes the body's supply of glutathione, then it follows that taking glutathione at the same time as taking **Acetaminophen** (or many other drugs), helps protect your ears from any resulting hearing loss, not to mention preventing or reducing damage to your liver. Note that since glutathione is not easily absorbed through your stomach, a good alternative is to take **N-acetyl-cysteine** (NAC) (a major building block of glutathione) instead, and let your body convert it to glutathione.

Furthermore, in emergency medicine, NAC is used as an antidote for **Acetaminophen** toxicity resulting from an **Acetaminophen** overdose. Mortality due to **Acetaminophen** toxicity has been shown to be virtually eliminated when NAC is promptly administered.[8]

Acetaminophen can cause profound hearing loss when ingested in large doses (e.g. 15 to 75 pills a day) over several weeks or months. Taken by itself, these large doses would kill the liver, and thus the person, before hearing loss became apparent. However, when taken in combination with **Hydrocodone** (e.g. *Vicodin*), the **Hydrocodone** somehow protects the liver. As a result, the person doesn't die and eventually massive hearing loss becomes apparent.[9] For further information on how **Acetaminophen** and **Hydrocodone** work together to cause massive hearing loss, see the explanation under the drug **Hydrocodone**.

It's hard to believe, but from the time **Acetaminophen** was first used until researchers realized that it was ototoxic and could cause massive hearing loss took an incredible 117 years!

Also, see Chapter 2 "Ototoxic Drugs—What Are They?"; the section entitled "The Story of Vicodin" in Chapter 8; and Chapter 10, "We 'Hear' With Our Eyes" for further information on **Acetaminophen**.

Anecdotal Reports:

A medical doctor explained, "I have been taking **Acetaminophen** 1,300 to 2,600 mg daily for past several weeks for persistent pain. I have noted an increase in tinnitus and variability in hearing at times lately. I'm going to stop the **Acetaminophen** and find other means for pain control such as boswellia and ashwagandha and acupuncture."

Acetazolamide

Pronunciation guide: ah-seet-ah-ZOLE-ah-myed

Drug classification: DIURETICS—CARBONIC ANHYDRASE INHIBITORS (see section 30.5.1 in Table 19-1)

Brand names: *Diamox*

Ototoxic effects:
- Cochlear:
  - Hearing disorder: (CPS, PDR)
  - Hearing loss: (PDR) (12 cases reported to FDA [FMR])
  - Phonophobia: (4 cases reported to FDA [FMR])
  - Tinnitus: (CPS, PDR) (28 cases reported to FDA [EHM])
- Vestibular:
  - Ataxia/Gait disturbance: (CPS, NDH) (45 cases reported to FDA [FMR])
  - Balance disorder: (18 cases reported to FDA [FMR])
  - Dizziness: (BNF, CPS) (120 cases reported to FDA [FMR])
  - Nystagmus: (3 cases reported to FDA [FMR])
  - Vertigo: (8 cases reported to FDA [FMR])
- Outer/Middle Ear:
  - Ear infection: (3 cases reported to FDA [FMR])

Risk assessment: Class 1.5

Notes:

See Chapter 10, "We 'Hear' With Our Eyes" for further information on this drug.

Anecdotal Reports:

Although **Acetazolamide** does not have many reports of tinnitus (FMR), it causes tinnitus in many people who take this drug for Idiopathic Intracranial Hypertension (IIH). One lady in a IIH support group with 3,000+ members reported that "pretty much everyone who takes **Acetazolamide** has ringing in their ears." She further explained, "We took an informal poll and most reported they did not have ringing in their ears before they began taking **Acetazolamide**. There were a few who said they already had tinnitus and the **Acetazolamide** made it worse, while still others explained that whenever they take higher doses, their tinnitus gets worse."

A lady explained, "I took **Acetazolamide**—one dose in the morning and another late in the afternoon. My tinnitus began within hours of the second dose. It has not stopped. I took another dose the next morning. I only took ¼ dose that night. I felt horrible. (Each dose of **Acetazolamide** made me feel very drugged.) Over the two days I took 3¼ pills. My tinnitus has been constant since the second dose—non-stop high pitch in one ear. My tinnitus is still the same frequency and intensity 8 days later, I'm wondering whether it will go away."

A lady wrote, "I started taking **Acetazolamide** and several hours later I noticed high-pitched ringing in both of my ears."

Acetic acid

Pronunciation guide: ah-SEE-tik ASS-id

Drug classification: Acetic acids (see section 1.1.1 in Table 19-1)

Brand names: *Acetasol HC* [1], *VoSoL* [1], *VoSoL HC* [1]

Ototoxic effects:
- Cochlear:
  - Hearing loss: (3 cases reported to FDA [EHM])
  - Tinnitus: (2 cases reported to FDA [EHM])
- Vestibular:
  - Ataxia/Gait disturbance: (13 cases reported to FDA [FMR])
  - Dizziness: (27 cases reported to FDA [FMR])
  - Vertigo: (3 cases reported to FDA [FMR])
- Outer/Middle Ear:
  - Eustachian tube dysfunction: (34 cases reported to FDA [FMR])
  - Otitis media: (17 cases reported to FDA [FMR])
  - Otorrhagia: (16 cases reported to FDA [FMR])
- Unspecified/General Ear Conditions:
  - Ear disorder: (4 cases reported to FDA [FMR])
  - Ototoxicity: [2]

Risk assessment: Class 0.5

Notes:

[1] *VoSoL* is a combination of **Acetic acid** (2%), **Propylene glycol** (3%) and **Benzethonium** (0.02%). *VoSoL HC* and *Acetasol HL* are the same as *VoSoL* but has **Hydrocortisone** (1%) added. (See the generic drugs **Benzethonium**, **Hydrocortisone** and **Propylene glycol** for their specific ototoxic properties.)

[2] **Acetic acid** seems to be ototoxic. It's ototoxicity especially increases when combined with **Propylene glycol** (*VoSoL*).[10]

Acetic acid has produced small (appreciable) auditory brainstem threshold shifts (hearing loss) in guinea pigs. When **Acetic acid** is combined with **Propylene glycol** (*VoSoL*), the ototoxic effects have been shown to increase substantially.[11]

Acetic acid is toxic to outer hair cells.[12]

Do not use if your eardrum is perforated.

Acetylcarnitine (Acetyl-L-Carnitine)

Pronunciation guide: ah-SEE-til-KAR-nih-teen

Drug classification: NUTRACEUTICAL PRODUCTS (see section 75.9 in Table 19-1)

Brand names: *Neuroactil*

Ototoxic effects:
- Cochlear:
  - Hearing loss: (22 cases reported to FDA [FMR])
  - Tinnitus: (22 cases reported to FDA [FMR])
- Vestibular:
  - Ataxia/Gait disturbance: (23 cases reported to FDA [FMR])
  - Dizziness: (21 cases reported to FDA [FMR])

Risk assessment: Class 1

Acetylcysteine (N-acetyl-cysteine [NAC])

Pronunciation guide: ah-SEE-til-SIS-teen

Drug classification: ACETAMINOPHEN ANTIDOTES (see section 72.1.1 in Table 19-1)

Brand names: *ACC Long*, *Acetadote*, *Exomuc*, *Fluimucil*, *Mucomyst*

Ototoxic effects:
- Cochlear:
  - Hearing loss: (23 cases reported to FDA [FMR])
  - Hyperacusis: (4 cases reported to FDA [FMR])
  - Tinnitus: (10 cases reported to FDA [FMR])

Vestibular:
Ataxia/Gait disturbance: (DFC) (86 cases reported to FDA [FMR])
Balance disorder: (18 cases reported to FDA [FMR])
Dizziness: (147 cases reported to FDA [FMR])
Labyrinthitis: (9 cases reported to FDA [FMR])
Vertigo: (21 cases reported to FDA [FMR])
Vestibular disorder: (9 cases reported to FDA [FMR])
Outer/Middle Ear:
Ear discomfort/Ear pain: 1% (DFC) (22 cases reported to FDA [FMR])
Ear infection: (3 cases reported to FDA [FMR])
Otitis media: (16 cases reported to FDA [DCC])

Risk assessment: Class 1.5

Notes:

Ataxia is a symptom of acute toxicity (overdose).

Acetyldigoxin

Pronunciation guide: ah-SEE-til-die-JOKS-in

Drug classification: CARDIAC GLYCOSIDES (see section 20.4.1 in Table 19-1)

Brand names: —

Ototoxic effects:
Vestibular:
Ataxia/Gait disturbance: (3 cases reported to FDA [FMR])
Balance disorder: (3 cases reported to FDA [FMR])
Dizziness: (5 cases reported to FDA [FMR])

Risk assessment: Class 0.5

Acetylleucine (Acetyl-D-leucine)

Pronunciation guide: ah-SEE-til-LOO-seen

Drug classification: AMINO ACIDS (see section 75.1 in Table 19-1)

Brand names: *Tanganil*

Ototoxic effects:
Vestibular:
Ataxia/Gait disturbance: (4 cases reported to FDA [FMR])
Balance disorder: (5 cases reported to FDA [FMR])
Dizziness: (3 cases reported to FDA [FMR])
Vertigo: (6 cases reported to FDA [FMR])

Outer/Middle Ear:
Otitis externa: (3 cases reported to FDA [DCC])

Risk assessment: Class 0.5

Acetylsalicylic acid (Aspirin)

Pronunciation guide: ah-SEE-till-sal-ih-SILL-ik ASS-id

Drug classification: SALICYLATES (see section 1.1.16 in Table 19-1)

Brand names: *222*[1], *282*[1], *282 MEP*[2], *292*[1], *692*[3], *Aggrenox*[4], *Alka-Seltzer*, *Anacin*[5], *ASA*, Asaflow, *Asasantine*[4], *Ascriptin*, Aspegic, *Aspirin*[6], *Aspirin Backache*[7], *Astrix*, *BayAspirin*, *Bayer Aspirin*, *BC Powder*[8], *Bufferin*, *Cardioaspirin*, *Cardiprin*, *Cardirene*, *Coated Aspirin*, *Darvon Compound-65*[9], *Disprin*, *Easprin*, *Ecosprin*, *Ecotrin*, *Ecotrin Enteric-coated Aspirin*, *Entrophen*, *Excedrin Back & Body*[10], *Excedrin Extra Strength*[10], *Excedrin Migraine*[10], *Kardegic*, *MSD Enteric coated ASA*, *Norgesic*[11], *Nu-Seals*, *Robaxisal*[12], *Somalgin*, *St. Joseph Aspirin*, *Thomapyrin N*[13], *Trombyl*, *Vanquish Extra Strength Pain Reliever*[13]

Ototoxic effects:
Cochlear:
Auditory hallucinations: (233 cases reported to FDA [FMR])
Hearing disorder: (51 cases reported to FDA [FMR])
Hearing loss: >10% (NDH, PDR) (2,412 cases reported to FDA [FMR])
Hyperacusis: (39 cases reported to FDA [FMR])
Phonophobia: (21 cases reported to FDA [FMR])
Tinnitus: >10% (NDH, PDR) (1,286 cases reported to FDA [FMR])
Vestibular:
Ataxia/Gait disturbance: (4,877 cases reported to FDA [FMR])
Balance disorder: (2,316 cases reported to FDA [FMR])
Dizziness: <5% (CPS, PDR) (14,567 cases reported to FDA [FMR])
Labyrinthitis: (151 cases reported to FDA [FMR])
Nystagmus: (111 cases reported to FDA [FMR])
Oscillopsia: (7 cases reported to FDA [FMR])
Vertigo: (CPS, PDR) (1,769 cases reported to FDA [FMR])
Vestibular disorder: (67 cases reported to FDA [FMR])
Outer/Middle Ear:
Ceruminosis: (272 cases reported to FDA [FMR])
Ear blocked: 1% (CPS) (55 cases reported to FDA [FMR])
Ear discomfort/Ear pain: (CPS) (755 cases reported to FDA [FMR])
Ear infection: (244 cases reported to FDA [FMR])
Eustachian tube dysfunction: (122 cases reported to FDA [FMR])
Otitis externa: (159 cases reported to FDA [FMR])
Otitis media: (217 cases reported to FDA [FMR])

Otorrhagia: (80 cases reported to FDA [FMR])
Otorrhea: (78 cases reported to FDA [FMR])
Perforated eardrum: (31 cases reported to FDA [FMR])
Unspecified/General Ear Conditions:
Ear disorder: (161 cases reported to FDA [FMR])
Meniere's disease: (82 cases reported to FDA [FMR])
Ototoxicity: (7 cases reported to FDA [FMR])

Risk assessment: Class 3.5

Notes:

[1] *222, 282* and *292* are combinations of **ASA** (**Aspirin**), **Caffeine** and **Codeine**. (See the generic drugs **Caffeine** and **Codeine** for their specific ototoxic properties.)

[2] *282 MEP* is a combination of **ASA** (**Aspirin**) and **Meprobamate**. (See the generic drug **Meprobamate** for its specific ototoxic properties.)

[3] *692* is a combination of **ASA** (**Aspirin**), **Caffeine** and **Propoxyphene**. (See the generic drugs **Caffeine** and **Propoxyphene** for their specific ototoxic properties.)

[4] *Asasantine* and *Aggrenox* are both combinations of **ASA** (**Aspirin**) and **Dipyridamole**. (See the generic drug **Dipyridamole** for its specific ototoxic properties.)

[5] *Anacin* is a combination of **ASA** (**Aspirin**) and **Caffeine**. (See the generic drug **Caffeine** for its specific ototoxic properties.)

[6] *Aspirin* is a brand name of the Bayer Company in Canada. **Acetylsalicylic acid** (**ASA**) is the generic name. At the same time, **Aspirin** is also an official generic drug name designation in the United States.

[7] *Aspirin Backache* is a combination of **ASA** (**Aspirin**) and **Methocarbamol**. (See the generic drug **Methocarbamol** for its specific ototoxic properties.)

[8] *BC Powder* is a combination of **ASA** (**Aspirin**), **Hydroxybenzamide** (**Salicylamide**) and **Caffeine**. (See the generic drugs **Caffeine** and **Hydroxybenzamide**)for their specific ototoxic properties.)

[9] *Darvon Compound-65* is a combination of **ASA** (**Aspirin**), **Caffeine** and **Propoxyphene**. (See the generic drugs **Caffeine** and **Propoxyphene** for their specific ototoxic properties.)

[10] *Excedrin* is a combination of **ASA** (**Aspirin**), **Acetaminophen** and **Caffeine**. (See the generic drugs **Acetaminophen** and **Caffeine** for their specific ototoxic properties.)

[11] *Norgesic* is a combination of **ASA** (**Aspirin**), **Orphenadrine** and **Caffeine**. (See the generic drugs **Caffeine** and **Orphenadrine** for their specific ototoxic properties.)

[12] *Robaxisal* is a combination of **ASA** (**Aspirin**), **Methocarbamol** and sometimes **Codeine**. (See the generic drugs **Methocarbamol** and **Codeine** for their specific ototoxic properties.)

[13] *Vanquish Extra Strength Pain Reliever* and *Thomapyrin N* are combinations of **ASA** (**Aspirin**), **Acetaminophen** and **Caffeine** (PDR-N). (See the generic drugs **Acetaminophen** and **Caffeine** for their specific ototoxic properties.)

There are many other **ASA** (**Aspirin**) brand names and compounds too numerous to list here. The ones listed here are a few of the more common ones.

Acetylsalicylic acid (Aspirin) is not easy on your ears. In just 9 years the FDA received 29,123 reports of ototoxicity (see above). And that's just the ototoxic side effects that were reported. Much fewer than 1% are ever reported, so you probably could safely multiply this figure by 1,000. That's probably 29,000,000 people whose ears were damaged by this one drug in just 9 years.

If your ears begin to ring or buzz (tinnitus), or if hearing loss occurs, consult your doctor before you take any more **ASA** (**Aspirin**) (CPS, PDR). If you already have the typical high-frequency hearing loss, you may have difficulty perceiving tinnitus. In such cases, you can't rely on the presence of tinnitus to warn you of damage to your ears from this drug (PDR). Tinnitus does not usually begin until your **ASA** (**Aspirin**) serum level is 19.6 mg/L (200 mcg/ml) or higher [13] (PDR). Plasma levels above 30 mg/L (300 mcg/ml) are clearly toxic (PDR). Taking 6 to 8 *Aspirin* a day can cause ringing in your ears and temporary hearing loss.[14]

Salicylate-induced hearing loss involves bilateral loss of pure tone sensitivity for all sound frequencies. Hearing losses generally range from 20-40 dB. Hearing loss occurs initially at a serum salicylate concentration of about 200 mcg/ml and increases with increasing concentrations. Maximum hearing loss occurs most frequently at a serum salicylate concentration of about 400 mcg/ml (AHF).

SALICYLATE ototoxicity generally appears as a high-pitched or hissing tinnitus accompanied by hearing loss. Sometimes it will also affect your balance.[15] If you are taking **ASA** (**Aspirin**) and notice you now have tinnitus, hearing loss and/or dizziness, this indicates that your blood SALICYLATE concentrations are reaching or exceeding the upper limit of the therapeutic range (CP2). These three symptoms most frequently indicate chronic **ASA** (**Aspirin**) intoxication. They usually occur in people taking large doses, or doses for a long time. Also, increased serum levels of **ASA** (**Aspirin**) can result in SALICYLATE toxicity (salicylism). Symptoms of salicylism include nausea, vomiting, headaches, tinnitus, hearing loss, mental dullness, confusion, quickened pulse and increased respirations.[16]

High doses of **ASA** (**Aspirin**) typically produce both a flat hearing loss of up to 40 dB in both ears and some reduction in speech discrimination. As a general rule, the greater the blood serum levels of **ASA** (**Aspirin**), the worse the resulting tinnitus and/or hearing loss (CP2, CPS). Usually, but not always, the hearing loss and accompanying tinnitus are completely reversible within 24 to 72 hours after you stop taking **ASA** (**Aspirin**), although permanent hearing loss can occur.[17] There have been reports of permanent sudden sensorineural hearing loss (SSHL) and tinnitus from taking **ASA** (**Aspirin**).[18]

Using **ASA** (**Aspirin**) regularly over time can increase your risk of hearing loss. For example, in one study of 26,917 men between the ages of 40 and 75 at the beginning of the study, men that used **ASA** (**Aspirin**) at least twice a week had a 22% increased risk of hearing loss over men who were not regular users of **ASA** (**Aspirin**). However, when only men under the age of 50 were considered, the risk factor for hearing loss jumped to 33%.[19]

Taking **ASA** (**Aspirin**) results in abnormal outer hair cell function and decreased cochlear blood flow.[20]

You are at greater risk of **ASA** ototoxicity if you take high doses, are elderly or are dehydrated. The incidence of ototoxicity is about 1%.[21]

Salicylates such as **ASA** (**Aspirin**) can increase the effects of other ototoxic drugs (e.g. **Vancomycin**). You should avoid taking **ASA** (**Aspirin**) at the same time or following any ototoxic drugs because hearing loss may occur and may progress to deafness even after the medication is stopped. Although these effects may be reversible, they are usually permanent (CPS). That's the bad news.

The good news is that researchers have recently discovered that **ASA** (**Aspirin**) may actually help protect our ears from the damaging effects of taking Aminoglycoside antibiotics such as **Streptomycin**, **Gentamicin** and **Neomycin**.

Here is how it works. Aminoglycoside antibiotics bind iron in our bodies. When they do this, they produce free radicals that can damage or kill cells. The tiny hair cells in our inner ears are particularly vulnerable to free radical damage. When these hair cells die, the result is permanent hearing loss. **ASA** (**Aspirin**) quickly breaks down in our bodies to produce Salicylate, a compound that soaks up any extra iron and thereby prevents the Aminoglycosides from forming free radicals.

The results in animal studies are impressive. Guinea pigs receiving **Gentamicin** alone had severe hearing loss of up to 70 dB and almost complete destruction of the outer hair cells in their cochlea. In contrast, guinea pigs given both **Gentamicin** and **ASA** (**Aspirin**) had minor hearing loss of less than 20 dB and minimal hair cell damage.[22] Current research is now determining if **ASA** (**Aspirin**) affords the same protection in humans. Let's hope it does!

Note: **ASA** (**Aspirin**) is still ototoxic and can damage your ears as shown earlier. However, if the choice is between relatively minor ear damage while taking a necessary course of AMINOGLYCOSIDE antibiotics and **ASA** (**Aspirin**) in order to save your life, as opposed to major ear damage from taking the same antibiotics without the protection **ASA** (**Aspirin**) seems to afford, the choice seems obvious.

For additional information see **Salix spp.** in the "Ototoxic Herbals" chapter.

See Chapter 2 "Ototoxic Drugs—What Are They"; Chapter 5 "Are You at Risk"; the section "What Does Rare Really Mean"; in Chapter 6 "The Incidence of Side Effects Is Grossly Under-reported"; Chapter 10, "We 'Hear' With Our Eyes"; Chapter 11, "The Sinister Partnership Between Ototoxic Agents and Noise"; and Chapter 12, "Aminoglycoside Antibiotics are the Ototoxic 'Bad boys'" for further information on this drug.

Anecdotal Reports:

A lady reported she got permanent tinnitus from taking **Aspirin**. She wrote, "I took 2 **Aspirin** every 4 hours for exactly 24 hours when I was 18. My ears started with a "static" ringing, and haven't stopped. I'm 57 now, so it doesn't look promising [that my tinnitus will be temporary]."

A lady who had been taking very large doses of **ASA** (**Aspirin**) for headaches reported that this had been going on for about five years. She had put her hearing loss down to other causes, never thinking the **ASA** (**Aspirin**) was the culprit. However, when I suggested that taking **ASA** (**Aspirin**) could be causing much of her hearing loss, she stopped taking it. Just six days after she stopped taking **ASA** (**Aspirin**), she wrote, "I have noticed that I am hearing better now. I have the TV volume set at level 18 instead of the usual 24. The ringing in my ears is still there but it is not as bad." Three days later she added, "Today when someone was talking behind me, I heard every word he said. My hearing still isn't perfect but it is better than it was."

Acitretin

Pronunciation guide: ah-sih-TREE-tin

Drug classification: VITAMIN A ANALOGS (see section 23.4 in Table 19-1)

Brand names: *Soriatane*

Ototoxic effects:
- Cochlear:
  - Hearing loss: <1% (CPS, PDR) (10 cases reported to FDA [EHM])
  - Tinnitus: 1-10% (CPS, PDR) (3 cases reported to FDA [EHM])
- Vestibular:
  - Ataxia/Gait disturbance: <1% (CPS, PDR) (26 cases reported to FDA [FMR])
  - Balance disorder: (16 cases reported to FDA [FMR])
  - Dizziness: <1% (CPS, PDR) (22 cases reported to FDA [FMR])

Outer/Middle Ear:
Ceruminosis: 1-10% (CPS, PDR)
Ear discomfort/Ear pain: 1-10% (CPS, PDR)
Otitis externa: <1% (CPS, PDR)
Otitis media: <1% (DFC, PDR)

Risk assessment: Class 1

Adalimumab

Pronunciation guide: ay-dah-LIM-yoo-mab

Drug classification: TNF-ALPHA INHIBITORS (see section 7.17.8.1 in Table 19-1)

Brand names: *Humira, Trudexa*

Ototoxic effects:
Cochlear:
Auditory hallucinations: (12 cases reported to FDA [FMR])
Hearing disorder: (13 cases reported to FDA [FMR])
Hearing loss: <0.1% [1, 2] (661 cases reported to FDA [FMR])
Hyperacusis: (18 cases reported to FDA [FMR])
Tinnitus: 0.1-1% [1, 2, 3] (328 cases reported to FDA [FMR])
Vestibular:
Ataxia/Gait disturbance: (2,061 cases reported to FDA [FMR])
Balance disorder: (405 cases reported to FDA [FMR])
Dizziness: 1-10% [1] (3,380 cases reported to FDA [FMR])
Labyrinthitis: (64 cases reported to FDA [FMR])
Nystagmus: (70 cases reported to FDA [FMR])
Vertigo: 0.1-10% (GIP) [2] (512 cases reported to FDA [FMR])
Vestibular disorder: (6 cases reported to FDA [FMR])
Outer/Middle Ear:
Ceruminosis: (17 cases reported to FDA [FMR])
Cholesteatoma: (4 cases reported to FDA [FMR])
Ear blocked: (38 cases reported to FDA [FMR])
Ear discomfort/Ear pain: 0.1-1% [1, 2] (548 cases reported to FDA [FMR])
Ear infection: (543 cases reported to FDA [FMR])
Otitis externa: (29 cases reported to FDA [FMR])
Otitis media: (63 cases reported to FDA [FMR])
Otorrhagia: (23 cases reported to FDA [FMR])
Otorrhea: (49 cases reported to FDA [FMR])
Perforated eardrum: (33 cases reported to FDA [FMR])
Unspecified/General Ear Conditions:
Ear disorder: (32 cases reported to FDA [FMR])
Meniere's disease: (19 cases reported to FDA [FMR])

Risk assessment: Class 4

Notes:

[1] **Adalimumab** can cause dizziness (including vertigo), tinnitus, ear discomfort (including pain and swelling) and hearing loss.[23]

[2] **Adalimumab** can cause dizziness, ear or hearing problems, tinnitus and vertigo.[24]

Anecdotal Reports:

[3] A man who was put on **Adalimumab** 40 mg shots every two weeks reported that his tinnitus was bad during this time, but he attributed it to stress. Recently, he had an injection after not having had one for about a month. He explains, "Coincidently, my tinnitus was getting better during that period. A few hours after the shot my tinnitus acted up again, and has been very loud 24/7."

A man reported, "I started taking *Humira* 40 mg. Approximately 4 weeks after the first shot, I started having severe vertigo and dizziness along with tinnitus. My balance has been an issue ever since. After taking **Adalimumab** injections for 17 months I decided to stop taking the injections. Since stopping the injections, my symptoms have gradually subsided, although I am not completely free of them".

A lady explained, "I have always had tinnitus since I was a baby but it's much, much louder now since I took my first two shots of *Humira* (yesterday). I can't believe how loud it is now."

A lady wrote, "My doctor wants to increase my dose of **Adalimumab**, but I am suspicious since my tinnitus has worsened since the time I started *Humira* injections."

A man reported, "For the last 3 years I have had rheumatological problems. The doctor said maybe I'm a candidate for *Humira*. I got the 2-shot pack and Monday evening took the first shot. The next day I felt the same, but that night, about 24 hours later , I was sitting there and bang—it was like my tinnitus volume turned up to a 6-7 from my existing tinnitus level of a 2-3. It changed pitch to a 10 kHz tone. It's now positional with movement, with harmonics all over the place and debilitating. My rheumatologist said, 'Oh, I have never heard of this'. He looked on his computer at WebMD.com and shook his head 'No'. I said, 'Google *Humira* and tinnitus'. He did, and bang, hundreds of hits. He was shocked. It's been 1 month now and my life is ruined, I would never recommend this drug to anyone. Be aware and read up before you consider taking it."

A lady explained, "I have been on *Humira* approximately one year. 10 months into the shots I developed severe vertigo, ear pressure, and sinus infections. I still did one more shot 2 weeks later. Now I have peripheral neuropathy, weakness in both legs, all kinds of problems. Bad, bad drug. I wish I never ever went on it."

A lady wrote, "After starting *Humira* I have been getting a loud buzzing sound in my ears."

A lady reported, "After 7 injections of *Humira*, I now have a loud buzzing in my left ear."

A lady explained, "I have been on *Humira* injection 2 times a month now for 11 months. I had tinnitus before I started the medication. Last night in my left ear I had very loud ringing and now I'm left with very little hearing in that ear. I went to the emergency room, but they found no reason for the hearing loss."

A man reported, "I took *Humira* from September 2007 to January 2017. Since then, I've been diagnosed with tinnitus, vertigo, dizziness and ear pain. But when I brought it up to my doctors, they all dismissed the fact that *Humira* is the cause of it. My tinnitus sounds like popcorn or guns firing."

A man observed, "I've been on *Humira* for a few years and never had an issue until recently, I've developed extremely annoying tinnitus in my left ear. After my last few injections, it's getting worse and worse."

A man explained, "After taking *Humira* for 6 years I suddenly got tinnitus in my left ear. At first I didn't relate it to *Humira* but after taking a break for a month and then taking another shot, it got worse. I found a report of a patient with tinnitus who was treated with a high dose of **Methylprednisolone**. Because of my medical condition I took **Prednisolone** in a lower dose and it reduced my tinnitus loudness significantly."

Adapalene

Pronunciation guide: ah-DAP-ah-leen

Drug classification: Dermatological drugs (see section 23 in Table 19-1)

Brand names: *Differin*

Ototoxic effects:
- Cochlear:
  - Hearing loss: (32 cases reported to FDA [FMR])
  - Tinnitus: (34 cases reported to FDA [FMR])
- Vestibular:
  - Ataxia/Gait disturbance: (9 cases reported to FDA [FMR])
  - Dizziness: (19 cases reported to FDA [FMR])
  - Vertigo: (7 cases reported to FDA [FMR])
- Outer/Middle Ear:
  - Ear discomfort/Ear pain: (35 cases reported to FDA [FMR])
  - Ear infection: (3 cases reported to FDA [FMR])

Eustachian tube dysfunction: (30 cases reported to FDA [FMR])
Otitis media: (3 cases reported to FDA [FMR])

Risk assessment: Class 1.5

Adefovir

Pronunciation guide: ah-DEF-oh-veer

Drug classification: Anti-retroviral reverse transcriptase inhibitors (see section 7.17.1.4 in Table 19-1)

Brand names: *Hepsera*

Ototoxic effects:
Cochlear:
Hearing loss: (11 cases reported to FDA [FMR])
Tinnitus: (9 cases reported to FDA [FMR])
Vestibular:
Ataxia/Gait disturbance: (53 cases reported to FDA [FMR])
Balance disorder: (5 cases reported to FDA [FMR])
Dizziness: (13 cases reported to FDA [FMR])
Vertigo: (4 cases reported to FDA [FMR])

Risk assessment: Class 1

Adenosine

Pronunciation guide: ah-DEN-oh-seen

Drug classification: Anti-arrhythmics (Heart rhythm regulators) (see section 20.4 in Table 19-1)

Brand names: *Adenocard*, *Adenoscan*, *Adetphos*

Ototoxic effects:
Cochlear:
Hearing loss: (4 cases reported to FDA [EHM])
Tinnitus: (6 cases reported to FDA [FMR])
Vestibular:
Ataxia/Gait disturbance: (14 cases reported to FDA [FMR])
Dizziness: 1-12% (CPS, PDR) (47 cases reported to FDA [FMR])
Vertigo: (4 cases reported to FDA [FMR])
Outer/Middle Ear:
Ear discomfort/Ear pain: <1% (CPS, PDR)
Unspecified/General Ear Conditions:
Meniere's disease: (7 cases reported to FDA [FMR])

Risk assessment: Class 1

Aflibercept (Afibercept)

Pronunciation guide: af-LIH-ber-sept

Drug classification: MACULAR DEGENERATION THERAPY ADJUNCT (see section 56.1.1 in Table 19-1)

Brand names: *Eylea, Vegf Trap*

Ototoxic effects:
  Vestibular:
    Dizziness: (5 cases reported to FDA [FMR])
    Vertigo: (4 cases reported to FDA [FMR])

Risk assessment: Class 0.5

Agalsidase alfa

Pronunciation guide: ah-GAL-sih-dase AL-fah

Drug classification: ENZYMES (see section 32.1 in Table 19-1)

Brand names: *Replagal*

Ototoxic effects:
  Cochlear:
    Hearing loss: (CPS)
    Tinnitus: (CPS, GIP)
  Vestibular:
    Dizziness: (CPS)
    Vertigo: 1.8% (CPS, GIP)
  Outer/Middle Ear:
    Ear discomfort/Ear pain: (CPS)

Risk assessment: Class 0.5

Agalsidase beta

Pronunciation guide: ah-GAL-sih-dase BAY-tah

Drug classification: ENZYMES (see section 32.1 in Table 19-1)

Brand names: *Fabrazyme*

Ototoxic effects:
  Cochlear:
    Hearing disorder: (9 cases reported to FDA [FMR])
    Hearing loss: (DFC, PDR) (152 cases reported to FDA [FMR])
    Tinnitus: 8% [5% above placebo results] (GIP, PDR) (30 cases reported to FDA [FMR])

Vestibular:
Ataxia/Gait disturbance: (PDR) (29 cases reported to FDA [FMR])
Balance disorder: (33 cases reported to FDA [FMR])
Dizziness: 5-21% [<11% above placebo results] (CPS, PDR) (127 cases reported to FDA [FMR])
Nystagmus: (3 cases reported to FDA [FMR])
Vertigo: 1-4% (CPS, PDR) (26 cases reported to FDA [FMR])
Vestibular disorder: (3 cases reported to FDA [FMR])
Outer/Middle Ear:
Ear discomfort/Ear pain: (4 cases reported to FDA [FMR])
Ear infection: (15 cases reported to FDA [FMR])
Otitis media: (5 cases reported to FDA [FMR])
Otorrhagia: (5 cases reported to FDA [FMR])
Unspecified/General Ear Conditions:
Ear disorder: (4 cases reported to FDA [FMR])

Risk assessment: Class 2

Agomelatine

Pronunciation guide: AH-goe-MEL-ah-teen

Drug classification: Anti-depressant drugs (see section 60.1 in Table 19-1)

Brand names: *Valdoxan*

Ototoxic effects:
Vestibular:
Ataxia/Gait disturbance: (4 cases reported to FDA [FMR])
Dizziness: (7 cases reported to FDA [FMR])
Vertigo: (4 cases reported to FDA [FMR])

Risk assessment: Class 0.5

Albendazole

Pronunciation guide: al-BEN-dah-zole

Drug classification: Anthelmintic drugs (see section 7.1 in Table 19-1)

Brand names: *Albenza*

Ototoxic effects:
Vestibular:
Ataxia/Gait disturbance: (29 cases reported to FDA [FMR])
Balance disorder: (13 cases reported to FDA [FMR])
Dizziness: 1% (DFC, PDR) (47 cases reported to FDA [FMR])
Vertigo: 1% (DFC, PDR) (8 cases reported to FDA [FMR])

Risk assessment: Class 0.5

Notes:

Caution: Eating grapefruit or drinking grapefruit juice during the time you are taking this drug may make the listed side effects worse than shown here.

See Chapter 16, "Grapefruit Juice and Ototoxic Drugs" for further information on this drug.

Albuterol (Salbutamol)

Pronunciation guide: al-BYOO-ter-ole (sal-BYOO-tah-mole)

Drug classification: Bronchodilators—beta adrenergic agonists (see section 63.4 in Table 19-1)

Brand names: *AccuNeb*, *Airomir*, *Asmavent*, *ProAir HFA*, *Proventil*, *Sultanol*, *Ventolin*, *Volmax*

Ototoxic effects:

Cochlear:

- Auditory hallucinations: (140 cases reported to FDA [FMR])
- Hearing disorder: (7 cases reported to FDA [FMR])
- Hearing loss: (645 cases reported to FDA [FMR])
- Hyperacusis: (14 cases reported to FDA [FMR])
- Phonophobia: (11 cases reported to FDA [FMR])
- Tinnitus: <3% (CPS, PDR) (499 cases reported to FDA [EHM])

Vestibular:

- Ataxia/Gait disturbance: <3% (CPS, PDR) (1,417 cases reported to FDA [FMR])
- Balance disorder: (740 cases reported to FDA [FMR])
- Dizziness: 1-7% [placebo 0] (CPS, PDR) (4,234 cases reported to FDA [FMR])
- Labyrinthitis: (28 cases reported to FDA [FMR])
- Nystagmus: (26 cases reported to FDA [FMR])
- Vertigo: (CPS, PDR) (522 cases reported to FDA [FMR])
- Vestibular disorder: (11 cases reported to FDA [FMR])

Outer/Middle Ear:

- Ceruminosis: (58 cases reported to FDA [FMR])
- Ear blocked: (9 cases reported to FDA [FMR])
- Ear discomfort/Ear pain: <3% (AHF, PDR) (407 cases reported to FDA [FMR])
- Ear infection: (188 cases reported to FDA [FMR])
- Eustachian tube dysfunction: (34 cases reported to FDA [FMR])
- Otitis externa: (76 cases reported to FDA [FMR])
- Otitis media: 0.9-4.3% [placebo 0] (AHF, PDR) (169 cases reported to FDA [FMR])
- Otorrhagia: (25 cases reported to FDA [FMR])
- Otorrhea: (44 cases reported to FDA [FMR])
- Perforated eardrum: (25 cases reported to FDA [FMR])

Unspecified/General Ear Conditions:
Ear disorder: <3% (AHF, PDR) (53 cases reported to FDA [FMR])
Meniere's disease: (19 cases reported to FDA [FMR])

Risk assessment: Class 3.5

Notes:

See the section "Manipulating the Placebo and Nocebo Effects" in Chapter 7 for further information on this drug.

Alclofenac

Pronunciation guide: al-kloe-FEN-ak

Drug classification: Acetic acids (see section 1.1.1 in Table 19-1)

Brand names: *Mervan*

Ototoxic effects:
Cochlear:
Tinnitus: (San, She)
Unspecified/General Ear Conditions:
Ototoxicity: (San)

Risk assessment: Class 0.5

Alclometasone

Pronunciation guide: al-kloe-MET-ah-sone

Drug classification: Glucocorticoids (see section 40.1.4 in Table 19-1)

Brand names: *Aclovate*

Ototoxic effects:
Cochlear:
Tinnitus: (3 cases reported to FDA [FMR])
Vestibular:
Ataxia/Gait disturbance: (4 cases reported to FDA [FMR])
Balance disorder: (3 cases reported to FDA [FMR])
Dizziness: (9 cases reported to FDA [FMR])
Vertigo: (3 cases reported to FDA [FMR])

Risk assessment: Class 0.5

Aldesleukin

Pronunciation guide: al-dess-LOO-kin

Drug classification: Interleukins (see section 14.12.1 in Table 19-1)

Brand names: *Proleukin*

Ototoxic effects:
  Cochlear:
    Hearing loss: (4 cases reported to FDA [FMR])
  Vestibular:
    Ataxia/Gait disturbance: (PDR) (8 cases reported to FDA [FMR])
    Dizziness: 11% (PDR) (11 cases reported to FDA [FMR])
    Vertigo: (4 cases reported to FDA [FMR])
  Outer/Middle Ear:
    Ear infection: (4 cases reported to FDA [FMR])

Risk assessment: Class 0.5

Aldioxa

Pronunciation guide: al-dee-OKS-ah

Drug classification: DERMATOLOGICAL DRUGS (see section 23 in Table 19-1)

Brand names: *Isalon*

Ototoxic effects:
  Vestibular:
    Ataxia/Gait disturbance: (12 cases reported to FDA [FMR])
    Dizziness: (15 cases reported to FDA [FMR])
    Nystagmus: (4 cases reported to FDA [FMR])

Risk assessment: Class 0.5

Alefacept

Pronunciation guide: al-eh-FAY-sept

Drug classification: IMMUNOSUPPRESSANT DRUGS (see section 43 in Table 19-1)

Brand names: *Amevive*

Ototoxic effects:
  Cochlear:
    Hearing loss: (5 cases reported to FDA [FMR])
    Tinnitus: (5 cases reported to FDA [FMR])
  Vestibular:
    Ataxia/Gait disturbance: (3 cases reported to FDA [FMR])
    Dizziness: (50 cases reported to FDA [FMR])
    Vertigo: (7 cases reported to FDA [FMR])
  Outer/Middle Ear:
    Ear infection: (3 cases reported to FDA [FMR])

Risk assessment: Class 1

Alemtuzumab

Pronunciation guide: ah-lem-TOO-zoo-mab

Drug classification: MONOCLONAL ANTIBODIES (see section 7.17.8 in Table 19-1)

Brand names: *Campath*, *MabCampath*

Ototoxic effects:
- Cochlear:
  - Auditory hallucinations: (10 cases reported to FDA [FMR])
  - Hearing loss: (CPS, PDR) (26 cases reported to FDA [FMR])
- Vestibular:
  - Ataxia/Gait disturbance: (PDR) (51 cases reported to FDA [FMR])
  - Dizziness: 1-12% (CPS, PDR) (98 cases reported to FDA [FMR])
  - Labyrinthitis: (6 cases reported to FDA [FMR])
  - Vertigo: 3% (CPS) (13 cases reported to FDA [FMR])
  - Vestibular disorder: (4 cases reported to FDA [FMR])
- Outer/Middle Ear:
  - Ear discomfort/Ear pain: (3 cases reported to FDA [FMR])
  - Ear infection: (3 cases reported to FDA [FMR])
  - Otitis media: (PDR) (3 cases reported to FDA [FMR])

Risk assessment: Class 1.5

Alendronate (Alendronic Acid)

Pronunciation guide: ah-LEN-droh-nate (al-len-DROH-ik ah-sid)

Drug classification: BISPHOSPHONATES (see section 50.1.1 in Table 19-1)

Brand names: *Bonalon*, *Fosamac*, *Fosamax*, *Fosavance* [1]

Ototoxic effects:
- Cochlear:
  - Auditory hallucinations: (109 cases reported to FDA [FMR])
  - Hearing disorder: (173 cases reported to FDA [FMR])
  - Hearing loss: (4,217 cases reported to FDA [FMR])
  - Hyperacusis: (14 cases reported to FDA [FMR])
  - Tinnitus: [2, 3, 4] (2,220 cases reported to FDA [FMR])
- Vestibular:
  - Ataxia/Gait disturbance: (5,539 cases reported to FDA [FMR])
  - Balance disorder: (2,210 cases reported to FDA [FMR])
  - Dizziness: 0.1–1.0% [placebo 0] (CPS, PDR) (7,303 cases reported to FDA [FMR])
  - Labyrinthitis: (404 cases reported to FDA [FMR])
  - Nystagmus: (58 cases reported to FDA [FMR])
  - Oscillopsia: (58 cases reported to FDA [FMR])
  - Vertigo: (CPS, PDR) (2,668 cases reported to FDA [FMR])
  - Vestibular disorder: (246 cases reported to FDA [FMR])

Outer/Middle Ear:
- Ceruminosis: (1,429 cases reported to FDA [FMR])
- Cholesteatoma: (30 cases reported to FDA [FMR])
- Ear blocked: (6 cases reported to FDA [FMR])
- Ear discomfort/Ear pain: (2,313 cases reported to FDA [FMR])
- Ear infection: (579 cases reported to FDA [FMR])
- Eustachian tube dysfunction: (642 cases reported to FDA [FMR])
- Otitis externa: (700 cases reported to FDA [FMR])
- Otitis media: (1,266 cases reported to FDA [FMR])
- Otorrhagia: (97 cases reported to FDA [FMR])
- Otorrhea: (356 cases reported to FDA [FMR])
- Otosclerosis: (15 cases reported to FDA [FMR])
- Perforated eardrum: (218 cases reported to FDA [FMR])

Unspecified/General Ear Conditions:
- Ear disorder: (819 cases reported to FDA [FMR])
- Meniere's disease: (125 cases reported to FDA [FMR])

Risk assessment: Class 5

Notes:

[1] *Fosavance* is a combination of **Alendronate** and **Cholecalciferol**. (See the generic drug **Cholecalciferol** for its specific ototoxic properties.)

Alendronate is one of the most commonly reported ototoxic drugs. A whopping 33,756 ototoxic side effects were reported to the FDA in the 9-year period between 2004 and 2012 (see above).

Between 2004 and 2012 a total of 166.4 million prescriptions were written in the USA for **Alendronate**. In contrast only 27.4 million prescriptions were written for **Ibandronate** (2006-2014). When comparing the number of tinnitus reports for **Alendronate** as compared to **Ibandronate** (2,220 vs. 145) and taking into account the fact that there were 6.07 times more prescriptions written for **Alendronate**, the normalized number of tinnitus reports for **Ibandronate** was 880 (6.07 x 145). Thus, there were about 2.5 times the number of tinnitus reports for **Alendronate** as for **Ibandronate**, indicating that **Ibandronate** is only about 40% as ototoxic as **Alendronate**. Therefore, if you need to take a Bisphosphonate class of drugs, **Ibandronate** would be a less ototoxic choice. (The comparable figure for hearing loss between these two drugs is about 3.6 times (4,217 vs. 1,171), thus **Ibandronate** is only about 28% as ototoxic as **Alendronate**.[25]

Anecdotal Reports:

[2] A man reported that his physician thought his tinnitus resulted from taking **Alendronate**.

[3] A lady thought her tinnitus resulted from taking **Alendronate**.

[4] A man reported his tinnitus was "raging again" a few hours after he took **Alendronate**.

Alfacalcidol (1-Hydroxycholecalciferol)

Pronunciation guide: AL-fah-KAL-sih-doll
(ONE-hie-DROKS-ee-KOE-leh-kal-SIF-er-all

Drug classification: Vitamins (see section 75.4 in Table 19-1)

Brand names: *Alfarol, D-alfa, Etalpha, OneAlfa*

Ototoxic effects:
- Cochlear:
  - Auditory hallucinations: (3 cases reported to FDA [FMR])
  - Hearing loss: (31 cases reported to FDA [FMR])
  - Tinnitus: (19 cases reported to FDA [FMR])
- Vestibular:
  - Ataxia/Gait disturbance: (151 cases reported to FDA [FMR])
  - Balance disorder: (8 cases reported to FDA [FMR])
  - Dizziness: (186 cases reported to FDA [FMR])
  - Vertigo: (GIP) (24 cases reported to FDA [FMR])
- Outer/Middle Ear:
  - Otitis media: (11 cases reported to FDA [FMR])

Risk assessment: Class 1.5

Notes:

Alfacalcidol is a form of Vitamin D.

Alfaxalone

Pronunciation guide: al-FAKS-ah-lone

Drug classification: General anesthetics (see section 4.8 in Table 19-1)

Brand names: *Alfaxan*

Ototoxic effects:
- Vestibular:
  - Ataxia/Gait disturbance: (15 cases reported to FDA [FMR])
  - Dizziness: (9 cases reported to FDA [FMR])
  - Labyrinthitis: (14 cases reported to FDA [FMR])
  - Vertigo: (17 cases reported to FDA [FMR])

Risk assessment: Class 0.5

Alfentanil

Pronunciation guide: al-FEN-tah-nil

Drug classification: Opiate agonist drugs (see section 1.4.1 in Table 19-1)

Brand names: *Rapifen*

Ototoxic effects:
- Cochlear:
  - Tinnitus: (DIO)
- Vestibular:
  - Ataxia/Gait disturbance: (RXL)
  - Dizziness: 3-9% (DIO, RXL) (12 cases reported to FDA [EHM])
  - Vertigo: (GIP) (12 cases reported to FDA [EHM])

Risk assessment: Class 0.5

Alfuzosin

Pronunciation guide: al-foo-ZOE-sin

Drug classification: Alpha-adrenergic blocking drugs (Alpha blockers) (see section 20.8.1 in Table 19-1)

Brand names: *Uroxatral, Xatral*

Ototoxic effects:
- Cochlear:
  - Hearing loss: (23 cases reported to FDA [FMR])
  - Tinnitus: (19 cases reported to FDA [FMR])
- Vestibular:
  - Ataxia/Gait disturbance: (83 cases reported to FDA [FMR])
  - Balance disorder: (57 cases reported to FDA [FMR])
  - Dizziness: 5.7% [2.9% above placebo results] (CPS) (344 cases reported to FDA [FMR])
  - Vertigo: 0.1-1% (CPS,GIP) (29 cases reported to FDA [FMR])
- Outer/Middle Ear:
  - Ear discomfort/Ear pain: (17 cases reported to FDA [FMR])
- Unspecified/General Ear Conditions:
  - Meniere's disease: (11 cases reported to FDA [FMR])

Risk assessment: Class 1

Alglucosidase alfa

Pronunciation guide: al-gloo-KOE-sih-dase al-fah

Drug classification: Enzymes (see section 32.1 in Table 19-1)

Brand names: *Lumizyme*, *Myozyme*

Ototoxic effects:
  Cochlear:
    Hearing loss: [1] <11.9% (CPS) (26 cases reported to FDA [FMR])
    Tinnitus: (8 cases reported to FDA [FMR])
  Vestibular:
    Ataxia/Gait disturbance: (16 cases reported to FDA [FMR])
    Balance disorder: (4 cases reported to FDA [FMR])
    Dizziness: 6.7% (CPS) (31 cases reported to FDA [FMR])
    Nystagmus: (39 cases reported to FDA [FMR])
    Vertigo: (9 cases reported to FDA [FMR])
  Outer/Middle Ear:
    Ear discomfort/Ear pain: 5.1% (CPS)
    Ear infection: (9 cases reported to FDA [FMR])
    Otitis media: 40.7% (CPS, DFC) (5 cases reported to FDA [FMR])
    Otorrhagia: 5.1% (CPS)

Risk assessment: Class 1.5

Notes:

[1] Hearing loss may be conductive or sensorineural. Hearing loss seems more related to the high incidence of middle ear infections in the people with Pompe Disease taking **Alglucosidase alfa**, rather than from the **Alglucosidase** therapy itself (CPS).

Aliskiren

Pronunciation guide: ah-LIS-keh-ren

Drug classification: Renin inhibitors (see section 20.8.36 in Table 19-1)

Brand names: *Rasilez*, *Tekturna*, *Tekturna HZT* [1], *Valturna* [2]

Ototoxic effects:
  Cochlear:
    Auditory hallucinations: (11 cases reported to FDA [FMR])
    Hearing loss: (14 cases reported to FDA [FMR])
    Tinnitus: (45 cases reported to FDA [FMR])
  Vestibular:
    Ataxia/Gait disturbance: (161 cases reported to FDA [FMR])
    Balance disorder: (18 cases reported to FDA [FMR])
    Dizziness: 2.3% [1.3% above placebo results] (PDR) (689 cases reported to FDA [FMR])
    Vertigo: 1.2% [0.7% above placebo results] (CPS, PDR) (78 cases reported to FDA [FMR])

Outer/Middle Ear:
Ceruminosis: (4 cases reported to FDA [FMR])
Ear discomfort/Ear pain: (13 cases reported to FDA [FMR])
Perforated eardrum: (4 cases reported to FDA [FMR])
Unspecified/General Ear Conditions:
Ear disorder: (5 cases reported to FDA [FMR])

Risk assessment: Class 1.5

Notes:

[1] *Tekturna HCT* is a combination of **Aliskiren** and **Hydrochlorothiazide**. (See the generic drug **Hydrochlorothiazide** for its specific ototoxic properties.)

[2] *Valturna* is a combination of **Aliskiren** and **Valsartan**. (See the generic drug **Valsartan** for its specific ototoxic properties.)

Caution: Eating grapefruit or drinking grapefruit juice during the time you are taking this drug may make the listed side effects worse than shown here. See Chapter 16, "Grapefruit Juice and Ototoxic Drugs" for further information on this drug.

Alizapride

Pronunciation guide: ah-LEE-zah-pride

Drug classification: DOPAMINE ANTAGONISTS (see section 53.26 in Table 19-1)

Brand names: *Vergentan*

Ototoxic effects:
Vestibular:
Dizziness: (7 cases reported to FDA [FMR])
Vertigo: (GIP) (3 cases reported to FDA [FMR])

Risk assessment: Class 0.5

Allopurinol

Pronunciation guide: al-oh-PURE-ih-nole

Drug classification: XANTHINE OXIDASE INHIBITORS (see section 46.10 in Table 19-1)

Brand names: *Alositol, Jenapurinol, Zyloprim, Zyloric*

Ototoxic effects:
Cochlear:
Auditory hallucinations: (37 cases reported to FDA [FMR])
Hearing disorder: (7 cases reported to FDA [FMR])
Hearing loss: (330 cases reported to FDA [FMR])
Hyperacusis: (5 cases reported to FDA [FMR])

Phonophobia: (4 cases reported to FDA [FMR])
Tinnitus: <1% (AHF, PDR) (361 cases reported to FDA [EHM])

Vestibular:
Ataxia/Gait disturbance: (CPS) (807 cases reported to FDA [FMR])
Balance disorder: (237 cases reported to FDA [FMR])
Dizziness: <1% (CPS, PDR) (1,796 cases reported to FDA [FMR])
Labyrinthitis: (5 cases reported to FDA [FMR])
Nystagmus: (20 cases reported to FDA [FMR])
Vertigo: <1% (CPS, PDR) (245 cases reported to FDA [FMR])
Vestibular disorder: (11 cases reported to FDA [FMR])

Outer/Middle Ear:
Ceruminosis: (38 cases reported to FDA [FMR])
Ear blocked: (5 cases reported to FDA [FMR])
Ear discomfort/Ear pain: (173 cases reported to FDA [FMR])
Ear infection: (55 cases reported to FDA [FMR])
Eustachian tube dysfunction: (12 cases reported to FDA [FMR])
Otitis externa: (45 cases reported to FDA [FMR])
Otitis media: (30 cases reported to FDA [FMR])
Otorrhagia: (4 cases reported to FDA [FMR])
Otorrhea: (24 cases reported to FDA [FMR])
Perforated eardrum: (10 cases reported to FDA [FMR])

Unspecified/General Ear Conditions:
Ear disorder: (17 cases reported to FDA [FMR])
Meniere's disease: (12 cases reported to FDA [FMR])
Ototoxicity: (3 cases reported to FDA [FMR])

Risk assessment: Class 3.5

Notes:

See Chapter 10, "We 'Hear' With Our Eyes" for further information on this drug.

Almotriptan

Pronunciation guide: al-moh-TRIP-tan

Drug classification: Serotonin-receptor agonists (see section 53.32 in Table 19-1)

Brand names: *Almogran, Axert*

Ototoxic effects:

Cochlear:
Hyperacusis: 0.1-1% (DFC, PDR)
Phonophobia: (8 cases reported to FDA [FMR])
Tinnitus: 0.1-1% (DFC, PDR)

- Vestibular:
  - Ataxia/Gait disturbance: <0.1% (PDR) (4 cases reported to FDA [FMR])
  - Balance disorder: (14 cases reported to FDA [FMR])
  - Dizziness: >1% (NDH, PDR) (30 cases reported to FDA [FMR])
  - Nystagmus: <0.1% (DFC, PDR)
  - Vertigo: 0.1-10% (GIP, PDR) (9 cases reported to FDA [FMR])
- Outer/Middle Ear:
  - Ear discomfort/Ear pain: 0.1-1% (DFC, PDR)
  - Otitis media: <0.1% (DFC, PDR)

Risk assessment: Class 1

Alosetron

Pronunciation guide: ah-LOSS-eh-tron

Drug classification: Serotonin-receptor antagonists (see section 34.1.4 in Table 19-1)

Brand names: *Lotronex*

Ototoxic effects:

- Vestibular:
  - Balance disorder: (3 cases reported to FDA [FMR])
  - Dizziness: (13 cases reported to FDA [FMR])
- External/Middle Ear:
  - Ear discomfort/Ear pain: (3 cases reported to FDA [FMR])
  - Ear infection: (PDR)
- Unspecified/General Ear Conditions:
  - Ear disorder: <0.1% (PDR)

Risk assessment: Class 0.5

Alpha 1-proteinase inhibitor

Pronunciation guide: AL-fah 1-PROE-tee-nase in-HIB-ih-tor

Drug classification: Respiratory drugs (see section 63 in Table 19-1)

Brand names: *Prolastin, Zemaira*

Ototoxic effects:

- Cochlear:
  - Tinnitus: (6 cases reported to FDA [FMR])
- Vestibular:
  - Dizziness: (59 cases reported to FDA [FMR])
  - Labyrinthitis: (4 cases reported to FDA [FMR])

Risk assessment: Class 0.5

Alpha lipoic acid

Pronunciation guide: AL-fah lih-PROE-ik ASS-id

Drug classification: NUTRACEUTICAL PRODUCTS (see section 75.9 in Table 19-1)

Brand names: *Thioctic acid*

Ototoxic effects:
- Cochlear:
  - Hearing loss: (75 cases reported to FDA [FMR])
  - Tinnitus: (25 cases reported to FDA [FMR])
- Vestibular:
  - Ataxia/Gait disturbance: (36 cases reported to FDA [FMR])
  - Balance disorder: (12 cases reported to FDA [FMR])
  - Dizziness: (82 cases reported to FDA [FMR])
  - Vertigo: (33 cases reported to FDA [FMR])
- Outer/Middle Ear:
  - Ceruminosis: (3 cases reported to FDA [FMR])
  - Ear blocked: (3 cases reported to FDA [FMR])
  - Otitis media: (8 cases reported to FDA [FMR])

Risk assessment: Class 1.5

Alprazolam

Pronunciation guide: al-PRAH-zoe-lam

Drug classification: BENZODIAZEPINES (see section 60.12.8 in Table 19-1)

Brand names: *Alzam*, *Apraz*, *Constan*, *Frontal*, *Solanax*, *Xanax*, *Xanax TS*, *Xanor*, *Zolam*

Ototoxic effects:
- Cochlear:
  - Auditory hallucinations: (252 cases reported to FDA [FMR])
  - Hearing disorder: (12 cases reported to FDA [FMR])
  - Hearing loss: (662 cases reported to FDA [FMR])
  - Hyperacusis: [1, 2] (64 cases reported to FDA [FMR])
  - Phonophobia: (5 cases reported to FDA [FMR])
  - Tinnitus: 6.6% (CPS, PDR) (858 cases reported to FDA [DCC])
- Vestibular:
  - Ataxia/Gait disturbance: >1% (NDH, PDR) (1,886 cases reported to FDA [FMR])
  - Balance disorder: (1,150 cases reported to FDA [FMR])
  - Dizziness: 0.8->10% (NDH, PDR) (4,691 cases reported to FDA [FMR])
  - Labyrinthitis: (101 cases reported to FDA [FMR])
  - Nystagmus: (37 cases reported to FDA [FMR])

Vertigo: 1-10% (GIP, NDH) (632 cases reported to FDA [FMR])
Vestibular disorder: (34 cases reported to FDA [FMR])

Outer/Middle Ear:

Ceruminosis: (30 cases reported to FDA [FMR])
Ear blocked: (59 cases reported to FDA [FMR])
Ear discomfort/Ear pain: (422 cases reported to FDA [FMR])
Ear infection: (141 cases reported to FDA [FMR])
Eustachian tube dysfunction: (70 cases reported to FDA [FMR])
Otitis externa: (63 cases reported to FDA [FMR])
Otitis media: (178 cases reported to FDA [FMR])
Otorrhagia: (41 cases reported to FDA [FMR])
Otorrhea: (77 cases reported to FDA [FMR])
Perforated eardrum: (24 cases reported to FDA [FMR])

Unspecified/General Ear Conditions:

Ear disorder: (42 cases reported to FDA [FMR])
Meniere's disease: (29 cases reported to FDA [FMR])

Risk assessment: Class 3.5

Notes:

Caution: Eating grapefruit or drinking grapefruit juice during the time you are taking this drug may make the listed side effects worse than shown here. See Chapter 16, "Grapefruit Juice and Ototoxic Drugs" for further information on this drug.

Also, see Chapter 5 "Are You at Risk"; and Chapter 13 "Beware of the Benzodiazepines—Nasty Time Bombs for additional information on this drug.

Anecdotal Reports:

[1] If you stop taking **Alprazolam** "cold turkey" instead of weaning off it very slowly, you may experience tinnitus and/or hyperacusis. As one lady explained, "I have seen countless people that have stopped taking *Xanax* develop tinnitus, hyperacusis or both".

[2] A man wrote, "When I first acquired hyperacusis/tinnitus my ENT put me on *Xanax*. It was a godsend for about a year. At that point the interdose withdrawals [short half-life] of the medication were too much for me to put up with. I'd take 3 tablets a day, and after about 4 hours of taking a tablet I'd start getting increased hyperacusis."

Long term use of **Alprazolam** can result in various ototoxic side effects. As one lady explained, "About 15 years ago I started having panic attacks and began taking **Alprazolam** (*Xanax*) at 1.5 mg/day and have been on it ever since. Two years ago I had some really bad panic attacks so my doctor doubled my *Xanax* medication to 3 mg/day. Now everything is out of control for some reason. In the past year or two, in spite of the increased dose, things have been getting much worse to the point I don't feel normal any more. My hearing is a lot worse, I have vertigo and balance problems. I feel unsteady on my feet. My ears are ringing. They are also supersensitive to sounds [hyperacusis]. As a result, I can't wear a hearing aid in one ear anymore."

One man reported, "**Alprazolam** (*Xanax*) is a really dangerous drug, physically and mentally. My wife lost hearing permanently while on it and I lost my wife permanently while she was on it. I would rank it on a par with heroin and crack, and worse than coke. Do not use it!"

Alprostadil

Pronunciation guide: al-PROS-tah-dill

Drug classification: Vasodilators (see section 20.8.40 in Table 19-1)

Brand names: *Caverject*

Ototoxic effects:
 Cochlear:
  Hearing loss: (10 cases reported to FDA [FMR])
  Tinnitus: (3 cases reported to FDA [FMR])
 Vestibular:
  Ataxia/Gait disturbance: (6 cases reported to FDA [FMR])
  Dizziness: (38 cases reported to FDA [FMR])
  Vertigo: (GIP)

Risk assessment: Class 0.5

Alteplase

Pronunciation guide: AL-teh-playss

Drug classification: Anti-clotting drugs (see section 36.1 in Table 19-1)

Brand names: *Activase, Cathflo-Activase*

Ototoxic effects:
 Cochlear:
  Hearing loss: (13 cases reported to FDA [FMR])
  Tinnitus: (3 cases reported to FDA [FMR])
 Vestibular:
  Ataxia/Gait disturbance: (77 cases reported to FDA [FMR])
  Balance disorder: (26 cases reported to FDA [FMR])
  Dizziness: (42 cases reported to FDA [FMR])
  Vertigo: (9 cases reported to FDA [FMR])

Outer/Middle Ear:
Ear discomfort/Ear pain: (11 cases reported to FDA [FMR])

Risk assessment: Class 1

Altretamine

Pronunciation guide: al-TRET-ah-meen

Drug classification: ALKYLATING DRUGS (see section 14.1 in Table 19-1)

Brand names: *Hexalen*

Ototoxic effects:
Vestibular:
Ataxia/Gait disturbance: (AHF, PDR)
Dizziness: (AHF, PDR)
Vertigo: (AHF, PDR)

Risk assessment: Class 0.5

Aluminum chloride

Pronunciation guide: ah-LOO-mih-num KLOR-eyed

Drug classification: ANTIPERSPIRANTS (see section 23.10 in Table 19-1)

Brand names: *Drysol*

Ototoxic effects:
Cochlear:
Hearing loss: (12 cases reported to FDA [FMR])
Tinnitus: (12 cases reported to FDA [FMR])
Vestibular:
Dizziness: (31 cases reported to FDA [FMR])
Outer/Middle Ear:
Cholesteatoma: (12 cases reported to FDA [FMR])
Ear discomfort/Ear pain: (12 cases reported to FDA [FMR])

Risk assessment: Class 1

Aluminum hydroxide

Pronunciation guide: ah-LOO-mih-num hie-DROKS-eyed

Drug classification: ANTACIDS (see section 34.32 in Table 19-1)

Brand names: *Gaviscon* [1], *Mylanta* [2], *Nephrox*

Ototoxic effects:
Cochlear:
Auditory hallucinations: (10 cases reported to FDA [FMR])

Hearing loss: (37 cases reported to FDA [FMR])
Tinnitus: (14 cases reported to FDA [FMR])
Vestibular:
Ataxia/Gait disturbance: (73 cases reported to FDA [FMR])
Balance disorder: (57 cases reported to FDA [FMR])
Dizziness: (185 cases reported to FDA [FMR])
Labyrinthitis: (7 cases reported to FDA [FMR])
Vertigo: (33 cases reported to FDA [FMR])
Outer/Middle Ear:
Ear blocked: (4 cases reported to FDA [FMR])
Ear discomfort/Ear pain: (34 cases reported to FDA [FMR])
Unspecified/General Ear Conditions:
Meniere's disease: (6 cases reported to FDA [FMR])

Risk assessment: Class 1

Notes:

[1] *Gaviscon* is a combination of **Aluminum hydroxide** and Magnesium carbonate. **Aluminum hydroxide** is the ototoxic agent.)

[2] *Mylanta* is a combination of **Aluminum hydroxide**, Magnesium hydroxide and **Simethicone**. (See the generic drug **Simethicone** for its specific ototoxic properties.)

Amantadine

Pronunciation guide: ah-MAN-tah-deen

Drug classification: ANTI-VIRAL DRUGS (see section 7.17 in Table 19-1)

Brand names: *Mantidan, Symmetrel*

Ototoxic effects:
Cochlear:
Auditory hallucinations: (24 cases reported to FDA [FMR])
Hearing loss: (83 cases reported to FDA [FMR])
Tinnitus: (12 cases reported to FDA [FMR])
Vestibular:
Ataxia/Gait disturbance: 1-5% (CPS, PDR) (274 cases reported to FDA [FMR])
Balance disorder: (125 cases reported to FDA [FMR])
Dizziness: 5-10% (CPS, PDR) (256 cases reported to FDA [FMR])
Labyrinthitis: (3 cases reported to FDA [FMR])
Vertigo: (GIP) (93 cases reported to FDA [FMR])
Vestibular disorder: (6 cases reported to FDA [FMR])
Outer/Middle Ear:
Ceruminosis: (3 cases reported to FDA [FMR])
Ear discomfort/Ear pain: (7 cases reported to FDA [FMR])

Ear infection: (3 cases reported to FDA [FMR])
Otitis externa: (17 cases reported to FDA [FMR])
Perforated eardrum: (3 cases reported to FDA [FMR])

Risk assessment: Class 1.5

Notes:

Ataxia may be a sign of **Amantadine** overdose (PDR).

See Chapter 10, "We 'Hear' With Our Eyes" for further information on this drug.

Ambrisentan

Pronunciation guide: AM-brih-SEN-tan

Drug classification: Pulmonary anti-hypertensive drugs (see section 20.8.22 in Table 19-1)

Brand names: *Letairis*

Ototoxic effects:
Cochlear:
Auditory hallucinations: (3 cases reported to FDA [FMR])
Hearing loss: (153 cases reported to FDA [EHM])
Tinnitus: (110 cases reported to FDA [FMR])
Vestibular:
Ataxia/Gait disturbance: (41 cases reported to FDA [FMR])
Balance disorder: (19 cases reported to FDA [FMR])
Dizziness: (329 cases reported to FDA [FMR])
Vertigo: (14 cases reported to FDA [FMR])
Outer/Middle Ear:
Ear discomfort/Ear pain: (20 cases reported to FDA [FMR])

Risk assessment: Class 2

Ambroxol

Pronunciation guide: AM-broks-all

Drug classification: Mucolytic drugs (see section 63.16 in Table 19-1)

Brand names: *Mucosolvan*

Ototoxic effects:
Cochlear:
Auditory hallucinations: (10 cases reported to FDA [FMR])
Hearing loss: (8 cases reported to FDA [FMR])
Tinnitus: (3 cases reported to FDA [FMR])
Vestibular:
Ataxia/Gait disturbance: (10 cases reported to FDA [FMR])

Balance disorder: (3 cases reported to FDA [FMR])
Dizziness: (66 cases reported to FDA [FMR])
Vertigo: (GIP) (3 cases reported to FDA [FMR])
Outer/Middle Ear:
Perforated eardrum: (3 cases reported to FDA [FMR])

Risk assessment: Class 0.5

Amezinium

Pronunciation guide: ah-meh-ZIN-ee-um

Drug classification: SYMPATHOMIMETIC DRUGS (see section 17.16 in Table 19-1)

Brand names: *Risumic, Tenfortan*

Ototoxic effects:
Cochlear:
Tinnitus: (She)
Vestibular:
Ataxia/Gait disturbance: (20 cases reported to FDA [FMR])
Dizziness: (24 cases reported to FDA [FMR])
Vertigo: (3 cases reported to FDA [FMR])

Risk assessment: Class 0.5

Amifostine

Pronunciation guide: AM-ih-FOS-teen

Drug classification: ANTI-NEOPLASTIC DETOXIFYING AGENTS (see section 14.44 in Table 19-1)

Brand names: *Ethyol*

Ototoxic effects:
Cochlear:
Hearing loss: (3 cases reported to FDA [FMR])
Tinnitus: (3 cases reported to FDA [EHM])
Vestibular:
Ataxia/Gait disturbance: (19 cases reported to FDA [FMR])
Dizziness: (23 cases reported to FDA [FMR])
Vertigo: (GIP)
Outer/Middle Ear:
Ear discomfort/Ear pain: (40 cases reported to FDA [FMR])
Otitis media: (3 cases reported to FDA [FMR])
Perforated eardrum: (4 cases reported to FDA [FMR])
Unspecified/General Ear Conditions:
Ototoxicity: (3 cases reported to FDA [FMR])

Risk assessment: Class 1

Amikacin

Pronunciation guide: am-ih-KAY-sin

Drug classification: AMINOGLYCOSIDES (see section 7.4.1 in Table 19-1)

Brand names: *Amikin, Amiklin, Novamin*

Ototoxic effects:
- Cochlear:
  - Hearing loss: (CPS, PDR) (88 cases reported to FDA [FMR])
  - Tinnitus: (CPS, PDR) (7 cases reported to FDA [FMR])
- Vestibular:
  - Ataxia/Gait disturbance: (CPS) (19 cases reported to FDA [FMR])
  - Balance disorder: (CPS, PDR) (17 cases reported to FDA [FMR])
  - Dizziness: (CPS, PDR) (108 cases reported to FDA [FMR])
  - Nystagmus: (CPS, PDR) (7 cases reported to FDA [FMR])
  - Vertigo: (CPS, PDR) (14 cases reported to FDA [FMR])
- Outer/Middle Ear:
  - Ear blocked: (CPS, PDR)
- Unspecified/General Ear Conditions:
  - Ototoxicity: (CPS, NDH) (9 cases reported to FDA [FMR])

Risk assessment: Class 4

Notes:

If you are taking **Amikacin**, you should be under close medical observation. The incidence of ototoxicity in **Amikacin** is up to 13.9%.[26]

You have a greater chance of having vestibular (balance) problems and permanent hearing loss in both ears if you have pre-existing kidney damage, or if you have normal kidney function but are being treated at higher doses and/or for longer periods than those recommended (CPS, PDR).

Therefore, before taking **Amikacin**, tell your doctor if you have any of these risk factors—pre-existing hearing loss, ear damage from previously prescribed drugs, impaired kidney function, advanced age or dehydration (CPS, PDR). Any of these risk factors may make your ears more susceptible to damage from **Amikacin** than would be expected in the general population.

The side effects of **Amikacin** can result in hearing loss, loss of balance or both. **Amikacin** primarily affects auditory function. Cochlear damage includes high-frequency hearing loss and usually occurs before clinical hearing loss can be detected. Initially, high-frequency audiometric testing is the only way to detect hearing loss (CPS, PDR).

Be aware that hearing loss (and other ear damage) may develop without warning while you are taking **Amikacin** (PDR). In order to reduce the chances of ototoxicity, you should only take **Amikacin** for 7 to 10 days. Your doctor should stop this medication if there is no definite clinical response within 3 to 5 days of therapy.[27]

Since hearing loss from taking **Amikacin** is often permanent, you need your hearing checked both **before** and **during** treatment (serial high-frequency audiograms) in order that your doctor may take appropriate action to minimize the risk of permanent hearing loss (CPS). This is particularly true if you already have any hearing or balance problems or problems with your kidneys (PDR).

You should know that you may not have any symptoms such as hearing loss or vertigo while you are taking **Amikacin** to warn you that you are damaging your ears. Total or partial hearing loss in both ears, or disabling vertigo may not show up until several weeks after you have stopped taking **Amikacin**. Such damage to your ears is usually permanent. Because of this risk, immediately check with your doctor if you detect any signs of hearing loss, dizziness, tinnitus or feeling of fullness in your ears, stop taking **Amikacin** and immediately notify your doctor (PDR). If you have any of these signs, your doctor should strongly consider stopping treatment immediately or adjust the dosage (CPS, PDR).

The risk of permanent hearing loss and kidney damage increases when you take **Amikacin** at the same time as rapidly-acting diuretic (water pills), nephrotoxic (kidney-damaging) or ototoxic (ear damaging) drugs. You can quickly lose your hearing if you have poor kidney function and are treated at the same time with **Amikacin** and one of the rapidly-acting diuretic drugs given intravenously such as **Ethacrynic acid**, **Furosemide** or **Mannitol** (CPS).

You should not use other neurotoxic (nerve damaging) or nephrotoxic (kidney damaging) drugs, particularly **Amphotericin B**, **Bacitracin**, Cephaloridine, **Cisplatin**, **Colistin**, **Paromomycin**, **Polymyxin B**, **Vancomycin**, **Viomycin**, or other Aminoglycoside antibiotics at the same time as, or following, taking **Amikacin** (PDR).

See Chapter 12, "Aminoglycoside Antibiotics are the Ototoxic 'Bad boys'" for further information on this drug.

Amiloride

Pronunciation guide: ah-MILL-oh-ride

Drug classification: Diuretics—potassium-sparing (see section 30.5.8 in Table 19-1)

Brand names: *Apo-Amiloride*, Co-Amilofruse, *Frumil, Midamor, Moduret*[1], *Moduretic*[1], *Normorix*

Ototoxic effects:

Cochlear:

Hearing loss: (31 cases reported to FDA [FMR])

Tinnitus: <1% (CPS, PDR) (17 cases reported to FDA [FMR])

Vestibular:
Ataxia/Gait disturbance: (61 cases reported to FDA [FMR])
Balance disorder: (34 cases reported to FDA [FMR])
Dizziness: 1-8% (CPS, PDR) (200 cases reported to FDA [FMR])
Vertigo: <1% (CPS, PDR) (37 cases reported to FDA [FMR])
Outer/Middle Ear:
Ear discomfort/Ear pain: (3 cases reported to FDA [FMR])

Risk assessment: Class 1.5

Notes:

[1] *Moduret, Moduretic* and *Normorix* are combinations of **Amiloride** and **Hydrochlorothiazide**. (See the generic drug **Hydrochlorothiazide** for its specific ototoxic properties.)

Aminocaproic acid

Pronunciation guide: ah-MEE-noe-kah-PROE-ik ASS-id

Drug classification: ANTI-FIBRINOLYTIC DRUGS (see section 36.4 in Table 19-1)

Brand names: *Amicar*

Ototoxic effects:
Cochlear:
Hearing loss: (AHF, PDR)
Tinnitus: (CPS, PDR)
Vestibular:
Dizziness: (CPS, PDR) (30 cases reported to FDA [FMR])
Vertigo: (13 cases reported to FDA [FMR])

Risk assessment: Class 0.5

Aminoglutethimide

Pronunciation guide: ah-MEE-noe-gloo-TETH-ih-myed

Drug classification: ADRENAL CORTICOSTEROID INHIBITORS (see section 40.1.2.1 in Table 19-1)

Brand names: *Cytadren*

Ototoxic effects:
Vestibular:
Ataxia/Gait disturbance: (BNF, CPS)
Dizziness: (BNF, CPS)
Vertigo: (CPS)

Risk assessment: Class 0.5

Aminophylline

Pronunciation guide: ah-mih NOFF-ih-lin

Drug classification: BRONCHODILATORS—BETA ADRENERGIC AGONISTS (see section 63.4 in Table 19-1)

Brand names: *Phyllocontin, Truphylline*

Ototoxic effects:
- Vestibular:
  - Ataxia/Gait disturbance: (7 cases reported to FDA [FMR])
  - Dizziness:(21 cases reported to FDA [FMR])
  - Vertigo: (6 cases reported to FDA [FMR])

Risk assessment: Class 0.5

Aminopyrine

Pronunciation guide: ah-MEE-noe-PYE-reen

Drug classification: ANALGESIC DRUGS (PAINKILLERS) (see section 1 in Table 19-1)

Brand names: *Ampyrone*

Ototoxic effects:
- Cochlear:
  - Hearing loss: (NTP) (3 cases reported to FDA [FMR])
  - Tinnitus: (NTP) (7 cases reported to FDA [FMR])
- Vestibular:
  - Ataxia/Gait disturbance: (47 cases reported to FDA [FMR])
  - Dizziness: (NTP) (72 cases reported to FDA [FMR])
  - Labyrinthitis: (4 cases reported to FDA [FMR])
  - Vertigo: (6 cases reported to FDA [FMR])

Risk assessment: Class 0.5

Notes:

In the USA, the FDA has removed this drug from use. It was formerly used in both human and veterinary medicine.

Amiodarone

Pronunciation guide: am-ee-OH-dah-rohn

Drug classification: ANTI-ARRHYTHMICS (HEART RHYTHM REGULATORS) (see section 20.4 in Table 19-1)

Brand names: *Ancoron, Cordarone, Novo-Amiodarone, Pacerone*

Ototoxic effects:
Cochlear:
Auditory hallucinations: (24 cases reported to FDA [FMR])
Hearing loss: (208 cases reported to FDA [FMR])
Hyperacusis: (6 cases reported to FDA [FMR])
Tinnitus: <1% (CPS) (87 cases reported to FDA [FMR])
Vestibular:
Ataxia/Gait disturbance: 4-9% (CPS, PDR) (562 cases reported to FDA [FMR])
Balance disorder: (273 cases reported to FDA [FMR])
Dizziness: 4-9% (CPS, PDR) (1,357 cases reported to FDA [FMR])
Labyrinthitis: (3 cases reported to FDA [FMR])
Nystagmus: (AHF) (26 cases reported to FDA [FMR])
Vertigo: (BNF, CPS) (198 cases reported to FDA [FMR])
Vestibular disorder: (4 cases reported to FDA [FMR])
Outer/Middle Ear:
Ceruminosis: (9 cases reported to FDA [FMR])
Ear discomfort/Ear pain: (79 cases reported to FDA [FMR])
Ear infection: (6 cases reported to FDA [FMR])
Otitis externa: (59 cases reported to FDA [FMR])
Otitis media: (6 cases reported to FDA [FMR])
Unspecified/General Ear Conditions:
Ear disorder: (70 cases reported to FDA [FMR])
Meniere's disease: (13 cases reported to FDA [FMR])

Risk assessment: Class 3

Notes:

Vertigo occurs frequently at the beginning of therapy when high doses are used (CPS).

Caution: Eating grapefruit or drinking grapefruit juice during the time you are taking this drug may make the listed side effects worse than shown here. See Chapter 16, "Grapefruit Juice and Ototoxic Drugs" for further information on this drug.

Amisulpride

Pronunciation guide: AH-mih-SUL-pride

Drug classification: Second generation (atypical) antipsychotic drugs (see section 60.8.3.2 in Table 19-1)

Brand names: *Solian*

Ototoxic effects:
Cochlear:
Auditory hallucinations: (80 cases reported to FDA [FMR])

Hearing loss: (5 cases reported to FDA [FMR])
Tinnitus: (4 cases reported to FDA [EHM])
Vestibular:
Ataxia/Gait disturbance: (43 cases reported to FDA [FMR])
Balance disorder: (31 cases reported to FDA [FMR])
Dizziness: (77 cases reported to FDA [FMR])
Vertigo: (GIP) (9 cases reported to FDA [FMR])
Outer/Middle Ear:
Ear discomfort/Ear pain: (5 cases reported to FDA [FMR])
Ear infection: (18 cases reported to FDA [FMR])
Otorrhea: (4 cases reported to FDA [FMR])

Risk assessment: Class 1

Amitriptyline

Pronunciation guide: ah-mee-TRIP-tih-leen

Drug classification: Tricyclic anti-depressants (see section 60.1.8 in Table 19-1)

Brand names: *Amitril, Amitrip, Amytril, Elavil, Elavil Plus*[1], *Endep, Etrafon*[1], *Laroxyl, Limbitrol*[2], *Triavil*[1], *Triptanol, Tryptizol*

Ototoxic effects:
Cochlear:
Auditory hallucinations: (104 cases reported to FDA [FMR])
Hearing disorder: [3] (20 cases reported to FDA [FMR])
Hearing loss: (389 cases reported to FDA [FMR])
Hyperacusis: (9 cases reported to FDA [FMR])
Phonophobia: (4 cases reported to FDA [FMR])
Tinnitus: >1% (NDH, PDR) (293 cases reported to FDA [FMR])
Vestibular:
Ataxia/Gait disturbance: >1% (NDH, PDR) (963 cases reported to FDA [FMR])
Balance disorder: (649 cases reported to FDA [FMR])
Dizziness: >1%(NDH, PDR) (2,351 cases reported to FDA [FMR])
Labyrinthitis: (23 cases reported to FDA [FMR])
Nystagmus: [4] (CPS) (49 cases reported to FDA [FMR])
Vertigo: (CPS, GIP) (331 cases reported to FDA [FMR])
Vestibular disorder: (13 cases reported to FDA [FMR])
Outer/Middle Ear:
Ceruminosis: (64 cases reported to FDA [FMR])
Cholesteatoma: (12 cases reported to FDA [FMR])
Ear blocked: (21 cases reported to FDA [FMR])
Ear discomfort/Ear pain: (280 cases reported to FDA [FMR])
Ear infection: (62 cases reported to FDA [FMR])
Eustachian tube dysfunction: (61 cases reported to FDA [FMR])

Otitis externa: (17 cases reported to FDA [FMR])
Otitis media: (81 cases reported to FDA [FMR])
Otorrhagia: (26 cases reported to FDA [FMR])
Otorrhea: (58 cases reported to FDA [FMR])
Perforated eardrum: (12 cases reported to FDA [FMR])
Unspecified/General Ear Conditions:
Ear disorder: (23 cases reported to FDA [FMR])
Meniere's disease: (39 cases reported to FDA [FMR])

Risk assessment: Class 3.5

Notes:

[1] *Elavil Plus*, *Etrafon* and *Triavil* are combinations of **Amitriptyline** and **Perphenazine.** (See the generic drug **Perphenazine** for its specific ototoxic properties.)

[2] *Limbitrol* is a combination of **Amitriptyline** and **Chlordiazepoxide**. (See the generic drug **Chlordiazepoxide** for its specific ototoxic properties.)

[3] There is a report of a change in the ability to perceive tones.[28]

[4] Nystagmus may be a symptom of **Amitriptyline** overdose (CPS).

Caution: Eating grapefruit or drinking grapefruit juice during the time you are taking this drug may make the listed side effects worse than shown here. See Chapter 16, "Grapefruit Juice and Ototoxic Drugs" for further information on this drug.

Also see Chapter 5 "Are You at Risk?" for additional information on this drug.

Anecdotal Reports:

A man reported distorted hearing, hearing loss and tinnitus after taking his first 40 mg dose of **Amitriptyline** after being on it for 2 weeks at 10, 20 and 30 mg.

A lady who had been taking **Amitriptyline** for 12 years wrote, "Lately I have noticed several symptoms which I'm sure are linked to this drug. I suddenly started getting chronic ear infections in my left ear at least once every couple of months, and this has continued for the last few years. I also have terrible tinnitus, worse in the problem left ear, and what I believe is hyperacusis. I find watching the television even at low volumes causes my ears to have a full feeling and my tinnitus to increase quite severely."

A lady reported she has "screaming tinnitus" whenever she takes **Amitriptyline**. Her tinnitus changes in both sounds and pitch. She also hears different sounds in each ear, sometimes more than one at a time.

A man began taking **Amitriptyline** which resulted in severe tinnitus. When he stopped taking the drug, he joyfully reported that 12 days later his tinnitus went away.

A lady reported annoying tinnitus occurred when her doctor put her on double her previous dose of **Amitriptyline**.

A lady wrote, "I took only one 10 mg **Amitriptyline** tablet and experienced a massive tinnitus spike that dropped down to a low level a day or two later."

Another lady also took just one **Amitriptyline** capsule. The next morning she got whistling tinnitus in her right ear that never stopped. She wrote this 25 years later. Fortunately she habituated to her tinnitus.

A man explained, "About 6 months ago I had a hearing test and the result surprised the doctor as being so acute for someone of my age (65). My medicine regime didn't change until a few weeks after my hearing test when I was prescribed **Amitriptyline**. Within 2 days I had severe tinnitus and my hearing went fuzzy. After taking the drug for 5 days I was told to stop taking it. I was referred to the hearing clinic and tests showed a marked decrease on my hearing to the extent that I now need hearing aids. I've had the hearing aids now for 3 months so the hearing loss appears to be permanent."

Amlodipine

Pronunciation guide: am-LOE-dih-peen

Drug classification: CALCIUM CHANNEL-BLOCKING DRUGS (CCBs) (see section 20.8.16 in Table 19-1)

Brand names: *Amlodin, Amlor, Amturnide* [1], *Azor, Caduet* [2], *Exforge* [3], *Exforge HCT* [4], *Istin, Lotrel* [5], *Norvasc, Norvask, Tekamlo* [6]

Ototoxic effects:
- Cochlear:
  - Auditory hallucinations: (168 cases reported to FDA [FMR])
  - Hearing disorder: (18 cases reported to FDA [FMR])
  - Hearing loss: (799 cases reported to FDA [FMR])
  - Hyperacusis: (20 cases reported to FDA [FMR])
  - Phonophobia: (6 cases reported to FDA [FMR])
  - Tinnitus: 0.1-2% (CPS, PDR) (985 cases reported to FDA [EHM])
- Vestibular:
  - Ataxia/Gait disturbance: <0.1% (CPS, PDR) (2,368 cases reported to FDA [FMR])
  - Balance disorder: (841 cases reported to FDA [FMR])
  - Dizziness: 1.1-4.5% [<2.9% above placebo results] (CPS, PDR) (6,592 cases reported to FDA [FMR])
  - Labyrinthitis: (70 cases reported to FDA [FMR])
  - Nystagmus: (52 cases reported to FDA [FMR])
  - Vertigo: 0.1-2% (CPS, PDR) (798 cases reported to FDA [FMR])
  - Vestibular disorder: (18 cases reported to FDA [FMR])

Outer/Middle Ear:
- Ceruminosis: (59 cases reported to FDA [FMR])
- Cholesteatoma: (5 cases reported to FDA [FMR])
- Ear blocked: (18 cases reported to FDA [FMR])
- Ear discomfort/Ear pain: >0.2% (PDR) (309 cases reported to FDA [FMR])
- Ear infection: (159 cases reported to FDA [FMR])
- Eustachian tube dysfunction: (29 cases reported to FDA [FMR])
- Otitis externa: (89 cases reported to FDA [FMR])
- Otitis media: (127 cases reported to FDA [FMR])
- Otorrhagia: (8 cases reported to FDA [FMR])
- Otorrhea: (37 cases reported to FDA [FMR])
- Perforated eardrum: (41 cases reported to FDA [FMR])

Unspecified/General Ear Conditions:
- Ear disorder: (50 cases reported to FDA [FMR])
- Meniere's disease: (76 cases reported to FDA [FMR])
- Ototoxicity: (4 cases reported to FDA [FMR])

Risk assessment: Class 2.5

Notes:

[1] *Amturnide* is a combination of **Aliskiren**, **Amlodipine** and **Hydrochlorothiazide**. (See the generic drugs **Aliskiren** and **Hydrochlorothiazide** for their specific ototoxic properties.)

[2] *Caduet* is a combination of **Amlodipine** and **Atorvastatin**. (See the generic drug **Atorvastatin** for its specific ototoxic properties.)

[3] *Exforge* is a combination of **Amlodipine** and **Valsartan**. (See the generic drug **Valsartan** for its specific ototoxic properties.)

[4] *Exforge HCT* is a combination of **Amlodipine, Valsartan and Hydrochlorothiazide**. (See the generic drugs **Valsartan** and **Hydrochlorothiazide** for their specific ototoxic properties.)

[5] *Lotrel* is a combination of **Amlodipine** and **Benazepril**. (See the generic drug **Benazepril** for its specific ototoxic properties.)

[6] *Tekamlo* is a combination of **Aliskiren** and **Amlodipine**. (See the generic drug **Aliskiren** for its specific ototoxic properties.)

Caution: Eating grapefruit or drinking grapefruit juice during the time you are taking this drug may make the listed side effects worse than shown here. Taking **Amlodipine** with grapefruit juice can increase the potency of **Amlodipine** up to 16%. See Chapter 16, "Grapefruit Juice and Ototoxic Drugs" for further information on this drug.

Anecdotal Reports:

A lady explained, "I started taking **Amlodipine** two days ago and am now experiencing a high pitched whirring in my head and ears and my balance is off."

A man wrote, "I've been on **Amlodipine** for about a year and a half. Early this week while sitting at my home computer, I became aware of a high-pitched squealing in my hearing. The sound was at the frequency of crickets, but continuous and more on the side of 'electric'. I discovered (by going off and on this drug a couple of times) that the noise promptly returned each time I took the 5 mg daily dose."

A man questioned, "I have been taking **Amlodipine** 5 mg for 3 years now. Several weeks ago, I started having a high pitched sound. Could the side effect of tinnitus develop 3 years after taking it?"

A lady reported, "I took **Amlodipine** for two days, experienced severe side effects including tinnitus, ear pain, hearing loss and loss of balance among other side effects. I stopped after 2 days. The symptoms began clearing in a few hours. My hearing seemed to return to normal. I tried again for one day. Same thing happened. I stopped taking the **Amlodipine** and the side effects cleared. After about two weeks, I tried again for about 10 days. I had worse, frightening side effects including loss of balance. I missed work. Some days I could not leave home. I stopped taking the **Amlodipine** the third time. My hearing mostly returned in one ear within a day. However, I have some tinnitus and significant hearing loss in my other ear still even after 2 months. I also still have continuing balance problems."

A man lamented, "I have been taking **Amlodipine** 5 mg a day. Now for the past two weeks, I have had whistling in my ears. It's driving me nuts. I can't sleep at night. I stopped taking the **Amlodipine** but still the noise continues."

A man began taking **Amlodipine** and he began hearing a "roaring" or "wind blowing" type of noise. When he stopped taking the **Amlodipine**, the roaring sounds stopped.

A lady reported she got tinnitus and hearing loss after taking **Amlodipine**. She told her doctor and he said, "Not a side effect of **Amlodipine**," and blew her off.

A lady explained, "I was prescribed **Amlodipine** for blood pressure about 2 years ago. Approximately 2 hours after I took the first dose I developed severe tinnitus and extreme pain in both ears, loss of hearing in both ears and vertigo. I staggered and could not walk without holding onto the wall or furniture. I could not leave my home and missed a week of work. I did not take a second dose, my hearing partially returned but the tinnitus continued. My doctor insisted I continue with the **Amlodipine**. A second one-time dose resulted in the same symptoms, only worse. After the 3rd attempt, with even worse results, I stopped taking it and now after two years I have incomplete improvement. My hearing in one ear is very diminished and I continue to have some tinnitus and balance problems. This medication has negatively impacted many aspects of my life."

A lady explained, "I have been on **Amlodipine** for several years. Three years ago I developed hearing loss and tinnitus in my left ear. The loss was significant. I went to my ENT and the doctor could not find the cause of my hearing loss. In addition, I was suffering from severe aches in my lower legs and right hand. My lower legs were constantly swollen and had what looked like a red rash. I saw several doctors and not one said anything about the **Amlodipine**. I saw the nurse practitioner at my doctor's office and pointed out my red swollen legs to her. She said, "**Amlodipine** can cause that. Let's try something else. I don't even know why doctor's still prescribe it". Not thinking about my hearing, I stopped the **Amlodipine**. Within a week my tinnitus was significantly less and I could hear from my left ear! I could actually hold the phone up to my ear and hear the person clearly on the other end. The redness and swelling in my legs was also gone. I could walk without pain.

For over 2 years I had suffered from what seems to be horrific side effects from **Amlodipine** and I didn't even realize it. Today my hearing is just about perfect. However, I still have a bit of ringing in my ears. In addition, the redness in my legs is gone, and the aches and pains are gone as well. I wish it hadn't taken me over 2 years to realize what was happening and stop taking the **Amlodipine**. I am now feeling healthy again."

A lady reported, "I have been taking **Amlodipine** for 2 months. Yesterday I woke with high-pitched ringing and loud noise in my ears. One side of my head and ear felt like concrete."

A man explained, "I started taking **Amlodipine** 2 months ago. I started to experience tinnitus in my right ear and then in my left ear. I also got hearing loss. I am now wearing hearing aids."

A man reported, "I took **Amlodipine** for approximately 1½ months and noticed tinnitus and a fullness in my ears. Read your article and replies and spoke with my MD about getting off the drug. After being off the 2.5 mg of **Amlodipine** for 2½ weeks, my hearing is 100% restored!"

A man explained, "I was on **Amlodipine** for about a month. Shortly after, I started hearing a high-pitched sound that won't go away. My doctor took me off the **Amlodipine** 3 months ago, but I am still having ear problems."

A man recounted, "After taking **Amlodipine** for weeks (which **did** effectively lower my blood pressure and keep it down) although with somewhat unpleasant but tolerable side effects such as flushing, mildly burning eyelids, hot flashes and fatigue, one day out of the blue, I experienced sudden and profound hearing loss followed by extreme tinnitus. My hearing has not come back."

A lady began taking **Amlodipine** one day, and woke up the next morning with "loud ringing in my ears".

A man reported, "I started taking **Amlodipine** and a few days later I started to get fullness in my right ear. Within two more weeks I had terrible headache pain from temple to temple and vertigo. My blood pressure improved with diet and exercise so I cut down the **Amlodipine** to 2.5. My headache decreased so I totally got off it and within 3 days hardly any headache, but I still have ear fullness from time to time. Hopefully, someday I will be able to hear again out of my right ear."

A man commented, "I had a sudden increase in high-pitched tinnitus literally feeling it in the top center of my head. It began after I started taking *Norvasc* blood pressure medication."

A lady explained, "I developed tinnitus two weeks after being on 5 mg of **Amlodipine**. I thought I was going crazy. I've stopped taking the **Amlodipine** and have noticed my tinnitus is getting less and less every day."

Ammonium lactate

Pronunciation guide: ah-MOE-nee-um LAK-tate

Drug classification: Dermatological drugs (see section 23 in Table 19-1)

Brand names: *Lac-Hydrin*

Ototoxic effects:
- Cochlear:
  - Auditory hallucinations: (3 cases reported to FDA [FMR])
  - Hearing loss: (21 cases reported to FDA [FMR])
  - Tinnitus: (15 cases reported to FDA [FMR])
- Vestibular:
  - Dizziness: (36 cases reported to FDA [FMR])
- Outer/Middle Ear:
  - Cholesteatoma: (12 cases reported to FDA [FMR])
  - Ear blocked: (4 cases reported to FDA [FMR])
  - Ear discomfort/Ear pain: (21 cases reported to FDA [FMR])
  - Otitis externa: (5 cases reported to FDA [FMR])

Risk assessment: Class 1

Amobarbital

Pronunciation guide: am-oh-BAR-bi-tal

Drug classification: Barbiturates (see section 60.12.4 in Table 19-1)

Brand names: *Amytal*

Ototoxic effects:
  Vestibular:
    Ataxia/Gait disturbance: (5 cases reported to FDA [FMR])
    Dizziness: (CPS, Med) (8 cases reported to FDA [FMR])
    Vertigo: (CPS)

Risk assessment: Class 0.5

Amonafide (Nafidimide)

Pronunciation guide: ah-MON-ah-fide (nah-FIH-dih-myed)

Drug classification: ANTI-NEOPLASTICS (ANTI-CANCER DRUGS) (see section 14 in Table 19-1)

Brand names: *Quinamed*

Ototoxic effects:
  Cochlear:
    Tinnitus: 1-10% [1] (San, She)
  Vestibular:
    Dizziness: 1-10% [1]

Risk assessment: Class ?1

Notes:

[1] Can cause tinnitus and dizziness.[29]

Amoxapine

Pronunciation guide: ah-MOKS-ah-peen

Drug classification: TRICYCLIC ANTI-DEPRESSANTS (see section 60.1.8 in Table 19-1)

Brand names: Amoxan, *Asendin*

Ototoxic effects:
  Cochlear:
    Auditory hallucinations: (5 cases reported to FDA [FMR])
    Tinnitus: <1% (CPS, PDR)
  Vestibular:
    Ataxia/Gait disturbance: >1% (PDR) (13 cases reported to FDA [FMR])
    Balance disorder: (3 cases reported to FDA [FMR])
    Dizziness: >1% (CPS, PDR) (27 cases reported to FDA [FMR])
    Nystagmus: (5 cases reported to FDA [FMR])

Risk assessment: Class 0.5

Amoxicillin/Clavulanate

Pronunciation guide: a-MOKS-ih-SILL-in/KLAV-yoo-lah-nate

Drug classification: PENICILLINS (see section 7.4.40 in Table 19-1)

Brand names: *Amoclav, Amox, Amoxil, Augmentin* [1], *Clamoxyl, Curam, Helipak* [2], *Klavocin* [1], *Larotid, Moxatag, Sawacillin, Trimox, Vimox* [1]

Ototoxic effects:

- Cochlear:
  - Auditory hallucinations: (67 cases reported to FDA [FMR])
  - Hearing loss: (604 cases reported to FDA [FMR])
  - Hyperacusis: (3 cases reported to FDA [FMR])
  - Phonophobia: (15 cases reported to FDA [FMR])
  - Tinnitus: (477 cases reported to FDA [EHM])
- Vestibular:
  - Ataxia/Gait disturbance: (907 cases reported to FDA [FMR])
  - Balance disorder: (283 cases reported to FDA [FMR])
  - Dizziness: (RXL) (1,840 cases reported to FDA [FMR])
  - Labyrinthitis: (47 cases reported to FDA [FMR])
  - Nystagmus: (24 cases reported to FDA [FMR])
  - Vertigo: (GIP) (484 cases reported to FDA [FMR])
  - Vestibular disorder: (20 cases reported to FDA [FMR])
- Outer/Middle Ear:
  - Ceruminosis: (57 cases reported to FDA [FMR])
  - Cholesteatoma: (13 cases reported to FDA [FMR])
  - Ear blocked: (25 cases reported to FDA [FMR])
  - Ear discomfort/Ear pain: (502 cases reported to FDA [FMR])
  - Ear infection: (241 cases reported to FDA [FMR])
  - Eustachian tube dysfunction: (36 cases reported to FDA [FMR])
  - Otitis externa: (126 cases reported to FDA [FMR])
  - Otitis media: (222 cases reported to FDA [FMR])
  - Otorrhagia: (32 cases reported to FDA [FMR])
  - Otorrhea: (12 cases reported to FDA [FMR])
  - Perforated eardrum: (20 cases reported to FDA [FMR])
- Unspecified/General Ear Conditions:
  - Ear disorder: (49 cases reported to FDA [FMR])
  - Meniere's disease: (8 cases reported to FDA [FMR])
  - Ototoxicity: (3 cases reported to FDA [FMR])

Risk assessment: Class 3

Notes:

[1] *Augmentin, Klavocin* and *Vimox* are combinations of **Amoxicillin** and the beta-lactamase inhibitor Clavulanic acid.

[2] *Helipak* is a combination of **Amoxicillin** , **Clarithromycin** and **Lansoprazole**. (See the generic drugs **Clarithromycin** and **Lansoprazole** for their specific ototoxic properties.)

Anecdotal Reports:

A man got mild tinnitus when he took *Augmentin* for pneumonia.

A lady reported, "I just took *Augmentin* and the volume of my tinnitus went up. I don't think I can bear this level of tinnitus."

A lady explained, "I just took a 14 day course of *Augmentin* for diverticulitis and last night my right ear just started to have a strange sensation of being stopped up. I was sitting on my bed and I stood up, and it felt like deep inside of my ear was vibrating (a low dull sound with throbbing)."

A lady wrote, "I was on *Augmentin* in January and subsequently lost partial hearing in my right ear. Not thinking there was any correlation, I went on it again in October. Now I am confirmed 100% deaf in my right ear."

A man explained, "I experienced the onset of tinnitus the day after starting **Amoxicillin/Clavulanate**. My ENT confirmed loss of hearing in my left ear only (everything above 1 kHz is attenuated). Six months later I still have the ringing and hearing loss in that ear."

A man's tinnitus went from a 2 (out of 10) to an 8 after he took a course of *Augmentin* for his sinusitis.

A lady reported, "I took a course of *Augmentin Duo Forte* tablets and have had severe tinnitus since day two of taking the medication."

A man wrote, "My doctor gave me a 5 day course (2 a day) of *Alphaclav Duo Forte* for an infection. The actual course of the antibiotics didn't bring on any tinnitus, but I did get it about 5 days after stopping. Anyways, it's now been about a week and a half since the tinnitus onset, and last night my tinnitus was the best it's been—fading almost completely for several hours in the evening, and barely returning at night. It's now done this two days in a row so hopefully it's fading away."

A man explained, "My doctor recently prescribed *Augmentin* for sinusitis, and I took a complete course. Result: loss of hearing in both ears, with volume and clarity diminished significantly across all frequency ranges, but especially in the highs. I now have to cup my ears to hear clearly what people are saying. The loss set in motion is progressive, in other words it's getting worse from day to day, even though I ceased the course a week ago."

A lady reported, "I have been ravaged with moderate bilateral tinnitus ever since taking *Augmentin XR* about 4 years ago".

A man explained, "I am on day 4 of *Augmentin* 875 mg for bacterial Actinomyces. I have previous low level tinnitus in my right ear. Today, with the *Augmentin*,

I've had acute onset of loud tinnitus in my left ear that comes and goes in waves."

A lady wrote, "I was prescribed 1 g (as against 625 mg) dose of *Augmentin* for a persistent typhoid infection. On the last day of the two-week regime, I lost 80% hearing in my left ear as well as developed tinnitus. I went to three separate ENT specialists, where I was told it was not the *Augmentin* when I was pretty sure that my hearing was perfect before taking the drug. It's been almost 2 years since then and my hearing has not come back, but the ringing is still there in my left ear."

A man reported, "My wife took **Amoxicillin** about a year ago for an infected tooth and has had tinnitus ever since. I just finished six days of the same and tonight my ears started ringing as well."

A man wrote: "I have never had any hearing problem until a month ago when I took *Augmentin* for a sinus infection. I noticed tinnitus had begun and it has never ceased 24-7. It clearly caused my hearing loss and tinnitus."

A man wrote, "I had flu and tried to blow my nose and had my ear full of air pressure so I visited my ENT and he prescribed *Augmentin*. After 3 days I had a high level of tinnitus."

A man reported, "I have acquired partial hearing loss and tinnitus from taking *Augmentin*. Also, I have a pulsating pressure sensation in my ears. I can hear the tone of the tinnitus change as the pressure fluctuates."

A man explained, "I took *Augmentin* for a foot infection. Within a day I had loud ringing in my ears. I checked online and found the possibility it could be from taking *Augmentin* so stopped taking it within 36 hours. It is now two months later, and the ringing hasn't stopped."

Amphetamine

Pronunciation guide: am-FET-ah-meen

Drug classification: AMPHETAMINES (see section 53.44.1 in Table 19-1)

Brand names: *Adderall* [1]

Ototoxic effects:
- Cochlear:
  - Auditory hallucinations: (39 cases reported to FDA [FMR])
  - Hearing loss: (26 cases reported to FDA [FMR])
  - Hyperacusis: (6 cases reported to FDA [FMR])
  - Tinnitus: (40 cases reported to FDA [FMR])
- Vestibular:
  - Ataxia/Gait disturbance: (87 cases reported to FDA [FMR])
  - Balance disorder: (35 cases reported to FDA [FMR])

Dizziness: (381 cases reported to FDA [FMR])
Vertigo: (36 cases reported to FDA [FMR])
Outer/Middle Ear:
Cholesteatoma: (11 cases reported to FDA [FMR])
Ear discomfort/Ear pain: (35 cases reported to FDA [FMR])
Ear infection: (23 cases reported to FDA [FMR])
Otitis externa: (3 cases reported to FDA [FMR])
Otitis media: (8 cases reported to FDA [FMR])
Unspecified/General Ear Conditions:
Ear disorder: (5 cases reported to FDA [FMR])

Risk assessment: Class 1.5

Notes:

[1] *Adderall* is a combination of **Amphetamine** and **Dextroamphetamine**. (See the generic drug **Dextroamphetamine** for its specific ototoxic properties.)

Amphotericin B

Pronunciation guide: am-foe-TER-ih-sin

Drug classification: ANTI-FUNGAL ANTIBIOTICS (see section 7.10 in Table 19-1)

Brand names: *Abelcet, AmBisome, Amphotec, Fungizone*

Ototoxic effects:
Cochlear:
Auditory hallucinations: (4 cases reported to FDA [FMR])
Hearing loss: (CPS, PDR) (67 cases reported to FDA [FMR])
Tinnitus: 1-5% (DFC, PDR) (13 cases reported to FDA [FMR])
Vestibular:
Ataxia/Gait disturbance: (33 cases reported to FDA [FMR])
Balance disorder: (8 cases reported to FDA [FMR])
Dizziness: 7-10.3% (CPS, PDR) (69 cases reported to FDA [FMR])
Nystagmus: (3 cases reported to FDA [FMR])
Vertigo, transient: (CPS, PDR) (6 cases reported to FDA [FMR])
Outer/Middle Ear:
Ear discomfort/Ear pain: (3 cases reported to FDA [FMR])
Ear infection: (3 cases reported to FDA [FMR])
Otitis media: (4 cases reported to FDA [FMR])
Unspecified/General Ear Conditions:
Ear disorder: (DFC, PDR)

Risk assessment: Class 1.5

Notes:

See Chapter 5 "Are You at Risk?" for further information on this drug.

Ampicillin

Pronunciation guide: am-pih-SILL-in

Drug classification: PENICILLINS (see section 7.4.40 in Table 19-1)

Brand names: *Ampicin*, *Unacid*[1], *Unasyn*[1], *Viccillin*

Ototoxic effects:
- Cochlear:
  - Hearing loss: (99 cases reported to FDA [FMR])
  - Tinnitus: (41 cases reported to FDA [FMR])
- Vestibular:
  - Ataxia/Gait disturbance: (174 cases reported to FDA [FMR])
  - Balance disorder: (42 cases reported to FDA [FMR])
  - Dizziness: (166 cases reported to FDA [FMR])
  - Nystagmus: (4 cases reported to FDA [FMR])
  - Vertigo: (28 cases reported to FDA [FMR])
- Outer/Middle Ear:
  - Ceruminosis: (20 cases reported to FDA [FMR])
  - Ear discomfort/Ear pain: (46 cases reported to FDA [FMR])
  - Ear infection: (21 cases reported to FDA [FMR])
  - Eustachian tube dysfunction: (19 cases reported to FDA [FMR])
  - Otitis externa: (6 cases reported to FDA [FMR])
  - Otitis media: (45 cases reported to FDA [FMR])
  - Otorrhea: (4 cases reported to FDA [FMR])
- Unspecified/General Ear Conditions:
  - Ear disorder: [2] (18 cases reported to FDA [FMR])
  - Ototoxicity: (CPS)

Risk assessment: Class 2 (Class 4 in high doses)

Notes:

[1] *Unacid* and *Unasyn* are combinations of **Ampicillin** and **Sulbactam**. (See the generic drug **Sulbactam** for its specific ototoxic properties.)

Ampicillin may be ototoxic when given intravenously in very high doses (CPS).

[2] The above ear disorders include 3 cases of ear malformation, 2 cases of low-set ears and 2 cases of microtia (small or missing external ears).

See Chapter 5 “Are You at Risk?” for further information on this drug.

Amprenavir

Pronunciation guide: am-PREN-ah-veer

Drug classification: ANTI-RETROVIRAL PROTEASE INHIBITORS (see section 7.17.1.1 in Table 19-1)

Brand names: *Agenerase*

Ototoxic effects:
Vestibular:
Balance disorder: (8 cases reported to FDA [FMR])
Dizziness: (4 cases reported to FDA [FMR])
Nystagmus: (15 cases reported to FDA [FMR])

Risk assessment: Class 0.5

Notes:

Caution: Eating grapefruit or drinking grapefruit juice during the time you are taking this drug may make the listed side effects worse than shown here. See Chapter 16, “Grapefruit Juice and Ototoxic Drugs” for further information on this drug.

Amtolmetin

Pronunciation guide: am-TOLE-met-in

Drug classification: Acetic acids (see section 1.1.1 in Table 19-1)

Brand names: *Artromed, Eufans*

Ototoxic effects:
Cochlear:
Tinnitus: (She)

Risk assessment: Class 0.5

Anabolic androgenic steroids (AAS)

Pronunciation guide: ah-nah-BOL-ik AN-droe-JEN-ik STAIR-roids

Drug classification: Androgens (Male sex hormones) (see section 40.4 in Table 19-1)

Brand names: —

Ototoxic effects:
Cochlear:
Hearing loss: (3 cases reported to FDA [FMR])
Vestibular:
Ataxia/Gait disturbance: (13 cases reported to FDA [FMR])
Balance disorder: (5 cases reported to FDA [FMR])
Dizziness: (35 cases reported to FDA [FMR])
Labyrinthitis: (4 cases reported to FDA [FMR])

Risk assessment: Class 0.5

Anagrelide

Pronunciation guide: a-NAG-reh-lied

Drug classification: PLATELET INHIBITOR DRUGS (see section 36.24 in Table 19-1)

Brand names: *Agrylin*

Ototoxic effects:
  Cochlear:
    Hearing loss: (8 cases reported to FDA [FMR])
    Tinnitus: 1-5% (CPS, PDR) (7 cases reported to FDA [EHM])
  Vestibular:
    Dizziness: 14.5-15.4% (CPS, PDR) (44 cases reported to FDA [FMR])
    Vertigo: 1-10% (GIP) (21 cases reported to FDA [FMR])
    Vestibular disorder: (18 cases reported to FDA [FMR])
  Outer/Middle Ear:
    Otitis externa: (35 cases reported to FDA [FMR])
  Unspecified/General Ear Conditions:
    Ear disorder: (CPS)

Risk assessment: Class 1.5

Anakinra

Pronunciation guide: an-nah-KIN-rah

Drug classification: ANTI-RHEUMATIC DRUGS (see section 46.1 in Table 19-1)

Brand names: *Kineret*

Ototoxic effects:
  Cochlear:
    Hearing loss: (15 cases reported to FDA [EHM])
    Tinnitus: (12 cases reported to FDA [EHM])
  Vestibular:
    Ataxia/Gait disturbance: (5 cases reported to FDA [FMR])
    Dizziness: (21 cases reported to FDA [FMR])
    Vertigo: (5 cases reported to FDA [FMR])

Risk assessment: Class 1

Anastrozole

Pronunciation guide: an-ASS-troe-zole

Drug classification: AROMATASE INHIBITORS (see section 14.24 in Table 19-1)

Brand names: *Arimidex*

Ototoxic effects:
  Cochlear:
    Auditory hallucinations: (9 cases reported to FDA [FMR])
    Hearing loss: (173 cases reported to FDA [FMR])
    Tinnitus: (133 cases reported to FDA [EHM])
  Vestibular:
    Ataxia/Gait disturbance: (544 cases reported to FDA [FMR])
    Balance disorder: (143 cases reported to FDA [FMR])
    Dizziness: (684 cases reported to FDA [FMR])
    Labyrinthitis: (33 cases reported to FDA [FMR])
    Nystagmus: (12 cases reported to FDA [FMR])
    Vertigo: (154 cases reported to FDA [FMR])
  Outer/Middle Ear:
    Ceruminosis: (11 cases reported to FDA [FMR])
    Ear blocked: (7 cases reported to FDA [FMR])
    Ear discomfort/Ear pain: (176 cases reported to FDA [FMR])
    Ear infection: (4 cases reported to FDA [FMR])
    Eustachian tube dysfunction: (9 cases reported to FDA [FMR])
    Otitis externa: (9 cases reported to FDA [FMR])
    Otitis media: (83 cases reported to FDA [FMR])
    Otorrhagia: (3 cases reported to FDA [FMR])
    Otorrhea: (3 cases reported to FDA [FMR])
  Unspecified/General Ear Conditions:
    Ear disorder: (17 cases reported to FDA [FMR])
    Meniere's disease: (3 cases reported to FDA [FMR])

Risk assessment: Class 3

Androstenedione

Pronunciation guide: an-droe-STEEN-ee-dee-ohn

Drug classification: ANDROGENS (MALE SEX HORMONES) (see section 40.4 in Table 19-1)

Brand names: *Andros*

Ototoxic effects:
  Vestibular:
    Dizziness: (8 cases reported to FDA [FMR])
  Outer/Middle Ear:
    Ear infection: (6 cases reported to FDA [FMR])

Risk assessment: Class 0.5

Anistreplase

Pronunciation guide: an-EYE-strep-lase

Drug classification: Coagulation drugs (see section 36.16 in Table 19-1)

Brand names: *Eminase*

Ototoxic effects:
  Vestibular:
    Dizziness: <10% (CPS, PDR)
    Vertigo: <10% (CPS, PDR)

Risk assessment: Class 0.5

Antihemophilic factor

Pronunciation guide: AN-tee-hee-moe-FILL-ik FAK-tor

Drug classification: Anti-fibrinolytic drugs (see section 36.4 in Table 19-1)

Brand names: *Advate*, *Helixate*, *Koate*, *Kogenate*, *Xyntha*

Ototoxic effects:
  Vestibular:
    Dizziness: (NDH, PDR) (18 cases reported to FDA [FMR])
    Vertigo: (4 cases reported to FDA [FMR])
  Outer/Middle Ear:
    Otitis media: (PDR) (3 cases reported to FDA [FMR])

Risk assessment: Class 0.5

Anti-thymocyte globulin

Pronunciation guide: AN-tee-THY-moe-site GLOB-yoo-lin

Drug classification: Immunosuppressant drugs (see section 43 in Table 19-1)

Brand names: *Thymoglobulin*

Ototoxic effects:
  Cochlear:
    Hearing loss: (17 cases reported to FDA [FMR])
    Tinnitus: (5 cases reported to FDA [FMR])
  Vestibular:
    Ataxia/Gait disturbance: (20 cases reported to FDA [FMR])
    Dizziness: (25 cases reported to FDA [FMR])
    Vertigo: (4 cases reported to FDA [FMR])
  Outer/Middle Ear:
    Ear discomfort/Ear pain: (11 cases reported to FDA [FMR])
    Otitis media: (5 cases reported to FDA [FMR])

Risk assessment: Class 1

Apixaban

Pronunciation guide: ah-PIKS-ah-ban

Drug classification: ANTI-THROMBOTIC DRUGS (see section 36.8 in Table 19-1)

Brand names: *Eliquis*

Ototoxic effects:
  Cochlear:
    Hearing loss: (331 cases reported to FDA [EHM])
    Tinnitus: (60 cases reported to FDA [EHM])
  Vestibular:
    Dizziness: 1-10% (DIO) (13 cases reported to FDA [FMR])
    Vertigo: 1-10% (DIO)

Risk assessment: Class 2.5

Notes:

Caution: Eating grapefruit or drinking grapefruit juice during the time you are taking this drug may make the listed side effects worse than shown here. See Chapter 16, "Grapefruit Juice and Ototoxic Drugs" for further information on this drug.

Anecdotal Reports:

Apixaban (*Eliquis*) caused one man to have even worse tinnitus.

A lady explained, "My pulsatile tinnitus resulted from taking the anticoagulant, **Apixaban** (*Eliquis*). My ENT is a pulsatile tinnitus specialist and said it's more commonly a whooshing/roaring sound (which I also got from time to time), but can in rare cases be more of a ring and whistle. Mine was like a symphony of ugly sounds—beeps, flat-toned frequency, weird static noise, whirring, and what sounded like whistling or chirping. The intensity and volume of the sound was sometimes so loud I could catch the sound on my lapel microphone just by putting it **near** (not even inside) my ear. My ENT said blood thinners can sometimes cause this, especially if the dosage is too high. My hematologist lowered my anticoagulant dosage by just 1/5 and the ringing reduced to the point of being almost non-existent, and so there's hope that it'll go away completely once I'm off this drug."

Apomorphine

Pronunciation guide: ah-poe-MOR-feen

Drug classification: DOPAMINE RECEPTOR AGONISTS (see section 53.16.1 in Table 19-1)

Brand names: *Apokyn*

Ototoxic effects:
  Vestibular:
    Ataxia/Gait disturbance: (12 cases reported to FDA [FMR])
    Dizziness: (43 cases reported to FDA [FMR])

Risk assessment: Class 0.5

Apraclonidine

Pronunciation guide: ah-prah-KLAH-nih-deen

Drug classification: OPHTHALMIC GLAUCOMA DRUGS (see section 56.1.4 in Table 19-1)

Brand names: *Lopidine*

Ototoxic effects:
  Vestibular:
    Ataxia/Gait disturbance: (DIO)
    Dizziness: 1-10% (DIO)
    Vertigo: 0.1-1% (GIP)

Risk assessment: Class 0.5

Aprepitant (and Fosaprepitant)

Pronunciation guide: ah-PRE-pit-ant, foss-ah-PRE-pit-ant

Drug classification: P/NEUROKININ-1 RECEPTOR ANTAGONISTS (see section 34.1.2 in Table 19-1)

Brand names: *Emend, Emend IV*

Ototoxic effects:
  Cochlear:
    Auditory hallucinations: (4 cases reported to FDA [FMR])
    Hearing loss: (8 cases reported to FDA [FMR])
    Hyperacusis: (3 cases reported to FDA [FMR])
    Tinnitus: <1%-3.7% (NDH, PDR) (18 cases reported to FDA [FMR])
  Vestibular:
    Ataxia/Gait disturbance: (22 cases reported to FDA [FMR])
    Dizziness: <1%-6.6% [<2.2% above placebo results] (NDH, PDR) (128 cases reported to FDA [FMR])
    Vertigo: (GIP) (8 cases reported to FDA [FMR])

Risk assessment: Class 1

Notes:

Fosaprepitant is very similar to **Aprepitant** and has essentially the same ototoxic side effects.

Aprotinin

Pronunciation guide: ah-proe-TYE-nin

Drug classification: ANTI-FIBRINOLYTIC DRUGS (BLOOD CLOTTING DRUGS) (see section 36.4 in Table 19-1)

Brand names: *Trasylol*

Ototoxic effects:
Cochlear:
Hearing loss: (22 cases reported to FDA [FMR])
Vestibular:
Ataxia/Gait disturbance: (9 cases reported to FDA [FMR])
Balance disorder: (31 cases reported to FDA [FMR])
Dizziness: (4 cases reported to FDA [FMR])
Vertigo: (4 cases reported to FDA [FMR])
Unspecified/General Ear Conditions:
Ototoxicity: (13 cases reported to FDA [FMR])

Risk assessment: Class 1

Arformoterol

Pronunciation guide: ar-for-MOTE-er-ol

Drug classification: BRONCHODILATORS—BETA ADRENERGIC AGONISTS (see section 63.4 in Table 19-1)

Brand names: *Brovana*

Ototoxic effects:
Cochlear:
Hearing loss: (3 cases reported to FDA [FMR])
Vestibular:
Ataxia/Gait disturbance: (10 cases reported to FDA [FMR])
Balance disorder: (6 cases reported to FDA [FMR])
Dizziness: (34 cases reported to FDA [FMR])
Outer/Middle Ear:
Ear infection: (3 cases reported to FDA [FMR])

Risk assessment: Class 0.5

Argatroban

Pronunciation guide: are-GAH-troe-ban

Drug classification: ANTI-THROMBOTIC DRUGS (see section 36.8 in Table 19-1)

Brand names: *Acova*

Ototoxic effects:
  Cochlear:
    Auditory hallucinations: (7 cases reported to FDA [FMR])
    Hearing loss: (4 cases reported to FDA [EHM])
  Vestibular:
    Ataxia/Gait disturbance: (4 cases reported to FDA [FMR])
    Dizziness: (12 cases reported to FDA [FMR])

Risk assessment: Class 0.5

Aripiprazole

Pronunciation guide: air-eh-PIP rah-zole

Drug classification: SECOND GENERATION (ATYPICAL) ANTIPSYCHOTIC DRUGS (see section 60.8.3.2 in Table 19-1)

Brand names: *Abilify*

Ototoxic effects:
  Cochlear:
    Auditory hallucinations: (424 cases reported to FDA [FMR])
    Hearing loss: 0.01-0.1% (PDR) (58 cases reported to FDA [FMR])
    Hyperacusis: (18 cases reported to FDA [FMR])
    Tinnitus: 0.1-1% (DFC, PDR) (52 cases reported to FDA [EHM])
  Vestibular:
    Ataxia/Gait disturbance: 0.1-1% (NDH, PDR) (424 cases reported to FDA [FMR])
    Balance disorder: (171 cases reported to FDA [FMR])
    Dizziness: 8-11% [3% above placebo results] (NDH, PDR) (906 cases reported to FDA [FMR])
    Labyrinthitis: (3 cases reported to FDA [FMR])
    Nystagmus: (10 cases reported to FDA [FMR])
    Vertigo: 0.1-10% (GIP, PDR) (114 cases reported to FDA [FMR])
  Outer/Middle Ear:
    Ear blocked: (24 cases reported to FDA [FMR])
    Ear discomfort/Ear pain: 0.1-1% (NDH, PDR) (46 cases reported to FDA [FMR])
    Ear infection: (18 cases reported to FDA [FMR])
    Eustachian tube dysfunction: (4 cases reported to FDA [FMR])
    Otitis externa: (DFC) (14 cases reported to FDA [FMR])
    Otitis media: (DFC) (29 cases reported to FDA [FMR])
    Otorrhea: (4 cases reported to FDA [FMR])
    Perforated eardrum: (4 cases reported to FDA [FMR])
  Unspecified/General Ear Conditions:
    Meniere's disease: (12 cases reported to FDA [FMR])

Risk assessment: Class 2

Armodafinil

Pronunciation guide: are-moe-DAF-ih-nil

Drug classification: Psychostimulants (see section 60.20 in Table 19-1)

Brand names: *Nuvigil*

Ototoxic effects:
- Cochlear:
  - Auditory hallucinations: (7 cases reported to FDA [FMR])
  - Hearing loss: (16 cases reported to FDA [FMR])
  - Hyperacusis: (4 cases reported to FDA [FMR])
  - Tinnitus: (19 cases reported to FDA [EHM])
- Vestibular:
  - Ataxia/Gait disturbance: (68 cases reported to FDA [FMR])
  - Balance disorder: (38 cases reported to FDA [FMR])
  - Dizziness: (209 cases reported to FDA [FMR])
  - Vertigo: (19 cases reported to FDA [FMR])
- Outer/Middle Ear:
  - Ceruminosis: (7 cases reported to FDA [FMR])
  - Ear discomfort/Ear pain: (8 cases reported to FDA [FMR])
  - Eustachian tube dysfunction: (3 cases reported to FDA [FMR])
  - Otitis media: (3 cases reported to FDA [FMR])
- Unspecified/General Ear Conditions:
  - Meniere's disease: (4 cases reported to FDA [FMR])

Risk assessment: Class 1.5

Arsenic trioxide

Pronunciation guide: ARE-seh-nik try-OKS-eyed

Drug classification: Anti-neoplastics (Anti-cancer drugs) (see section 14 in Table 19-1)

Brand names: *Trisenox*

Ototoxic effects:
- Cochlear:
  - Hearing loss: (Ryb)
  - Tinnitus: 5% (DFC, PDR)
- Vestibular:
  - Ataxia/Gait disturbance: (8 cases reported to FDA [FMR])
  - Dizziness: 23% (DFC, PDR) (9 cases reported to FDA [FMR])
- Outer/Middle Ear:
  - Ear discomfort/Ear pain: 8% (DFC, PDR)

Risk assessment: Class 0.5

Notes:

Hearing losses caused by **Arsenic** are concentrated in the low frequencies—125 Hz to 500 Hz (Ryb).

Exposure to **Arsenic** and loud noise at the same time can result in greater hearing loss than would normally result from exposure to both **Arsenic** and noise separately (Nia).

See further information under **Arsenic** in the Chemicals section.

Artemether/Lumefantrine

Pronunciation guide: are-TEM-mah-ther/loo-meh-FAN-treen

Drug classification: ANTI-MALARIAL DRUGS (see section 7.14.8 in Table 19-1)

Brand names: *Coartem*

Ototoxic effects:
- Cochlear:
  - Tinnitus: <3% (NDH, PDR)
- Vestibular:
  - Ataxia/Gait disturbance: <3% (NDH, PDR)
  - Dizziness: 4-39% (NDH, PDR)
  - Nystagmus: <3% (NDH, PDR)
  - Vertigo: 3% (NDH, PDR)
- Outer/Middle Ear:
  - Ear infection: >1% (NDH)

Risk assessment: Class 0.5

Articaine

Pronunciation guide: ARE-tih-kane

Drug classification: AMIDES (see section 4.1 in Table 19-1)

Brand names: *Septocaine, Ultracaine*[1]

Ototoxic effects: [30]
- Cochlear:
  - Tinnitus: (CPS, GIP)
- Vestibular:
  - Ataxia/Gait disturbance: (9 cases reported to FDA [FMR])
  - Balance disorder: (12 cases reported to FDA [FMR])
  - Dizziness: <1% (CPS, DFC) (29 cases reported to FDA [FMR])
  - Vertigo: (GIP) (7 cases reported to FDA [FMR])

Outer/Middle Ear:
- Ear discomfort/Ear pain: <1% (DFC) (3 cases reported to FDA [FMR])
- Ear infection: (13 cases reported to FDA [FMR])

Risk assessment: Class 0.5

Notes:

[1] *Ultracaine* is a combination of **Articaine** and **Epinephrine**. (See the generic drug **Epinephrine** for its specific ototoxic properties.)

Artificial tears

Pronunciation guide: are-tih-FIH-shal teers

Drug classification: Ophthalmic lubricants (see section 56.1.6 in Table 19-1)

Brand names: *Bion tears*

Ototoxic effects:
- Cochlear:
  - Hearing loss: (4 cases reported to FDA [FMR])
  - Tinnitus: (4 cases reported to FDA [FMR])
- Vestibular:
  - Dizziness: (4 cases reported to FDA [FMR])

Risk assessment: Class 0.5

Ascorbic acid (Vitamin C)

Pronunciation guide: ass-KOR-bik ASS-id

Drug classification: Vitamins (see section 75.4 in Table 19-1)

Brand names: *Ester-C*

Ototoxic effects:
- Cochlear:
  - Hearing disorder: (3 cases reported to FDA [FMR])
  - Hearing loss: (220 cases reported to FDA [FMR])
  - Hyperacusis: (4 cases reported to FDA [FMR])
  - Tinnitus: (396 cases reported to FDA [FMR])
- Vestibular:
  - Ataxia/Gait disturbance: (611 cases reported to FDA [FMR])
  - Balance disorder: (335 cases reported to FDA [FMR])
  - Dizziness: (1,412 cases reported to FDA [FMR])
  - Labyrinthitis: (17 cases reported to FDA [FMR])
  - Nystagmus: (13 cases reported to FDA [FMR])
  - Vertigo: (215 cases reported to FDA [FMR])
  - Vestibular disorder: (4 cases reported to FDA [FMR])

Outer/Middle Ear:
Ceruminosis: (36 cases reported to FDA [FMR])
Ear blocked: (5 cases reported to FDA [FMR])
Ear discomfort/Ear pain: (83 cases reported to FDA [FMR])
Ear infection: (30 cases reported to FDA [FMR])
Eustachian tube dysfunction: (17 cases reported to FDA [FMR])
Otitis externa: (7 cases reported to FDA [FMR])
Otitis media: (36 cases reported to FDA [FMR])
Otorrhagia: (5 cases reported to FDA [FMR])
Otorrhea: (12 cases reported to FDA [FMR])
Unspecified/General Ear Conditions:
Ear disorder: (18 cases reported to FDA [FMR])
Meniere's disease: (4 cases reported to FDA [FMR])
Ototoxicity: (4 cases reported to FDA [FMR])

Risk assessment: Class 3.5

Asenapine

Pronunciation guide: ah-SEN-ah-peen

Drug classification: SECOND GENERATION (ATYPICAL) ANTIPSYCHOTIC DRUGS (see section 60.8.3.2 in Table 19-1)

Brand names: *Saphris, Sycrest*

Ototoxic effects:
Cochlear:
Auditory hallucinations: (20 cases reported to FDA [FMR])
Hearing loss: (16 cases reported to FDA [EHM])
Tinnitus: (16 cases reported to FDA [EHM])
Vestibular:
Ataxia/Gait disturbance: (49 cases reported to FDA [FMR])
Balance disorder: (20 cases reported to FDA [FMR])
Dizziness: (196 cases reported to FDA [FMR])
Vertigo: (6 cases reported to FDA [FMR])

Risk assessment: Class 1

Asparaginase

Pronunciation guide: ah-SPAR-ah-jih-nase

Drug classification: ANTI-NEOPLASTICS (ANTI-CANCER DRUGS) (see section 14 in Table 19-1)

Brand names: *Elspar*

Ototoxic effects:
Vestibular:
Ataxia/Gait disturbance: (19 cases reported to FDA [FMR])
Dizziness: (15 cases reported to FDA [FMR])
Vertigo: (3 cases reported to FDA [FMR])

Risk assessment: Class 0.5

Astromicin

Pronunciation guide: ass-troe-MY-sin

Drug classification: AMINOGLYCOSIDES (see section 7.4.1 in Table 19-1)

Brand names: *Fortimicin*[1]

Ototoxic effects:
Cochlear:
Hearing loss: 0.1% [2]
Tinnitus: 0.1% [2]
Vestibular:
Vertigo: 0.1%[2]
Vestibular disorder: [2]
Outer/Middle Ear:
Ear blocked: [2]

Risk assessment: Class ?3.5

Notes:

[1] *Fortimicin* is a fairly new drug. Actually, there is a whole family of them numbered A, B, C, D and KE. These drugs are used in Japan and the Far East.

[2] Reported as "feeling of fullness in ears" by the manufacturer, Kyowa Hakko Kogyo Co, Ltd. in Japan.[31]

You should not take **Astromicin** if you have had previous ear damage from taking any AMINOGLYCOSIDE antibiotic, or if you already have a hearing loss. You are at greater risk if you are elderly, if you have kidney problems, if you take this drug for a long time or if you take it in high doses. If any of these risk factors apply to you, you should have your hearing tested. Note that AMINOGLYCOSIDE-induced hearing loss normally begins in the high frequencies and works its way down the hearing frequency spectrum.[32]

See Chapter 12, "Aminoglycoside Antibiotics are the Ototoxic 'Bad boys'" for further information on this drug.

Atazanavir

Pronunciation guide: ah-tah-ZAN-ah-veer

Drug classification: Anti-retroviral protease inhibitors (see section 7.17.1.1 in Table 19-1)

Brand names: *Reyataz*

Ototoxic effects:
- Cochlear:
  - Hearing loss: (3 cases reported to FDA [FMR])
  - Tinnitus: (3 cases reported to FDA [FMR])
- Vestibular:
  - Ataxia/Gait disturbance: (43 cases reported to FDA [FMR])
  - Balance disorder: (10 cases reported to FDA [FMR])
  - Dizziness: (110 cases reported to FDA [FMR])
  - Vertigo: 0.1-1% (GIP) (189 cases reported to FDA [FMR])

Risk assessment: Class 1

Atenolol

Pronunciation guide: ah-TEN-oh-lawl

Drug classification: Beta-adrenergic blocking drugs (Beta Blockers) (see section 20.8.12 in Table 19-1)

Brand names: *Normiten, Noten, Ormidol, Tenolin, Tenoretic*[1], *Tenormin, Venapulse*

Ototoxic effects:
- Cochlear:
  - Auditory hallucinations: (116 cases reported to FDA [FMR])
  - Hearing disorder: (7 cases reported to FDA [FMR])
  - Hearing loss: [33] (511 cases reported to FDA [FMR])
  - Hyperacusis: (15 cases reported to FDA [FMR])
  - Phonophobia: (9 cases reported to FDA [FMR])
  - Tinnitus: <1% (CPS) (794 cases reported to FDA [EHM])
- Vestibular:
  - Ataxia/Gait disturbance: <1% (CPS) (1,381 cases reported to FDA [FMR])
  - Balance disorder: (670 cases reported to FDA [FMR])
  - Dizziness: 3-13% [<7% above placebo results] (CPS, PDR) (4,274 cases reported to FDA [FMR])
  - Labyrinthitis: (42 cases reported to FDA [FMR])
  - Nystagmus: (41 cases reported to FDA [FMR])
  - Vertigo: 2% [1.5-1.8% above placebo results] (CPS, PDR) (500 cases reported to FDA [FMR])
  - Vestibular disorder: (22 cases reported to FDA [FMR])

Outer/Middle Ear:
- Ceruminosis: (64 cases reported to FDA [FMR])
- Ear blocked: (21 cases reported to FDA [FMR])
- Ear discomfort/Ear pain: (227 cases reported to FDA [FMR])
- Ear infection: (66 cases reported to FDA [FMR])
- Eustachian tube dysfunction: (36 cases reported to FDA [FMR])
- Otitis externa: (41 cases reported to FDA [FMR])
- Otitis media: (108 cases reported to FDA [FMR])
- Otorrhagia: (36 cases reported to FDA [FMR])
- Otorrhea: (5 cases reported to FDA [FMR])
- Perforated eardrum: (28 cases reported to FDA [FMR])

Unspecified/General Ear Conditions:
- Ear disorder: (36 cases reported to FDA [FMR])
- Meniere's disease: (17 cases reported to FDA [FMR])
- Ototoxicity: (4 cases reported to FDA [FMR])

Risk assessment: Class 3

Notes:

[1] *Tenoretic* is a combination of **Atenolol** and **Chlorthalidone**. (See the generic drug **Chlorthalidone** for its specific ototoxic properties.)

Atenolol can also distort your perception of music so that you hear music in the wrong key.

See Chapter 6 "The Incidence of Side Effects Is Grossly Under-reported," for further information on this drug.

Anecdotal Reports:

One man explained, "I take **Atenolol**—25mg—and my tinnitus stays at baseline. If I try to increase the **Atenolol** dose, my tinnitus gets worse."

Peggy's doctor prescribed **Atenolol** and she suffered serious ototoxic side effects. She wrote, "I was given **Atenolol** for some little irregular heart-beats. Within a few days, my perfectly normal ears started to give me all kinds of noise, roaring and muffledness. Within a week, I woke up one morning stone cold deaf in one ear. I had pressure in my head so extreme that it felt like my head was stuffed with bricks. The hearing in my other ear was distorted." Fortunately, in Peggy's case, she stopped taking the **Atenolol** and her hearing eventually came back.

A man explained, "I was on **Atenolol** (100 mg once a day) for 4 years before bad side effects appeared. Mine started about a year ago when all of a sudden I just lost hearing in my left ear. I went to bed and the next morning it was back to normal. However, a few months later I started to develop ringing and hissing in my right ear. About 6 or 8 weeks ago all of a sudden I felt an intense pressure in my head and my pulse dropped dangerously low. I went to the

Emergency room 4 times within a 2 week period. One Doctor finally told me they thought it was due to the **Atenolol**. I have been off of it completely now for almost 2 weeks and I have noticed a huge change in the way I feel—just a little bit of the fullness in the left side of my head and a little bit of tinnitus in the left ear."

A lady wrote, "I have been taking **Atenolol** for 3 years and I am having intense ringing in my ears. I never thought the silence could be so loud! I also experienced a hissing sound. I thought the hissing was something in the house or outside the window. My hearing has faded in and out."

A man got tinnitus "some years after my doctor prescribed **Atenolol** for high blood pressure. I have thought for some time that this beta blocker may be the cause of my tinnitus."

In a somewhat similar case a lady reported, "I started taking **Atenolol** in November, 2005. In June, 2007, out of nowhere, tinnitus kicked in and never left. I am suspicious that it may be the beta blocker."

A man explained, "In November I was given **Atenolol**. By December I had vertigo, right ear hearing loss, short term memory problems and anxiety issues. In January I switched to **Metoprolol** and the **Atenolol** side effects went away except for the hearing loss."

A man wrote, "I have been taking **Atenolol** for about 3 years with no ill effects—until recently. Over the last month the hearing in my left ear has come and gone—and now there is a constant ringing. I went off the **Atenolol** for about a week and my hearing returned about 75%. I took another 25 mg of **Atenolol** this morning and the ringing returned along with the associated loss of hearing in my left ear."

A medical doctor explained that he had been taking **Atenolol** for some years and was now experiencing a weird set of symptoms as a result. A few times a year he would suddenly get loud tinnitus in one ear that seemed to come out of nowhere and for no reason. Then his hearing would begin to fade away. This would last an hour or two, then his tinnitus would fade away and his hearing would come back.

A man wrote, "I have been taking 12.5 mg of **Atenolol** for the last two years. For the past two or three months my ears have been ringing off and on, and I get a hissing sound in my right ear every now and then. My hearing would be off one day and ok the next. I went to doctor several times—no ear infections, no fluid. He said it must be Eustachian tube dysfunction. I really didn't think so because I can pop my ears at will. I never thought about the **Atenolol**! I won't be taking **Atenolol** anymore. It has caused me enough misery these last few months!"

A man explained, “I only take one blood pressure pill, **Atenolol**. I’ve been on it for 8 years now. My tinnitus has been pretty steady for the last 5 years, but I get these spikes. I usually get pressure in my ears, muffled hearing and louder tinnitus. It usually lasts 24 hours and then I am back to my normal level. The spikes really upset me to the point that I feel hopeless and scared, always wondering if it will go back down. I can have them about once a week.”

In another “weirdly” similar case, a man reported, “I was taking **Atenolol** 10 mg for 8 years. I stopped about 3 years ago and within a week my left ear began ringing. It is bad for a couple of days, then virtually disappears for a day or two. Then comes back. It has been this same cycle since day 1. My tinnitus only changes when I’m asleep for some reason. I will go to bed without any ringing, then wake up with it ringing. And vice-versa. It never changes while I’m awake.”

A man explained how he had been taking a low dose of **Atenolol** (25 mg) for 12 years without noticing any side effects. His doctor recently increased his dose of **Atenolol** to 50 mg, and within a couple of weeks his hearing became muffled and distorted.

A man reported, “I started on **Atenolol** three weeks ago, 25 mg at first then to a higher dose, and now back to 25 mg The result was severe ringing in both ears. My ears were great before. Now I feel like I am in a bell factory!”

A lady reported, “I have taken 50 mg of **Atenolol** daily for nearly twenty years. Shortly after beginning the medication, my hearing deteriorated rapidly. Because my mother had hearing problems, I assumed it was my destiny. Interestingly enough she has taken **Atenolol** for many years too.”

A lady wrote, “I have been taking **Atenolol** for a few years. About five years ago my ears started having a “full” sensation. I thought it was allergies. My MD prescribed nose spray, and antihistamines, but it continually got worse and I had a few bouts of vertigo here and there. I started to see my MD with complaints of the vertigo. He sent me to an ENT who diagnosed me with Meniere’s disease. I came across the Center’s website and feel now that **Atenolol** is the cause. My ENT doesn’t seem to think so. The ringing and noise was almost unbearable. The vertigo was coming on closer and closer together. The ENT even injected **Prednisone** in ear to no avail. After 5 days off the **Atenolol** I feel that I can hear better and the noise has somewhat calmed down at least to be tolerable. I am praying that all of the symptoms go away.”

A wife wrote, “My husband’s hearing loss got much worse after his doctor put him on **Atenolol**.”

A lady explained, “I take 25 mg of **Atenolol**. I do not have tinnitus, but my hearing is so bad, even with hearing aids, that I am giving up many activities. I am calling my doctor today to see about changing to another medication for slightly elevated blood pressure.”

A man reported, "I've been taking 25 mg of **Atenolol** for 11 years and about 3 years ago began to experience hearing loss in my left ear. It gradually became worse and I also began to experience fullness in my left ear. I went to several ENT's and the audiograms showed hearing loss in my left ear. The past several months I have begun to experience pressure behind my left eye, pressure in my left temple and on top of my head. This did come and go but recently it remained pretty steady day and night. My wife came across your site and I immediately stopped the **Atenolol** and now 4 days later I am feeling much better and the headaches, pressure in the left temple and behind the left eye has all but disappeared."

A lady explained that she had been on **Atenolol** and taking this drug resulted in hearing loss, vertigo and other ear problems. When she had her doctor switch her from the **Atenolol** to **Nebivolol** her hearing mostly returned and her vertigo and other ear problems went away.

A lady lamented, "My doctor switched me from another blood pressure medication to **Atenolol**. Within four days, I was dizzy, confused, weak and experiencing chest tightness. The ringing in my ears was horrible too. I stopped two days ago and the ringing in my ears is still continuing but not as strong. This is a horrible drug! I could not function at work during those four days. I would not recommend this drug to anyone."

A man found that when he took **Atenolol** at higher doses his ears heard music at the wrong pitch. When he lowered the dose to 12.5 mg this pitch distortion didn't occur.

Another man reported, "I take **Atenolol** daily for hypertension and this has contributed to my loss of pitch (strangely bass notes only) when gigging in my rock band?"

A lady was put on a high dose of **Atenolol** which resulted in "tinnitus so bad I cannot think or sleep, and my hearing has faded."

A lady reported, "I have recently had my **Atenolol** increased from 50 mg per day to 75 and all of a sudden my tinnitus is much worse."

A man started taking 25 mg of **Atenolol** and soon after both of his ears began ringing.

A lady had been on **Atenolol** for more than 10 years when she noticed a plugged ear feeling. She told her cardiologist and her cardiologist took her off the drug and stated that she had a lot of patients with ear problems from taking **Atenolol**. Twenty days after stopping the **Atenolol** she reported, "My ears are 50% better, but I still get the crackling when I open my mouth, and the feeling of fullness remains.

A man explained, "I had been taking **Atenolol** twice a day for 2 months when the high-pitched siren started. It is worst in quiet rooms but at work I barely notice it. I stopped the **Atenolol** with permission from my cardiologist. The ringing lessened in a week. It's no longer unbearable."

A lady wrote, "I've been on 25 mg of **Atenolol** for about 4.5 years. A year ago a hissing ear sound started but my doctor said not to worry about it. My left ear gets full and loses hearing, my throat swells up on the left side and I get face hot flashes. This also affects my left eye and loses eye sight (sight gets blocked and blurry, double vision) and I get a mild headache. Now a year later the tinnitus and all symptoms are getting worse. I've also had vertigo attacks which were very scary. I'm also getting pins and needles now."

Atomoxetine

Pronunciation guide: ah-toe-MOKS-ah-teen

Drug classification: Selective Norepinephrine Reuptake Inhibitors (see section 60.1.24 in Table 19-1)

Brand names: *Strattera*

Ototoxic effects:
- Cochlear:
  - Auditory hallucinations: (123 cases reported to FDA [FMR])
  - Hearing loss: (47 cases reported to FDA [FMR])
  - Hyperacusis: (20 cases reported to FDA [FMR])
  - Tinnitus: (56 cases reported to FDA [FMR])
- Vestibular:
  - Ataxia/Gait disturbance: (25 cases reported to FDA [FMR])
  - Balance disorder: (98 cases reported to FDA [FMR])
  - Dizziness: 5-6% [<4% above placebo results] (AHF, CPS) (783 cases reported to FDA [FMR])
  - Vertigo: (GIP) (26 cases reported to FDA [FMR])
- Outer/Middle Ear:
  - Ear infection: 1-3% [<2% above placebo results] (CPS, NDH)
  - Ear discomfort/Ear pain: (22 cases reported to FDA [FMR])
  - Ear infection: (35 cases reported to FDA [FMR])
  - Otitis media: (12 cases reported to FDA [FMR])
- Unspecified/General Ear Conditions:
  - Meniere's disease: (3 cases reported to FDA [FMR])

Risk assessment: Class 2

Atorvastatin

Pronunciation guide: ah-TOR-vah-stah-tin

Drug classification: HMG-CoA reductase inhibitors (see section 20.12.8 in Table 19-1)

Brand names: *Cardyl, Citalor, Lipitor, Sortis, Tahor, Torvast, Zarator*

Ototoxic effects:

Cochlear:

Auditory hallucinations: (159 cases reported to FDA [FMR])
Hearing disorder: (38 cases reported to FDA [FMR])
Hearing loss: <2% (PDR) (1,105 cases reported to FDA [FMR])
Hyperacusis: (13 cases reported to FDA [FMR])
Phonophobia: (7 cases reported to FDA [FMR])
Tinnitus: <2% (CPS, PDR) (1,066 cases reported to FDA [EHM])

Vestibular:

Ataxia/Gait disturbance: (1,172 cases reported to FDA [DCC])
Balance disorder: (3,824 cases reported to FDA [FMR])
Dizziness: >2% (CPS, PDR) (6,191 cases reported to FDA [FMR])
Labyrinthitis: (86 cases reported to FDA [FMR])
Nystagmus: (67 cases reported to FDA [FMR])
Vertigo: (GIP) (777 cases reported to FDA [FMR])
Vestibular disorder: (22 cases reported to FDA [FMR])

Outer/Middle Ear:

Ceruminosis: (123 cases reported to FDA [FMR])
Ear blocked: (28 cases reported to FDA [FMR])
Ear discomfort/Ear pain: (421 cases reported to FDA [FMR])
Ear infection: (117 cases reported to FDA [FMR])
Eustachian tube dysfunction: (72 cases reported to FDA [FMR])
Otitis externa: (70 cases reported to FDA [FMR])
Otitis media: (128 cases reported to FDA [FMR])
Otorrhagia: (45 cases reported to FDA [FMR])
Otorrhea: (22 cases reported to FDA [FMR])
Perforated eardrum: (20 cases reported to FDA [FMR])

Unspecified/General Ear Conditions:

Ear disorder: (114 cases reported to FDA [FMR])
Meniere's disease: (40 cases reported to FDA [FMR])

Risk assessment: Class 2

Notes:

Since statin drugs deplete your body's stores of Co-enzyme Q10 (CoQ10), if you take a statin, it would be wise to also take CoQ10 supplements to replace what the drug destroys. The best form of CoQ10 is called Ubiquinol.

Caution: Eating grapefruit or drinking grapefruit juice during the time you are taking this drug may make the listed side effects worse than shown here. In fact, taking **Atorvastatin** with grapefruit juice can increase the potency of **Atorvastatin** by as much as 250%. See Chapter 11, "Grapefruit Juice and Ototoxic Drugs" for further information on this drug.

Also see Chapter 2 "Ototoxic Drugs—What Are They" for additional information on this drug.

Anecdotal Reports:

A lady who got tinnitus from taking **Atorvastatin** explained, "*Lipitor* caused my 'bilateral aural fullness' which left me with tinnitus. I have gone 2 months with this condition thinking everyday it would go away. Finally, after looking up and researching and seeing that *Lipitor* could be the culprit, I stopped taking it. Guess what? My tinnitus is slowly getting better. In a few weeks I'm sure it will be gone."

One person reported, "I was taking 20 mg **Atorvastatin**. When the dosage was doubled to 40 mg I started experiencing pulsatile tinnitus and other tinnitus noises and music."

A lady reported, "I was placed on **Atorvastatin** for high cholesterol. Within a month I developed tinnitus in my right ear. I stopped taking it for a few months. When I saw my doctor again he said I should try and restart it, which I did. My original tinnitus had never subsided and when I restarted **Atorvastatin** again my tinnitus became much worse within 4 days, and is now pulsatile. In addition I am experiencing a feeling of fullness in my right ear with hearing loss. It is now 4 weeks later with no decrease in symptoms. My ENT really made out that it was no big deal and didn't see an association with the medication [little he knows]."

Atosiban

Pronunciation guide: ah-TOS-ih-ban

Drug classification: Oxytocin antagonist drugs (see section 40.36.3 in Table 19-1)

Brand names: *Tractocile*

Ototoxic effects:
- Vestibular:
  - Dizziness: (MED)
  - Vertigo: 1-10% (GIP)

Risk assessment: Class 0.5

Atovaquone

Pronunciation guide: ah-TOE-vah-kwon

Drug classification: Anti-protozoals (see section 7.14 in Table 19-1)

Brand names: *Malarone*[1], *Mepron*[1], *Wellvone*

Ototoxic effects:
  Cochlear:
    Auditory hallucinations: (6 cases reported to FDA [FMR])
    Hearing loss: (20 cases reported to FDA [FMR])
    Tinnitus: (She) (11 cases reported to FDA [EHM])
  Vestibular:
    Ataxia/Gait disturbance: (8 cases reported to FDA [FMR])
    Balance disorder: (5 cases reported to FDA [FMR])
    Dizziness: 3-8% (CPS, PDR) (151 cases reported to FDA [FMR])
    Vertigo: (16 cases reported to FDA [FMR])
  Outer/Middle Ear:
    Ear infection: (5 cases reported to FDA [FMR])
    Otitis externa: (17 cases reported to FDA [FMR])
  Unspecified/General Ear Conditions:
    Ototoxicity: (12 cases reported to FDA [FMR])

Risk assessment: Class 1

Notes:

[1]*Malarone* and *Mepron* are combinations of **Atovaquone** and **Proguanil**. (See the generic drug **Proguanil** for its specific ototoxic properties.)

Atracurium

Pronunciation guide: ah-trah-KYOO-ree-um

Drug classification: NEUROMUSCULAR BLOCKING AGENTS (see section 53.36.3 in Table 19-1)

Brand names: —

Ototoxic effects:
  Vestibular:
    Dizziness: (6 cases reported to FDA [FMR])
    Nystagmus: (3 cases reported to FDA [FMR])

Risk assessment: Class 0.5

Atropine

Pronunciation guide: AH-troe-peen

Drug classification: ANTI-CHOLINERGIC DRUGS (see section 17.1 in Table 19-1)

Brand names: *AtroPen, Atropisol, Co-Phenotrope*[1], *Donnatal*[2], *Lomotil*[1], *Lonox*[1]

Ototoxic effects:
  Cochlear:
    Auditory hallucinations: (8 cases reported to FDA [FMR])
    Hearing loss: (90 cases reported to FDA [FMR])

Hyperacusis: (3 cases reported to FDA [FMR])
Tinnitus: (50 cases reported to FDA [FMR])
Vestibular:
Ataxia/Gait disturbance: <10% (NDH) (262 cases reported to FDA [FMR])
Balance disorder: (186 cases reported to FDA [FMR])
Dizziness: >10% (NDH, PDR) (514 cases reported to FDA [FMR])
Nystagmus: (7 cases reported to FDA [FMR])
Vertigo: (GIP) (66 cases reported to FDA [FMR])
Vestibular disorder: (6 cases reported to FDA [FMR])
Outer/Middle Ear:
Ceruminosis: (3 cases reported to FDA [FMR])
Ear blocked: (13 cases reported to FDA [FMR])
Ear discomfort/Ear pain: (56 cases reported to FDA [FMR])
Ear infection: (5 cases reported to FDA [FMR])
Eustachian tube dysfunction: (22 cases reported to FDA [FMR])
Otitis externa: (29 cases reported to FDA [FMR])
Otitis media: (26 cases reported to FDA [FMR])
Otorrhagia: (16 cases reported to FDA [FMR])
Perforated eardrum: (3 cases reported to FDA [FMR])
Unspecified/General Ear Conditions:
Ototoxicity: [34] (San)

Risk assessment: Class 2

Notes:

[1] *Co-Phenotrope*, *Lomotil* and *Lonox* are combinations of **Atropine** and **Diphenoxylate**. (See the generic drug **Diphenoxylate** for its specific ototoxic properties.)

[2] *Donnatal* is a combination of **Atropine**, **Hyoscyamine**, **Phenobarbital** and **Scopolamine**. (See the generic drugs **Hyoscyamine**, **Phenobarbital** and **Scopolamine** for their specific ototoxic properties.)

See Chapter 10, "We 'Hear' With Our Eyes" for further information on this drug.

Auranofin

Pronunciation guide: ore-RAIN-oh-fin

Drug classification: ANTI-RHEUMATIC DRUGS (see section 46.1 in Table 19-1)

Brand names: *Ridaura*

Ototoxic effects:
Cochlear:
Tinnitus: (Ka8)

Vestibular:
Dizziness: (8 cases reported to FDA [FMR])
Unspecified/General Ear Conditions:
Ototoxicity: [35] (Str)

Risk assessment: Class 0.5

Avanafil

Pronunciation guide: ah-VAN-ah-fil

Drug classification: PHOSPHODIESTERASE TYPE 5 (PDE5) INHIBITORS (see section 20.8.28.3 in Table 19-1)

Brand names: *Spedra*, *Stendra*

Ototoxic effects:
Cochlear:
Hearing loss: [1] <2% (DIO, RXL)
Tinnitus: [1] <2% (DIO, RXL)
Vestibular:
Dizziness: 1%-2% (DIO, RXL)
Vertigo: <2% (DIO, RXL)

Risk assessment: Class 1

Notes:

[1] Use of PDE5 inhibitors has been associated with sudden decrease or loss of hearing, which may be accompanied by tinnitus or dizziness. Physicians should advise patients to stop taking PDE5 inhibitors, including *Stendra*, and seek prompt medical attention in the event of sudden decrease or loss of hearing.

Anecdotal Reports:

A man reported, "I took the smallest recommended dose of 50 mg, and while it worked as intended, it also turned my mild tinnitus that I have had for a couple of years into something much worse—very loud and intrusive."

Axitinib

Pronunciation guide: aks-ih-TEE-nib

Drug classification: TYROSINE KINASE INHIBITORS (see section 14.40 in Table 19-1)

Brand names: *Inlyta*

Ototoxic effects:
- Vestibular:
  - Ataxia/Gait disturbance: (9 cases reported to FDA [FMR])
  - Dizziness: (3 cases reported to FDA [FMR])

Risk assessment: Class 0.5

Azacitidine

Pronunciation guide: ay-zah-SYE-tih-deen

Drug classification: ANTI-NEOPLASTICS (ANTI-CANCER DRUGS) (see section 14 in Table 19-1)

Brand names: *Vidaza*

Ototoxic effects:
- Cochlear:
  - Hearing loss: (13 cases reported to FDA [EHM])
  - Tinnitus: (7 cases reported to FDA [EHM])
- Vestibular:
  - Ataxia/Gait disturbance: (21 cases reported to FDA [FMR])
  - Balance disorder: (10 cases reported to FDA [FMR])
  - Dizziness: (48 cases reported to FDA [FMR])
  - Vertigo: (7 cases reported to FDA [FMR])
- Outer/Middle Ear:
  - Ear discomfort/Ear pain: (3 cases reported to FDA [FMR])
  - Ear infection: (3 cases reported to FDA [FMR])

Risk assessment: Class 1

Azapropazone

Pronunciation guide: ah-zah-PROE-pah-zone

Drug classification: NON-STEROIDAL ANTI-INFLAMMATORY DRUGS (NSAIDs) (see section 1.1 in Table 19-1)

Brand names: *Rheumox*

Ototoxic effects:
- Cochlear:
  - Tinnitus: (BNF)
- Vestibular:
  - Dizziness: (BNF)
  - Vertigo: [36] (BNF)

Risk assessment: Class 0.5

Azatadine

Pronunciation guide: ah-ZAH-tah-deen

Drug classification: H_1 RECEPTOR ANTAGONISTS (see section 10.1 in Table 19-1)

Brand names: *Optimine*, *Rynatan*[1], *Trinalin*[1]

Ototoxic effects:
  Cochlear:
    Hearing loss: (4 cases reported to FDA [FMR])
    Tinnitus: (CPS, PDR)
  Vestibular:
    Ataxia/Gait disturbance: (CPS)
    Dizziness: (CPS, PDR)
    Labyrinthitis, acute: (PDR)
    Vertigo: (PDR) (4 cases reported to FDA [FMR])
  Outer/Middle Ear:
    Eustachian tube dysfunction: (4 cases reported to FDA [FMR])

Risk assessment: Class 1

Notes:

[1] *Rynatan* and *Trinalin* are both combinations of **Azatadine** and **Pseudoephedrine**. (See the generic drug **Pseudoephedrine** for its specific ototoxic properties.)

Azathioprine

Pronunciation guide: ay-zah-THYE-oh-preen

Drug classification: ANTIRHEUMATICS (see section 43.1 in Table 19-1)

Brand names: *Azasan*, *Imuran*, *Imurek*, *Imurel*

Ototoxic effects:
  Cochlear:
    Auditory hallucinations: (4 cases reported to FDA [FMR])
    Hearing loss: (99 cases reported to FDA [FMR])
    Tinnitus: (114 cases reported to FDA [EHM])
  Vestibular:
    Ataxia/Gait disturbance: (287 cases reported to FDA [FMR])
    Balance disorder: (92 cases reported to FDA [FMR])
    Dizziness: (453 cases reported to FDA [FMR])
    Nystagmus: (19 cases reported to FDA [FMR])
    Vertigo: (GIP) (50 cases reported to FDA [FMR])
  Outer/Middle Ear:
    Ceruminosis: (11 cases reported to FDA [FMR])
    Cholesteatoma: (3 cases reported to FDA [FMR])

Ear discomfort/Ear pain: (70 cases reported to FDA [FMR])
Ear infection: (33 cases reported to FDA [FMR])
Otitis externa: (22 cases reported to FDA [FMR])
Otitis media: (26 cases reported to FDA [FMR])

Risk assessment: Class 2

Azelastine

Pronunciation guide: ah-ZELL-ass-teen

Drug classification: H_1 RECEPTOR ANTAGONISTS (see section 10.1 in Table 19-1)

Brand names: *Astelin, Astepro, Optivar*

Ototoxic effects:
Cochlear:
Auditory hallucinations: (19 cases reported to FDA [FMR])
Hearing loss: (77 cases reported to FDA [FMR])
Tinnitus: (49 cases reported to FDA [EHM])
Vestibular:
Ataxia/Gait disturbance: (80 cases reported to FDA [FMR])
Balance disorder: (56 cases reported to FDA [FMR])
Dizziness: 2% [0.6% above placebo results] (PDR) (256 cases reported to FDA [FMR])
Vertigo: <2% (PDR) (46 cases reported to FDA [FMR])
Outer/Middle Ear:
Ceruminosis: (6 cases reported to FDA [FMR])
Ear discomfort/Ear pain: (24 cases reported to FDA [FMR])
Ear infection: (31 cases reported to FDA [FMR])
Eustachian tube dysfunction: (16 cases reported to FDA [FMR])
Otitis externa: (10 cases reported to FDA [FMR])
Otitis media: (19 cases reported to FDA [FMR])
Otorrhea: (25 cases reported to FDA [FMR])
Unspecified/General Ear Conditions:
Ear disorder: (23 cases reported to FDA [FMR])
Meniere's disease: (3 cases reported to FDA [FMR])

Risk assessment: Class 2

Azelnidipine

Pronunciation guide: AH-zel-NID-ih-peen

Drug classification: CALCIUM CHANNEL BLOCKING DRUGS (CCBs) (see section 20.8.16 in Table 19-1)

Brand names: *Calblock*

Ototoxic effects:
  Cochlear:
    Hearing loss: (3 cases reported to FDA [FMR])
  Vestibular:
    Ataxia/Gait disturbance: (10 cases reported to FDA [FMR])
    Dizziness: (40 cases reported to FDA [FMR])
    Vertigo: (4 cases reported to FDA [FMR])

Risk assessment: Class 0.5

Azithromycin

Pronunciation guide: ay-zih-throe-MYE-sin

Drug classification: Macrolide antibiotics (see section 7.4.32 in Table 19-1)

Brand names: *Zithromax*, Zitromax, Zmax, *Z-Pak*

Ototoxic effects:
  Cochlear:
    Auditory hallucinations: (47 cases reported to FDA [FMR])
    Hearing disorder: (3 cases reported to FDA [FMR])
    Hearing loss: <1% (CPS, PDR) (515 cases reported to FDA [FMR])
    Hyperacusis: (13 cases reported to FDA [FMR])
    Phonophobia: (3 cases reported to FDA [FMR])
    Tinnitus: <1% (CPS, PDR) (277 cases reported to FDA [FMR])
  Vestibular:
    Ataxia/Gait disturbance: (581 cases reported to FDA [FMR])
    Balance disorder: (246 cases reported to FDA [FMR])
    Dizziness: 1.1-3.9% (CPS, PDR) (1,277 cases reported to FDA [FMR])
    Labyrinthitis: (35 cases reported to FDA [FMR])
    Nystagmus: (11 cases reported to FDA [FMR])
    Vertigo: <1% (CPS, PDR) (196 cases reported to FDA [FMR])
    Vestibular disorder: (3 cases reported to FDA [FMR])
  Outer/Middle Ear:
    Ceruminosis: (51 cases reported to FDA [FMR])
    Ear blocked: (30 cases reported to FDA [FMR])
    Ear discomfort/Ear pain: (278 cases reported to FDA [FMR])
    Ear infection: (159 cases reported to FDA [FMR])
    Eustachian tube dysfunction: (58 cases reported to FDA [FMR])
    Otitis externa: (46 cases reported to FDA [FMR])
    Otitis media: >1% (PDR) (177 cases reported to FDA [FMR])
    Otorrhagia: (33 cases reported to FDA [FMR])
    Otorrhea: (13 cases reported to FDA [FMR])
    Perforated eardrum: (7 cases reported to FDA [FMR])

Unspecified/General Ear Conditions:
Ear disorder: (44 cases reported to FDA [FMR])
Ototoxicity: (13 cases reported to FDA [FMR])

Risk assessment: Class 3

Notes:

Hearing loss may be reversible (CP2).

Hearing loss has been reported in some people receiving long-term high-dose **Azithromycin** (i.e., 500 – 600 mg daily for up to 9 months) (AHF).

Hearing loss generally develops within 1½ to 20 weeks. If the hearing loss is temporary, hearing typically returns within 5 weeks after stopping the **Azithromycin** (AHF).

Anecdotal Reports:

A lady with a serious infection was given mega-doses of **Azithromycin** (8 grams per day). As a result, her hearing dropped to almost nothing.

A lady got tinnitus after taking **Azithromycin** for a sinus infection.

A man who had an eye infection and used eye drops containing **Azithromycin** for 3 weeks was told to rub the solution on the top and bottom eyelids of his right eye. During this time, he noticed a blocked feeling in his right ear. Subsequent hearing testing revealed he had lost the hearing in his right ear.

A lady reported, "I was treated with **Azithromycin** (*Zithromax*) for five days for a pneumonia infection. The day after I began the **Azithromycin**, I began experiencing hearing loss. I told my doctor and he just said, 'Oh, that's the medicine.' I received no warnings or advice about this being a possible side effect. I'd have chosen to suffer through the pneumonia longer rather than to become permanently hearing impaired."

A man explained, "I took a 3-pak of **Azithromycin** for a sore throat and my existing tinnitus went up from a 3 out of 10 to a 4. In addition, I got intermittent hyperacusis for about 3 days."

Azosemide

Pronunciation guide: ah-ZOE-seh-myed

Drug classification: Diuretics—loop (see section 30.5.4 in Table 19-1)

Brand names: *Diart*

Ototoxic effects:
Cochlear:
Auditory hallucinations: (5 cases reported to FDA [FMR])

Vestibular:
Ataxia/Gait disturbance: (8 cases reported to FDA [FMR])
Dizziness: (21 cases reported to FDA [FMR])
Vertigo: (3 cases reported to FDA [FMR])
Unspecified/General Ear Conditions:
Ototoxicity: [37]

Risk assessment: 0.5

Notes:

Azosemide can deplete your body's stores of magnesium. This can lead to worse ototoxic side effects. Therefore, if you are going to be taking **Azosemide**, taking magnesium supplements at the same time and for 2 or 3 weeks afterwards is probably wise. Note: Magnesium threonate is the most bioavailable form of magnesium. Avoid magnesium oxide as it is the least bioavailable form.

Aztreonam

Pronunciation guide: az-TREE-oh-nam

Drug classification: Monobactams (see section 7.4.12.4 in Table 19-1)

Brand names: *Azactam*

Ototoxic effects:
Cochlear:
Hearing loss: (AHF) (7 cases reported to FDA [EHM])
Tinnitus: <1% (DFC, PDR) (3 cases reported to FDA [EHM])
Vestibular:
Ataxia/Gait disturbance: (9 cases reported to FDA [FMR])
Dizziness: <1% (DFC, PDR) (14 cases reported to FDA [FMR])
Vertigo: <1% (DFC, PDR)
Outer/Middle Ear:
Ceruminosis: (3 cases reported to FDA [FMR])
Ear discomfort/Ear pain: (6 cases reported to FDA [FMR])

Risk assessment: Class 0.5

Bacampicillin

Pronunciation guide: bah-kam-pih-SILL-in

Drug classification: Penicillins (see section 7.4.40 in Table 19-1)

Brand names: *Penglobe*

Ototoxic effects:
- Vestibular:
  - Dizziness: 0.6-1.2% (CPS)
  - Vertigo: 0.6-1.2% (CPS)

Risk assessment: Class 0.5

Bacillus Calmette-Guerin (BCG) (Tuberculosis) Vaccine

Pronunciation guide: bah-SILL-us KAL-met-guer-ON (too-BER-kyoo-loe-sis) VAK-seen

Drug classification: VACCINES (see section 70.8 in Table 19-1)

Brand names: *TheraCys*

Ototoxic effects:
- Cochlear:
  - Hearing loss: (4 cases reported to FDA [FMR])
  - Tinnitus: (3 cases reported to FDA [FMR])
- Vestibular:
  - Ataxia/Gait disturbance: (42 cases reported to FDA [FMR])
  - Balance disorder: (10 cases reported to FDA [FMR])
  - Dizziness: (26 cases reported to FDA [FMR])
  - Labyrinthitis: (6 cases reported to FDA [FMR])
  - Vertigo: (6 cases reported to FDA [FMR])

Risk assessment: Class 0.5

Bacitracin

Pronunciation guide: bass-ih-TRAY-sin

Drug classification: BACITRACINS (see section 7.4.4 in Table 19-1)

Brand names: *Baciguent*

Ototoxic effects:
- Cochlear:
  - Hearing loss: (GIP) (5 cases reported to FDA [EHM])
  - Tinnitus: (3 cases reported to FDA [EHM])
- Vestibular:
  - Ataxia/Gait disturbance: (39 cases reported to FDA [FMR])
  - Balance disorder: (7 cases reported to FDA [FMR])
  - Dizziness: (39 cases reported to FDA [FMR])
  - Vertigo: (3 cases reported to FDA [FMR])
- Outer/Middle Ear:
  - Ear discomfort/Ear pain: (12 cases reported to FDA [FMR])
  - Otitis media: (9 cases reported to FDA [FMR])

- Unspecified/General Ear Conditions:
  - Ototoxicity: (Str)

Risk assessment: Class 1

Baclofen

Pronunciation guide: BAK-low-fen

Drug classification: Skeletal muscle relaxants (see section 53.36 in Table 19-1)

Brand names: *Lioresal, Mylan-Baclofen*

Ototoxic effects:

- Cochlear:
  - Auditory hallucinations: (51 cases reported to FDA [FMR])
  - Hearing loss: (101 cases reported to FDA [EHM])
  - Hyperacusis: (14 cases reported to FDA [FMR])
  - Tinnitus: 0.1-1% (CPS, PDR) (401 cases reported to FDA [EHM])
- Vestibular:
  - Ataxia/Gait disturbance: <10% (CPS, PDR) (1,022 cases reported to FDA [FMR])
  - Balance disorder: (469 cases reported to FDA [FMR])
  - Dizziness: 1.7-15% (CPS, PDR) (1,071 cases reported to FDA [FMR])
  - Nystagmus: <10% (CPS, PDR) (43 cases reported to FDA [FMR])
  - Oscillopsia: (3 cases reported to FDA [FMR])
  - Vertigo: (AHF,GIP) (111 cases reported to FDA [FMR])
  - Vestibular disorder: (4 cases reported to FDA [FMR])
- Outer/Middle Ear:
  - Ceruminosis: (13 cases reported to FDA [FMR])
  - Ear blocked: (6 cases reported to FDA [FMR])
  - Ear discomfort/Ear pain: (50 cases reported to FDA [FMR])
  - Ear infection: (43 cases reported to FDA [FMR])
  - Eustachian tube dysfunction: (3 cases reported to FDA [FMR])
  - Otitis externa: (6 cases reported to FDA [FMR])
  - Otitis media: (6 cases reported to FDA [FMR])
  - Otorrhagia: (5 cases reported to FDA [FMR])
  - Perforated eardrum: (7 cases reported to FDA [FMR])
- Unspecified/General Ear Conditions:
  - Ear disorder: (13 cases reported to FDA [FMR])
  - Meniere's disease: (15 cases reported to FDA [FMR])

Risk assessment: Class 3

Bamifylline

Pronunciation guide: BAH-mih-FILL-in

Drug classification: Bronchodilators—beta adrenergic agonists (see section 63.4 in Table 19-1)

Brand names: *Bamifix*

Ototoxic effects:
  Vestibular:
    Ataxia/Gait disturbance: (4 cases reported to FDA [FMR])
    Dizziness: (8 cases reported to FDA [FMR])
  Outer/Middle Ear:
    Otorrhea: (6 cases reported to FDA [FMR])

Risk assessment: Class 0.5

Barbexaclone

Pronunciation guide: bar-BEKS-ah-klone

Drug classification: Barbiturate Derivatives (see section 60.12.4.1 in Table 19-1)

Brand names: —

Ototoxic effects:
  Vestibular:
    Ataxia/Gait disturbance: (4 cases reported to FDA [FMR])
    Dizziness: (7 cases reported to FDA [FMR])
    Nystagmus: (7 cases reported to FDA [FMR]
    Oscillopsia: (4 cases reported to FDA [FMR])

Risk assessment: Class 0.5

Barnidipine

Pronunciation guide: bar-NIH-dih-peen

Drug classification: Calcium channel blocking drugs (CCBs) (see section 20.8.16 in Table 19-1)

Brand names: *Hypoca, Osipine*

Ototoxic effects:
  Vestibular:
    Ataxia/Gait disturbance: (6 cases reported to FDA [FMR])
    Dizziness: (13 cases reported to FDA [FMR])

Risk assessment: Class 0.5

Basiliximab

Pronunciation guide: bah-sih-LIKS-ih-mab

Drug classification: Interleukin inhibitors (see section 7.17.8.3 in Table 19-1)

Brand names: *Simulect*

Ototoxic effects:
  Vestibular:
    Ataxia/Gait disturbance: (34 cases reported to FDA [FMR])
    Dizziness: (22 cases reported to FDA [FMR])
  Outer/Middle Ear:
    Ear discomfort/Ear pain: (8 cases reported to FDA [FMR])
    Otitis media: (4 cases reported to FDA [FMR])

Risk assessment: Class 0.5

Becaplermin

Pronunciation guide: beh-KAP-ler-min

Drug classification: DERMATOLOGICAL DRUGS (see section 23 in Table 19-1)

Brand names: *Regranex*

Ototoxic effects:
  Vestibular:
    Vertigo: (7 cases reported to FDA [FMR])
  Outer/Middle Ear:
    Ceruminosis: (4 cases reported to FDA [FMR])
    Ear discomfort/Ear pain: (4 cases reported to FDA [FMR])

Risk assessment: Class 0.5

Beclomethasone (Beclometasone)

Pronunciation guide: beh-kloe-METH-ah-sone

Drug classification: GLUCOCORTICOIDS (see section 40.1.4 in Table 19-1)

Brand names: *Apo-Beclomethasone*, *Beclovent*, *Beconase*, *Becotide*, *Clenil*, *Cuvar*, *Inuvair*[1], *Qvar*, *Vancenase*, *Vanceril*

Ototoxic effects:
  Cochlear:
    Auditory hallucinations: (28 cases reported to FDA [FMR])
    Hearing loss: (12 cases reported to FDA [FMR])
    Tinnitus: 2-3% [placebo 0] (PDR) (28 cases reported to FDA [FMR])
  Vestibular:
    Ataxia/Gait disturbance: (107 cases reported to FDA [FMR])
    Balance disorder: (47 cases reported to FDA [FMR])
    Dizziness: (CPS) (312 cases reported to FDA [FMR])
    Nystagmus: (9 cases reported to FDA [FMR])
    Vertigo: (33 cases reported to FDA [FMR])
    Vestibular disorder: (3 cases reported to FDA [FMR])

Outer/Middle Ear:
Burning/stinging: (CPS)
Ear blocked: (42 cases reported to FDA [FMR])
Ear discomfort/Ear pain: <2% (DFC, PDR) (37 cases reported to FDA [FMR])
Ear infection: (15 cases reported to FDA [FMR])
Otitis externa: (6 cases reported to FDA [FMR])
Otitis media: (7 cases reported to FDA [FMR])
Perforated eardrum: (5 cases reported to FDA [FMR])
Unspecified/General Ear Conditions:
Ear disorder: (12 cases reported to FDA [FMR])
Meniere's disease: (14 cases reported to FDA [FMR])

Risk assessment: Class 2

Notes:

[1] *Inuvair* is a combination of **Beclomethasone** and **Formoterol**. (See the generic drug **Formoterol** for its specific ototoxic properties.)

Stinging and burning have been reported rarely when the medication has gained access to the middle ear (CPS).

Belimumab

Pronunciation guide: beh-LIM-you-mab

Drug classification: Monoclonal antibodies (see section 7.17.8 in Table 19-1)

Brand names: *Benlysta*

Ototoxic effects:
Vestibular:
Ataxia/Gait disturbance: (4 cases reported to FDA [FMR])
Balance disorder: (8 cases reported to FDA [FMR])
Dizziness: (40 cases reported to FDA [FMR])
Vertigo: (3 cases reported to FDA [FMR])
Outer/Middle Ear:
Ear infection: (3 cases reported to FDA [FMR])

Risk assessment: Class 0.5

Belladonna alkaloids

Pronunciation guide: bell-ah-DON-ah AL-ka-loids

Drug classification: Anti-cholinergic drugs (see section 17.1 in Table 19-1)

Brand names: *Atropa*, *Bellamine S*[1], *Bellergal*[1]

Ototoxic effects:
  Cochlear:
    Hearing loss: (21 cases reported to FDA [FMR])
    Tinnitus: (11 cases reported to FDA [FMR])
  Vestibular:
    Ataxia/Gait disturbance: (31 cases reported to FDA [FMR])
    Dizziness: (28 cases reported to FDA [FMR])
    Labyrinthitis: (3 cases reported to FDA [FMR])
  Outer/Middle Ear:
    Ear discomfort/Ear pain: (3 cases reported to FDA [FMR])
    Otitis externa: (17 cases reported to FDA [FMR])

Risk assessment: Class 1

Notes:

[1]*Bellamine* and *Bellergal* are combinations of **Belladonna alkaloids**, **Ergotamine** and **Phenobarbital**. (See the generic drugs **Ergotamine** and **Phenobarbital** for their specific ototoxic properties.)

Belladonna alkaloids come from the Deadly Nightshade (Atropa belladonna) plant.

Benazepril

Pronunciation guide: beh-NAH-zah-pril

Drug classification: ANGIOTENSIN-CONVERTING ENZYME (ACE) INHIBITORS (see section 20.8.8 in Table 19-1)

Brand names: *Cibadrex, Lotensin, Lotensin HCT*[1]

Ototoxic effects:
  Cochlear:
    Auditory hallucinations: (7 cases reported to FDA [FMR])
    Hearing disorder: (3 cases reported to FDA [FMR])
    Hearing loss: (65 cases reported to FDA [FMR])
    Tinnitus: 0.3-1% (CPS, PDR) (52 cases reported to FDA [EHM])
  Vestibular:
    Ataxia/Gait disturbance: (150 cases reported to FDA [FMR])
    Balance disorder: (79 cases reported to FDA [FMR])
    Dizziness: 3.6-6.3% [1.2-2.9% above placebo results] (CPS, PDR) (537 cases reported to FDA [FMR])
    Labyrinthitis: (17 cases reported to FDA [FMR])
    Nystagmus: (10 cases reported to FDA [FMR])
    Vertigo: 1.1%-1.5% [0.6% above placebo results] (CPS, PDR) (72 cases reported to FDA [FMR])

Outer/Middle Ear:
Ceruminosis: (4 cases reported to FDA [FMR])
Ear blocked: (12 cases reported to FDA [FMR])
Ear discomfort/Ear pain: (43 cases reported to FDA [FMR])
Ear infection: (14 cases reported to FDA [FMR])
Eustachian tube dysfunction: (6 cases reported to FDA [FMR])
Otitis externa: (16 cases reported to FDA [FMR])
Otitis media: (11 cases reported to FDA [FMR])
Unspecified/General Ear Conditions:
Meniere's disease: (12 cases reported to FDA [FMR])

Risk assessment: Class 2.5

Notes:

[1] *Lotensin HCT* is a combination of **Benazepril** and **Hydrochlorothiazide**. (See the generic drug **Hydrochlorothiazide** for its specific ototoxic properties.)

Bendamustine

Pronunciation guide: ben-dah-MUS-teen

Drug classification: ALKYLATING DRUGS (see section 14.1 in Table 19-1)

Brand names: *Treanda*

Ototoxic effects:
Cochlear:
Hearing loss: (9 cases reported to FDA [EHM])
Hyperacusis: (3 cases reported to FDA [FMR])
Tinnitus: (8 cases reported to FDA [EHM])
Vestibular:
Ataxia/Gait disturbance: (10 cases reported to FDA [FMR])
Balance disorder: (11 cases reported to FDA [FMR])
Dizziness: (37 cases reported to FDA [FMR])
Vertigo: (3 cases reported to FDA [FMR])
Outer/Middle Ear:
Otitis externa: (3 cases reported to FDA [FMR])

Risk assessment: Class 1

Bendazac

Pronunciation guide: BEN-dah-zak

Drug classification: ACETIC ACIDS (see section 1.1.1 in Table 19-1)

Brand names: —

Ototoxic effects:
Vestibular:
Ataxia/Gait disturbance: (3 cases reported to FDA [FMR])
Dizziness: (3 cases reported to FDA [FMR])
Vertigo: (3 cases reported to FDA [FMR])

Risk assessment: Class 0.5

Bendroflumethiazide (formerly Bendrofluazide)

Pronunciation guide: ben-droh-floo-meh-THYE-ah-zide

Drug classification: THIAZIDE-RELATED DIURETIC (see section 30.5.12 in Table 19-1)

Brand names: *Aprinox, Centyl, Corzide* [1], *Salures*

Ototoxic effects:
Cochlear:
Hearing loss: (Eps) (4 cases reported to FDA [FMR])
Hyperacusis: (4 cases reported to FDA [FMR])
Tinnitus: (Eps) (17 cases reported to FDA [FMR])
Vestibular:
Ataxia/Gait disturbance: (38 cases reported to FDA [FMR])
Balance disorder: (91 cases reported to FDA [FMR])
Dizziness: (DFC, PDR) (306 cases reported to FDA [FMR])
Nystagmus: (9 cases reported to FDA [FMR])
Vertigo: (DFC, PDR) (46 cases reported to FDA [FMR])
Outer/Middle Ear:
Ear discomfort/Ear pain: (9 cases reported to FDA [FMR])
Ear blocked: (7 cases reported to FDA [FMR])
Otorrhea: (5 cases reported to FDA [FMR])
Unspecified/General Ear Conditions:
Ear disorder: (3 cases reported to FDA [FMR])

Risk assessment: Class 1.5

Notes:

[1] *Corzide* is a combination of **Bendroflumethiazide** and **Nadolol**. (See the generic drug **Nadolol** for its specific ototoxic properties.)

Bendroflumethiazide can deplete your body's stores of magnesium. This can lead to worse ototoxic side effects. Therefore, if you are going to be taking **Bendroflumethiazide**, taking magnesium supplements at the same time and for 2 or 3 weeks afterwards is probably wise. Note: Magnesium threonate is the most bioavailable form of magnesium. Avoid magnesium oxide as it is the least bioavailable form.

Benefiber

Pronunciation guide: BEN-ee-FIE-ber

Drug classification: NUTRACEUTICAL PRODUCTS (see section 75.9 in Table 19-1)

Brand names: —

Ototoxic effects:
- Cochlear:
  - Hearing loss: (24 cases reported to FDA [FMR])
- Vestibular:
  - Ataxia/Gait disturbance: (14 cases reported to FDA [FMR])
  - Balance disorder: (26 cases reported to FDA [FMR]) (BNF)
  - Dizziness: (56 cases reported to FDA [FMR]) (BNF)
- Outer/Middle Ear:
  - Ear infection: (3 cases reported to FDA [FMR])
  - Perforated eardrum: (9 cases reported to FDA [FMR])

Risk assessment: Class 1

Benexate

Pronunciation guide: beh-NEKS-ate

Drug classification: ANTI-ULCER DRUGS (see section 34.8 in Table 19-1)

Brand names: *Ulgut*

Ototoxic effects:
- Vestibular:
  - Ataxia/Gait disturbance: (5 cases reported to FDA [FMR])
  - Dizziness: (5 cases reported to FDA [FMR]) (BNF)

Risk assessment: Class 0.5

Benfluorex

Pronunciation guide: ben-FLOOR-eks

Drug classification: ANTI-HYPERLIPIDEMIC AGENTS (see section 20.12 in Table 19-1)

Brand names: *Mediator*

Ototoxic effects:
- Vestibular:
  - Ataxia/Gait disturbance: (13 cases reported to FDA [FMR])
  - Dizziness: (9 cases reported to FDA [FMR]) (BNF)
  - Vertigo: (8 cases reported to FDA [FMR]) (BNF)

Risk assessment: Class 0.5

Benidipine

Pronunciation guide: beh-NID-ih-peen

Drug classification: Calcium channel blocking drugs (CCBs) (see section 20.8.16 in Table 19-1)

Brand names: *Coniel*

Ototoxic effects:
- Cochlear:
  - Hearing loss: (6 cases reported to FDA [FMR])
- Vestibular:
  - Ataxia/Gait disturbance: (40 cases reported to FDA [FMR])
  - Dizziness: (67 cases reported to FDA [FMR]) (BNF)
  - Vertigo: (3 cases reported to FDA [FMR]) (BNF)

Risk assessment: Class 0.5

Benorilate (Benorylate)

Pronunciation guide: be-NOE-ril-ate

Drug classification: Salicylates (see section 1.1.16 in Table 19-1)

Brand names: *Benoral*

Ototoxic effects:
- Cochlear:
  - Tinnitus: [38] (Ka7, San)
- Vestibular:
  - Dizziness: (BNF)
  - Vertigo: (BNF)
- Unspecified/General Ear Conditions:
  - Ototoxicity: (San)

Risk assessment: Class 0.5

Benoxaprofen

Pronunciation guide: ben-OKS-ah-PROE-fen

Drug classification: Propionic acids (see section 1.1.13 in Table 19-1)

Brand names: *Oraflex*

Ototoxic effects:
- Cochlear:
  - Tinnitus: (Ka7)

Risk assessment: ?0.5

Benzalkonium

Pronunciation guide: ben-zal-KOE-nee-um

Drug classification: ANTI-BACTERIAL DRUGS (see section 7.4 in Table 19-1)

Brand names: *Ilube, Ony-clear, Zephiran*

Ototoxic effects:
- Cochlear:
  - Hearing loss: (8 cases reported to FDA [FMR])
- Vestibular:
  - Dizziness: (4 cases reported to FDA [FMR])
- Unspecified/General Ear Conditions:
  - Ototoxicity: (Str)

Risk assessment: 0.5

Notes:

Ototoxicity can occur when **Benzalkonium** is applied to the middle ear in concentrations of only 0.1%.[39]

Benzbromarone

Pronunciation guide: benz-BROM-ah-rone

Drug classification: URICOSURIC DRUGS (see section 30.14 in Table 19-1)

Brand names: *Urinorm*

Ototoxic effects:
- Vestibular:
  - Ataxia/Gait disturbance: (15 cases reported to FDA [FMR])
  - Dizziness: (15 cases reported to FDA [FMR])

Risk assessment: 0.5

Benzethonium

Pronunciation guide: ben-zeh-THOH-nee-um

Drug classification: ANTI-BACTERIAL DRUGS (see section 7.4 in Table 19-1)

Brand names: *Buro-sol, VoSoL* [1]

Ototoxic effects:
- Unspecified/General Ear Conditions:
  - Ototoxicity: [40]

Risk assessment: ?0.5

Notes:

[1] *VoSoL* is a combination of **Benzethonium** (0.02%), **Acetic acid** (2%) and **Propylene glycol** (3%) (See the generic drugs **Acetic acid** and **Propylene glycol** for their specific ototoxic properties.)

Benzocaine

Pronunciation guide: BEN-zoe-kane

Drug classification: ESTERS (see section 4.4 in Table 19-1)

Brand names: *Americaine Otic, Cepacol, Orajel, Tympagesic*[1]

Ototoxic effects:
  Cochlear:
    Tinnitus: (5 cases reported to FDA [FMR])
  Vestibular:
    Dizziness: (9 cases reported to FDA [FMR]) (BNF)
  Outer/Middle Ear:
    Burning/stinging: (PDR, USP)

Risk assessment: Class 0.5

Notes:

[1] *Tympagesic* is a combination of **Benzocaine**, **Antipyrine** and **Phenylephrine**. (See the generic drug **Phenylephrine** for its specific ototoxic properties.)

Antipyrine (an-tee-PYE-reen) in combination with **Benzocaine** may cause tinnitus (PDR). **Antipyrine** is an ANALGESIC DRUG (PAINKILLER) (see section 1 in Table 19-1).

Benzocaine can cause burning, stinging, redness, oozing sores in ear canal if you have contact dermatitis and/or hypersensitivity to **Benzocaine** (PDR, USP).

Benzonatate

Pronunciation guide: ben-ZOE-nah-tate

Drug classification: ANTITUSSIVE DRUGS (see section 63.1 in Table 19-1)

Brand names: *Tessalon*

Ototoxic effects:
  Cochlear:
    Auditory hallucinations: (4 cases reported to FDA [FMR])
    Hearing loss: (27 cases reported to FDA [FMR])
    Tinnitus: (41 cases reported to FDA [EHM])

Vestibular:
  Ataxia/Gait disturbance: (77 cases reported to FDA [FMR])
  Balance disorder: (49 cases reported to FDA [FMR])
  Dizziness: (183 cases reported to FDA [FMR])
  Labyrinthitis: (14 cases reported to FDA [FMR])
  Vertigo: (24 cases reported to FDA [FMR])
Outer/Middle Ear:
  Ceruminosis: (4 cases reported to FDA [FMR])
  Ear discomfort/Ear pain: (11 cases reported to FDA [FMR])
  Ear infection: (13 cases reported to FDA [FMR])
  Eustachian tube dysfunction: (5 cases reported to FDA [FMR])
  Otitis externa: (5 cases reported to FDA [FMR])
  Otitis media: (13 cases reported to FDA [FMR])
  Otorrhea: (3 cases reported to FDA [FMR])

Risk assessment: Class 1.5

Benzoyl peroxide

Pronunciation guide: BEN-zoe-il per-OKS-eyed

Drug classification: Dermatological drugs (see section 23 in Table 19-1)

Brand names: *Benzac, Brevoxyl, Triaz*

Ototoxic effects:
Cochlear:
  Hearing loss: (20 cases reported to FDA [FMR])
Vestibular:
  Ataxia/Gait disturbance: (9 cases reported to FDA [FMR])
  Dizziness: (17 cases reported to FDA [FMR])
Outer/Middle Ear:
  Ear discomfort/Ear pain: (3 cases reported to FDA [FMR])
  Ear infection: (3 cases reported to FDA [FMR])
  Otitis media: (8 cases reported to FDA [FMR])

Risk assessment: Class 1

Benztropine (Benzatropine)

Pronunciation guide: BENZ-troe-peen (BEN-zah-TROE-peen)

Drug classification: Anti-cholinergic drugs (see section 17.1 in Table 19-1)

Brand names: *Cogentin*

Ototoxic effects:
Cochlear:
  Auditory hallucinations: (185 cases reported to FDA [FMR])

Hearing loss: (134 cases reported to FDA [FMR])
Tinnitus: (14 cases reported to FDA [EHM])
Vestibular:
Ataxia/Gait disturbance: (CPS) (154 cases reported to FDA [FMR])
Balance disorder: (56 cases reported to FDA [FMR])
Dizziness: (CPS) (279 cases reported to FDA [FMR])
Labyrinthitis: (5 cases reported to FDA [FMR])
Vertigo: (88 cases reported to FDA [FMR])
Outer/Middle Ear:
Ceruminosis: (8 cases reported to FDA [FMR])
Ear discomfort/Ear pain: (7 cases reported to FDA [FMR])
Ear infection: (3 cases reported to FDA [FMR])
Otitis externa: (4 cases reported to FDA [FMR])
Otitis media: (9 cases reported to FDA [FMR])

Risk assessment: Class 2.5

Bepridil

Pronunciation guide: BEH-prih-dill

Drug classification: Calcium channel blocking drugs (CCB) (see section 20.8.16 in Table 19-1)

Brand names: *Vascor*

Ototoxic effects:
Cochlear:
Tinnitus: 6.5% [4.2% above placebo results] (PDR)
Vestibular:
Ataxia/Gait disturbance: (4 cases reported to FDA [FMR])
Dizziness: 11.6-27.2% [4.8-20.4% above placebo results] (PDR)
Vertigo: 0.5-2% (PDR)

Risk assessment: Class 0.5

Beraprost

Pronunciation guide: BEER-ah-prost

Drug classification: Platelet inhibitor drugs (see section 36.24 in Table 19-1)

Brand names: *Dorner, Procylin*

Ototoxic effects:
Cochlear:
Auditory hallucinations: (9 cases reported to FDA [FMR])
Hearing loss: (5 cases reported to FDA [FMR])

Vestibular:
Ataxia/Gait disturbance: (11 cases reported to FDA [FMR])
Dizziness: (35 cases reported to FDA [FMR])

Risk assessment: Class 0.5

Betacarotene

Pronunciation guide: BAY-tah-KAR-oh-teen

Drug classification: VITAMIN A ANALOGS (see section 23.4 in Table 19-1)

Brand names: *Difrarel*

Ototoxic effects:
Cochlear:
Auditory hallucinations: (4 cases reported to FDA [FMR])
Hearing loss: (7 cases reported to FDA [FMR])
Vestibular:
Ataxia/Gait disturbance: (3 cases reported to FDA [FMR])
Balance disorder: (12 cases reported to FDA [FMR])
Dizziness: (23 cases reported to FDA [FMR])
Vertigo: (6 cases reported to FDA [FMR])
Outer/Middle Ear:
Otitis media: (7 cases reported to FDA [FMR])

Risk assessment: Class 1

Betahistine

Pronunciation guide: BAY-tah-HISS-teen

Drug classification: H_1 RECEPTOR ANTAGONISTS (see section 10.1 in Table 19-1)

Brand names: *Betaserc, Labirin, Merislon, Serc, Vertix*

Ototoxic effects:
Cochlear:
Tinnitus: (38 cases reported to FDA [FMR])
Vestibular:
Ataxia/Gait disturbance: (38 cases reported to FDA [FMR])
Balance disorder: (21 cases reported to FDA [FMR])
Dizziness: (223 cases reported to FDA [FMR])
Labyrinthitis: (41 cases reported to FDA [FMR])
Nystagmus: (4 cases reported to FDA [FMR])
Vertigo: (52 cases reported to FDA [FMR])
Unspecified/General Ear Conditions:
Meniere's disease: (3 cases reported to FDA [FMR])

Risk assessment: Class 1.5

Made in the USA
Monee, IL
16 October 2024

67375910R00324